Hollywood by Hollywood

Hollywood by Hollywood

*The Backstudio Picture and
the Mystique of Making Movies*

Steven Cohan

OXFORD
UNIVERSITY PRESS

OXFORD
UNIVERSITY PRESS

Oxford University Press is a department of the University of Oxford.
It furthers the University's objective of excellence research, scholarship,
and education by publishing worldwide. Oxford is a registered trade mark of
Oxford University Press in the UK and in certain other countries.

Published in the United States of America by Oxford University Press
198 Madison Avenue, New York, NY 10016, United States of America.

© Oxford University Press 2019

Library of Congress Cataloging-in-Publication Data
Names: Cohan, Steven, 1948– author.
Title: Hollywood by Hollywood : the backstudio picture and the mystique of
    making movies / Steven Cohan.
Description: New York : Oxford University Press, [2019] | Includes
    bibliographical references and index.
Identifiers: LCCN 2018005300 (print) | LCCN 2018007709 (ebook) | ISBN
    9780190865795 (updf) | ISBN 9780190865801 (epub) | ISBN 9780190865771
    (pbk. : alk. paper) | ISBN 9780190865788 (cloth : alk. paper)
Subjects: LCSH: Motion picture industry in motion pictures. | Hollywood (Los
    Angeles, Calif.)—In motion pictures. | Motion pictures—United
    States—History.
Classification: LCC PN1995.9.M65 (ebook) | LCC PN1995.9.M65 C64 2019 (print)
    | DDC 791.4309794/93—dc23
LC record available at https://lccn.loc.gov/2018005300

9 8 7 6 5 4 3 2 1

Printed by Sheridan Books, Inc.
United States of America

For my sister and in memory of our mother

Contents

Acknowledgments

I presented portions of this book at several conferences of the Society of Cinema and Media Studies as well as at conferences organized by Console-ing Passions, the Modern Languages Association, and the Modernism/Modern Studies Association. In addition, I presented excerpts about *A Star Is Born* at the Cultural Studies Now! symposium hosted by the University of Pittsburgh in honor of Jane Feuer and at the Classical Hollywood Studies in the 21st Century conference at Wilfred Laurier University. I discussed the film's trailer on *In Media Res*. As valuable to this book's gestation, an invitation to speak at the University of Kentucky in 2010 gave me my first opportunity to think about films about Hollywood, and some of that early material has remained in my mind and in the book these many years later. I wish to take this opportunity to thank the organizers of these events for giving me these occasions at which I was able to try out my ideas about the backstudio picture.

Numerous friends and colleagues also shared their insights and provided helpful feedback (or just their friendship and support) during the long process of writing. I wish to thank Julie Abraham, Sarah Barkin, Harry Benshoff, Michael DeAngelis, Lindsey Decker, Mary Desjardins, Steven Doles, Mike Dwyer, Mike Goode, Sean Griffin, Julie Grossman, Karen Hall, Chris Hanson, Ina Hark, Nicola Jones, Coran Klaver, Barbara Klinger, Amy Lang, David Lugowski, Erin Mackie, Neepa Majumber, Adrienne McLean, Jolynn Parker, Andrea Scheibel, Linda Shires, Gohar Siddiqui, Jill Simpson, Staci Stutsman, T. J. West, and Pamela Wojcik. A special shout-out to Roger Hallas, Matt Fee, and Will Scheibel, who were always ready to talk Hollywood with me; our conversations over the years were of great value to this project from beginning to end. Merrill Schleier, Karen McNally, and Alan Nadel read all or parts of the book manuscript and provided very helpful comments. My work and Alan's often cover similar ground, and I have benefited from his comments or questions at various stages of this book's composition. Josh

Stenger provided some invaluable source material and good advice as I began. Samantha Hake pointed out to me how *Barton Fink* is legible as a blacklist film. Eric Hoyt found material for me in the Lantern at the Media History Digital Library. I also don't want to forget Scotty Nicolini, Sarah Parsons, Mark Strodel, Vanessa Watts, and my friends at the dog park. Let me thank as well Norm Hirschy, my editor at Oxford University Press, whose excitement about this project never waned; and the people at the press who saw the book through production—Lauralee Yeary, Judith Hoover, Celine Aenlle-Rocha, and, of course, Joellyn Ausanka. I should not forget the anonymous reviewers whose comments helped me to see more clearly what I have accomplished here.

Finally, I wish to thank the undergraduate students in the two versions of the course based on this book: your enthusiastic responses to the films were infectious and, in many instances, prompted me to linger on some in ways I had not anticipated, just as I know that your lively discussions in class remained in my mind afterward as I wrote certain sections. If you read this book you know who you are.

A portion of chapter 6 was first published as part of my article " 'This Industry Lives on Gossip and Scandal': Female Star Narratives and the Marilyn Monroe Biopic," which appeared in 2017 in *Celebrity Studies,* volume 8, pp. 527–43, and on the journal's website, http://www.tandfonline.com/doi/full/10.1080/19392397.2017.1370827.

About the Companion Website

www.oup.com/us/hollywoodbyhollywood

Oxford University Press has created a website to accompany *Hollywood by Hollywood: The Backstudio Picture and the Mystique of Making Movies*. In addition to the illustrations included in the book, on the website there are more than two hundred additional frame captures and twenty short film clips; these are indicated by the symbol ⊙ in the text.

Hollywood by Hollywood

Introduction

The Backstudio Picture

In 1937 the *New York Times* critic (and future Oscar-nominated screenwriter) Frank Nugent wrote a column about "the surprising number of back-studio pictures which have been dashing down the Times Square pike in the last few months." Although Nugent acknowledged that the cycle did have its antecedents, he believed that William Wellman's *A Star Is Born* (1937), still considered the quintessential backstudio picture, "is commonly supposed to have started things.... Where the process will end, for the cycle apparently is just beginning, no one—this round-eyed corner least of all—can predict with any assurance" (Nugent 1937).

Today the end point of backstudio pictures is as unpredictable as it seemed in 1937. The prospect of making a movie about making movies has apparently fascinated some of Hollywood's most respected directors: King Vidor's *Show People* (1928), George Cukor's *What Price Hollywood?* (1933) and the remake of *A Star Is Born* (1954), Preston Sturges's *Sullivan's Travels* (1941), Nicholas Ray's *In a Lonely Place* (1950), Billy Wilder's *Sunset Boulevard* (1950) and *Fedora* (1978), Vincente Minnelli's *The Bad and the Beautiful* (1952) and *Two Weeks in Another Town* (1962), Gene Kelly and Stanley Donen's *Singin' in the Rain* (1952), Joseph L. Mankiewicz's *The Barefoot Contessa* (1954), Robert Aldrich's *The Big Knife* (1955), *What Ever Happened to Baby Jane?* (1962), and *The Legend of Lylah Clare* (1968), Elia Kazan's *The Last Tycoon* (1976), Peter Bogdanovich's *Nickelodeon* (1976) and *The Cat's Meow* (2001), Woody Allen's *Stardust Memories* (1980), *The Purple Rose of Cairo* (1985), and *Hollywood Ending* (2002), Blake Edwards's *S.O.B.* (1981) and *Sunset* (1988), Clint Eastwood's *White Hunter, Black Heart* (1990), Joel and Ethan Coen's *Barton Fink* (1991), Robert Altman's *The Player* (1992), and Barry Levinson's *Wag the Dog* (1997) and *What Just Happened* (2008).

In 2011 the backstudio picture received attention once again from another *Times* critic, Manohla Dargis, due to that year's leading award contenders: Martin Scorsese's *Hugo*, Simon Curtis's *My Week with Marilyn*, and the eventual Oscar winner, Michel Hazanavicius's *The Artist*, a riff on *Singin' in the Rain* (Dargis 2011). Another backstudio picture, Ben Affleck's *Argo* (2012), which uses the cover of a movie shoot to conceal a CIA rescue action, took the top Oscar again the following year. Two years later the big prize went to still another backstudio picture of sorts, this time about a former movie star trying for a Broadway comeback but haunted by his superhero character: Alejandro G. Iñárritu's *Birdman or (The Unexpected Virtue of Ignorance)* (2014). Two years after that saw the Coen brothers' *Hail, Caesar!* (2016), Allen's *Café Society* (2016), Warren Beatty's *Rules Don't Apply* (2016), and the front runner in the 2017 Oscar race, Damien Chazelle's *La La Land* (2016).

My title, *Hollywood **by** Hollywood*, means to reflect both the enduring industrial authorship of such films throughout the history of American filmmaking and their institutional self-reflexivity.

Since it originates in the silent era with shorts by Charles Chaplin and Mack Sennett appearing in the 1910s and extends to twenty-first-century Academy Award competitions a hundred years later, the backstudio picture ought to be considered a genre in its own right. But while the film about making movies has persisted from decade to decade and from one transition to another (from silent to talkies, black and white to Technicolor, Academy ratio to CinemaScope, studio-era Hollywood to media conglomerate-era Hollywood, celluloid to digital), no name describing it has stuck. Whereas Nugent called this type of film a "back-studio picture," David O. Selznick referred to *A Star Is Born* as his "Hollywood picture" (Behlmer 1973, 143). Four decades later, Patrick Donald Anderson wrote his dissertation on "the Hollywood film" (Anderson 1976). Film scholars concurrent with or following Anderson have most often called this genre "movies about the movies" (Davis 1977; Ames 1997; Shiel 2012) or "movies on movies" (Meyers 1978), while also coining various alternatives, such as "the Hollywood-on-Hollywood" film (Parrish and Pitts, 1978; Ames 1997), "Hollywood-focused films" (Braudy 2011), and the "Hollywood about Hollywood" genre (Sklar 2012). As for the movies themselves, the advertising for *Sunset Boulevard* subtitled Wilder's insider's view "A Hollywood Story," while a character in William Castle's *Hollywood Story* (1951) refers to "backcamera stories." Because of its comparability with the backstage musical, I prefer Nugent's "back-studio" designation, even though, until Dargis revived the term in 2011, it has apparently not caught on with scholars, other reviewers, or filmmakers.

Like the backstage musical, the backstudio picture, as Nugent recognized in his column, purports to demystify the production of entertainment as a condition for re-mystifying it. At its simplest, a backstudio story represents Hollywood either by glamor-izing or satirizing the industry's present-day conditions or by remembering its history with tongue-in-cheek parody or outright nostalgia. Truth be told, backstudio pictures often appear in the guise of other genres, such as the musical, melodrama, comedy, biopic, film noir, or horror. But uniting those disparate types of narratives is their shared setting in Hollywood with plots that focus on making a motion picture or, if characters leave the soundstage, on dramatizing the industry's impact on people who have worked for it. Many backstudios thus recount the making or breaking of careers in film. When the production of an indie film occurs outside a studio setting, as in *Living in Oblivion* (1995), at least one leading character still hails from or is aiming for Hollywood. Similarly, a variant of the genre occurs when a leading character is narratively important because of his or her identification with Hollywood even if the film is not set there, as in *Notting Hill* (1999).

Backstudio pictures, in other words, share what Rick Altman calls a "semantics"—a common setting in Los Angeles, recurring themes about ambition, success, power, and labor, a predictable set of character types, and a self-reflexive mode of representation—but do not necessarily feature a common "syntax" or underlying structure determining a plot and its aesthetic and ideological forms. Backstudio pictures do not need to share a formal structure to be viewed as a genre because films move through multiple and overlapping signifying fields that exceed purely formal considerations but still powerfully determine one's appreciation of their generic identities: not only the industry's own standardization of narrative types and star vehicles but also advertising and promotion, reviews and criticism, audience expectations, fan discourses, and so forth (see Altman 1999; Neale 1999; Cohan 2012). As the example of film noir proves, too, with reception determined by such factors a motion picture genre can cohere belatedly and retrospectively over time.

Additionally, their longevity as a Hollywood product pretty much demands that backstudios be considered a genre in their own right, despite Nugent's viewing them in 1937 as part of a temporary cycle following the release of *A Star Is Born*. Although production of numerous backstudios have occurred cyclically, as I discuss later in this introduction, due to its enduring continuity throughout the history of American movies the backstudio picture cannot be called a film cycle despite the ease with which it masquerades as other genres. As Amanda Ann Klein points out, "Because they are so dependent on audience desires, film cycles are also subject to defined time constraints: most film cycles are financially viable for only five to ten years. After that point, a cycle must be updated or altered in order to continue to turn a profit." (Klein 2011, 4). Thus, whereas film cycles "exist to please their audiences" (10) and so "repeat the same images and plots over and over within a relatively short period of time" (13), film genres survive because they ultimately can withstand (even as they modify themselves in response to) the "interludes of audience apathy, exhaustion, or annoyance" that cause the demise of cycles (15).

Furthermore, while, as Thom Anderson's documentary *Los Angeles Plays Itself* (2003) shows, backstudios can be considered Los Angeles films, as are many film noirs and police procedurals, not all Los Angeles films are backstudios. What gives backstudios their overall coherence as a distinctive genre, albeit one not strictly defined according to a shared, conventionalized formal structure, is their fascination with the mystique of commercial filmmaking in Hollywood. Because they each make that fascination their subject matter, the backstudio picture shares an obvious kinship with what literary critics have named "the Hollywood novel" (Slide 1995; Springer 1995). However, in terms of their viewpoints and industrial contexts, the two are distant cousins.

In its so-called traditional form—that is, when its presence as a literary genre was simultaneous with the heyday of the studio system—the Hollywood novel was often written by screenwriters who, bearing grudges against an industry that paid little heed to their talent or artistry, tended to write about filmmaking from the perspective of a jaundiced, cynical outsider—the novelist or playwright brought to Hollywood but with no control over his or her work (Fox 1985, 7). In its postmodern incarnation, by comparison, "recent contributions to the genre are 'insider' novels, offering a wealth of details about contemporary moviemaking in the midst of its absurdity" (Ames 2008, 164). Although most backstudios tend to be filmed from original screenplays, a few Hollywood novels, such as Nathanael West's *The Day of the Locust* (1939) and F. Scott Fitzgerald's unfinished *The Last Tycoon* (1941) from the earlier, more traditional era and Michael Tolkin's *The Player* (1988) and Art Hinsen's *What Just Happened? Bitter Tales from the Hollywood Front Lines* (2008) from the more recent period, were subsequently adapted for the screen with their authorial viewpoints reasonably intact; but only *The Player* was a notable critical and commercial success. Regardless, the adaptations prove the kinship *and* the distance between the literary endeavor and cinematic product, for the latter is always produced by the very institution being celebrated or castigated.

For a backstudio picture nothing matters except the movies. But matters for whom? One might assume simply as a matter of course that this genre has always been enormously popular. After all, as the scholar John L. Sullivan observes, "Myths about Hollywood have excited the public imagination since the early twentieth century. The popular media and the movie studios' own marketing have continually portrayed motion picture production as magical and fantastic, heralding the individual achievement of a few creative individuals. This celebration continues despite the realities of industrialized division of labor and creative outsourcing which are prominent features of today's media production environment" (Sullivan 2009, 39). Yet with a few exceptions, such as *The Way We Were* (1973), the genre has not produced blockbuster hits on a regular basis; some of the most memorable titles, in fact, such as the much acclaimed (and for their time successful) *Sunset Boulevard* and *Singin' in the Rain* on one hand, and the much derided (and less successful) *Myra Breckinridge* (1970) and *Mommie Dearest* (1981) on the other, earned their present-day critical or cultish reputations sometime after their initial theatrical releases. Among the more than two hundred feature films and short subjects I have watched for this book, I have to conclude that some backstudios are artfully executed and deserve their canonical standing today, while others are, admittedly, mediocre because they recycle stock plots and characters or become mired in tonal and thematic confusion (or suffer from both problems). Most, however, fall somewhere in between these two poles: they have their moments of originality, insight, even audacity, but in one way or another they get caught up in clichés about Hollywood and typically end on a note of ideological conformity or narrative incoherence.

The rather narrow, not to say narcissistic concerns of the backstudio picture may account for its overall limited commercial appeal and often lackluster artistic results, suggesting that films about Hollywood are usually of greater interest to those *making* movies than to those *paying* to see them. Explaining his claim that the 1937 "*A Star Is Born* is the closest thing we have to an ideal of the movies: what they meant to the people who worked in them and to the people who went to see them," Ronald Haver describes the myopia as well as insularity of "the Hollywood movie colony":

> The people who inhabited it were concentrated close to each other and confronted with themselves and their work every single day, on the screen, in the papers, and on the radio. The lore of the town was rife with successes, has-beens, comebacks, ruined marriages, and tragic deaths, and after years and years of retelling and being gossiped about and clucked over, these events and people took on a kind of romantic patina, becoming the authentic legends of Hollywood, making winners out of losers and giving some of them an immortality that transcended anything they might have actually done in pictures. (Haver 1980, 191)

These comments do not seem disapproving but, on the contrary, equate the intensity of the people who make the movies with that of fans thoroughly caught up with the images flickering on the screen before them. Thus when Haver later concludes, "In *A Star Is Born*, Hollywood—the time, the place, and the attitude—was flawlessly presented as conceived by its audience" (206), it is not clear whether he has in mind an audience in Chicago, Syracuse, or St. Paul, or the more self-interested one watching this film in a Wilshire Boulevard theater or Beverly Hills screening room.

Its unabashed self-interest and failure to be successfully named over the decades may explain why backstudios have not received much concerted scholarly attention as a coherent and long-standing genre. The general consensus is that, at the end of the day, the backstudio picture is two-faced in its message: its self-reflexivity as a movie about the movies represents Hollywood as the modern-day fulfillment of the American dream at the same time that it insists upon the industry's soulless cynicism and ruthless ambition as the insider's truth about what really happens once inside the studio gates. "The best films about Hollywood," Christopher Ames states, "struggle with ambivalences that our culture has about movies and their roles in our lives: the viability of the American dream of material success, the cultural struggle between highbrow and lowbrow definitions of art and entertainment, and the conflict between corporate capitalism and the belief in individual heroes or creative geniuses" (Ames 1997, 12). True enough. Yet doesn't this conclusion reiterate the genre's own contradictory message about Hollywood, as *The Bad and the Beautiful* so well illustrates through its ambivalently viewed protagonist, Jonathan Shields (Kirk Douglas), who is at once loathsome and irresistible? The genre's cynicism about Hollywood, its artisans, and their product may be Hollywood's ultimate expression of self-mystification.

Like *The Bad and the Beautiful*, nearly every movie about filmmaking declares that it is tearing the veil from the face of Hollywood's celebrated mystique; nearly every one of those movies then removes one veil only to disclose several more underneath. In his *Times* column about backstudios, Nugent referred to this tactic as "the Hollywood strip-tease," since for all the apparent behind-the-scene revelations, the goal is still "to preserve the glamorous illusion" and protect "the greatest of its mysteries" (Nugent 1937). However, safeguarding the egos and mystifying the labor of the movie industry is not necessarily the sole end game of Hollywood's striptease act. For as David Raksin, who composed the musical score for *The Bad and the Beautiful*, once observed, "It isn't that people in Hollywood wish to lie to themselves, but that they suspect the truth is not very glamorous.... Talent is the point, not truth.... The things that really matter about Hollywood are those things few people would care about because they involve the drudgery of doing something decently or respectably. Hollywood prefers to think of its glamour and all kinds of jazzy things going on. Also, Hollywood is very cognizant of the world's notions of its myths" (quoted in Behlmer and Thomas 1975, 325).

That deliberated and conscious self-mystification may seem outmoded now, a characteristic of the studio system that produced films like MGM's all-star, Oscar-winning *Bad and the Beautiful*. Nonetheless such self-mystification continues to determine how the industry thinks about itself, although not with the sole purpose of glamorizing what is otherwise the drudgery of repetitive labor, as the anthropologist Sherry B. Ortner has discovered. Ortner reports that the present-day Hollywood community is still "deeply invested in discourses and practices that both define and constantly construct insideness and outsideness." These boundaries serve the need, first, to maintain a competitive advantage over rivals within the industry and, second, to preserve for those outside the industry the very "illusions" that define the product (i.e., the films and their stars). Spatially, the inside/ outside division manifests itself in the walled exteriors of the studios and stars' estates: "The whole conceit of 'star tours' is to take tourists past locations where nothing is visible at all." Discursively, the binary is supported by the argot of trade publications, notably the punning headlines and condensed phrasing that were long the hallmark of *Variety*. Psychologically, this division makes itself evident in the social hierarchies that govern production at all stages of the process. Ortner learned to her frustration that it is practically impossible for "an outsider" to gain entrance "inside." Insiders may at times talk off the record, but they are reluctant to take outsiders behind the scenes, allowing them to sit in on story conferences or production meetings, say. Even when Ortner finally gained access to a shoot after two years of trying, she learned that one can be on a set yet still be "some distance away from where the action is taking place," that is, kept away from where the director watches what is being filmed on video monitors in a tented enclosure called "video village." In short, "it seems there is always an inside further inside the inside" (Ortner 2009, 176–78).

Is anyone ever allowed "inside the inside" to see the wizard? The backstudio picture purports to share that view behind the curtain with audiences. In doing so, the genre raises some provocative questions about its ongoing depiction of Hollywood as an institution that, on one hand, is enduringly mythic in its cultural currency and, on the other, is economically driven and subject to change. In the chapters to follow, I reexamine the mystique that drives the backstudio genre but take a different approach than those characterizing previous studies. The many movies about filmmaking made during and after the studio era, I argue, have functioned in large part to sell Hollywood to audiences as an institutional brand, one exceeding individual studio authorship and secondary product differentiation. Furthermore, it should go without saying that backstudios reflect the ongoing racialization of Hollywood as a white enterprise.

Obviously, branding has always played a central role in the production and marketing of films. During the era of oligopolistic domination, the studios made a point of differentiating their product according to their cohort of stars, the genres they specialized in, and their reputation (e.g., their track records of box-office successes and award-winning, prestigious productions). The companies' distinctive logos—Warners' shield, MGM's lion, Twentieth Century-Fox's searchlight, RKO's radio tower, Paramount's mountain, Columbia's Statue of Liberty, Universal's globe—not only served as signatures opening their films but were heavily featured in trade advertisements in *Variety* and *Box-Office*, in trailers, and on occasion in local newspaper ads.

This same means of branding films through product and studio differentiation holds true today. "Despite changes in the industrial climate," Paul Grainge comments about the transformation of old Hollywood into the new era of Big Media, "entertainment branding retained important continuities with the studio system in its focus on stars and stories" just as "name" actors and directors along with "pre-sold properties" have continued to determine "the branding of individual film events" (Grainge 2008, 46). As further illustration of this continuity, Grainge notes the resilience of those old studio logos, which have regained their prominence in today's promotion of films, as when featured fleetingly at the start of trailers and then as the sole opening credit of a film, whether alone or as the first in a sequence of logos indicating a major studio's financial partnerships with multiple independent companies. The revitalized studio logos enable the multimedia conglomerates "to claim propriety rights over Hollywood's past, a form of brand annexation tied to the appropriation and circulation of competing logos" (77).

No more or less than other studio product, backstudio pictures have always been subject to this type of studio authorship as a sign of their corporate ownership (Schatz 1988; Christensen 2012). The genre's function in branding "Hollywood," on the other hand, goes beyond that. I have in mind how scholars like Grainge have analyzed the complex signification of contemporary brands—in his case, studio logos—according to "the degree to which a product or company can naturalize an emotional relation or set of values" (Grainge 2008, 48). This conceptualization of the brand as both sign and solicitation of an irresistible emotional relation between consumer and consumable, one that typically exceeds the properties of the object itself, is indebted to Naomi Klein's influential study of how today's corporations are now in the business of selling "*images* of their brands" and not their product. Beginning in the mid-1980s, Klein observes, "their real work lay not in manufacturing [things] but in marketing [them]" (Klein 2000, 4). Whereas the manufacturing age turned to branding as "an important add-on," first for product standardization (as manufacturers assumed the role formerly fulfilled by the local general store) and then for product differentiation (as the manufacturers became big companies that competed with each other in merchandising the same type of product), the marketing age has capitalized upon the truism, already evident to the advertising industry if not to their clients at mid-century, that "corporations may manufacture products, but what consumers buy are brands" (7).

It therefore follows for today's corporate thinking, as Christine Harold puts it, that "products are the *vehicles* that deliver their brands to consumers, rather than vice versa" (Harold 2007, xxii). To take this metaphor further, branding mystifies who is actually in the driver's seat and even what is being driven. For as Klein points out, "The old paradigm had it that all marketing was selling a product. In the new model, however, the product always takes a back seat to the real product, the brand, and the selling of the brand acquired an extra component that can only be described as spiritual. Advertising is about hawking product. Branding, in its truest and most advanced incarnations, is about corporate transcendence" (Klein 2000, 21). Put simply, the product is no longer a marketable thing but the pretext for branding the corporate enterprise itself in order to invest it with extra-added value.

In this context, one has to recognize how the Hollywood film industry charts the pattern described by Klein and others; just recall the well-studied transformation of the studio era's systematic means of manufacturing movies into the marketing priorities and outsourcing practices of today's global Hollywood. Yet even back in the days of the moguls Hollywood was never in the business of simply manufacturing a "thing" since film, its main product, is a highly intangible object, to say the least. Hollywood, as Grainge's comments on logos suggests, has always positioned itself halfway between an industry devoted to manufacturing a standardized product and an institution participating in something much more ephemeral. After all, at least until the introduction of home video, Hollywood's output had a limited shelf life in terms of its availability to consumers; more profoundly, as a practice of representation, that output was instrumental in the circulation of cultural meanings, values, and attitudes not too different from how brand theorists now analyze "the brand as experience, as life style" (Klein 2000, 21). As an industry that early on learned how to exploit product endorsement by its leading stars and product placement in the mise en scène, Hollywood has long operated as a vehicle delivering manufacturers' brands to consumers by investing the brands with "an extra component," namely, the strong emotional associations with a filmic experience and the stars embodying it. In trading on the value of branding before the Age of the Brand, studio-era Hollywood was already ahead of the curve, nowhere more so than when it came to branding *itself* on film so openly and unapologetically in backstudio pictures.

Despite its commercial unreliability, the backstudio picture has been an enduring genre for the industry precisely because of its ability to brand American filmmaking with the Hollywood mystique, soliciting consumers' strong investment in the movies. This is not to say, however, that the backstudio genre was deliberately conceived as a branding initiative or that it was subsequently viewed in this light by the industry at large, although individual films may have served such a purpose for a producer like David O. Selznick with *A Star Is Born* in 1937 or a studio like Twentieth Century-Fox with its several back-studios in the 1930s and 1940s featuring a studio head explicitly modeled on Darryl F. Zanuck. Indeed, as early as the 1910s numerous Mack Sennett slapstick shorts and occasional features were already mythifying "the mechanics of moviemaking" to suit "the corporate concerns" of his Keystone Film Company (D'haeyere 2014, 84).

As a point of comparison to what I am claiming about the backstudio picture, consider one of Hollywood's more transparent collective branding programs from the studio era. In the late summer of 1938 the major and minor studios organized a four-month promotion entitled "Motion Pictures' Greatest Year." The campaign was designed as an institutional effort to combat the severe fall-off in attendance that had begun the year before, ostensibly due to Hollywood's increasingly mediocre and irrelevant fare, which had caused widespread concern that consumers had begun to shake off the weekly moviegoing habit. The majors' theater chains and many independents heavily promoted and also helped to fund the centerpiece of this campaign, a movie quiz contest with a $250,000 pot that required entrants to see at least a third of the industry's output of more than ninety pictures during the last several months of 1938.

"Motion Pictures' Greatest Year" was a consciously orchestrated rebranding effort on the part of the studios. Circumstantially, along with falling grosses there were two additional factors at work motivating this institutional effort. The campaign began shortly after the notorious trade ad by exhibitors in the *Hollywood Reporter* declared that glamorous stars like Joan Crawford, Greta Garbo, and Katharine Hepburn were box-office poison, and this project of bringing together major theater chains with independents and major studios with minor ones became an idea one week after the federal government first filed its antitrust suit against the majors (Jurca 2012, 15–37). With this 1938 campaign the industry hoped to identify itself anew with a concern for quality filmmaking and with movies that jettisoned the outlandish glamour and unrealistic escapism that had apparently caused box-office receipts to nosedive (even though the new films themselves, which ranged from superspecials to inexpensive B pictures, were all at least in the preproduction stage before the campaign was conceived). The campaign's overall goal "was not just to get the public to love the film industry like a favorite star but to persuade it to embrace the making of commercial entertainment as a significant, stable, and indispensable enterprise" (183). The effects of this rebranding campaign were negligible, however. As it turned out, the planners were short-sighted; scholars and popular culture have since branded 1939 as the truly "greatest year" of the studio era.

But as a branding campaign, "The Motion Pictures' Greatest Year" is still illuminating. To kick off the campaign studio organizers prepared several large newspaper advertisements trumpeting Hollywood's relevance from numerous perspectives, such as its commitment to quality, to movies that played out on a very human scale, and to its understanding of a mass audience that was actually segmented according to differences of taste and opinion. One advert in particular turned inward with the spirit of a backstudio, calling attention to the collaboration, hard work, professionalism, and innovation at the heart of movie production. Yet as Catherine Jurca notes about this promotion in her excellent account of the campaign, "the word *Hollywood* does not once appear in the ads, while references to the *Motion Picture Industry* are everywhere. *Hollywood* evoked the insubstantial culture of the movies, the people and behavior that fueled gossip columnists and inspired reformers. The *Motion Picture Industry* communicated permanence and respectability, highlighting the solid economic structure behind the shadows on the screen" (Jurca 2012, 64).

Although never an organized institutional PR endeavor like this 1938 campaign, or subsequent ones like the November 1957 celebration of Hollywood's fifty-year anniversary with a "Golden Jubilee Month," through their narratives, character types, settings, and themes, backstudios have repeatedly and successfully had a significant *residual* effect of branding the motion picture industry as "Hollywood" and Hollywood as "the motion picture industry." This is as true today as it was in the 1930s with films like *A Star Is Born* and the cycle Nugent believed this backstudio picture had started.

Taking off from its self-interested premise, the backstudio genre focuses its point of view on the allure of movies and the industry manufacturing them, and this perspective, in turn, invests the idea of "Hollywood" with its powerful cultural cachet. This exchange of values, moreover, is reciprocal and hence circular: moviemaking is imagined as a larger-than-life, enthralling activity because of Hollywood's great mystique. In the twenty-first century the aspirations directed toward Hollywood—namely, to achieve the social and economic empowerment represented by the lifestyles that reward the industry's stars, creatives, and other assorted players for their passionate love of the movies—continues to make Los Angeles the magnet for ambitious young wannabe stars and filmmakers who head to the West Coast directly after their college graduation. Inspiring that ambition in the early twentieth century by giving it narrative form, the backstudio picture has given emotional heft to filmmaking as the quintessential (if almost always white) American success story: anyone with a creative hunger and single-minded drive, the genre shows, can make it in the movies. It therefore matters little at the generic level if the ambition and greed motivating success in Hollywood is valorized or damned in a particular film; either way the brand remains intact and appealing.

Regardless of whether it aims its lens on the present or the past, then, a backstudio picture views "Hollywood" simultaneously as (1) a geographic locale in the Los Angeles metropolitan area, (2) a business dedicated to the standardized production of motion pictures, and (3) an enduring cultural fantasy about fame, leisure, consuming, sexuality, artistry, and modernity. This overlapping of the literal (the locale) onto the material (the business) and the symbolic (the fantasy) registers the impact of the film industry's transformations as an institution even when the genre mystifies these changes in story terms, as in the many tales of stars being born, made, or falling apart. Just as important, that overlaying of perspectives is a primary means by which the genre authenticates the industry's representation of its own labor, in large part by conflating through the glamorous mystique of the film capital how "Hollywood" is at once the place where movies are made and "a dynamic social system, replete with status relationships, hierarchies, unrest and conflict, and unique personalities" (Sullivan 2009, 45). The backstudio picture, in short, is deeply concerned with shaping extrafilmic perceptions of how the industry works, with masking how its product depends upon industrial labor, including stardom, and with determining how that work's value accrues from the Hollywood brand stamped onto the product.

In presenting this set of arguments, I do not mean to imply that backstudios have been indifferent to their historical conditions. *A Star Is Born* (1937) may be the quintessential backstudio picture but, Nugent's impression notwithstanding, it was by no means the genre's starting point. The genre began in earnest in the silent era with several full-length features released during the 1920s, and then flourished during the robust studio system of the 1930s and 1940s. Afterward the terms of its subsequent renewals corresponded to significant crises in and transformations of the political economy of US film production: the studio system's breakdown in the 1950s and 1960s; the takeovers by and mergers with nonentertainment corporations in the 1970s; and the film industry's absorption into Big Media, which began in the late 1980s, became more pronounced during the 1990s, and is the status quo of the present century's media conglomerates, with their global reach.

There were, to be sure, films about making movies even before the chronology I just outlined. Sennett directed Mabel Normand in the short *Mabel's Dramatic Career* (1913). Chaplin made shorts that took his character on set (*A Film Johnnie*, 1914; *The Masquerader*, 1914; *His New Job*, 1915; *Behind the Screen*, 1916), and so did Tom Mix (*Movie Picture Cowboy*, 1914; *Sage Brush Tom*, 1915; *A Mix-Up in the Movies*, 1916; *Shooting Up the Movies*, 1916) (Meyers 1978, 44, 96–98; Barbas 2001, 116–17). According to my research, the first feature-length film that shows a great deal of behind-the-scenes work at a studio was the hour-long *A Girl's Folly* (1917), but it was made and takes place in Fort Lee, New Jersey. As for feature-length treatments of Hollywood, *Merton of the Movies* (a 1919 novel, 1922 Broadway adaptation, and 1924 Paramount feature film that is now lost) set a comedic prototype for the silent era of "the innocent who stumbles into stardom" (Anderson 1978, 2). A year before the screen version of that hit play appeared, in 1923 *The Extra Girl* and *Souls for Sale* both featured young women seeking stardom in Hollywood. *Ella Cinders* adapted the Cinderella template to a backstudio setting in 1926. Two years later, at the very moment Hollywood was introducing sound technology in features, the silent comedy *Show People* (1928) returned to that premise of the inexperienced young woman arriving in the film capital with hopes of making it in the movies. That same year *The Last Command* (1928) took a more melodramatic look at filmmaking, using a studio setting to frame a Russian Revolution backstory. Following upon these silent iterations of the backstudio picture, a more discernible cycle began in earnest concurrently with the industry's widespread conversion to sound: *The Talk of Hollywood* (1929), *Show Girl in Hollywood* (1930), and *Free and Easy* (1930). It is worth noting that production of these early backstudios corresponds with the evolving identification of the movie industry with "Hollywood," as two of those talkies indicate with their titles.

It seems evident to me from how this cycle gathered momentum during the 1930s that one of the ways the industry responded to the challenges of the Great Depression—including New Deal regulations, federal investigations of the film industry's vertical integration, burgeoning unionism and popular front radicalism, and the studios' own actual or near bankruptcies arising from their expensive conversion to sound and expanding theater circuits—was by producing numerous backstudios to promulgate the Hollywood mystique. These included *Movie Crazy* (1932), *Make Me a Star* (1932), *Once in a Lifetime* (1932), *Lost Squadron* (1932), *Lucky Devils* (1932), *What Price Hollywood?* (1932), *Lady Killer* (1933), *Bombshell* (1933), *Let's Fall in Love* (1933), *Going Hollywood* (1933), *Broadway to Hollywood* (1933), *Sitting Pretty* (1933), *365 Nights in Hollywood* (1934), *Hollywood Party* (1934), *Music Is Magic* (1935), *In Person* (1935), *Hollywood Boulevard* (1936), *Stand-In* (1937), *A Star Is Born* (1937), *Hollywood Hotel* (1937), *Pick a Star* (1937), *Go West Young Man* (1937), *Boy Meets Girl* (1938), *Crashing Hollywood* (1938), *The Goldwyn Follies* (1938), *The Affairs of Annabel* (1938), *Annabel Takes a Tour* (1938), *Hollywood Cavalcade* (1939), *Second Fiddle* (1939), *Star Dust* (1940), *Never Give a Sucker an Even Break* (1941), *Sullivan's Travels* (1941), and *World Premiere* (1941). Additionally there were B-versions of the genre produced by the majors and the minor companies like Columbia: *Scarlet River* (1933), *The Preview Murder Mystery* (1935), *The Cowboy Star* (1936), *It Happened in Hollywood* (1937), *Talent Scout* (1937), *Super Sleuth* (1937), *Hollywood Cowboy* (1937), *Hollywood Round-up* (1937), *The Jones Family in Hollywood* (1939), and *Shooting High* (1940). The all-star patriotic musicals produced during World War II and set in the film industry, notably *Star Spangled Rhythm* (1942), *Thank Your Lucky Stars* (1943), and *Hollywood Canteen* (1944), kept the genre visible in wartime. At war's end, the backstudio picture returned as *The Jolson Story* (1945), *Anchors Aweigh* (1945), *Without Reservations* (1945), *Hollywood and Vine* (1945), another remake of *Merton of the Movies* (1947), *On an Island with You* (1948), *Miracle of the Bells* (1948), *You're My Everything* (1949), *Dancing in the Dark* (1949), *Slightly French* (1949), and *It's a Great Feeling* (1949).

However fanciful or tame their revelations may seem at times, these 1930s and 1940s films about the industry promote Hollywood as a brand shared by all the studios. The genre achieves this purpose by equating the studio system with stardom via Hollywood, which verifies the stars' authentic presence since "Hollywood" is where they work, live, love, and recreate. On one hand, the identification of stardom with industrial Hollywood makes both appear equally fixed and unchanging. On the other hand, the centrality of female stardom in so many of these films registers the economic importance of women's labor for the studio system while indirectly contextualizing it in the tumultuous conflicts with the guilds and unions that challenged the studios' authority in the 1930s, were somewhat deferred but never entirely so during the Second World War, and were then revived shortly before the war ended.

By contrast, starting in 1950 with *In a Lonely Place* and *Sunset Boulevard* a second cycle began, this time comprising much less celebratory films about Hollywood that debunked the first cycle's interconnected myths of success, stardom, and the studio system as a thriving and well-functioning dream factory (Anderson 1978, 2–3, 200–201). This second cycle of "exposés" of the industry's hypocritical, self-mystifying ways—which also includes *Hollywood Story* (1951), *Dreamboat* (1952), *The Star* (1952), *The Bad and the Beautiful* (1952), *Singin' in the Rain* (1952), a remake of *A Star Is Born* (1954), *The Barefoot Contessa* (1954), *The Big Knife* (1955), *Love Me or Leave Me* (1955), *Will Success Spoil Rock Hunter?* (1957), *The Fuzzy Pink Nightgown* (1957), *Too Much Too Soon* (1958), *The Female Animal* (1958), and *The Goddess* (1958)—refracted the studio system's imminent break-down following the government's successful antitrust suit against Paramount and the other film companies in 1948, which forced the five majors to spin off their exhibition chains, a significant source of profit. The system's collapse was then made evident in the widening gap between the film product, the Hollywood brand, and the industry's shrinking audi-ence (itself the result of many congruent factors, starting with the rise in prices and un-employment, not to say strikes, following the war, suburban migration, the baby boom, competition from television and other forms of recreation and entertainment, and the greater availability of international art films). The grotesque female star narratives char-acterizing this cycle during the 1960s, such as *What Ever Happened to Baby Jane?* (1962), *The Carpetbaggers* (1964), *Inside Daisy Clover* (1965), two versions of *Harlow* (1965), *Valley of the Dolls* (1967), and *The Legend of Lylah Clare* (1968), registered even more dra-matically the incoherence of Hollywood as a brand, especially when still seen as being organized principally around female stardom.

The old system of production had completely eroded by the end of the 1960s. The financially troubled studios, moreover, had by this point merged with or been taken over by large corporations (Gulf and Western, Transamerica, Kinney), which knew very little about making movies or running a movie studio. Intensifying a postwar trend that had begun with the government's dismantling of the studio-era oligopoly in 1948, the in-dustry transitioned in the 1970s "from a studio system where moguls exercised consider-able control over production rosters and technical and creative talent, to a package-unit system where studios came to finance and distribute film projects put together by agents" (Grainge 2008, 46). As this shift occurred, much of the product ceased to be manufac-tured in Hollywood, a trend already started with the runaway production of the 1960s. As if aiming to brighten the tarnished Hollywood brand by evoking its storied past, a new cycle of backstudios concentrated quite intently on the industry's salad days, riding a wave of nostalgia for "what in the 1970s was rapidly becoming a wildly decentralized his-tory" (Braudy 2011, 148). Not coincidentally, this nostalgia boom happens to be the decade when the genre itself first received the most scholarly attention, and both occurred at the time the new academic discipline of film studies was becoming more formalized by col-lege teaching across the United States and in the United Kingdom (Ames 1997, 11).

The backstudio pictures of this third cycle included *The Way We Were* (1973), *That's Entertainment!* (1974), *The Wild Party* (1975), *The Day of the Locust* (1975), *Hearts of the West* (1975), *The Great Waldo Pepper* (1975), *W. C. Fields and Me* (1976), *Gable and Lombard* (1976), *The Last Tycoon* (1976), *Silent Movie* (1976), *Good-bye Norma Jean* (1976), *Won Ton*

Ton, the Dog That Saved Hollywood (1976), *Nickelodeon* (1976), *The World's Greatest Lover* (1977), *Fedora* (1978), *Mommie Dearest* (1981), *Under the Rainbow* (1981), and *Frances* (1982). This third cycle actively discounts the uncertain economic and artistic conditions of what had already been called "the New Hollywood." Instead of depicting the present-day state of affairs for the industry, backstudios of this period take a nostalgic view that glamorizes the heyday of the studio system as the industry's golden age and remembers the prior silent era as a time of industrial and technological innocence or even chaos. Simply put, the films in this cycle respond to a period of corporate mismanagement and fiscal uncertainty in Hollywood by displacing that crisis from view.

During the "golden" studio era memorialized by this third cycle, Hollywood turned out one type of product, motion-picture entertainment; it manufactured that product within the bounded, self-enclosed physical spaces of the studio, an industrial plant composed of multiple soundstages and a sprawling backlot; and it maintained its commercial domination of that product through an oligopolistic economic system. The globalized Hollywood of the present day, in comparison, is controlled by financial interests that have proliferated so far beyond production alone that the main investment in filmmaking seems mostly to do with the regulation and control of movies solely for their value as protected intellectual properties, especially those with recognizable brands.

In the pages of any twentieth-first-century issue of the now defunct print version of *Daily Variety* everything and everybody—studios, networks, production companies, genres, franchises, TV series, animated characters, celebrities, TV hosts, and stars—were routinely called "brands" or "branded identities" by the executives who are in the business of selling, nurturing, and protecting their "properties." Writing a column to explain why movies with stars like Bruce Willis, Matt Damon, and Sandra Bullock were looking "downright torpid at the box-office," the former Paramount and MGM executive and former *Variety* editor-in-chief Peter Bart explained the failure of their star vehicles: "Stars don't resonate just as actors any more, they are brands that produce multiple revenue streams. Further, the actor-brands must compete with toy brands (like Barbie) or game brands (like Asteroids), so career problems occur, not just when movies tank but when the brand tanks" (Bart 2009, 2).

It is no exaggeration now to describe the multimedia conglomerates that own the motion picture studios as "the copyright industries" (Maltby 2003, 195)—although "the trademark industries" could equally apply. In fact, whereas the Motion Picture Association of America once tirelessly made Hollywood safe for the moral consensus of Middle America by vetting every studio film according to the Hays Production Code, today this organization assigns ratings to films but mainly serves as both the industry's watchdog for video piracy and a powerful lobby in Congress representing the multimedia corporations' interests in revision or extension of copyright law. Likewise the Alliance of Motion Picture and Television Producers (AMPTP) represents a unified bargaining position for all the studios whenever the time comes to negotiate new contracts with the creative guilds (directing, writing, acting) or technical unions, as happened in 2007-8 when the writers went on strike, in large part over their demand for an equitable share in new media distribution of scripts, which they write but do not legally own as authors (Stahl 2009; Banks 2015). Historically, writers have received residuals in exchange for transferring their "authorship" to the production companies that copyrighted the material. The AMPTP's agenda in every contract negotiation is to maximize the studios' share of profit from its intellectual properties just as much as it is to control wages and benefits.

While the giant multimedia companies still own soundstages and a backlot, their movie studios for the most part have been reduced to their stylized logos, which signify the corporate brand as the source of ownership and not, as in the past, a physical space in the Los Angeles region where filmmaking happens. More often than not, in popular usage outside of Los Angeles, "Hollywood" designates escapist, contrived, glossy, and expensive product dominating global markets. As a branded location the Hollywood of today, in comparison with that of the past, seems even more emblematic than geographic, even more virtual than actual. Universal Studios in the San Fernando Valley is as much a theme-park attraction, complete with its own satellite shopping center, multiplex cinema, and amphitheater, as it is an industrial plant dedicated to manufacturing movies and TV series—which is why in 1990 the studio identity could so easily be shared with its fabricated twin in Orlando, Florida, without any loss to the original of its symbolic value as "Hollywood." As Alison Trope points out, although during the 1980s entertainment corporations besides Universal and Disney had already begun investing in themed environments and storefronts tied to the movies, "the 1990s, the age of conglomerates, corporatization, and franchising, exploded with theme parks that replicated and reinterpreted this interest in backstage Hollywood access as well as the fantasy and magic generically tied to Hollywood and its history.... These theme parks appropriate iconic figures, images, and landmarks as stand-ins for a historical era, but more importantly, they use decidedly ahistorical symbols of glamour and star power" (Trope 2011, 98, 103).

In the 1980s and 1990s, too, the talent agencies—the two most powerful ones then were Creative Artists Agency and International Creative Management—effectively took over what had been the studios' former role in originating production and managing stardom (Hozic 2001, 109). While the agencies' names have since changed as a result of mergers and newly created firms, their role in packaging productions has not. On their part, the distribution outlets of the conglomerates' film companies now plan their annual theatrical lineup around expensive seasonal tentpoles, few of which the companies finance wholly by themselves. Usually these titles are presold synergistic productions or franchises relying on CGI effects, oversized spectacle, and 3-D exhibition and Imax, and are built upon narratives that can ideally (if not always so easily) migrate across media platforms. At the same time, the conglomerates have ceased to build their annual output around middlebrow dramas and comedies; the burden for those have fallen on "Indiewood," the independent film industry that typically sells its fare to the few remaining studio subsidiaries and small bona fide independent companies at festivals like Sundance in the winter and Toronto in the fall.

In this contemporary institutional setting of "virtual Hollywood," the backstudio picture has again been revived, this time mostly but not always as a source of postmodern satire, parody, or pastiche: *Who Framed Roger Rabbit?* (1988), *The Big Picture* (1989), *Postcards from the Edge* (1990), *Barton Fink* (1991), *The Hard Way* (1991), *The Player* (1992), *The Last Action Hero* (1993), *Ed Wood* (1994), *Swimming with Sharks* (1994), *Living in Oblivion* (1995), *Get Shorty* (1995), *Wag the Dog* (1997), *Boogie Nights* (1997), *Burn Hollywood Burn* (1998), *Bowfinger* (1999), *S1m0ne* (2002), *Looney Tunes: Back in Action* (2003), *Straight Jacket* (2004), *Baadasssss!* (2004), *The Last Shot* (2004), *For Your Consideration* (2006), *Tropic Thunder* (2008), *What Just Happened?* (2008), *The Artist* (2011), *The Congress* (2013), *Birdman* (2014), *Hail, Caesar!* (2016), *Rules Don't Apply* (2016), and *La La Land* (2016). In their different ways, the films included in this latest cycle all engage in some form of deconstructing Hollywood's authenticity, but they demystify only to remystify the industry's art of simulation along with its internal politics, while representing what amounts to the corporate hollowing out of Hollywood's culture, whether viewed spatially, economically, or artistically.

Admittedly my chronological summary still sketches these four cycles in broad strokes, but I do so in order to make evident how the genre's renewal at key moments in Hollywood's history helps to identify the backstudio picture's long-standing currency for the industry, if not always for audiences. There are nonetheless some revealing inconsistencies in my schematic account that I do not want to ignore. Most obviously, while female characters focus most Hollywood narratives from the 1930s through the 1960s, some films, such as *In a Lonely Place*, *The Bad and the Beautiful*, *The Big Knife*, *Two Weeks in Another Town*, and *The Oscar* (1966), follow men in crisis. Before then, although the premise of *Merton of the Movies* was quickly adapted to suit female characters (*The Extra Girl*, *Ella Cinders*, and *Show People*), both *Make Me a Star* and *Movie Crazy*, each essentially an early talkie remake of *Merton*, propel an overly earnest male movie fan into unexpected stardom. *Lady Killer* has James Cagney leaving his gangster past behind him for a new life as a movie star. Additionally, while Norman Maine in the first *A Star Is Born* is probably the most famous fictional male star from this era who crashes and burns, *Hollywood Boulevard* and *It Happened in Hollywood* feature a male counterpart of Norma Desmond—a star washed up after the talkies begin—nearly fifteen years before the creation of *Sunset Boulevard*. Likewise, despite the centrality of the female star narrative in the 1930s and 1940s, some notable examples of the genre, such as *Once in a Lifetime*, *Boy Meets Girl*, *Stand-In*, and *Sullivan's Travels,* make the acting profession secondary in importance to other aspects of production, writing or producing in particular. And while the female star narrative may have lost its dominance after the 1980s—this disappearance coinciding with the studios' growing disinterest in female audiences for their major theatrical releases—it did not fade away entirely but instead migrated to TV and cable as biopics: after *The Jayne Mansfield Story* aired in 1980 it was followed by *Rita Hayworth: The Love Goddess* (1983), *White Hot: The Mysterious Murder of Thelma Todd* (1991), *Liz: The Elizabeth Taylor Story* (1995), *Introducing Dorothy Dandridge* (1999), *The Audrey Hepburn Story* (2000), *Life with Judy Garland: Me and My Shadows* (2001), *The Mystery of*

Natalie Wood (2004), and, more recently, *The Girl* (2012). And a lot of Marilyn Monroe biopics: *Marilyn: The Untold Story* (1980), *Marilyn and Me* (1991), *Marilyn & Bobby: Her Final Affair* (1993), *Norma Jean & Marilyn* (1996), *Blonde* (2001), and *The Secret Life of Marilyn Monroe* (2015).

The four cycles, moreover, are not entirely separable from each other even though my chronological scheme may suggest otherwise. Nostalgic histories of Hollywood surely characterize the 1970s, beginning with 1973's box-office hit *The Way We Were*, but this cycle can be seen already emerging in 1969 with *The Comic*, a fictional biopic of a silent star evoking memories of Buster Keaton, whose life story had already been recounted by *The Buster Keaton Story* in 1957, the same year as the Lon Chaney biopic, *The Man of a Thousand Faces*. And we cannot forget that studio-era pictures had already started to fashion a history of Hollywood pivoting around the arrival of sound: *Hollywood Cavalcade*, *The Jolson Story*, *You're My Everything*, and, of course, *Singin' in the Rain*. As the cycle of histories in the 1970s runs its course, moreover, there are exceptions that rightfully stand out, notably *The Stunt Man* in 1980 and *S.O.B.* the year afterward. In their responses to the chaos of 1970s Hollywood, those two films predict (and can thus more properly be said to belong to) the subsequent cycle beginning in the late 1980s. Nor are Hollywood histories strictly confined to the 1970s, as *Sunset* (1988), *White Hunter, Black Heart* (1990), *Guilty by Suspicion* (1991), *Chaplin* (1992), *Gods and Monsters* (1998), *RKO 281* (1999), *The Cat's Meow* (2002), *The Aviator* (2004), *Hollywoodland* (2006), and *Hitchcock* (2012) make evident later on. For that matter, several decades before the comedies more characteristic of the 1990s and 2000s, Jerry Lewis ran wild on a Hollywood soundstage in *Hollywood or Bust* (1956) and *The Errand Boy* (1961), and Lewis was following in the slapstick footsteps of Buster Keaton in *Free and Easy* and Harold Lloyd in *Movie Crazy*. And *Who Framed Roger Rabbit* is as much nostalgic history as it is a start to the fourth cycle of deconstructive comedies, satires, and pastiches.

So even while appreciating the genre's historical vitality according to the chronology I sketched through the four major cycles of its production, I fully recognize the fluidity within that cyclical development. The continuity and historicity of backstudio pictures are equally important factors to keep in mind when examining how the genre works to foster the Hollywood mystique as a brand. As I argue throughout this study, the backstudio picture's history as a genre reveals the extent to which the Hollywood mystique not only determined how the old studio era imagined itself on screen *in the past* but still determines how the new Hollywood of giant multimedia conglomerates wants to think of itself *in the present*, if only as a means of effacing the outsourced basis of today's film production and financing so that the globalized product remains identifiable as American-made entertainment. The studio compound—the backlot, soundstages, front office, and gated entry—is still most immediately recognizable as "Hollywood," just as the infrastructure of the studio system from the first half of the twentieth century still provides the ground for backstudios to comment on the present conditions of Hollywood even when a film is set in the past, as Joel and Ethan Coen's recent *Hail, Caesar!* illustrates. Despite

Hollywood's industrial transformations during the past century, or perhaps because of them, the specter of old Hollywood haunts the genre.

The following chapters develop these arguments about the backstudio picture's branding of Hollywood and its mystique. In order to keep the genre's periodization always in mind as I move from one chapter to the next, I build my overarching argument by discussing broad topics as they get refracted through the backstudio picture's history of four cyclical renewals. My intent, therefore, is to historicize this genre but without strictly following its chronology in my ordering of chapters.

Chapter 1, "Self-Reflexive Hollywood," begins *Hollywood by Hollywood* with a deliberately nonchronological overview of the genre; in demonstrating the multiple ways that backstudios authenticate their depictions of filmmaking by referring back to their own existence as Hollywood product, this chapter establishes the book's premise about the genre's self-reflexivity. The second chapter, "Imaginary Hollywood," examines how backstudios visualize Hollywood: first by locating it as a geographical space with identifiable landmarks like Grauman's Chinese Theatre; then by relocating Hollywood through a depiction of the bounded studio lot as a well-guarded because well-regulated, and hence "safe" and autonomous, industrial space; and finally, by imagining Hollywood as a state of mind.

The next three chapters treat the main players of the movie industry according to the stories told about them. Together, chapter 3, "Movie-Struck Hollywood," and chapter 4, "Monstrous Hollywood," trace the significance of managed and unmanageable female stardom as the defining element of star narratives from the early 1920s through the end of the 1960s. Chapter 5, "Masculine Hollywood," looks behind the camera at stories about male producers, writers, and directors, especially those depicted as "crazy" for being creative while also bucking studio control in one way or another. Whereas the star narratives ground stardom in fandom while also raising concerns about female agency within the industry, the narratives about filmmakers, which have dominated backstudios since the 1970s, work to masculinize Hollywood's appeal.

The final two chapters turn from the industry's above-the-line players to consider how backstudio pictures give cultural heft to Hollywood's mystique. Chapter 6, "Historical Hollywood," looks at the genre's treatments of the industry's past, with attention paid to events in 1929, 1951, and 1962 that have preoccupied the genre. Continuing this discussion, this chapter considers how gossip has provided an additional framework for recounting Hollywood's history. Finally, Chapter 7, "Virtual Hollywood," examines backstudios that move the virtual world of a movie off the screen, first by looking at several films that mesh the imaginary world of film characters with the real world of their spectators or human actors, and then turning to several others that take for their premise a state agency borrowing Hollywood's practices as a cover for their own covert operations.

So dim the lights, draw open the curtains...and roll 'em!

1

Self-Reflexive Hollywood

According to the backstudio picture, nothing and nobody are really what they seem, on screen or off. To verify this axiom, backstudios often self-knowingly acknowledge the sleight of hand necessitated by Hollywood's cinematic tricks and business practices, even going so far as to critique the industry, if not the ontology of cinema itself. But such critiques are always tentative and momentary, resulting in the genre's characteristic double talk with which it mystifies the movies' appeal even while it demystifies the manufacturing of motion pictures. This legerdemain is not a simple process, nor is it as straightforward as it seems. On the contrary, much of a backstudio's concreteness as a representation of Hollywood arises from persistent conventions of self-authentication that are as old and familiar as the genre itself. Backstudio pictures are self-reflexive, casting an insular and narcissistic gaze upon the movie industry, insofar as they take Hollywood as their subject while making it their sole frame of reference.

Regardless of the filmmakers' intent in truthfully exposing what happens "inside" Hollywood, a backstudio's ability to accommodate what it imagines as the "outside" is invariably compromised by its own medium. As Christopher Ames points out, "When certain elements of the Hollywood-on-Hollywood film represent the world of moviemaking and other elements represent the real world outside the cinematic illusion, we encounter the basic paradox of the genre: the supposedly extra-Hollywood reality cannot escape its Hollywood genesis" (Ames 1997, 17). Any scene depicting *how* a movie gets made can happen only within a movie that has itself already been filmed, edited, and processed with similar technological practices and under similar industrial protocols. Inevitably, a paradox arises whenever Hollywood pulls back the curtains on itself because of the backstudio picture's two competing ambitions: "showing how the trick works and still making the trick work" (6). For this reason, two of the most intricate self-reflexive backstudios—*Singin' in the Rain* (1952) and *Tropic Thunder* (2008), which I shall discuss at some length at the end of this chapter—quite knowingly make a problem of their own filmic transparency as a means of questioning Hollywood's. Nevertheless, if viewers are to take the revelations and insights of a backstudio story seriously and not simply as the industry's self-serving product, then a film about making movies still has to find ways to convince their audiences that whatever it portrays about Hollywood is not illusory, neither insincere nor glamorized, but authentic.

The resulting problematic can be considered an ongoing motor of the backstudio picture's self-defining, multilayered, and highly conventionalized system of tropes that establish a given film's referential grounding in Hollywood. From this perspective, the genre's self-reflexivity is not offering a metacommentary on the nature of cinema as an art form, a narrative medium, or a technology. Rather, in the circular logic by which the genre authenticates itself, what makes a backstudio picture convincingly authentic is the conviction with which it consciously reflects upon its own authenticity—and that of Hollywood as well. This circular mode of reference is an essential characteristic of a backstudio picture, and its effect is not so much to expose the artifice of Tinseltown in contrast with something more genuine existing outside the movies as to reiterate a conviction that the authenticity of Hollywood lies in its artifice and its insularity.

Transparent Hollywood

Diehard moviegoers have often expressed their passion for the movies as their ability to distinguish authentic from contrived representations of Hollywood, starting with their convictions about what they perceive as the real personalities behind the fabricated imagery of their favorite stars or as the personal intention of an auteur director. Whether that desire is voiced as a fan's, aficionado's, or cinephile's, it harks back to the starting point of fandom, not to say to the invention of movie stardom (Barbas 2001), and it has continued unabated to the present day.

Entertainment news magazines in print, on broadcast and cable television, and on the Internet keep in constant circulation industry-fed knowledge about itself that claims to distinguish the truthful "inside" from the illusory "outside" of Hollywood's mystique. Many of these venues are themselves owned by the same multimedia conglomerates running the film studios, networks, and music companies. The nonstop buzz emanating from inside Hollywood today encourages everyone to feel so knowledgeable about the entertainment industry that a contemporary backstudio can presume its audience not only has a great deal of familiarity with how movies are made but also knows all the intricacies of behind-the-scene deal making.

Insider knowledge of this kind is not necessarily a recent phenomenon, but it has been intensified by DVD packaging of supplements and commentaries as well as the Internet. According to Paul Grainge, the widespread availability of backstudio information accounts for "the regularity [with which] self-reflexive movies about Hollywood life tap a certain 'vernacular of understanding' of the film industry developed in the last two decades by such as the weekly reporting of box-office statistics, the growing newsworthiness of film within popular entertainment and business journalism, and the tendency of DVDs to present data and information about the production and marketing of movies" (Grainge 2008, 128). As a result, the industry's seeming transparency, as John Caldwell comments, "places so much of the self-consciousness on the screen, outside, and in public [that] it makes traditional scholarly questions about a 'behind-the-scenes' or 'authentic' industry 'inside' seem rather beside the point" (Caldwell 2008, 1).

Such transparency is not entirely new, as Caldwell recognizes. Nor, as already mentioned in the introduction, does it break through what, in undertaking an ethnographic study of the film industry, Sherry B. Ortner observes firsthand about the insider/outsider mentality still structuring Hollywood: "Although the community is delocalized, it has a very strong sense of its boundaries. It is deeply invested in discourses and practices that both define and constantly construct insideness and outsideness.... Further, the product of Hollywood—movies and the larger world of cultural mythology of which movies partake—are all about illusions, and the boundaries around the production process, and especially around actors, are important for maintaining those illusions" (Ortner 2009, 176).

With regard to examining movies about the film industry, one therefore has to ask if an "authentic" backstudio look behind the scenes ever was, let alone still is, the genre's point—just as one has to wonder if there is that much more genuine transparency about the inner workings of today's Hollywood than there was in the past. After all, backstudios from all periods of the industry's history give an impression of transparency, but that is simply to recognize the genre's long-standing complicity in perpetuating the very discourses about the film industry that have influenced what moviegoers already knew about Hollywood before they entered a movie palace in the past or a multiplex today.

DVD supplements, then, are by no means a new instance of the industry's taking its audience behind the scenes of film production. Caldwell mentions as an example Walt Disney's long-running television series (Caldwell 2008, 283). The weekly series premiered on ABC as *Disneyland* in the 1954–55 season, and its coverage of animation magic, live-action special effects, and the Anaheim theme park were usually tied in some way to one of Disney's older or recent films or cartoons. Alison Trope similarly looks back to the short-lived *Warner Bros. Presents* of that same period (Trope 2011, 127–31). Before then, comparable studio-produced short subjects about the industry's practices in the 1930s and 1940s, such as Warners' *A Trip thru a Hollywood Studio* (1935) and *Alice in Movieland* (1940) and Paramount's *Hollywood Extra Girl* (1935), filled out the movie palace's bill of fare. Even earlier, a newly formed Metro-Goldwyn-Mayer produced a silent tour of its Culver City studio in 1925. These short subjects about the manufacturing of motion pictures from the studio era continue to serve their original function of supplementing the daily program on the cable network Turner Classic Movies. Now making a reappearance as DVD supplements, too, these shorts were forerunners of the making-of documentaries and behind-the-scene interviews, themselves modeled on electronic press kits, which are part of the production process for today's filmmaking in order to amplify the eventual DVDs (Caldwell 2008, 283–306). In their own way, these new and old behind-the-scenes featurettes and DVD extras are backstudios, too, albeit in miniature. Feature-length backstudios draw on the same knowledge that such "insider" supplements disseminate, just as these supplements, in turn, frame their revelations with conventions and discourses already set in place by prior backstudios.

This insular framework for taking viewers behind the scenes is not confined to studio-era short subjects or documentaries and contemporary electronic press kits or DVD supplements. The press book from United Artists for *A Star Is Born* (1937) outlines several promotions for this backstudio that read like a blueprint for what would much later become the standard DVD fare filling out a menu with "extras," those shorts reusing clips and talking-head interviews to cover multiple aspects of a film's production.

Some suggestions in the press book for *A Star Is Born* are obvious ballyhoo, such as arranging for a contest in the newspapers asking readers to identify Hollywood landmarks like Grauman's Chinese Theatre that are featured in the film or for soliciting letters from young women to have them explain "Why I'd like to be a Movie Star." Other recommendations for exploitation are more elaborate. Exhibitors are advised to re-create a soundstage movie set in the theater lobby, perhaps even to invite a local drama group to perform a scene there. The press book also recommends playing up "Hollywood's own language: This is the kind of inside stuff that gives every picture fan a thrill." For use either as a newspaper plant or a giveaway, "A Glossary of Technical Movie Terms" lists definitions of Hollywood argot such as "gaffer," "gobo," and "grip" (*A Star Is Born* press book 1937, 11–12).

Additionally, articles to be fed to local newspapers suggest how, in its representation of a "real" Hollywood, *A Star Is Born* is like a hall of mirrors. One piece parallels star Janet Gaynor's "rise from extra ranks" with her character's; a photo still from the film of her character accepting the Academy Award recalls Gaynor's own Oscar win, with the caption stating, "History repeats itself." Another ersatz newspaper article exclaims, "Film within a Film on Set within a Set on Lot within Lot." "A motion picture within a motion picture," this article begins, "was made on a soundstage within a soundstage on a film lot within a film lot at Selznick International Studio recently" (*A Star Is Born* press book 1937, 19–21).

The most elaborately self-referential element of the publicity campaign, however, opens this press book with a full-page offering of "eight 22″ by 30″ pictorial displays lithographed on heavy stock paper in brown color." These displays, which an exhibitor can purchase singly or as set of eight, illustrate with photos or drawings "and descriptive captions" behind-the-scene perspectives of the Selznick production, foregrounding the manufacturing of *A Star Is Born* in much the same way that DVD supplements now claim transparency for contemporary pictures. Indeed the eight titles composing this promotion anticipate the typical slate of supplementary material on DVDs almost to the letter: "Famous Movieland Scenes, Background of the Picture," "Details in Preparation," "Preparing the Story," "Building the Sets," "Style Creations for Miss Gaynor," "Technical and Tonal Accuracy," "Behind the Scenes," and "Advertising and Publicity." (⊙ Figures 1.1–1.2)

These displays use *A Star Is Born*, a movie about the movies, to document the making of a movie from its various stages of preparation through to its eventual promotion. Even more striking is how these displays treat *A Star Is Born* as the authenticating referent for their documentation. The set "was prepared by the MPPDA [the Motion Picture Producers and Distributors of America, a forerunner of the Motion Picture Association of America] as part of its education campaign on films and film-making. These exhibits will be displayed simultaneously in 2000 Public Libraries, Schools, Clubs and Photoplay Study Groups in towns throughout the country" (*A Star Is Born* press book 1937, 3). According to the MPPDA, *A Star Is Born* accurately represents how movies are made, taking viewers behind the scenes to provide the full backstudio view; at the same time, the eight displays themselves substantiate the film's authenticity. The promotional discourse is so self-referential in its circularity that there no longer seems to be an outside to the insider's perspective.

The *Star Is Born* press book exemplifies the self-referentiality with which backstudio pictures from their beginnings to the present day establish their authenticity as an inside view of Hollywood. For instance, early movies about stardom already acknowledged what later backstudio plots, assisted by the post-1960s publishing industry's scandalous celebrity biographies and tell-all memoirs, now make much more of in their unflattering treatments of the star system: namely, how the studios' publicity machines authored stardom in collaboration with *Photoplay*, *Modern Screen*, and other monthly fan magazines and syndicated daily newspaper columns written by Hedda Hopper and Louella Parsons, among others. Studio-generated discourse planted by the publicity mavens established the fundamental elements of onscreen star narratives that the columnists and fan magazines reiterated: the concern with stars' authenticity, their geographic migration from the hinterlands to southern California, the ambiguity of their class affiliation as they emerge from the working class to attain great wealth and social prestige yet epitomize bourgeois tastes, the displacement of their labor onto their leisure, the attention to their excess in consumption of all kinds. Details change with the fashions, but that account of stardom, crystallized onscreen by the publicist Matt Libby when he and his studio cohort transform Esther Blodgett into Vicki Lester in *A Star Is Born*, still pretty much determines today's coverage of stardom in print, on television, and on the Internet.

Nor can one ignore how, as an extension of this star discourse, gossip about the industry supplies an ongoing intertext for the backstudio picture throughout its history. Gossip grounds accounts of Hollywood in what is sometimes called "semitruthful" reality. The most common interaction with gossip occurs when real-life Hollywood personalities appear as the source of fictional characters. John Barrymore or John Gilbert or Frank Fay may or may not have inspired the character of Norman Maine in *A Star Is Born* (1937), and that film's producer, David O. Selznick, probably inspired the character of producer Jonathan Shields in *The Bad and the Beautiful* (1952). The excerpt from *Queen Kelly* (1929) brings the real-life histories of Gloria Swanson and Erich von Stroheim on that aborted production into *Sunset Boulevard* (1950), much as the Joan Crawford–Bette Davis feud still intersects with *What Ever Happened to Baby Jane?* (1962). Similarly, gossip about Judy Garland and Ethel Merman informed the respective characters of Neely O'Hara (Patty Duke) and Helen Lawson (Susan Hayward, who replaced Garland) in *Valley of the Dolls* (1967). Dyan Cannon's character in *The Last of Sheila* (1973) was modeled on her own feisty and famous agent Sue Mengers, according to the *Los Angeles Times* gossip columnist Joyce Haber, a close friend of Mengers. In *S.O.B.* not only does Shelley Winters play another Mengers clone, but Loretta Swit impersonates a grotesque version of Haber, who had been finding every excuse to trash the director Blake Edwards and the star Julie Andrews in her column with as much frequency as she was pushing Mengers and Cannon.

Still another of the genre's recurring conventions for authenticating its insider's depiction of Hollywood is to show fictional characters interacting with real-life celebrities who, most typically, appear in cameo guest spots, which are sometimes billed and sometimes not. Perhaps the most famous examples are from *Sunset Boulevard*: Cecil B. DeMille directing a scene from *Samson and Delilah* (1949) on the Paramount lot; Hedda Hopper phoning in her story to the city desk at the *Los Angeles Times*; and the "waxworks"—Buster Keaton, Anna Q. Nilsson, and H. B. Warner—playing bridge with fellow has-been Norma Desmond (Gloria Swanson). *Hollywood Story* (1951) likewise features (to quote from the film) several "old time movie stars" such as Francis X. Bushman along with a "modern day movie star," Joel McCrae, shown working on set with a fictional character whose career began in silents, Roland Paul (Paul Cavanagh). *Pepe* (1960), with its cameos heavily advertised and promoted, features even more stars in guest appearances interacting with the title character (Cantinflas) to shore up its movieland setting. More than thirty years later, numerous stars appear throughout *The Player* (1992), whether working at or visiting the fictional studio's lot, attending private parties or gala industry events, or watching the film-within-the-film starring "real life" Julia Roberts, Bruce Willis, Susan Sarandon, and Peter Falk.

The cameo appearances in *Sunset Boulevard, Hollywood Story, Pepe*, and *The Player* are not unique to these films but a convention established by the backstudio genre early on. In *Souls for Sale* (1923), as heroine Mem Steddon (Eleanor Boardman) tries to break into pictures, she watches Erich von Stroheim show Jean Hersholt how to play a scene in *Greed* (1924); is hired as one of the five hundred extras whom Fred Niblo directs in *The Famous Mrs. Fair* (1923); and rides a horse for a day's pay in a scene directed by Charles Chaplin for *A Woman in Paris* (1923). When she finally gets a steady job as a member of director Frank Claymore's (Richard Dix) stock company, we see her in the commissary with Roy Barnes, Zasu Pitts, and other known players, eating and laughing. Chaplin shows up again alongside John Gilbert, Douglas Fairbanks, and a host of other stars, including Marion Davies playing herself in an encounter with her character, Peggy Pepper, in *Show People* (1928). Loretta Young, Al Jolson, and Ruby Keeler arrive at the premiere that closes *Show Girl in Hollywood* (1930), just as Tallulah Bankhead, Clive Brook, Claudette Colbert, Maurice Chevalier, Fredric March, and Gary Cooper appear briefly at various moments in *Make Me a Star* (1932). *It Happened in Hollywood* (1937), a Columbia programmer about a cowboy star (Richard Dix) thrown out of work by the arrival of talkies, forsakes star cameos and instead features the real-life stand-ins of Chaplin, Greta Garbo, Marlene Dietrich, Joan Crawford, Mae West, Myrna Loy, W. C. Fields, and others.

As these examples illustrate, the appeal of combining "real" with "reel" Hollywood has not waned over the years but is a recurring trope for authenticating a backstudio setting in a world of moviemaking. The columnist Louella Parsons appears in a simulation of her radio broadcast to document the "real" Hollywood of *Hollywood Hotel* (1937) and *Without Reservations* (1946). *Jolson Sings Again* (1949) has star Larry Parks playing himself interacting with his character, Al Jolson, as they make the film's predecessor, *The Jolson Story* (1946), while the real-life Jolson supplies Parks's singing voice, as he did in the earlier film. In *The Star* (1952), has-been 1940s star Margaret Elliot (Bette Davis) is said to lack "that fresh dewy quality"; the young ingénue who has it and gets the big role that Margaret openly covets is Barbara Lawrence, playing herself.

In an even more sustained use of this merging of "real" and "reel" Hollywood, *Fade-In,* aka *Iron Cowboy* (1968), the first film starring Burt Reynolds, was shot on the location shoot of the western *Blue* (1968). This story of a local rancher (Reynolds) romancing the visiting assistant editor (Barbara Loden) incorporates scenes of *Blue* actually being made (one is led to assume), with its actors (Joanna Pettet, Ricardo Montalban, Terence Stamp) addressed by the director (Silvio Narizzano, who also co-produced *Fade-In*) as they film on the fictional rancher's property. The Loden character's supervisor, moreover, is called "Stu" since the editor of *Blue* was Stu Linder.

This convention can lead to a veritable hall of mirrors, where any difference between "real" and "reel" Hollywood becomes a moot point at best. *Adaptation* (2002), written by Charlie Kaufman after being Oscar-nominated for his screenplay of *Being John Malkovich* (1999), opens on the set of that film with Catherine Keener and others working on a scene under Spike Jonze's direction while a nervous and insecure Kaufman (played by Nicholas Cage) watches. *Adaptation* returns to the *Malkovich* set midway through, this time to show John Malkovich himself working, then later depicts Keener relaxing at Charlie's home with his fictional twin brother, Donald (also Cage), and the latter's girlfriend. Then, in one more twist of playful, audacious conflation of the "real" with the "reel," because Donald dies at the end, *Adaptation* is dedicated to him; what is more, although he never existed, Donald shared screenwriting credit and an Oscar nomination with the real-life Charlie.

Far from simply being a postmodern self-reflexive trope, the convention of fictional and real-life Hollywood interacting had already inspired plot lines in several backstudios from Warner Bros. during the 1940s. In addition to its many cameos of Warners' stars appearing as themselves, *Hollywood Canteen* (1944) features a romance between "real" movie star Joan Leslie and the fictional Slim Green (Robert Hutton); this GI even meets Leslie's offscreen family, the parents played by actors and Leslie's sister by her actual sibling. Similarly, almost every star and director working at Warners after the war makes an appearance in *It's a Great Feeling* (1949), the plot of which has Jack Carson and Dennis Morgan playing themselves on the studio lot opposite Doris Day's fictional character, Judy Adams, whom the duo try to cast in their new movie. And the same studio's *Starlift* (1951) recounts a romance between fictional flier Rick Williams (Ron Haggerthy) and fictional starlet Nell Wayne (Janice Rule), whose close friends include top-billed real-life Doris Day and Ruth Roman along with other big names then working on the Warners lot.

Whether billed or not, guest stars ordinarily appear as themselves in a walk-on or, at best, just act as themselves in a scene, their purpose being to authenticate the Hollywood setting, but in these three backstudios Warners stars like Joan Leslie and Jack Carson play themselves as major characters in a narrative that has them interacting with fictional characters to move the plot along. These three Warners films anticipate *Fade-In* and *Adaptation* to some extent, but their influence can be most strongly felt on television, first in Lucy Ricardo's (Lucille Ball) trip to southern California on *I Love Lucy* (1951–57) in the mid-1950s, when the character draws real-life stars like William Holden, John Wayne, Rock Hudson, and Richard Widmark into her schemes and shenanigans, and several decades after that, in the HBO series *Entourage* (2004–11, a motion picture in 2015), which features characters interacting with one or two celebrity cameos in nearly every episode in order to authenticate the show's Hollywood setting.

In many films about Hollywood, too, the Motion Picture Academy's Oscar makes a guest appearance, usually receiving a special credit, as in the final title card of *The Bad and the Beautiful* (1952). Screenwriter Mark Christopher's (Dick Powell) Oscar even narrates *Susan Slept Here* (1954)! The convention of "real" life meeting "reel" life, meant to authenticate the extrafilmic "truthfulness" of the insider's backstudio view, treats cameo appearances on a par with the stock footage of Hollywood that typically signifies the setting's authentic location, as in the numerous establishing shots displaying the Hollywood sign or the imposing entrance to a movie studio such as the Bronson Gate at Paramount.

Along with gossip, cameos, clips, and stock footage, photojournalism and television coverage of southern California greatly contribute to what "authentic" Hollywood looks like on screen. This referentiality is reciprocal, as when familiar TV personalities like Mary Hart, Leeza Gibbons, and Maria Menounos (and before them Hedda and Louella) appear in fictive newscasts or when films incorporate simulated *Variety* front pages. The authenticity is convincing because, in circular fashion, it often refers back to filmic sources: when, for instance, documentaries recycle old movie footage in the public domain, such as the establishing shots of Hollywood from the 1937 *A Star Is Born*, or when *Vanity Fair* photo shoots of contemporary stars re-create studio-era glamour or scenes from classic films.

Inserted clips of old films help to establish the credibility of a star's character by bringing in an extrafictive backstory. Excerpts from Bette Davis's and Joan Crawford's early films document the screen careers of their characters in *What Ever Happened to Baby Jane?* Similarly, *Two Weeks in Another Town* (1962) is considered a follow-up of sorts to *The Bad and the Beautiful* because the same people (Kirk Douglas, Vincente Minnelli, John Houseman, MGM) made it; acknowledging that continuity, a clip from *The Bad and the Beautiful* is screened in *Two Weeks* in order to confirm for the rest of the company the Douglas character's past stardom—and to give this new version extrafilmic credibility through association with the earlier backstudio classic. As for *The Bad and the Beautiful*, before its main titles begin the MGM lion roars below the studio slogan *Ars Gratia Artis* and is then succeeded by the fictional Shields studio's logo—what else but a shield sporting the motto *Non: Sans: Droit.* This shield then remains behind the opening credits for their duration; the logo's placement there gives it a patina of authenticity prior to the narrative's beginning, thereby investing this fictional studio with the aura of a "real" Hollywood counterpart of Metro-Goldwyn-Mayer.

Extrafictive authenticity can result from many different types of self-referential quoting of Hollywood's immediate past, as the shield behind the credits of *The Bad and the Beautiful* illustrates. The 1954 remake of *A Star Is Born* authenticates its complex view of Hollywood through a network of quotations of its star (Judy Garland), its genre (the musical), and the studio most associated with it (Metro-Goldwyn-Mayer and its Arthur Freed production unit, which nurtured Garland). Jane Feuer points out that through its tempo, costuming, and male dancers, Garland's first number, "Gotta Have Me Go with You," quotes her last one in an MGM feature, "Get Happy" from *Summer Stock* (1950). Then the movement to "The Man That Got Away," the second number sung in a torchy, histrionic style never allowed at MGM, acknowledges the offscreen demystification of Garland's MGM star image following her termination, suicide attempt, and comeback in vaudeville at the Palace theater. Likewise, "Born in a Trunk," an MGM-style musical in miniature, evokes Garland's vaudeville background, her indelible identification with the musical genre, and her Palace theater comeback, but without parodying her talent or tarnishing the mystique of her stardom, which stands as the referential ground of Vicki Lester's (Feuer 1993, 119–20). Additionally, Garland's drag costume in the "Swanee" part of "Born in a Trunk" and in "Lose That Long Face" quotes from "A Couple of Swells" in *Easter Parade* (1948), which she also performed in her Palace act.

Gerald Mast calls *A Star Is Born* "a retrospective history of Judy Garland" but points out how it riffs on MGM's *Singin' in the Rain* as well. The two musicals open with search-lights beaming through the night sky to announce a gala industry event, and both close by returning full circle to the same theater where they began. Garland's ragamuffin newsboy in "Long Face" dances in puddles and is stopped by a cop, echoing Gene Kelly's performance of that other backstudio picture's title song. In its set design, themes, and narrative structure, "Born in a Trunk" liberally quotes from the big "Broadway Ballet" number in *Singin' in the Rain*, the difference being that Kelly's motto is "Gotta dance," whereas Garland's is "Gotta sing!" (Mast 1987, 275). Additionally, Garland's bricolage number, "Someone at Last," in which she single-handedly performs a big production number using whatever props she finds at hand in her living room, trumps in its scale the "Moses Supposes" bricolage number in *Singin' in the Rain* while parodying the big ballet number like the one in that musical; indeed before beginning, Garland/Vicki Lester mentions the ballet in *An American in Paris* (1951) as the prototype of the number she has been rehearsing at her studio.

As the physical settings of *The Bad and the Beautiful, Singin' in the Rain, A Star Is Born,* and scores of other such films serve to remind us, the home studio campus makes for a ready-at-hand location, one that immediately and automatically casts an air of authenticity on any backstudio picture. Often it is simply a matter of our knowing that a soundstage set is set on a real soundstage. But sometimes the studio becomes a kind of player in the picture due to its omnipresence throughout the diegesis. *The Studio Murder Mystery* (1929), *Star Spangled Rhythm* (1942), and *The Errand Boy* (1961) take their characters all over the Paramount studio lot, much as the three backstudios from Warners lead their characters around that Burbank lot. But it is a made-for-TV movie from the 1970s that makes the most self-referential use of footage of a real-life studio. *The Phantom of Hollywood* (1974), whose mystery plot is pretty much borrowed from *The Preview Murder Mystery* (1935), takes place at Worldwide Films, a stand-in for MGM, which produced this backstudio picture for airing on CBS.

Just as MGM was doing at this time, *The Phantom of Hollywood* opens as financially troubled Worldwide has sold Lot 3, is preparing to do the same with Lot 2, and is auctioning off its props and costumes. "The day of the Hollywood backlot is over," studio head Roger Cross (Peter Lawford) states, echoing a news reports shown at the start, which covers the fire sale at Worldwide and points out that audiences now expect "real locations." Later, actual documentary footage of the MGM auction and its second lot being bulldozed to make way for condominiums is intercut with new scenes shot for the movie that thematically link the famous company with the fictive Worldwide; reciprocally, such footage of "real locations" also refers back to MGM, substantiating the authenticity of Worldwide as the Culver City studio's transparent stand-in. As Cross takes the prospective buyers of Lot 2 on a tour of Worldwide, again informing everyone that "pictures are being made on actual locations now," the group travels along "actual locations" purportedly at Worldwide but still at MGM, where they are genuinely threatened by the sale of Lot 2, such as New England Street with Andy Hardy's house, Little Old New York, and Old Europe. Delivering the guided tour of Lot 2, "the backlot, as we call it," Cross's assistant links the sets to actual MGM films from the studio era, mentioning titles of several well-known MGM films. Underscoring his spiel, the soundtrack plays the familiar melodies of songs from MGM musicals. The deserted, weather-beaten sets standing in the present day illustrate the studio's (and studio system's) erosion, which "the Phantom" is trying to prevent by haunting Worldwide and killing the site surveyors and other contractors when they appear on Lot 2. "To destroy the back lot is to destroy yourself!" the Phantom warns Cross.

Aside from its extensive use of the Culver City backlot, both as remembered and as it was being dismantled, *The Phantom of Hollywood* sustains the equivalence of Worldwide and MGM by drawing on many of the other self-referencing conventions already discussed. As a means of documenting Worldwide's celebrated history for the diegesis, the film incorporates recognizable clips from MGM classics like *Grand Hotel* (1932) and *San Francisco* (1936) but attributes them to Worldwide. To commemorate its history while celebrating the sale (and demolition) of Lot 2, Worldwide prepares an anthology of excerpts from its treasure chest of old films, just as MGM was doing with its compilation

That's Entertainment! (1974), released theatrically that same year. The ultimate self-reflexive nod occurs via the casting. The actress playing Cross's daughter, whom the Phantom kidnaps, is Skye Aubrey. Her real-life father, James Aubrey, was the studio head who, acting with the blessing of the new owner, Kirk Kerkorian, had begun gutting MGM in the early 1970s, much as Cross does in this fictional account.

Only in the Movies

The various strategies for documenting an insider's view of Hollywood suggest that, in the final analysis, backstudios gain their authority by referring their depictions of filmmaking back to their own production as a backstudio picture. Trailers for some of the most memorable ones well illustrate, albeit in simple terms, how the genre's self-reflexivity, which I have so far only sampled, structures an insider's sense of authenticity for the films being advertised. This is not to imply that the trailers themselves are simplistic, however, for as Lisa Kernan notes, "trailers are where Hollywood displays its contradictions right to the point where its promotional message is most direct" (Kernan 2004, 9). In each case I will examine, a trailer uses its source, a major backstudio picture, to authenticate its message of taking viewers inside Hollywood. Furthermore, as studio marketing tools for promoting their films, these trailers give a good sense of the industry's understanding of the backstudio's relation to the real through the reel.

One common device in a trailer promoting a backstudio is to ride the coattails of the director's well-known credentials and equally well-known backstory as either an auteur or maverick, or both. For instance, we learn from the trailer for *S.O.B.* that "Blake Edwards, the man who gave the world *The Pink Panther* and then went on to create a perfect *Ten*, knows everything there is to know about Hollywood. That's why he wants to destroy it... the funniest way possible." This narration encourages us to infer, as the referential ground for *S.O.B.*, that, as was widely assumed at the time, Edwards's devastating satire of Hollywood acted out his rage at what Paramount's management had done to *Darling Lili* (1970), the failure of which had momentarily tarnished both his and Julie Andrews's standing in the industry, as Joyce Haber was continually reminding her readers in her daily gossip column. (▶ Clip 1)

The trailer for *The Player* (1992) similarly invests this film's take on Hollywood's insincere and backstabbing players with the authenticity of its director's reputation: "From director Robert Altman comes a story of Hollywood." Much like the one for *S.O.B.*, this trailer's guarantee of diegetic authenticity refers, on one hand, to an audience's familiarity with Altman's filmography while, on the other, it addresses an insider's or cinephile's more nuanced knowledge of the director's checkered studio career, one characterized by box-office triumphs and failures as well as maverick behavior matched by critical praise.

The Player's trailer further substantiates its claim of authenticity by proposing that life and the movies mirror each other within the Altman film. As clips of various pitches are shown, a narrator synopsizes Altman's "story of Hollywood" with these details: "Griffin

Mill is a hot-shot studio exec. He's heard every pitch. He knows all the angles and all the players. Now, he's about to star in his most unforgettable story yet. The trouble is…it's not a movie. It's his life." Playing into the conundrum that "life" not only imitates but is shaped by the logic of movies, a short scene follows with the two lead performers. Greta Scacchi asks Tim Robbins (as Griffin Mill), "Do places like this really exist?," and he replies, "Only in the movies." The trailer closes with another clip, this time of Robbins at a meal with several colleagues. He asks, "Can we talk about something besides Hollywood? We're educated people." His straight face breaks into a knowing laugh at his own pretentious sincerity, implicitly justifying the focus on diegetic *and* extra-diegetic Hollywood as a place that exists "only in the movies." At the same time, the movies supply the narrative model as well as the artistic inspiration for a life outside the movies yet lived entirely within Hollywood, which is ultimately, we are assured with some degree of self-conscious irony, "the most unforgettable story yet." (▶ Clip 2)

In comparison, the trailer advertising *The Bad and the Beautiful* may leave the impression that it promotes only this lavish melodrama's take on celebrity and power, not its backstudio account of Hollywood careers and betrayals. However, one ought not to ignore the footage excerpted from the film that visualizes what the trailer's voice-over describes. An announcer asks, "What goes on in the private lives of the famous, the notorious?" Then he tells us what to look for: "You'll share the laughter and the tears…of talented people who stop at nothing to attain success until success stops them…of romantic people who fight for love until love whips them." Although one might not immediately realize from the way it is being described that this upcoming MGM melodrama is about Hollywood, the clips visualizing the announcer's claims imply otherwise, providing a referential field for the big, unflinching, and indeterminate spoken pronouncements. "Never has anyone dared to put on the screen a story told with such boldness," the announcer exclaims as we see Lana Turner walking onto a darkened soundstage, or, he adds—and this second phrase is marked by a cut to a visible key light—"such frankness." "Never has anyone assembled such an array of fabulous players," he continues as a second shot now makes it look as if that light were being aimed at actors coming out for a bow. (It is actually taken from a scene within the film of characters arriving at a premiere.)

Consequently, when the voice concludes with booming earnestness, "Whenever and wherever you discuss great motion picture drama, the picture that will be talked about first will be…*The Bad and the Beautiful*," the trailer's references to fame and notoriety, talent and success, as well as bold and frank filmmaking by John Houseman and Vincente Minnelli and their fabulous group of players, implicitly point to the actual production of this "great motion picture drama" coming to theaters soon from MGM just as much as it hints at the film's more circumscribed narrative of heartless, ambitious people working in Hollywood at a studio like MGM. This doubled signification, moreover, is reversible. Because of the visual cues, the generalizations about "what goes on in the private lives of the famous, the notorious" refer one back to more specific questions about what goes on behind the studio gates in Hollywood, and vice versa. (▶ Clip 3)

The trailer for *Sunset Boulevard*, with its added (for advertising purposes only) subtitle "A Hollywood Story," betrays the same self-referential gesturing but does so more boldly. After an opening title card announces "the most unusual motion picture in many years," the trailer contrasts the phoniness of Hollywood with the more truthful representation of Hollywood found in this upcoming film. First, in a clip from the final moments of *Sunset Boulevard*, Hedda Hopper recites into a telephone her news story about a murder; then, in imitation of the film's own voice-over narration, William Holden refers to what follows onscreen, all those "big black headlines about Norma Desmond and this Hollywood scandal." Holden promises to reveal "the true story of the rest of us who are involved." With the same ironic distance used by his character in the film, Holden continues, "Well, we should have lived happily ever like they do in the movies. But this is different. Because this is a Hollywood story about the people who make the movies. The little ones you never hear of, like Betty [Shafer, played by Nancy Olson] and me. The great ones like Cecil B. DeMille. All those who knew Norma Desmond, a strange woman who left her mark on all of us who crossed her path."

Yet after Holden's declaration of this story's difference from "the movies," a new male voice returns us to *this* movie; the announcer's referential detachment from the actor's implied impersonation of his character enables fiction and reality to signify each other in an even tighter self-reflexive loop. The announcer praises "Gloria Swanson, one of the great personalities of this generation in a role that comes once in a lifetime" and announces that "a new star is born in *Sunset Boulevard*, Miss Nancy Olson." With this move, a fictional "Hollywood story" of "this generation" (and note the elision of the silent era as the ground of Swanson's career) celebrates the industry's continuity by virtue of Swanson's comeback and Olson's introduction. This recontextualization of *Sunset Boulevard* obviously means to bypass Billy Wilder's scathing critique of the institution for disregarding its past and trashing its former stars, but it nonetheless keeps *Sunset Boulevard* in view as a Hollywood product, that is, as "a Hollywood story about the people who made the movies," which was itself made by those very same people. According to the trailer, this backstudio's truthfulness rests upon its confirmation of Hollywood's institutional presence, as epitomized by new stars like Olson being "born" and great stars like Swanson returning in a "once in a lifetime" role. (▶ Clip 4)

Not surprisingly, given what I have already pointed out about its press book, an equally self-reflexive discourse structures the trailer for the earlier *A Star Is Born*. It begins with an introduction to Hollywood, California, "the most glamourous city on earth," via landmarks that by 1937 were already stock markers of "a city where men and women skyrocket to fame or plunge to oblivion. What happens amid such glamorous places as the Ambassador pool? The Trocadero on the Gold Coast of the film city? At the Brown Derby where famous stars meet? Or in the gay setting of Santa Anita Park? It's all part of the fantastic Hollywood at playtime." The trailer then juxtaposes such frivolous play with the seriousness of the industry's labor: "Here behind the walls of Selznick International Studio we see Hollywood at work."

Although this version of *A Star Is Born* views Hollywood's exploitation of stardom differently than *Sunset Boulevard*, from their trailers at least they seem to be viewing the institution through the same lens, which determines how "we see Hollywood at work" and, more to the point, what that work means to signify. Much as the *Sunset Boulevard* trailer crows that the Wilder film affords Swanson a comeback and Olson a breakout role, the one for *A Star Is Born* proudly announces, using footage of her character being made up for a screen test, that "a new Janet Gaynor is in the making, a Janet Gaynor never before seen on the screen." Following equal time for her costar Fredric March, "more swashbuckling than ever before," the trailer moves further behind the scenes, showing William Wellman directing his two stars. He gives instruction to "Freddy" on how to act in a love scene with Gaynor and shouts, "Roll 'em." We then immediately see a clip from the finished film but one now recontextualized by the trailer to make it seem as if we were watching the scene as it was being filmed by Wellman in the Selznick studio.

And just as the *Sunset Boulevard* trailer contrasts itself with other movies by referring to its industrial self-awareness and disdain for the phoniness of Hollywood endings, this one promises "Hollywood's first true story" and then warns audiences, "But don't come to see *A Star Is Born* expecting to find a Cinderella story or a glorification of motion pictures. Instead, you will be shocked by the price that must be paid in heartbreak and tears for every moment of triumph in Hollywood." Elaborating upon this theme, the announcer refers to this film's "bold revelations of how screen careers are ruined," all the while casting these revelations as a "rich human interest story," one showing that "Hollywood is filled with happiness and despair, joy and tragedy, a crazy quilt of madness, sanity, laughter, and tears." Ultimately, the announcer promises, "Janet Gaynor and Fredric March in *A Star Is Born* give you a Hollywood the world has not known. They answer for the first time the question, What is the cold fear clutching the hearts of the famous?"

Similar to the plans for exploitation laid out by its press book, the trailer for *A Star Is Born* crystallizes how the genre's self-referentiality works to authenticate both its back-studio revelations and its branding of the film industry as "Hollywood." But so do the other examples I have offered. In each trailer, the extrafictive guarantee of truthfulness lies in the film itself, which is then viewed doubly as a diegetic representation (the fictional story referring in one way or another to real-life practices, people, histories) and as an objective correlative of both the industry (the product perpetuating the mystique of the movies) and its location (that "glamorous city" in California). Thus scenes from *A Star Is Born* (such as Gaynor in a makeup chair and, later on, of her accepting an Oscar and March interrupting the ceremony to plead for a job) illustrate what the announcer says about the "new" Gaynor or about the eventual payment "in heartbreak and tears for every moment of triumph in Hollywood." With these claims so illustrated by the Selznick production, the trailer wants us to see how *A Star Is Born* is capable of merging fiction and reality. It is not the Selznick studio's refusal to offer "a Cinderella story" but its manufacturing of *A Star Is Born* that contrasts with both the frivolity of Hollywood "playtime" and the make-believe that "a glorification of motion pictures" perpetuates. (▶ Clip 5)

All the same, the *Star Is Born* trailer *is* glorifying motion pictures through its self-reflexivity. This strategy performs the symbolic condensation that gives "Hollywood" its currency as a place (the initial display of southern California landmarks), which in turn is understood to be equivalent to the film industry (the Selznick studio at work, shown making this film) while also being synonymous with the fantasy that glorifies the work, enabling it to signify as an institution ("the rich human interest story of Hollywood," which turns out to comprise the triumphs and tragedies of stardom for characters and actors alike). The process of recounting what happens behind the scenes secures the import of Hollywood through its product. This trailer, in sum, fully recognizes that the ultimate referent of *A Star Is Born* is its own material existence as a film about making movies. This is ultimately how the genre's self-reflexivity authors "Hollywood," producing what it means in order to sustain the term's circulation as a value-heavy brand. At once a material place and ephemeral fantasy, "Hollywood" is presumed to represent the film industry overall, which is also to say that it works as the industry's stand-in.

Inside Hollywood

Few backstudios are as thoroughly and consistently self-regarding as those trailers, but most of them in one way or another at least momentarily let slip the genre's self-reflexive logic. The already noted inclusion of clips from previous films, as in *Sunset Boulevard*, *What Ever Happened to Baby Jane?*, *Two Weeks in Another Town*, and *The Phantom of Hollywood*, automatically opens up a self-reflexive circuit as a means of documenting an authentic Hollywood, but such literal "quoting" is not the only means of achieving that impression. To borrow the phrase from the *Star Is Born* press book, a backstudio picture aims to document Hollywood by speaking in its "own language."

Although the text of *A Star Is Born* supplies almost all the imagery for its trailer, the film itself is much more illusionistic and, aside from the speeches about the price of stardom in heartbreak or the odds against breaking into the movies, is much less openly defensive about its authenticity in going behind the scenes to recount the opposite of a "Cinderella story." Even so, *A Star Is Born* opens and closes with pages from its final shooting script, and this trope discursively frames the film's authenticity as self-knowing Hollywood product (Smyth 2006, 269). The script not only invents but also transcribes the final speech just delivered by Janet Gaynor on film: "This is Mrs. Norman Maine." Although an artifact of filmmaking, the script as visualized has the first *and* last word on Hollywood. (▶ Figures 1.3–1.6 and 1.7–1.10)

Additionally, the opening establishing shots of Hollywood as a beckoning El Dorado, used in the trailer, slyly reveal this film's self-reflexive texture: as the camera pans across the swimming pool of what is probably the Ambassador Hotel, we come to realize that the pool is also being used as a location for a film shoot. Not stopping with this kind of self-reflexive framing, *A Star Is Born* uses Hollywood's own discourse to document the authenticity of Esther's and Norman Maine's presence as stars. Throughout, inserts of industrial texts document her rise, their marriage, and his fall through billboards (when signage with Vicki Lester's name effaces Norman Maine's from original advertising for *The Enchanted Hour*); tabloid newspaper headlines ("VICKI LOVES IN TRAILER!"); gossip columns ("What famous male star has stopped gargling the grog and is now taking a non-alcoholic honeymoon?"); a seasonal program for exhibitors ("Mr. Exhibitor, Here's a message of vital importance to you: Get Rich with Oliver Niles Productions!"); and the trades ("Norman Maine Contract with Niles Cancelled").

For all their overt dramatization of Hollywood chicanery and hypocrisy, then, back-studio pictures never break free of Hollywood's own discourse; on the contrary, their claims to authenticity rest on incorporation of that discourse, a convention firmly in place by the early 1930s. *What Price Hollywood?* (1932) uses a montage of theater marquees to record Mary Evans's (Constance Bennett) success in films as "America's Pal" and then does something similar with newspaper headlines to document her fall from stardom following a scandal. Like *A Star Is Born*, *What Price Hollywood?* also inserts "Hollywood documents, both private (film call sheets and script inserts) and public (gossip columns and excerpts from *Variety*)" (Smyth 2006, 259). *Bombshell* (1933), which deliberately blurs the difference between Jean Harlow and her character, movie star Lola Burns, opens with a montage to establish Lola's stardom by embedding it with visual allusions to Harlow's; later in the film, Lola goes to her studio to do reshoots on *Red Dust* (1932), the film Harlow had made the year before with Clark Gable, who himself is referred to as Lola's costar. Similarly, the frenetic farce *Boy Meets Girl* (1938) parodies the already established "star-is-born" narrative of *What Price Hollywood?* and *A Star Is Born* with a hilarious faux trailer that recounts Baby Happy's rapid rise to stardom at the expense of adult cowboy costar Larry Toms (Dick Foran).

It is also worth noting about this convention that the short subject *Hollywood Extra Girl* is itself a trailer of sorts for Cecil B. DeMille's latest epic. It recounts how an extra girl, Suzanne Emery, happens to meet DeMille on the Paramount set of *The Crusades* (1935), and their meeting may result in her first big break. Aside from being a mini-backstudio, *Hollywood Extra Girl* is an example of how "DeMille authored the trailers for his sound features as ten-minute 'story shorts,' providing audience members with a backstage look at the director at work" (Kenaga 2011, 86). With that in mind, it is hard not to consider his later and more famous cameo appearance in *Sunset Boulevard*, when he meets Norma Desmond on the set of *Samson and Delilah* (1949), as another DeMille "story short." The scene in question not only garners publicity for the director's new blockbuster, in effect acting as its trailer, but it dramatically mirrors and so refers back to the earlier *Extra Girl* short. In both we see DeMille at work on the Paramount soundstage, barking orders to assistants and technicians; then, when the woman gets his attention, he stops what he is doing to talk to her privately and paternally about the movie business. True, the two women couldn't be more different. Norma is bitter at being forgotten by Hollywood but remembered by the below-the-line workers, whereas Suzanne is earnest but not yet recognized, standing out to DeMille initially because of a dresser's error with the young

The pool shots from the Los Angeles montage in *A Star Is Born*. Note the presence of a movie crew in the second shot. (*A Star Is Born* ©1937 United Artists)

A STAR IS BORN

Scene 1

FADE IN:

MOONLIGHT. LONG SHOT EXPANSE OF SNOW.

In the foreground a wolf silhouetted in the moonlight.

In the background the isolated farmhouse of the Blodgetts.

As we hear the melancholy howling of the wolf, we

DISSOLVE TO:

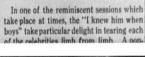

CINEMA SIDELIGHTS
BY ARTIE CARVER

What famous male star has stopped gargling the grog and is now taking a non-alcoholic honeymoon? But why do friends think his bride came about six performances too late as far as the public is concerned?

• • •

In one of the reminiscent sessions which take place at times, the "I knew him when boys" take particular delight in tearing each of the celebrities limb from limb. A non-

ARTIE CARVER

Examples of Hollywood discourse quoted by *A Star Is Born*: the screenplay, a tabloid newspaper, a gossip column, a billboard, an exhibitor's manual, a trade paper. (*A Star Is Born* ©1937 United Artists)

woman's wig. But the shared discursive frame of the DeMille "story short" forges a comparison between the two women that makes Norma's obsolescence all the more poignant—just as it makes DeMille's ability to retain his stature in Hollywood all the more patriarchal: On the basis of these two studio scenes, little has changed for *him* in fifteen years.

In more contemporary backstudios, the inclusion of faux TV news magazine reports, often featuring the actual anchors of *Extra* or *Access Hollywood*, now perform the same expositional function of those inserted faux trailers, gossip columns, trade paper headlines, and montages in framing stardom through Hollywood's discourse. Even so, references to trailers, themselves still a staple for marketing films, have not disappeared. *America's Sweethearts* (2001) begins with faux trailers to characterize the star power of its Hollywood couple (Catherine Zeta-Jones and John Cusack), only to contrast that illusory union with the diegetic reality of their public separation, caused by her infidelity and resulting in his breakdown. The faux trailers supply exposition, but also, because they are so obviously bad versions of Hollywood spiel, they openly display the artifice that the diegesis then exposes and which the studio head and his lackeys try to contain by fabricating the couple's reunion for the press junket of their final film together. That film then reestablishes backstudio authenticity with still another reversal: the crazy director (Christopher Walken) has jettisoned all the story footage, replacing it with what he discretely shot when the actors thought they were off-camera, revealing their more authentic and unflattering personalities.

Related to the faux trailer as a self-authenticating stratagem is the inclusion of a film within a film, whether its plot function is a screen test, a studio screening of dailies, a rough cut, a sneak preview, or a gala premiere. These usually occur at some point during the backstudio narrative, usually to clinch a neophyte's success or represent the finished product. Christopher Ames calls this type of sequence the "framed screen" or "framed film" (Ames 2013, 214–15):

> Over time, a fairly consistent cinematic syntax has developed that shapes how framed films are depicted. The director has available a set repertoire of shots that shows the movie-within-the-movie: a full-screen shot in which the framed film occupies the entire screen; a framed shot in which the framed film occupies most of the screen but a frame (such as a theatre curtain or the edge of a television or monitor) is visible; a shot which includes the viewers (often from the rear or the side) in the frame along with the framed film; and, finally, a reverse-angle frontal shot of the audience watching the film (often illuminated by the light of the projector). (215).

Ames calls the reverse of this convention "a 'reality cut,' in which we don't know for certain that a full shot of a movie-within-a movie is indeed a framed film until we pull back or cut into a 'reality' which shows the frame or the audience" (215). In a famous example of this convention, *Sullivan's Travels* (1941) opens with shots of a steaming train roaring across a bridge. Two men viciously fight each other on top of a boxcar until one pulls a gun and shoots. Following a struggle, both fall into the waters below. "The End" appears on a screen. Now it is clear we have been watching a film-within-a-film as it was being screened. The scene dramatizes capital and labor destroying each other, or so John L. Sullivan (Joel McCrea) explains to his producers, using it to illustrate the kind of realism he now wants to write and direct.

The Last Tycoon (1976) opens much the same way. A mobster shoot-out filmed in black and white turns out to be footage being screened so that Monroe Stahr (Robert De Niro), a character modeled on MGM's boy genius, Irving Thalberg, can suggest cuts. In a variation of the "reality cut," Jeanne Moreau and Tony Curtis soon appear in another black-and-white scene until someone yells "Cut!" and a reverse shot in color shows the studio soundstage where this scene is being filmed. (⊙ Clip 6) Moreau's character then asks for another take and quarrels with her director (Dana Andrews), whom Stahr removes from the picture. A short while later this trope is more or less undercut when a tour guide (John Carradine) takes a group of sightseers around the studio lot. After he explains how the earthquake in *San Francisco* (1936) was manufactured on the company's largest stage, an actual earthquake strikes the studio, damaging a water tank that floods the soundstage and jeopardizes the lives of those visitors.

Variations of the framed screen and reality cut abound. In *Singin' in the Rain* color fades to black and white during the dubbing scenes in order to segue into the finished version of *The Dancing Cavalier*. This visual transformation distinguishes the film-within-the-film's "authentic" status as a 1927 product as it presumably exists within the diegesis from Hollywood's manufacturing of illusionism in 1952. *The Cat's Meow* (2001), on the other hand, does the reverse. It begins and closes with black-and-white imagery as a means of setting its historical narrative in the silent era. Another version of this convention occurs with regard to filming on a soundstage, as in the first scene of *Slightly French* (1949): the camera pulls back at the end of a musical number to reveal the cinematographer and other tech people recording its filming. Or when Jack Andrus (Kirk Douglas) first arrives at Cinecitta in *Two Weeks in Another Town*, the widescreen framing exposes the artifice of a supposed outdoor scene only to make us realize its authenticity moments afterward. For even though the scene being shot looks phony, the painted backdrop and the tank in which two actors sit in a rowboat are realistically part of the studio shoot.

A precursor of these examples happens on a studio soundstage in *Lucky Devils* (1933). Starring Bill Boyd shortly before he personified Hopalong Cassidy, it opens with a violent bank robbery: A gang member played by Boyd smashes a pane of the huge lobby's glass-domed ceiling, announcing, "This is a stick-up!" The scene, with close-ups such as an initial view of Boyd on the roof punctuating longer shots of tumultuous action occurring on what is a large, realistic-looking interior set, plays out like a typical early sound-era gangster film. As both the robbers and bank personnel take out their guns, people get shot and drop to the floor; others tumble or are pushed down a staircase from the offices on a second-floor landing; and Boyd's character, clinging to a chandelier, is shot and falls to the ground. But after that happens, a voice shouts, "All right, cut it! How's that for sound? Okay, print it!"

This bravura opening turns out to be a robbery scene being filmed on a soundstage with stuntmen taking on the most physical roles. "I never knew they took such chances," a surprised onlooker comments, approaching one of the female actors who had been thrown down the stairs—but "she" turns out to be one of the "lucky devils" team in drag, standing in for an actress who was spared taking that fall. The conundrum staged by the stunts in *Lucky Devils* is that, as the daredevil action increases in danger and intensity during the course of the narrative—and the stunts are, to say the least, pretty impressive— the actors playing stuntmen in these big scenes are themselves being played by their profes- sional counterparts; we are therefore invited to see through the diegesis at the same time that we may be just as amazed by its illusionism.

The Stunt Man (1980) likewise plays with the illusionism of moviemaking as a film crew prepares a battle scene for filming on the beach. A man with a megaphone tells the assembled crowd of observers that they can watch and take pictures as long as they don't move during the shot, and the assistant director's voice states that this is "a five-camera shot for scene number thirty-six, take one." After much firing of guns and explosions, the crowd applauds until the smoke clears, when they scream or gasp at what they see: the beach littered with mutilated bodies. Befitting his background as a Vietnam vet, the film's protagonist, Cameron (Steve Railsback), shouts for medics, believing the scene to be real. However, like the opening of *Lucky Devils*, the stunt director, Chuck (Charles Ball, a bona fide stuntman in his own right), shouts, "Cut, that's a print," and stuntmen rise from their sandy graves, removing the prosthetics, peeling off cosmetic wounds, or unhooding the burlap protecting their buried heads. After the crowd responds with relief and more ap- plause, a bystander states, "Great, but why do they always use so much blood? It ruins the realism, don't you think?" Cameron calls him an asshole as a helicopter with director Eli Cross (Peter O'Toole) whirls in the air offscreen.

Moments later Cameron watches an old woman walk along the edge of the embank- ment; jostled by the whirling blades of the helicopter, she falls into the water. Cameron rushes to rescue her. As he carries her out of the water, the woman pulls makeup off her face, revealing herself as the much younger actress Nina Franklin (Barbara Hershey), star of the movie being filmed. Startled by her transformation, Cameron drops her in the shallow water. Nina explains, "It's a makeup test," and he recognizes her from seeing her on television. "Rescue me," she pleads, adding that she always wanted to have someone rescue her. As he picks her up again, Cameron states, "This is just like in the movies," but Nina corrects him: "I *am* the movies."

These last examples reframe in movie terms an event that is initially presented as actually happening; as a self-conscious representation of Hollywood's manufacturing of the real, whether through stunt doubles, special effects, or postproduction processing, this tactic gives greater credibility to the film's acknowledgment of Hollywood's illusionism. *It Happened in Hollywood*, a minor backstudio about the revival of cowboy films in the

1930s, makes somewhat the same point narratively in its climax. Although he desperately needs the work, unemployed and broke cowboy star Tim Bart (Richard Dix) walked off a picture, quitting before his scene could be finished because, out of fidelity to his star image and its fan base of young boys, he could not bring himself to play a bank robber. Now he may be regretting his decision as he stands outside the same building that the film company had used as the location for that scene. The cowboy's motive for staring at the frontage of the bank, though, is not entirely clear: Does he intend to play the robber after all? Or in his desperation is he now thinking about robbing the bank himself? As it invariably happens in Hollywood, inside the bank a *real* robbery is underway; as "life" now imitates the movies, the cowboy not only stops the theft and brings the thieves to justice but, with this single heroic act, Tim Bart reclaims his former stardom from silent pictures *and* he revives the western's popularity. And a newspaper headline exclaims, "FILM HERO REAL HERO IN GUN BATTLE."

Admittedly the plot of *It Happened in Hollywood* is far-fetched in its framing of the real through Hollywood's logic, but it simply offers in very broad strokes what modern-day backstudios do with more subtlety or irony. In *The Player*, the screening of "Habeas Corpus" starring Bruce Willis and Julia Roberts betrays the diegetic filmmakers' original intention to make a gritty, realistic film without stars or a happy ending. But as well as confirming that for Hollywood the only reality is the dollar, *The Player's* own ending mirrors that of "Habeas Corpus," with Griffin Mill and his pregnant spouse repeating dialogue verbatim from that film-within-the film. The wicked truth of *The Player* is that, behind the camera and in the front office, the referential ground of a Hollywood film is always and only the film industry.

"Let's not talk about Hollywood," Griffin says with tongue in cheek in the restaurant scene excerpted for the trailer. "We're educated people." His joke is that they cannot talk about anything else, although according to *The Player* the joke is on him: He does not manipulate the Hollywood discourse as well as he thinks. Indeed the mise en scène of *The Player* repeatedly displays posters and photographs of old crime movies and thrillers, each in some way mirroring Griffin's increasingly agitated and guilty state of mind as the stalking narrative unfolds and explodes into his killing of David Kahane. While the posters may simply appear reflexive of Griffin's pathological subjectivity, making it more transparent to viewers but not to other characters, their presence can as easily be understood to explain, even determine, his unfocused guilt, moral ambiguity, and loss of control over events; these posters do so by incorporating an iconography associated with film noir to comment, often wryly, on Griffin's situation and his anxiety as a narcissistic Hollywood player obsessed with losing his job while indulging in the power it affords him. (▶ Figures 1.11–1.13)

While appearing several decades before the acclaimed self-reflexivity of *The Player*, *Sullivan's Travels* makes somewhat the same point about Hollywood's hold on its players. For most of this film Hollywood is the sole point of reference for the characters, dominating their language and hence their perception to signify their self-regarding insularity

The office of Griffin Mill (Tim Robbins). Note the poster of *Laura* hanging on the wall. (*The Player* ©1992 Fine Line)

from Depression-era America. Sullivan's producers give grudging consent for him to plan a film in the style of social realism but only "so long as there's a little sex in it," a phrase repeated several times for comic effect during the first scene. Sullivan himself thinks through Hollywood's discourse of storytelling. "How does the girl fit into this picture?" a police officer asks Sullivan about Veronica Lake's character, using the word "picture" figuratively to mean "scheme of things." "There's always a girl in the picture," Sullivan replies. "Haven't you been to the movies?" Sullivan's own self-reflexivity here refers both to the specific sense of "picture" as "motion picture" and Lake's plot purpose as "the girl" (her name in the cast list) accompanying the film director on his travels. Even at his lowest point, when sentenced to hard labor in the prison camp because he could not remember his Hollywood identity at his trial, Sullivan still thinks in terms of motion pictures: "If ever a plot needed a twist, this one does," he moans, merging his fictional life with the narrativity of Preston Sturges's scenario. When Hollywood (referring to both his studio and Sturges's crafting of a happy ending) rescues Sullivan from the prison camp and reunites him with the girl, this satisfying closure with "a little sex in it" vindicates escapist entertainment—it's all some people have, Sullivan opines—while justifying the film industry's self-regarding insularity.

Whereas characters in *Sullivan's Travels* speak in terms of Hollywood genres, plots, and narrative conventions, those in *S.O.B.* find their touchstones in marketing, grosses, and profitability. Following its precredit prologue, *S.O.B.* opens and closes with intertitles that frame its satire of Hollywood as a fable about the hypocrisies of the movie business. "Once upon a time in a wonderland called Hollywood there lived a very successful motion picture producer named Felix Farmer," the opening intertitle states. Married to a movie star (Julie Andrews) whom he also directs, and admired and beloved by everyone at his studio, Felix produced films that made everyone a lot of money until "one day he produced the biggest, most expensive motion picture of his career…and it flopped." By the end of *S.O.B.* every character, including his wife, will have betrayed Farmer, exposing their hypocritical and selfish motives. At first his friends, family, and colleagues contribute to his depression and suicide attempts; then they collude against or seek to exploit his frantic effort to transform his flop into the most expensive soft-porn Hollywood film ever made; and finally they trigger the circumstances that result in his being shot to death when, armed with a water pistol, he takes back his recut film from the studio that has, with his wife's help, reclaimed the negative. The final intertitle comments, with undisguised sarcasm, that this recut version of what had been Felix's turkey "became the biggest money-making film in motion picture history": his wife won another Oscar for daring to break with her Peter Pan star image, as Andrews herself was doing in this film by going topless, and the people running the studio "made a ton of money, and they all lived happily ever after…until the next movie."

A contrast to this anti-Hollywood fable is a running gag that establishes a reality outside of the movie business. An aged bit player, unobserved by everyone else, dies on the beach outside Felix's Malibu house and is guarded zealously by his faithful dog for the remainder of the film. While, as befitting the conventions of classical satire, the dog may epitomize the sympathetic, more humane norm against which Hollywood is being judged and found wanting in *S.O.B*, what authenticates the scathing depiction of movieland in this satire is not the running gag but the insularity of these characters, who, involved in every aspect of filmmaking, live only from one movie to the next. For them, there is no outside to the inside.

Remystifying Hollywood

The self-reflexivity of backstudio pictures gives an impression of overcoming the insularity observed somewhat differently by *It Happened in Hollywood*, *The Player*, *Sullivan's Travels*, and *S.O.B.*, but, as these films each point out, what the genre ultimately verifies is a recognition that the insider's authenticity is itself a Hollywood construct. Two backstudios admired for the self-reflexivity of their narratives as well as their styles—the studio-era *Singin' in the Rain* and conglomerate-era *Tropic Thunder*—exemplify the complexity with which this recognition plays itself out, starting with how each embeds a film-within-a-film bearing the same title and serving as a mirror refracting its backstudio story.

A memorable scene in *Singin' in the Rain* occurs when silent screen star Don Lockwood (Gene Kelly) leads movie fan and wannabe actress Kathy Selden (Debbie Reynolds) onto an empty soundstage. The locale establishes the proper setting for a love song, "You Were Meant for Me," the only means by which, Don confesses, he can reveal to Kathy the sincere lover hidden by his glamorous, loquacious, and phony movie-star persona—the persona on display in his radio interview with Dora Bailey at the Hollywood premiere that opens *Singin' in the Rain*. Before singing, in an implied parallel to what he is confessing to Kathy, Don reveals the machinery behind Hollywood's fakery—in this instance the props, colored lights, and mechanical devices, such as a wind machine, all working together to create the illusion of romance when he performs in the movies with his leading lady, Lina Lamont (Jean Hagen).

Paradoxically, while the love scene's demystification of movie magic seeks to guarantee the authenticity of Don's self-revelation, movie magic is immediately remystified once the dancing begins and the couple travels across the soundstage and through pools of colored lights: the effect of the number is precisely to achieve what Don has declaimed about movie artifice. Even more paradoxically, when Kathy and Don converse outside the soundstage before entering, Debbie Reynolds's scarf is blowing with the help of an unseen wind machine. Hollywood's magic, in short, falsifies Don's genuine personality and conceals his real talent while he is a picture personality of the silent screen, but that very magic—here in the form of a bare soundstage with its technology of romantic effects, all eloquently and gracefully manipulated by directors Stanley Donen and Kelly when filming this number—guarantees the authenticity of both character (Don Lockwood) and performer (Gene Kelly), and of the movie industry enveloping each, an industry newly energized in the diegesis of *Singin' in the Rain* by the double arrival of sound and musicals.

While *Singin' in the Rain* knowingly deconstructs the stability of origins and originality, moreover, its many winking references to MGM's past, from the recycled

Don Lockwood (Gene Kelly) shows off the elements of movie magic to Kathy Selden (Debbie Reynolds). (*Singin' in the Rain* ©1952 Metro-Goldwyn-Mayer)

Freed-Brown songs to the repurposed equipment, sets, and costumes formerly used at MGM in the 1920s, enables it to be viewed as camp, as I have analyzed at length elsewhere, or as an affectionate pastiche. Either way, the execution of "You Were Meant for Me" captures the dense self-reflexivity of *Singin' in the Rain*, which further extends to its metacommentary on the musical genre, that form's history, the star persona of Kelly, the invention of talkies, and the relations of dance to song and of voice to body (Cohan 2005, 183–245). At many points the filmmakers toy with the authenticity of cinema due to the fabricated unity of sound and image, and their playful irony occurs narratively (from Don's dishonest voice-over at the premiere that opens the film to the later dubbing of Lina by Kathy) and technologically (the sly way that Reynolds's voice is dubbed by two different women, one being Jean Hagen, who plays Lina, when Kathy is looping Lina's speaking voice).

As for leading man Don Lockwood, he crashes silent-era Hollywood as an on-set musician, but the studio takes notice of him due to his stunt work. Rather subtly mirroring the drama of voice doubling that the plot acts out through the female characters, Lockwood works as a stunt double much in the way Kelly himself relied on the services of a double for at least one stunt in the film (when Don jumps off a trolley and into Kathy's jalopy). Similarly, within the diegesis Don supposedly narrates the Broadway ballet to R. F. Simpson, the studio head, although we see it as a 1952 production number in Technicolor, in other words, not as it would have to appear in the diegesis for authenticity's sake since this ballet belies the crude sound technology of early talkies, with their static cinematography and lumbering choreography. The punchline calling attention to the anachronism occurs afterward, when Simpson confesses he cannot quite visualize it and Lockwood's pal, Cosmo Brown (Donald O'Connor), remarks, "On film it'll be better yet."

As Cosmo's ironic comment indicates, remystification is the means by which *Singin' in the Rain* endorses Hollywood movie magic, best epitomized by the spectacular musical numbers, which belie the labor, multiple takes, prerecorded singing, and postrecorded tapping that enable the dancing to appear seamless, uniting sound and image and making the body appear as their common origin. Don's singing and dancing, in fact, implicitly respond to Kathy's dismissal of silent film acting as "a lot of dumbshow" when she first meets him. "You're nothing but a shadow on the screen," she taunts Don. "A shadow." The seamless way in which musical numbers are filmed in *Singin' in the Rain*, by contrast, secures the illusion of a performer's full presence on screen. On the other hand, the plot's conflicts initially occur because of the instability of sound technology, as the hilarious sneak preview of *The Dueling Cavalier* makes explicit when the dialogue goes out of sync with the imagery, dislocating voices from their bodies. The solution—turn that turkey into a musical by dubbing Lina Lamont's voice—sidesteps the problems implied by Hollywood's reliance on industrial labor and technology insofar as such fakery challenges the authenticity of sound, not of moviemaking.

Consequently the plot of *Singin' in the Rain* restores one's confidence in sound by resecuring the stable relation of voices and bodies. To achieve this end, the narrative appears to look beyond the medium of film: in the climax, Don and his cronies pull back the curtain of Grauman's Chinese Theatre to reveal Kathy onstage singing for Lina, who was miming the lyrics to the song "Singin' in the Rain." In keeping with this backstudio's self-reflexivity, although this revelation occurs with reference to a live performance and the point is to expose Kathy's physical presence behind the curtain, *Singin' in the Rain* then immediately realigns this revelation with the medium of film. Don shouts to the moviegoing audience that the concealed young woman was the real star of the picture they had just wildly applauded, and he prevents Kathy from fleeing the theater in embarrassment. The final two-shot of Reynolds and Kelly inside the theater dissolves into an exterior shot of the same couple beneath a billboard advertising Don Lockwood and Kathy Selden starring in a new film musical also called "Singin' in the Rain." (▶ Figures 1.14–1.15)

Such self-reflexive differentiation of what is authentic from what is fabricated is complexly handled by *Singin' in the Rain*, but it is also typical of the backstudio genre overall. As already stated, one central trope by which a backstudio authenticates its perspective on Hollywood is by openly interrogating or at least pointing out the movies' manufacturing of reality. *Singin' in the Rain* is not singular in this regard, but it most famously and perhaps most playfully writes large the problematic motivating backstudio pictures as a genre, namely, that its knowingness about Hollywood arises from an ambivalent stance toward moviemaking due to the technological manipulation of imagery and sounds composing the finished print. Backstudio pictures usually make no effort to conceal the fact that what makes movies authentic is their illusionism; if the illusion is not viewed, as in *Singin' in the Rain*, as a technological effect required of the industrial production of movies, then, as this musical also has it, Hollywood's manufacturing of illusions is revealed to be part and parcel with its selling of movies and their stars.

Tropic Thunder aims for the same inside view of Hollywood that characterizes *Singin' in the Rain*, albeit with much more postmodern irony—and ambiguity; this parody of the war film and male stardom all too easily slides into a pastiche that celebrates what it initially mocks. Yet for this very reason *Tropic Thunder* is also a veritable catalog of conventions shaping a backstudio's self-reflexivity. It begins with a series of faux trailers that economically establish the Hollywood personages of its leading characters. In the same way that the typical multiplex program opens with an advert, here rapper Alpa Cino (Brandon T. Jackson) sells his Booty Sweat drink and Bustanut Bars. Three faux trailers—each linked to a real studio logo (Universal, New Line, Fox Searchlight), albeit not the companies (Paramount, DreamWorks) that produced *Tropic Thunder*—follow this commercial. The trailers parody contemporary genres that function as male star vehicles. Tugg Speedman (Ben Stiller) stars in a tired action film franchise, Jeff Portnoy (Jack Black) in a gross-out comedy that features him in multiple roles, and five-time Oscar winner Kirk Lazarus (Robert Downey Jr.) in an indie film about repressed gay monks. Hilariously sending up those genres and the personas of stars associated with them, these mockeries of Hollywood artifice, excess, and pretense, in turn, establish the greater authenticity of *Tropic Thunder*'s own backstudio account of a big-budget Vietnam War film, which also happens to be entitled "Tropic Thunder."

The long set-piece scene in Vietnam that follows the faux trailers initially appears to reiterate the self-authenticating strategy of *Lucky Devils'* first scene. (▶ Figure 1.16) A daring yet gruesome helicopter rescue of Four Leaf Tayback (played by Stiller as Tugg Speedman) from a Vietcong POW camp initially appears to be happening diegetically. However, Speedman and costar Kirk Lazarus—a white Australian actor who has had his skin pigmentation surgically altered in order to play an African American—break character and start bickering over Speedman's inability to emote and Lazarus's scene-stealing tears. As the stars' quarrelling abruptly stops the filming, the camera pulls back to reveal an expansive location shoot in present-day Vietnam. Here, filming on "Tropic Thunder," based on the memoir by Tayback, who lost both hands in the war (according to his memoir, the gruesome injuries happened during this climactic rescue), has gone way behind schedule, over budget, and horribly if hilariously out of control.

While director Damian Cockburn (Steve Coogan) tries to get his stars back to work, the pyrotechnic specialist, Cody Underwood (Danny McBride), accidentally triggers a series of explosions in the distance that are planned as the "money shots" of this rescue scene. The effects go off perfectly, blasting the Vietnamese landscape, but without any cameras running to record the scene. (▶ Figure 1.17). "Bungle in the Jungle!" exclaims Maria Menounos when reporting the incident on *Access Hollywood*. To circumvent mercurial producer Les Grossman's (Tom Cruise) threat of shutting down production if Cockburn cannot gain control of his cast, the real Tayback (Nick Nolte), present on the shoot as technical adviser, urges the director to take his lead actors into the Vietnamese jungle, where they can experience guerrilla wartime conditions firsthand, all the while being filmed with hidden cameras in the manner of today's reality TV. However, as soon as they leave the production site Cockburn is killed when he unknowingly steps on a real landmine as the five actors look on in disbelief.

From this point on, *Tropic Thunder* plays fast and loose with movie realism and the fakery enabling it. With the actors uncertain as to whether Cockburn's exploding body was real or just realistic looking, *Tropic Thunder* very cleverly begins deconstructing the illusionism of both its backstudio view and Hollywood realism. Speedman believes the body parts and blood are just props and syrup, the "smoke and mirrors" of "the movie factory," but Lazarus is convinced Cockburn really died. All the while trying to convince the others to go back, the hammy Australian still does not drop character. (He never does so, he explains, until he records the DVD commentary.) Lost in the jungle, Speedman, who cannot read a map, unknowingly leads the group out of Vietnam. In the meantime, Tayback and Underwood, who were to engineer the special effects during the actors' trek through the jungle, are captured by Flaming Dragon, a gang of pirates and heroin manufacturers. Right before their capture, moreover, Underwood learns that Tayback's memoir is all fabrication: the man had never been out of the United States before this shoot, never served in the army, and did not lose his hands. Thinking he is still making the movie, Speedman goes it alone after the other actors decide to turn back, and he too is overtaken by Flaming Dragon, although the hapless actor believes they are locals playing the Vietcong who capture his character in the script.

When the other actors rescue Speedman with the assistance of Tayback and Underwood (and, in a final joke, Speedman's agent), their strategy is inspired by the script they had been filming. In this climax, the "off-camera" diegetic action parallels step by step the helicopter rescue that was being filmed unsuccessfully "on camera" when *Tropic Thunder* began. This time, however, Speedman and Lazarus display authentic emotions, and the money shots—the explosions and gunfire Underwood engineers with his arsenal of special-effects technology—go off without a hitch, enabling everyone to escape. (⏵ Figure 1.16) As a result, while its satire of Hollywood discourages a viewer from taking the movie business seriously (save for the industry's ability to warp the characters' self-perceptions), ultimately *Tropic Thunder* confirms the authenticity of Hollywood's illusion making. To push home this viewpoint, the film's coda occurs at the Academy Awards ceremony, where a backstudio account of the bungled production of *Tropic Thunder*—a $400 million grosser entitled "Tropic Blunder: The True Story behind the Making of the Most Expensive Fake True Story Ever"—wins eight Oscars, including a best actor trophy for Speedman, thereby confirming the Hollywood mystique initially sent up for its inauthenticity. (⏵ Figures 1.19–1.20)

With its coda occurring at the Oscars, *Tropic Thunder* winks at its audience and congratulates itself for being able to puncture Hollywood's mystique but without tarnishing it. This backstudio skewers nearly every tried-and-true convention of the war movie, satirizes the pretentiousness and stupidity of movie actors, and mocks Hollywood's elephantine sense of scale. It nonetheless ends up redeeming as authentic what it parodies as inauthentic to start with. The climax affirms war movie conventions: the actors perform their courageous rescue of Speedman and, as befitting a war movie, through their heroic actions and homosocial bonding reclaim their masculinity. Furthermore, their improvisation in response to unexpected events once they go out into the jungle on their own improves upon without ignoring the script they think they are following, so in this sense they turn out to be better off without writers—and without a director too. In fact, the only writer we see at the shoot is Tayback, who has faked his memoir. Likewise the gargantuan spectacle required of Hollywood blockbusters is sent up by all the bungling in the jungle when Cockburn is at the helm, but audiences do get their bona fide money shots without much ironic punctuation during the final rescue in the movie's climax.

It may even be possible to view the effort to make a war film outside of studio control, which *Tropic Thunder* dramatizes, as a parable of sorts about modern-day filmmaking from the viewpoint of labor, not management (which is sent up by Tom Cruise's absurd, oversized physical characterization of Grossman, who is back in Hollywood). For the kind of impromptu war-like experience that the actors undergo when let loose in the jungle evokes, at least for insiders, the discourse of a Hollywood crew. John Caldwell notes that "the production war story" supplies the narrative template through which Hollywood's below-the-line workers in the technical crafts relate their experiences as crew members, "commonly tell[ing] their personal and professional stories via anecdotes and allegories that connect film/video creation to military struggle and war footing" (Caldwell 2008, 42). As Caldwell further explains, these workers talk of "the artist's 'boot camp experience'" and consider "innovation" the result of "breaking the rules" (42). Despite the characters' above-the-line status, the trope of a "production war story" describes what happens to them in *Tropic Thunder*, just as it is reflected in the eventual finished product that documents an impromptu creation out of broken rules and that gives Speedman the elusive Oscar and industry respect he has craved.

In parodying what it nonetheless wholeheartedly endorses, *Tropic Thunder* is contemporary in a slick, very postmodern sense; however, like *Singin' in the Rain* from an earlier era of film production, *Tropic Thunder* is drawn to Hollywood's self-mystifying ways despite being cynically suspicious of them. Much as in *Singin' in the Rain*, the self-reflexivity of *Tropic Thunder* tries to cut both ways. Consequently there is no doubt when watching either Hollywood satire that the filmmakers know perfectly well the extent to which their self-reflexive posturing is as highly conventionalized as the genres being sent up. This self-reflexivity, moreover, does not guarantee truthfulness and transparency, which is the naïve claim of the convention, so much as it composes a cover story: disguising the degree to which, through those same self-referential markers of authenticity, the backstudio picture performs its institutional work of remystifying both the Hollywood mystique and the industrial labor that manufactures it.

2

Imaginary Hollywood

One scene common to many early backstudio pictures depicts the arrival in Los Angeles of a newcomer looking for Hollywood. Sometimes this newcomer heads to the West Coast on her own initiative with a fierce ambition to crash the movies, but just as often she leaves her hometown with the belief, usually mistaken, that she has won a studio contract. Regardless of the plotted circumstances, although she first sets her sights on Hollywood Boulevard as her destination, the wannabe star discovers rather quickly that a career in the movies requires her to look beyond the commercial district. On the map "Hollywood" may designate a locale to the west of downtown, a suburb absorbed into the city limits in 1910, but the term also names a movie industry spread out across metropolitan Los Angeles. By the same token, in backstudios "Hollywood" can seem like a shapeshifting, imaginary locale that acquires its significance on film from its *lack* of any material basis in a "real" Los Angeles.

Show People (1928), for example, opens with an intertitle announcing this type of scene: "To hopeful hundreds there is a golden spot on the map called—HOLLYWOOD." We then see a Hollywood hopeful from Georgia, Peggy Pepper (Marion Davies), accompanied by her father, Colonel Pepper (Dell Henderson), driving along Hollywood Boulevard; they pass by more than a dozen stores and businesses affiliated with the neighborhood through their names. After gliding by these storefronts, the Peppers travel past the Bronson Gate of Paramount Pictures, the frontages of the William Fox Studio and First National Pictures, and finally the columned entrance to Metro-Goldwyn-Mayer (which released *Show People*). (▶ Figures 2.1–2.4) Once there, the seeming conclusion of their journey, the duo park on the street; from their automobile they watch a chauffeur drive John Gilbert through MGM's front gates, but when they attempt to enter, a guard stops them. (▶ Figures 2.5–2.6) Although Colonel Pepper asks the guard to direct him to the president of the company, he and Peggy are instead sent to the casting office, where hopefuls, some in costume and some not, wait on benches for the call to a day's work. Peggy gives a sample of her mimicry talents and fills out a casting card, but no employment follows. The segment concludes with another intertitle, this one explaining, "There is many a slip between the casting office card and a menu card—especially when one's capital has dwindled to forty cents."

Peggy Pepper (Marion Davies) and her father arriving in Hollywood. (*Show People* ©1928 Metro-Goldwyn-Mayer)

Many a slip between the casting office and hunger indeed! In addition to pointing out the gulf between ambition and success for aspiring talent in the movies, the opening montage of *Show People* performs four key condensations of place, and these subtle "slips," as it were, characterize the terms by which "Hollywood" as an alluring fantasy and as an industry are represented—both here, in this very witty film, and afterward, throughout the history of the backstudio picture more generally.

First, the *Show People* montage links the commercial district of Hollywood Boulevard and the enclosed industrial plants of the studios. To be sure, the famous street is itself a public space, accessible to every new arrival as well as local inhabitants and, by this point in the 1920s, already well identified with the movie business through the publicity surrounding premieres and nightclubs; it may therefore seem axiomatic—especially to non-Angelinos watching this film—that the boulevard should epitomize "Hollywood." Interestingly, though, the Peppers' arrival occurs in daylight, not a nighttime illuminated by klieg lights, and the montage displays the boulevard as a busy commercial venue, not a site of glamorous partying or red carpet promenading. There are no sightings of exotic Hollywood movie palaces like Grauman's Chinese and Egyptian theaters (the former opening in 1927, the latter in 1922). Rather, as the Peppers cruise the street, we see shots of more than a dozen shops, all identified by name with their neighborhood location:

"Hollywood Boot Shop, "Hollywood China Shop," "Hollywood Cafeteria," "Hollywood Hardware Co.," "Hollywood Public Market," "Hollywood Studio B'ld'g," and so on. "Hollywood" is made immediately legible as both the local main street of the district and the capital of movieland. "It must be Hollywood," Peggy exclaims, according to another intertitle, her mouth agape after viewing all these signs bearing that enticing name. The montage, this is also to say, visualizes how "the golden spot on the map" is itself nothing more than a sign, possibly implying that, as well as designating commercial enterprises, "Hollywood" is a commodity sold by the movies.

Second, this montage obscures the geographic distance between the boulevard and the motion picture studios that signify the allure of the industry drawing newcomers like the Peppers across the continent. As Mark Shiel notes, the montage is edited in a way that subordinates Los Angeles to Hollywood, thereby effacing the former's identity as a major urban center in its own right. Furthermore, the montage elides the distance between the individual studios themselves, "consolidating for the viewer a misleading sense that 'Hollywood' was a unified place," whereas in fact most of these compounds were or still are spread across the city and its suburbs, not located in Hollywood proper (Shiel 2012, 183). The long shots of automobile traffic in the montage, according to Shiel, are a composite of Hollywood and Washington boulevards. With the storefronts behind them, the Peppers seem to continue driving along Hollywood Boulevard, but they actually leave it. Once past the Bronson Gate of Paramount Pictures on Melrose to the south of Hollywood Boulevard, they reverse direction to drive northeast in order to reach Fox at Sunset and Western; then they head northwest to Burbank in the San Fernando Valley in order to gawk at the First National studio; then they reverse direction again, driving southwest to reach MGM on Washington Boulevard in Culver City. The editing disguises the distances traveled from one studio to the other as well as these multiple shifts on a compass. In fact, if we were to visualize "Hollywood" as mapped out by this montage, this "golden spot on the map" looks more like what will be, several decades later, the original layout of Disneyland, itself modeled on the standing sets of a studio backlot: the Peppers drive down an idyllic main street sporting an array of commercial establishments (Hollywood Boulevard), and this street ends at a quadrant leading to four enticing "lands" (in this case, the four studios: Paramount, Fox, First National, MGM). A veritable Movieland, indeed!

Third, the montage's attention to Hollywood Boulevard as it seems visually to organize and unify the Peppers' driving helps to minimize the impact of the closing revelation, namely, that as an industry Hollywood is not only geographically disparate but also inaccessible to outsiders. John Gilbert's chauffeured arrival at MGM leaves no doubt as to the guarded entrance's function in *Show People*. Once the Peppers park outside that studio, the restrictiveness of Hollywood is symbolized by the front gate. Here, with a wave of his hand or a nod of recognition, a security guard determines who has license to go inside and who gets kept out. The front gate spatially differentiates insiders from outsiders, and in doing so it marks the movie studio as a world unto itself, one that is not only bounded but also an instrument for regulating the industrial labor happening within its boundaries. As important, by denying access as well as safeguarding entrance, the front gate visualizes the marginalization of outsiders like the Peppers, which, in effect, forces the hapless wannabes back to the environs of Hollywood Boulevard, the starting point of the *Show People* montage. The financial desperation alluded to by the intertitle, which informs us that the Peppers have quickly slipped from casting card to menu card with only forty cents to their name, predicts all those rooming houses, rundown hotels, and cheaply furnished apartments on the side streets off of Hollywood Boulevard, where, as the genre builds momentum during the 1930s, unlucky wannabes in one backstudio picture after another wait anxiously for the elusive yet hoped-for phone call from a studio or Central Casting.

Fourth, and still with the front gate in mind, the bounded studio lot as it first appears in *Show People* serves as a protective barrier for Hollywood workers, guarding them from the hazards and curiosity of the outside world. Even when it satirizes producers as crass businessmen or buffoons, early backstudios typically characterize the movie studio as a benevolent and paternalistic institution, which indulges its stars while protecting them from the press, overzealous fans, and themselves. Conversely, or at least as later backstudio narratives tell it, those who reject or fail to receive the studio's safe haven as the trade-off for its regulation tend to find themselves in dire straits and with diminished agency, victims of their own self-destructiveness or self-delusions or of unforeseen events over which they have no control, as often happens in the genre when a project leaves the studio to shoot on location.

This chapter takes off from the opening of *Show People* to examine how, in representing Hollywood, the backstudio picture raises the query "Where is Hollywood?" Where does Hollywood reside cinematically for the genre? The answer is to be found on the boulevard *and* in an imaginary yet geographically unified "movieland" *and* at the borders established via the guarded front gate *and* inside the regulation and protection of the studio compound. Invariably the backstudio genre cheats when attempting to find Hollywood, rendering it simultaneously a place that can be named, mapped, and located by outsiders or tourists and one that is dispersed, guarded, and inaccessible to them.

"This Must Be Hollywood"

A few additional glimpses of Hollywood, this time from the backstudio picture's robust period in the 1930s.

In *Show Girl in Hollywood* (1930), Broadway chorine Dixie Dugan (Alice White) arrives in Los Angeles, gulled into thinking she has a firm studio contract. She immediately sends a postcard to her boyfriend, Jimmie Doyle (Jack Mulhall), who is still in Brooklyn: "Arrived safe. So this is Hollywood?" On the card's back is a picture of the Warners' theater at the intersection of Hollywood Boulevard and Wilcox. (This is a Warners–First National film, after all.) A dissolve from the postcard photo reveals a sightseeing bus traveling past the theater. In medium shot, the tour guide intones, "And now ladies and gentlemen, you are on one of the most famous streets in the world. The thoroughfare of motion picture stars—Hollywood Boulevard!" Another dissolve, this time to the sightseers, shows them staring at the landmarks pointed out by their guide. "On the right, ladies and gentlemen, you see the famous Roosevelt Hotel, patronized by the 'ee-lyte' of the motion picture stars.... And now, ladies and gentlemen, on your left you see the great Superb Motion Picture Studios." As the bus drives by, a dissolve shows Dixie walking up to that company's front entrance from the street. (▶ Figure 2.7) (▶ Clip 7)

Inside, Dixie is no nearer to the soundstages on which moviemaking occurs but instead finds herself in a hallway with marbled walls and floors and frosted-glass doors leading to executive offices or dressing rooms. On this same floor too, across from the studio head's office suite, is a telegraph office, which Dixie herself will use several times during the film to have telegrams wired to Jimmy at her own expense. A running gag involves a sign painter whose studio job is to scrape off the names on those frosted-glass doors as the front office sends a telegram firing them. In any event, later on in *Show Girl in Hollywood*, Dixie will be seen on a large soundstage that is draped in cables from ceiling to floor and bustling with all the people involved in or just watching the production number being filmed; however, according to this backstudio picture's first impression of what a studio looks like, the interior of Superb's main building is pretty indistinguishable from any other 1920s office building, and the exterior is readily accessible by tour bus since, at least as the editing implies, Superb abuts the main thoroughfare in Hollywood.

Show Girl in Hollywood is not the only early backstudio picture locating Hollywood by a bus route. Following shots of Hollywood Boulevard by day, of a nighttime premiere at Grauman's Chinese, and then of an overhead exterior shot of soundstages, when Merton Gill (Stuart Erwin) finally arrives in Los Angeles in *Make Me a Star* (1932) he takes a bus to his destination—which initially resembles the Lasky-DeMille studio on Selma and Vine (as described in Fox 1925, 32–40) before it was absorbed into the new Paramount studio complex on Melrose in 1926, where the film itself was shot. "You won't forget to let me know, will ya?" he asks the driver, who is visibly annoyed at the number of times Merton has asked to be let off at the studio where his idol, Buck Benson (Dink Templeton), works. And indeed, with a dissolve from the shot of the bus driver, the vehicle does stop at the front door of Majestic Studios. (▶ Figures 2.8–2.10) As Merton descends from the bus, Maurice Chevalier tells his driver to return for him at five. Yet while Chevalier can walk through the guarded front gate, Merton, told "No visitors allowed," is sent to the casting office, "first door on the left." There he finds a plain waiting room, much like the one in *Show People*. The receptionist, nicknamed "the Countess" (Ruth Donnelly), sits behind a glass window, looking a bit like a movie palace cashier as she screens extras for day work. A door reading "Studio Entrance" is the portal through which Buck Benson arrives to work (no explanation is offered for why the cowboy star does not drive through the front gate as Chevalier did) and from which Flips (Joan

Blondell) emerges, leaving the production area to head for "the Big Shot's office." The visual point is the room's access to the world of filmmaking inside the studio, while underscoring the prohibition on Merton's getting past this entryway.

Several other backstudio pictures from later in the 1930s similarly maintain the premise that the boulevard is the epicenter of Hollywood, at least for newcomers. In *Hollywood Hotel* (1937), after Ronnie Bowers (Dick Powell) departs from his hometown airport, armed with a ten-week contract at All Star Pictures, there is a cut to Hollywood Boulevard's street sign, then several successive dissolves, each superimposing the sign over an image from the district: a bird's-eye view, then a street-level view of the shops and department stores, then a shot of the Hollywood Bowl; this montage moves on to the Hollywood Brown Derby on Vine Street, cuts over to the Café Trocadero on the Sunset Strip past La Cienega, jumps back to Sardi's at Hollywood and Vine, then to Vendome Fine Foods on Sunset near Cherokee, detours to Wilshire nearer downtown for the Ambassador Hotel and its Coconut Grove nightclub, heads back to the Hollywood Hotel on Highland, slides over to "Harry's Personal Guide to Movie Star Homes" at 8245 Sunset, and returns to Grauman's Chinese back on the boulevard near the hotel. After all this zig-zagging, the editing moves from the commercial district to a movie set: a shot of a streetcar scene being filmed dissolves into an overhead view of a big studio (given the water tower, probably Warners' compound in Burbank, the former First National plant), itself superimposed over a street view of stucco buildings, and finally over footage of a director (Busby Berkeley?) on a boom filming dancers as part of a lavish production number. With a shift to the Grand Central Air Terminal in Glendale, Ronnie's plane lands. Significantly, although *Hollywood Hotel* revolves around movie stars and movie-making, it remains centered on the eponymous location on the boulevard, where stars, their lovers and assistants, their costumers and makeup artists, their producers and publicists, not to mention photographers and Louella Parsons, all gather as Hollywood types.

By comparison, in *Stand-In* (1937), Atterbury Dodd's (Leslie Howard) first taxi ride upon arriving in Los Angeles takes him along Wilshire Boulevard, not Hollywood, with reverse shots of him looking at the Coconut Grove's marquee outside the Ambassador Hotel, the Brown Derby's "Eat in the Hat" sign," a "Personal Guide to Movie Stars Homes Here" billboard at 9211 Wilshire in Beverly Hills, along with distinctive southern California architectural sights such as the signature windmill of a Van de Kamps bakery-café, a sphinx head near a realty company, and the dog symbolizing the Pup Eat 'n Sup. The many quick cuts and abrupt zooming in on each landmark simulates Dodd's dizziness as he, an easterner, confronts LA's amusement park–like landscape. Nonetheless, even though he is apparently on Wilshire all this time, when his taxi finally reaches a stoplight and comes to a momentary halt, it does so unexpectedly and incongruously but very noticeably at the Hollywood and Highland intersection.

Befitting its title, *Hollywood Boulevard* (1936) likewise pays a great deal of attention to its eponymous street in a long opening sequence, another of those montages "creating a seemingly cohesive image of a Hollywood world that doesn't really exist, by juxtaposing places miles apart" (Braudy 2011, 103). This film shows that Hollywood equals the boulevard even for longtime residents. It opens with an overhead view of the street's automobile traffic in daylight, which cuts to the title card, to multiple shots of people walking almost in step with the horns dominating the pulsating musical score, to an insert of the Hollywoodland sign, then to more shots of pedestrians looking up from the street toward the buildings at street corners. Following the cards identifying the cast members and cameos from the silent era, pairs of bathing beauties pose atop famous landmarks: in front of the Hollywood Bowl's acoustic shell and on the roof of the Broadway's department store branch on Hollywood Boulevard. From what looks like the latter's vantage point, a downward view of the Taft Building on Vine follows. The remaining credits are superimposed over images signifying film production: a camera popping open, a director seated in a chair, key lights, and so on. Intercut with these cards are still more shots of pedestrians, either pounding the pavement or dwarfed by the street's buildings, and of more bathing beauties now posed in precision-like formation. Finally, this montage concludes at the Hollywood street sign, with the "stop" command changing to "go." Outside the Brown Derby restaurant, a young woman's face appears in profile with the Broadway store's distinctive sign visible behind her. Cut to the restaurant's busy interior, then a closer view of the wall displaying the Derby's signature caricatures of movie stars. As a picture of Fred MacMurray is being installed there, the one of John Blakeford (John Halliday), a silent-era leading man now unemployed, falls off the wall, occasioning a remark by one waiter to another: "That's kind of funny, ain't it? Down with the old, up with the new." Noting that the ex-star has not been in lately, this waiter wonders what Blakeford is doing. "That's easy," his colleague replies. "Like all the old-timers, he's either out looking for a job or walking on Hollywood Boulevard."

Or doing both. A cut to the casting office of Modern Productions, Inc. reveals that nothing is on hand for Blakeford, and a panning shot of the boulevard that ends at Grauman's Chinese Theatre shows Blakeford happening to arrive there as the tradition of a new star's casting her hands and feet in cement continues with young Eleanor Whitney. "And now, my dear," the emcee informs her and his radio listeners, "you have left your immortal mark in Hollywood." "What does that mean?" a child in the crowd asks her mother, "'immortal mark in Hollywood'?" Momma replies, "It means that Hollywood has a new star whose name will be known forever," adding for further explanation that those "hands and feet written in cement will remain there always." In illustration there are cuts to the cement slabs (with tourists stepping over them) imprinted by Gloria Swanson, Norma Talmadge, Bill Hart, Douglas Fairbanks, Mary Pickford, Harold Lloyd, and the fictional Blakeford, dated 1929. (▶ Figure 2.11) When the child asks about Blakeford, the mother muses, "He used to be a big star," then spies him in the crowd and points him out to her daughter. "Oh, Momma, he's kinda old, isn't he?" the child observes. Hearing that reminder of his age and once "big" stardom, Blakeford leaves the crowd. As he passes Sardi's, a newspaper hawker informs him that his photo is in the day's paper, but it turns out to be a notice that Blakeford's tailor is suing him. The ex-star's stroll concludes with a cut to the Trocadero on the Sunset Strip, where, in another sign of his lost status, the doorman greets the former matinee idol coolly (due to an unpaid bar tab), in contrast with the warmer greeting afforded to two male guests who arrive just before him.

David O. Selznick feared that *Hollywood Boulevard*, which he called a cheap "quickie" from Paramount, had ruined the public's tolerance for backstudio pictures. Nor did the producer think that Warners' musical *Hollywood Hotel*, then in production, would renew their interest (Behlmer 1973, 143). As discussed in chapter 1, the trailer for *A Star Is Born* (1937) claims the greater authenticity of Selznick's take on Hollywood. All the same, *A Star Is Born* follows form with its treatment of Esther Blodgett's (Janet Gaynor) arrival in Los Angeles. It prepares for this moment with a title card that echoes *Show People*'s and then displays the same logic, condensing Hollywood Boulevard with the industry's mystique. As Esther departs from a dark, snow-covered train depot in North Dakota, an intertitle identifies her destination: "HOLLYWOOD!...the beckoning El Dorado... Metropolis of Make Believe in the California Hills" (ellipses in original). With Hollywood visualized as a utopian landscape of sun-drenched leisure and recreation, a montage reveals how all modes of transportation travel in the same direction: a bus, a train, a propeller plane, all bear signs with "City of Los Angeles" as their journey's end.

Noticeably, though, Hollywood, not Los Angeles, is named "the beckoning El Dorado," the new goal of the frontier myth propounded by Esther's grandmother (May Robson) when she sends Esther off to California with a speech that translates nineteenth-century manifest destiny into twentieth-century movie stardom. Additionally the sequence omits Esther's arrival at the city's train station and instead suggests that the real termination of her journey is Grauman's Chinese Theatre. With suitcase still in hand, apparently the first thing Esther does upon reaching LA is to head for that theater's forecourt. Only after she gazes at the celebrated footprints immortalized in cement does she look for lodgings, which she finds, as a classified ad states, at the "Oleander Arms, 1312 Marion St. nr. Hollywood Blvd." Upon checking in, Esther naïvely asks the desk clerk, "Are all the studios really near here?" He replies sarcastically, "All except Gaumont British."

The point made by the particularities of Esther's arrival in southern California, like that evident in the others I have looked at so far, is twofold. First, this sequence reiterates what has by this time become a convention of showing the boulevard as the gateway to a spatially unified Hollywood, which, in turn, serves as the portal to the restricted studio factories. Second, as the other side of this convention, the sequence establishes the palpable gulf between the boulevard and the studios. Until Norman Maine (Fredric March) intercedes and arranges for her screen test, Esther cannot get close to industrial Hollywood even though the studios may be "nr" her lodging at the Oleander Arms. She may try on for size Norman's footprints in Grauman's forecourt, but that memento of movie stardom is still just a slab of cement, a stand-in for the genuine article that marks his absence and her distance from the star-making machinery of Hollywood. A while later Esther sees Norman in the flesh but at another local recreational landmark, the Hollywood Bowl;

Straight from the train station, Esther Blodgett (Janet Gaynor) heads for Grauman's Chinese Theatre on Hollywood Boulevard. (*A Star Is Born* ©1937 United Artists)

there a highly inebriated Norman makes a scene before photographers that Esther witnesses as a spectator, as if it were a movie.

Undeterred by the discouragement she receives at Central Casting, Esther presses on, going through her savings and owing back rent to the Oleander Arms. With the help of a fellow tenant, assistant director Danny McGuire (Andy Devine), her first paid work is not in pictures but as a waitress at a Hollywood party, where, until Norman picks her up in the kitchen, she is still shut out of the film industry's world. As she circulates among the guests with a tray, no one pays attention to her imitations of the big female stars of the moment; they look at her curiously and go on with their conversations as if she were not present. In this context, when the film's ending returns Esther to Grauman's Chinese and Norman's footprints, her memorable final line, "This is Mrs. Norman Maine," harks back to her arrival on the boulevard to suggest that, putting her own fame aside, she willingly becomes another stand-in for Norman, a sign remembering his absence—and Hollywood's?—not unlike the cement slabs in the theater's forecourt.

What I find striking about these early backstudio pictures is their reluctance to show industrial Hollywood head-on and concretely to start with. To be sure, a few other early backstudios forgo Hollywood Boulevard to signify the industry's allure and set their action almost entirely in a studio. However, as in *Studio Murder Mystery* (1929) and *Lucky Devils* (1933), these plots typically involve characters already working in the industry; or, as in *Once in a Lifetime* (1932) and *Boy Meets Girl* (1938), they not only involve studio writers but are based on popular Broadway plays, transporting their more confined stage settings to the screen; or, more rarely, as in *The Lost Command* (1928), the studio setting is a framing device for a story happening elsewhere and at an earlier time.

Additionally, promotional short subjects of the early sound period purport to take a movie fan into the studios. Vitaphone's *A Trip thru a Hollywood Studio* (1935) opens with a bird's-eye view of Hollywood, while a voice-over observes that many folks would like to visit there but cannot: "Then allow us to bring Hollywood to you." The short condenses "Hollywood" into the industry, traveling past all the major studio compounds throughout the LA area before focusing on a guided tour of Warner Bros.–First National in Burbank. After acknowledging the cost and labor of production, the short takes a viewer step by step through the process of making a motion picture. The voice-over commentary goes from department to department to show the process of preparing to film a scene featuring Hugh Herbert (script, casting, rehearsal, makeup) until it reaches a soundstage. There, with Herbert performing the scene on set, the commentary explains the technologies of cinematography and sound recording; we see a microphone on a boom, from which a cable leads to the mixer's booth. Following this "eyewitness" demonstration, we learn that a "wet" negative is developed and sent to the cutter's room, where young women prepare a positive print for the (male) editor to view on a moviola. During all of these demonstrations, the short also aims to exhibit Rudy Vallee, Alice White, Pat O'Brien, James Cagney, Ann Dvorak, Busby Berkeley, and other Hollywood people in their "natural" habitat as working members of the film industry. At the conclusion, *A Trip thru a Hollywood Studio* demystifies the process of film production by showing, in all its polished illusionism, the finished scene with Herbert.

A movie studio is therefore not an inconsequential location for depicting Hollywood on film, and I shall have more to say about this locale shortly. Given the recurring type of backstudio picture about Hollywood hopefuls, though, it makes great story sense for a wannabe to view industrial Hollywood from the outside, at least initially—hence the presence of tourist activities, like the sightseeing bus in *Show Girl in Hollywood* and Grauman's Chinese in *A Star Is Born*. This type of backstudio picture has to place obstacles in the way of its protagonists, so it is not surprising that the wannabe characters fail to gain immediate entrance to a studio and cannot find employment so early in the plot. *Hollywood Boulevard* is of this story type; as this film begins, John Blakeford, while a one-time star, is now broke and essentially forgotten, despite the reminder of his stardom at Grauman's Chinese Theatre. Yet in all of my examples, from *Show People* to *A Star Is Born*, the significance of Hollywood Boulevard in the mise en scène exceeds plot purposes: the street's iconic equivalence with industrial Hollywood through imagery of consumption disavows the extent to which the movies' mystique, as opposed to the labor happening inside the studios, is potentially insubstantial, mostly ephemeral, and certainly illusory, much like the product itself.

Backstudio pictures do not deny this revelation. In *Show Girl in Hollywood*, a tour bus shows up a second time during Dixie's first day in Hollywood. After she leaves the Superb studios with a new friend, Donny Harris (Blanche Sweet), Dixie goes to the latter's spacious home in the hills for tea. The tour bus passes by, and along with Dixie we hear the guide's spiel, which essentially treats Donny's house as if it were a sight no different from those already pointed out on the boulevard. Dixie is pretty jazzed by all this. "You know, I'm getting a terrific kick out of Hollywood," she tells Donny. "Everything is new and beautiful. Everybody seems so happy." Donny, however, tries to demystify Hollywood for Dixie, stating that it is all a façade, "a land of make-believe": not only is youth the currency, which puts Donny over the hill and unemployed at age thirty-two, but her grand house is "a big lie" since most of it is closed to avoid the expense of caring for its numerous rooms. Yet Donny cannot bring herself to "sell the house and get out" because people would say "I guess she's through," and as a consequence, she confesses, "I *would* be through."

As this scene from *Show Girl in Hollywood* suggests, by locating a spatially unified if actually imaginary "Movieland" on or near the physical Hollywood Boulevard, early backstudio pictures visualize Hollywood's accessibility as a public space while hinting at its inaccessibility as an industrial space. Whether concerning the deceptive ease of getting inside Hollywood through bogus contracts or empty promises, or the masks still worn there even by those kicked out the door, the industry's reliance on illusions makes filmmaking "a big lie," starting with the mystification of its treatment of female labor. Another "big lie," this one evident in Dixie's arrival in town as well as in all my other examples, results from the visual legerdemain with which these films depict Hollywood's unification of the studio's factories through the boulevard. Given how these montages tend to jump back and forth between Hollywood Boulevard and Sunset, mid-Wilshire, Beverly Hills, the Hollywood hills, Culver City, and the San Fernando Valley, the editing seems random, the point being a display of the familiar iconography, not a coherent geography. However, as Shiel (2012) and Braudy (2011) each suggest with reference to different backstudio pictures, the editing is not haphazard at all. Rather, the joining together of disparate places invests geographic Hollywood with an illusory unity, giving it filmic solidity as a coherently defined space, what I have been calling "Movieland."

With its resonant title, *Hollywood Boulevard* is likewise illustrative of what I am pointing out. This backstudio imagines the irresistible pull of Hollywood as a state of mind emanating from the street. Blakeford's estranged daughter, Pat (Marsha Hunt), knew at age twelve that she "didn't want any part of Hollywood," which she associated with her father. Now that he is publishing his memoirs, embarrassing her mother and threatening their privacy in Santa Barbara, while being rewarded with his own comeback in films due to his new notoriety, Pat's anger has returned. Romancing Pat, screenwriter Jay Wallace (Robert Cummings) tries to reassure her that he has not been suckered into that same world. "You've got me all mixed up with Hollywood," he tells her. Rather, he intends to make his fortune writing for the screen and then will get out. Pat, however, knows better, warning him, "You're going to stay in Hollywood just as long as it wants you—and then you're going to stay longer. You love it. You love it because it's crazy and senseless and exciting."

Much later in the film, after Pat has momentarily broken with Jay when he does get drawn into Hollywood's craziness and Blakeford's public life against his will, the couple celebrate their reconciliation at a restaurant overlooking the boulevard, which is lit up behind them with numerous Hollywood signs. (▶ Figure 2.12) Jay comments, "There it is, honey. Hollywood. Just waiting for us to kick it around." And once again Pat advises caution: "Or waiting to kick us around." "Not us," Jay insists. "No, we've got a hex on it. It can't kick you around if you know what you're after." By now appreciating the reason for Pat's dislike of Hollywood, his observation, inspired by their view of the street, condenses the "crazy and senseless and exciting" world of the film industry into the boulevard, reiterating the point made by the opening sequence. "The craziest mile in the world, though," Jay comments. "Tomorrow their names up in lights. Other guys, up in lights today, tomorrow walking the boulevard, hoping their shoe leather lasts 'til the end of it. It can build you up, and it can let you down. It can give you the world with a fence around it in double time and knock it out from under you twice as fast. You know if I had to write a story about Hollywood I have the title right now: 'Too Much, Too Soon, Too Bad.'" Pat laughs at his last remark, and Jay responds in kind, suggesting a shared awareness that his inflated rhetoric here is not so much deep thought as it is part and parcel with the same sensationalized discourse characterizing the tabloid press that published the heavily revised and fictionalized version of Blakeford's Hollywood career.

"Made in Hollywood, USA"

In projecting an imagined unity for Hollywood as a place that is simultaneously geographic, industrial, and a state of mind, early backstudio pictures not only displace the mystique of the movies onto the boulevard, but they also ignore the district's historical obsolescence with regard to the film industry of the 1930s. Although early filmmaking occurred at numerous spots in Los Angeles, "quite quickly in the mid-1910s, Hollywood emerged as the most important concentration" (Shiel 2012, 32). "Hollywood" became the industry's term to identify film production even if a studio was situated in another part of the city. In 1918, for instance, the head of Metro Pictures announced "a new studio out in Hollywood," although the plant was in Culver City (Hallett 2013, 85). And by 1921 *Photoplay* already was using the term "to stand in for the industry and its personalities writ large" (151).

But whereas in the 1910s and early 1920s "the constant interplay between Hollywood, the real place, and Hollywood, the filmic place," had developed "a symbiotic relationship that facilitated and promoted the marketing of both," this mutually beneficial "partnership" had dissolved by the end of the 1920s (Charles and Watts 2000, 254). With the coming of sound and the need for new soundstages and self-enclosed backlots placed well away from traffic and other urban interference, by 1929 most of the major studios aside from Paramount and Columbia had left the Hollywood core, yet the geographic place remained identified with the film factories, "no matter where they might be in reality" (Shiel 2012, 54). Additionally, as stars moved west to the Beverly Hills environs, "residence in Hollywood became less and less an indicator of success and more associated with dreams deferred" (Charles and Watts 2000, 272). Hollywood Boulevard's association with and imagined geographic proximity to film *production* (instead of just its *consumption* in the movie palaces on the street) was therefore already an anachronism in these backstudio pictures from the 1930s, at least from the industry's perspective, if not from the tourist's or migrant's.

By the late 1920s, then, as the idiom of Dixie Dugan's dialogue and her film's title reflect, "Hollywood" was in widespread use as shorthand for the entire film industry—its production and consumption, its allure and addictiveness, its glamorous and privileged people. The name became synonymous with motion pictures in popular discourse much as Wall Street was shorthand for New York's financial institutions or Fleet Street for the British press or, later on, Nashville for country music and Madison Avenue for advertising (Braudy 2011, 54–55, 87). MGM's slogan for its twenty-fifth anniversary in 1949, "Made in Hollywood, USA by Metro-Goldwyn-Mayer," acknowledged the unmooring of Hollywood from Los Angeles and, in this case, its implicit reattachment to the nation via Culver City. The slogan celebrates "Hollywood, USA," as an industrial principle and guarantee of entertainment, not as a determinate place. As a state (of mind) in the USA, moreover, Hollywood's materiality clearly resides in a branding function; hence this slogan's continuing appearance at the end of MGM films for nearly a decade after the silver anniversary year. (▶ Figure 2.13)

Due to such widespread usage to designate the film industry in all its aspects and locales, by the 1930s Hollywood was already a very movable sign, easily detachable as a brand name for the industry from any grounding in geography. In 1933 the Chicago World's Fair hosted an exhibition devoted to motion pictures, simply called "Hollywood." Its souvenir program claimed to reveal the inner workings of the industry while indirectly underscoring its portability: "Never before has it been possible for the vast majority of people to visit the interior of a motion picture and broadcasting sound studio, and see for themselves exactly how the 'wheels go round'" (Alderton 1933, 8). Judging from its elaborate souvenir program, far from guaranteeing transparency, the Chicago exhibit was much like other short stage shows or presentations of this period (or those promotional displays tied to *A Star Is Born*, as discussed in chapter 1), which "illustrated what was purportedly framed as the entire filmmaking process." These similarly "portrayed

[Hollywood] as untouchable and magical, on the one hand, but accessible and knowable on the other" (Trope 2011, 104). The initial focus on the neighborhood of Hollywood Boulevard in these early backstudio pictures similarly betrays the secrecy and distance underlying the apparent openness and proximity with which Hollywood beckons characters from across the continent.

Despite the fact that, "when the studios and stars left Hollywood behind, they also took it with them" (Charles and Watts 2000, 272), for 1930s backstudios the boulevard location graphically keeps industrial Hollywood affixed to the city's urban geography *on film*. In these early backstudios, if the street sign does not appear, then its presence is implied by comparable signs of the street, like the forecourt of Grauman's Chinese. There is an undeniable sense to this repeated iconography, too, despite its obfuscation of the Hollywood district's historical relation to the film industry. By the 1930s the relatively new Grauman's Chinese Theatre was already "the most obvious and repeated icon of Hollywood" (Braudy 2011, 100). In epitomizing Movieland's glamour (the premieres), stardom (the forecourt), escapism (the Orientalist decor), and partying (the location close to both the Hollywood and Roosevelt hotels), the theater exemplified the physical presence of "Hollywood" so that it could seemingly be witnessed firsthand, even as the label became an increasingly immaterial shorthand reference to everything connected to the film industry yet located elsewhere. Although *Hollywood Boulevard* belabors that icon's branding function, the savvier *A Star Is Born*, made at around the same time, recognizes that Esther just needs to visit Grauman's in order to signify the intricate and dense network of feelings, ambitions, and dreams drawing her to Hollywood. Firmly identified with the industry as its iconic emblem, the boulevard exemplifies the degree to which the film industry is at once accessible and inaccessible for Esther, knowable and unknowable.

As for the Hollywood district itself? Within the city of Los Angeles, in the 1930s and then the 1940s, Hollywood was just another one of those proverbial suburbs looking for a city; its commerce on Hollywood Boulevard (movie theaters and office buildings, shops and branch department stores, bars and restaurants) was mostly aimed at local residents. Although Grauman's Chinese Theatre still hosted premieres, continued to add stars' cement blocks to its forecourt, and attracted tourists, from 1934 through 1953 the theater shared weekly first-run bookings with a downtown movie palace, and in 1942 a third venue on Wilshire was added to this arrangement. The lively nightclub scene on the Sunset Strip between La Cienega and San Vicente was not as easy a walk from the commercial Hollywood district as, say, *Hollywood Boulevard* makes it appear when Blakeford strolls there from Grauman's Chinese. In fact, the point of that transition in the film's opening montage may well be to imply that Blakeford *had* to walk to the Troc because he lacked his own car and driver.

All the same, just as studio imagery was never absent from early backstudio pictures but present at least as a secondary setting, Hollywood Boulevard never disappears entirely following the genre's big first cycle in the 1930s. Rather, the boulevard's association with industrial Hollywood's mystique remained stereotyped as part of the genre's short-hand. Consider *Hollywood and Vine* (1945), a B-picture from PRC. As its title announces, this minor backstudio focuses on the boulevard even while setting plot scenes in offices and soundstages at the fictional Lavish Studios. Told in flashback, the main story about the rapid stardom of a stray dog, Emperor (Daisy of the "Blondie" series), begins in a diner "on one of those roads leading to Hollywood." When Pop (Emmett Lynn), the character narrating at the start, gets his main character, Martha Manning (Wanda McKay), to Hollywood, his voice-over repeats almost verbatim what the intertitle of *A Star Is Born* claims about Hollywood's utopian appeal as "the land of make-believe, the glamorous mecca of enchantment." Similarly reiterating the viewpoint of *Hollywood Boulevard* as voiced by Jay Wallace, Pop goes on to state that Hollywood is "where paupers become princes and shop girls become queens." He likewise equates Hollywood the place with "the fabulous world of the movies, where careers are born and hearts are broken." According to Pop, Martha herself is in the mold of a Peggy Pepper, Dixie Dugan, or Esther Blodgett: "She was one of the never-ending stream that follows a gilded path to make their dreams come true." As Pop describes Hollywood in these by-now highly conventional terms, an accompanying montage puts together equally conventionalized images familiar from the 1930s: a shot of Hollywood from the hills, the boulevard with its traffic and buildings, a crowded hotel swimming pool, Sunset Strip nightclubs (Ciro's, Mocambo, and Trocadero), and finally, the front of Grauman's Chinese Theatre.

Additionally, the protagonist of *Hollywood and Vine*, Larry Winter (James Ellison), is a writer assigned by Lavish to write a Hollywood story. Told by his butler (Robert Greig) that "Hollywood is a state of mind," Larry goes to the intersection of Hollywood and Vine to interview pedestrians and boulevard inhabitants, starting with a paperboy who hires a bogus Lassie to prove to customers that stars do travel through this famous intersection. In fact, the Hollywood and Vine corner does turn out to be the world's crossroads as far as this film is concerned because at that intersection Larry accidentally bumps into Martha, whom he has been seeking since their first meeting in Pop's diner thirty miles away; furthermore, her lodging, like Esther's, is just off the boulevard. For all the import of industrial Hollywood in the plot of this mid-1940s backstudio picture, then, geographic Hollywood still absorbs the movies' mystique as Movieland.

Hollywood and Vine recycles the boulevard's shorthand meanings from 1930s backstudio pictures; like its formulaic plot, the exact equivalence that this B picture posits between geographic and industrial Hollywood was already well out of date by 1945. By then a simple shot or two of the boulevard was enough for the street to signify a backstudio picture. Subsequent backstudios, moreover, pretty much forgo stories about Hollywood hopefuls. These typically forsake the boulevard, always understood as a mecca for tourists, often beginning instead with second-unit footage of locations tied to particulars of the narrative, as in the close-up of the stenciled street name on the inside of a curb, which constitutes the title card of *Sunset Boulevard* (1950), or a manic Dixon Steele (Humphrey Bogart) driving on the Strip, where he nearly gets into a fistfight before arriving at Paul's (read Romanoff's, which was in Beverly Hills) restaurant in the opening of *In a Lonely Place* (1951). Other backstudios begin with actual signs of moviemaking. Shots of Fred Amiel (Barry Sullivan) seated on a boom on Stage Five, a costumed Georgia Lorrison (Lana Turner) in her dressing room, a pensive James Lee Bartlow (Dick Powell) in his office, and a front gate imprinted with the Shields logo already seen beneath the opening credits—this montage immediately establishes the setting of *The Bad and the Beautiful* (1952) in a movie studio, and that studio with Hollywood.

By mid-century it is common to find a backstudio picture opening with a visual tour of a gated film studio, this sequence explicitly fulfilling what had, throughout the 1930s, formerly been the boulevard's conventionalized function of symbolically organizing the spatial unity of Hollywood as a place and state of mind simultaneously. Now the studio compound functions onscreen to equate the film industry with other major industrial manufacturing corporations, such as for aircraft, while also effacing the imagery of the disorder caused by the strikes occurring at the studios immediately after the war.

It's a Great Feeling (1949), for instance, opens with an overhead shot of Warners' Burbank studio, the setting of this backstudio picture. An anonymous voice declares, "Just a few miles from Hollywood is the largest studio in the world, the home of Warner Bros. pictures." A dissolve takes us from an initial overhead shot of Warners' soundstages in Burbank to a ground view of the lot with a studio bus and truck, as well as a line of workers filing into the employee entrance, anchoring the change in perspective. The announcer continues, with a montage now illustrating what he goes on to describe: "This is the entrance to a world of glamour and enchantment. Through these portals pass the most beautiful trucks in the world, bringing to the studio the many different things necessary to produce a picture: equipment, costumes, everything, in fact, from an airplane to a hairpin."

Sliding from Hollywood to the Warners' plant in Burbank, this declaration projects the aura of Hollywood onto the studio setting, which limits entrance to insiders only. The voice-over addresses the audience as outsiders being given a privileged glimpse of that world. This Hollywood is industrial, the site of production, insofar as its "glamour and enchantment" is manufactured out of the "many different things" we see being transported inside the studio. The enclosed studio compound, this is also to say, presents to audiences an image of regulated labor that belies the tumult and violence of the Conference of Studio Unions strike at Warner Bros. just four years earlier, in 1945. As one observer of "Black Friday" (October 5, 1945) recalled, when strikers stormed the studio gates, "the hysterical response at Warners was to direct their studio police and fireman to point high pressure fire hoses at those who marched, knocking them down, pushing them across the street" (Spiro 1998, 416). Enraged, this observer joined the picket line.

The Studio Factory

Obviously the exchange of symbolic value from the neighborhood of Hollywood to the studio factories "a few miles away" did not happen overnight, and for a time after the burst of backstudio pictures during the 1930s, the two iconic emblems coexisted with shifting emphases. But by the 1950s, due to the Paramount decision, the major film companies were losing their dominance of the industry to independent production companies; the majors let lapse the contracts of longtime stars, laid off workers, and rented their facilities; yet in a visual assertion of its clout for the industry, the studio compound, depicted as bustling and prosperous, ultimately displaced the boulevard as the genre's shorthand for locating Hollywood as a concrete place. The long precredits prologue of Jerry Lewis's *The Errand Boy* (1961) self-consciously stages this transference of value from street to studio, illustrating the displacement on film of geographic Hollywood by its industrial likeness, the gated studio compound.

The prologue of *The Errand Boy* is structured by voice-over commentary:

> This is Hollywood, land of the real and the unreal. The unreal are the actors and the real, nothing more than a thing to put film on. From up here, I guess it doesn't look very different from your hometown. But how would you know? You don't go around looking at your hometown from a plane. This is a town where dedicated people spend every waking hour applying their varied talents to the making of a product, the only purpose of which is to take you away from the harsh realities of life into the wondrous land of make-believe. What's your pleasure? Westerns? Cheesecake? Suspense? Brutality? How about a love story? Yes, a love story.

The prologue opens with a view from the air looking down on Hollywood and Sunset boulevards; the distinctive Capitol Records tower on Vine just to the north of Hollywood Boulevard is visible, identifying the district. As the disembodied voice sets the scene, the montage jumps to closer views of Sunset near Vine (according to the blade sign for the Palladium), the top of the sign on the roof of the Roosevelt Hotel, the Hollywood Bowl, and the Hollywood Taft Building, with the Capitol tower looming behind it. Over these images the spoken discourse equates Hollywood with everyone's hometown in visual terms ("It doesn't look very different") while differentiating it referentially ("But how would you know?") according to its status as a company town (everyone here devotes themselves to "the making of a product," motion pictures). A shift to this product then motivates clips of the enumerated genres. When the speaker reaches the love story, he stops for a moment so that we can hear and see this excerpt as viewed in a crowded movie theater. Then, with a shot of a movie studio lot, the commentary resumes:

> Yes, this is Hollywood, where for just the price of a ticket, they will take you any place you want to go. Any place, that is, except one. Seldom will they let you inside one of those soundstages down there where their magic potion is brewed, and we'll show you why. Sometimes the good guys are afraid of horses. And if they're afraid of horses, they're certainly not going to let them use real rocks on them. Mistreated girl, you think? She was formerly middle-weight champion of the

marine corps. The lovers? In real life, these two are man and wife. Aside from the behind-the-scenes activities of the people that are constantly seen on the silver screen, we would like to show you the behind-the-scenes activities of the motion picture tsar and tsaresses and their *tzurises*. And so as not to make this in any way a dry and stilted documentary, we have acquired the services of one of the most prominent and highly intelligent idiots available.

Traveling from the neighborhood of Hollywood to a movie studio (at the exact point where the speaker intones, "Yes, this is Hollywood"), the montage now comprises images of studio buildings, soundstages, and the outdoor sets on a backlot adjacent to those structures. When the speaker takes viewers "inside" this space to reveal the ingredients of the movies' "magic potion," his comments demystify the genres previously shown. Instead of riding a horse in the western, the cowboy hero is affixed to a mechanical saddle operated by several crew members; the bad guys in the suspense clip toss lightweight boulders; the abused female in the "brutality" clip is a stuntman in drag; the onscreen lovers are a married couple bickering and hurling insults at each other between takes of their scene.

As the speaker moves on to the ultimate Hollywood demystification, that of the movie bosses who run the place ("the motion picture tsar and tsaresses"), the montage now passes by several bona fide studio locations: Desilu, Columbia Pictures, MGM, and Paramount. Three of these compounds (Columbia, Desilu, and Paramount) are on Gower in Hollywood, but the fourth (MGM) is in Culver City. Metro's inclusion in this quartet reiterates the geographic legerdemain of earlier backstudio pictures, and here too the inaccuracy goes unnoticed—and why not? After all, it had only been a few years since MGM had ceased describing its Culver City operation as "Hollywood, USA" in the final card of its motion pictures. In any event, since *The Errand Boy* is a Paramount production, the montage condenses the interiority of Hollywood into this studio's Bronson Gate entrance; as the camera flies over the gate, a sign reveals that the studio's name has slyly changed to the fictive Paramutual Pictures. Playing the title character, Jerry Lewis is ineptly putting up a poster with the star's name in gigantic letters on a Paramutual billboard facing the gated entrance. His "idiocy," which reassures us that this backstudio picture will not be a documentary but a clown comedy, marks the end of the prologue and the start of the main titles.

In *The Errand Boy*'s prologue, voice-over commentary, and visual montage work together to dramatize what, for the backstudio genre historically, amounted to a transformation of iconic representations of the industry as made evident in spatial terms: a transference of the mystique of filmmaking from the Hollywood Boulevard commercial district to the gated movie studios, to which only insiders have access. (⊙ Figures 2.14–2.15) As part of this transference of value from street to studio, the backstudio genre sustained the more mystical signification of "Hollywood" as a state of mind, a state that could be visualized as the spatial unity organizing the gated studio compound as "Movieland" for consumers, the value previously attached to the street setting in those early backstudio pictures I discussed.

As the prologue to *The Errand Boy* depicts, the motor of the exchange was, as always for Hollywood, consumption ("the price of a ticket" to the genres being excerpted), which allows the spoken commentary to belie the signification of Hollywood geography right after acknowledging it. The prologue travels past those first views of geographic Hollywood, with the speaker's language initially establishing it as a place similar to one's hometown yet different because of its special relation to manufacturing pleasurable illusions; that difference then enables the departure from the Hollywood district as the speaker jumps to film production. Within the studio the engineering, technology, and artifice of acting are openly exposed, as in other backstudio pictures going back to the genre's early decades and to shorts like *A Trip thru a Hollywood Studio*. Nonetheless the "real" Hollywood remains inaccessible, according to *The Errand Boy*, insofar as the industry's operation by top management is still closed off to outsiders. The behind-the-scenes activities of the people actually running the place and making things happen can only be fictionalized and exaggerated, handed over to the clown's comedy so as not to appear too "dry and stilted" in the manner of a documentary.

"The Tough Part's Getting In"

A ready-at-hand and "genuine" location set in immediate proximity to soundstages, backlots, and all the departments supporting production, the gated studio compound acquired increasingly iconic significance for the backstudio picture as the privileged space that specializes in manufacturing illusions and manipulating reality. After World War II, as both the openings of *It's a Great Feeling* and *The Errand Boy* illustrate, whenever Los Angeles was thought of as the film capital (as opposed to, say, as a major site of aerospace production for the defense industry in similarly huge and enclosed manufacturing spaces), the studio lot, often identified by a signature gate or water tower, was the recurring telltale image in the same way that a Hollywood Boulevard street sign had formerly been in the 1930s. And although the corporate identities and interests of the major studios have, since the days of New Hollywood, considerably altered in conjunction with profound changes to the economics of filmmaking and film financing, as the emblem of production the studio image retains its strong iconic currency today—if only as the referent for a company's logo.

"The studio," Aida Hozic observes, "inspired the idea of an enclosed space in which circumstances could not only be controlled but created from scratch" (Hozic 2001, 7). Built to function as a highly managed and self-contained space, the studio operated as a world unto itself, with its own post office, police force, fire department, and so forth. *A Trip thru a Hollywood Studio* claims the Fox studio "is built like a modern city," and rivals like MGM liked to describe themselves in similar terms. While the enclosed studio compound assured that filming could occur without interruption or interference, this protected space was also inseparable from the film industry's maintenance of the star system. Beyond its merchandising function of selling movies, the star system was designed to manage the well-paid labor of actors (59, 127), both to preserve a measure of respectability for (and hence secrecy about) actors' behavior in private and to represent their labor as leisure outside of the studio—in walled Beverly Hills estates and exclusive Sunset Strip nightclubs, or in what the press and fandom called "Hollywood."

The gated studio's importance as an emblem of industrial Hollywood resides in the way it signifies elements of production that, for the backstudio genre, characterize filmmaking institutionally: the manufacturing of illusions but with "the magic" left intact; the regulation and control of above- and below-the-line labor; direct and indirect protection from all sources of disruption and annoyance, including intrusions by the press and obsessive fans; and the physical means of not only defining an "inside" against the "outside" but also of establishing the top-down hierarchical order within the institution (of management to labor, of stars to neophytes and has-beens, of those with a studio job to those coveting one). These meanings, moreover, coalesce in how often a backstudio picture conceives of the studio as a safe haven: on one hand, a bubble enveloping those working *inside* with the Hollywood "state of mind" and, on the other, a buffer zone erected to shield them from the many perils awaiting *outside* Hollywood.

In a backstudio picture the difficulty of getting past the guard at a studio's front entrance immediately defines the space inside as like a gated community, with all that this comparison now implies about safety, privacy, and elitism. Typically, as in *Show People* and *Make Me a Star*, aspiring entrants are directed elsewhere, most often the casting office, or just turned away altogether. When a character tries to circumvent that directive by sneaking inside, the result in comedies is often a wild cat-and-mouse routine throughout the compound.

In *Free and Easy* (1930), Elmer Butts (Buster Keaton) needs to get inside MGM in order to meet with his one client, a starlet from his hometown named Elvira Plunkett (Anita Page). Elmer's position as her manager means nothing to the studio guard, however. He dutifully informs Elmer, "The only way to get inside the studio is to get a pass." Needing to find Elvira, who is inside being considered for a part, Elmer inquires, "But how do I do that?" The response is the catch-22 of studio security: "You have to come inside to get one." Thinking that this response is license to enter, Elmer pushes through the gate only to be told with a shove, "Outside and stay outside." Determined to find Elvira, Elmer tries alternative means of gaining entrance. First he follows below-the-line crew members going to work through the employees' entrance, but here too he is turned around and sent outside. Then he mingles with the crowd of extras at the Casting Office. This ruse is successful. Once Elmer is inside MGM's bounded lot, though, the guard from the front gate single-mindedly pursues him throughout the studio, and Elmer's attempts to elude his pursuer cause slapstick havoc on whichever set he stumbles upon.

Less comically than Elmer, Merton Gill in *Make Me a Star* is unwaveringly obedient to the security guard's policing authority for Majestic Studio. After waiting patiently but to no avail every day for two months inside the casting office, a broke Merton resorts to stuffing the holes in his shoes with newspaper pages and leaving his rented room through the window to avoid running into his landlady. Feeling sorry for him, Flips arranges for Merton to get a day job in a western, and he proudly strides over to the gateman to tell him he's now working on the lot and, hence, there legitimately. "It won't take me many days to get me familiar with the lot," Merton assures Flips, who replies, with Joan Blondell's characteristic hard-boiled candor, "No, the tough part's getting in." So much so that once inside, Merton is afraid to leave. Fired from the day job for not remembering his few lines or the director's blocking, Merton makes his way to the front gate, where he sees the guard turn away someone not working at the studio. Instead of leaving, Merton hides out at the studio. He finds shelter in a deserted soundstage at night, where the set affords him a place to sleep and scraps of prop food to eat. The next morning, as a horn calls people to work, Merton awakes, eats some cold, moldy beans for breakfast, and eludes the crew who arrive to strike the set.

After several days, Flips discovers an unshaved, disheveled Merton foraging for food through a pile of empty lunch boxes. Again pitying him, she takes him to the restaurant across the street for a meal. Looking wistfully at the gate from outside, he moans, "How am I going to get back on the lot again?" Since Merton will not listen to Flips's advice to forget Hollywood and return home, she gives him money for a shave and to have his clothes pressed, and she promises, "I'll have St. Peter pass you in at the gate." While Merton responds with deep appreciation—"Oh, gee, that's the nicest thing you could do"—his earlier anxiety about *not* getting back on the lot resonates with the pathos of his situation in the face of the studio's impenetrability as epitomized by the authority invested in the guard at the front gate. As much to the point, while hiding *inside* as a squatter, Merton finds the studio to be a source of prop food and shelter; that the studio offers him this comforting safe haven, however crude, make-shift, transient, and unauthorized, merely adds more pathos to his anxious question, "How am I going to get back on the lot again?"

The locked and gated studio has other implications for Hollywood as well, especially in the context of the union movement within the industry, starting in the 1930s. *Stand-In* begins with a sort of riff on the convention of the movie-struck hopeful heading west to Hollywood. Leslie Howard's character, Atterbury Dodd, is a wunderkind efficiency expert sent to Los Angeles by Pettypacker & Sons, the bank financing Colossal Studio. Dodd's mission in going to Hollywood is to find out why Colossal is losing money and correct its mismanagement, thereby protecting the interests of the company's 30,202 stockholders. In the name of those stockholders, moreover, Dodd gets the bank to postpone the decision to sell Colossal for $5 million to Ivor Nassau (C. Henry Gordon), who buys successful independent film studios in order to dismantle them, selling off their assets for his profit and thus putting the companies out of business at a loss to their stockholders. To motivate the bank's willingness to sell Colossal, Nassau is in cahoots with its one big star, Thelma Cherie (Marla Shelton), and her incompetent, egotistical director-fiancé,

Kosovsky (Alan Mowbray). Using her contractual approval of all aspects of her latest production, "Sex and Satan," the pair have forced it to go a million dollars over budget and
way behind schedule, preventing the studio from paying back its loans. Nassau's tactic of
bleeding the studio to force a fire sale is no secret in Hollywood since a radio announcer
gives his listeners "the lowdown" that "Colossal is not sick, it's dying from slow poison."
He further confides, "It's an inside job engineered by an outsider chiseler with the aid of
which fading feminine supersexed star and what cheese director with a phony foreign
accent." Colossal's future rests on this one troubled picture finally reaching completion
and becoming a hit.

Inside the studio, whenever he finds evidence of Hollywood inefficiency (numerous
retakes, reshoots, and rewrites; unnecessary delays and tantrums by the star or director;
expensive props or set adornments that will not register on screen), Dodd is repeatedly
told, "That's the picture business." He finds an ally in a disillusioned producer, Doug
Quintain (Humphrey Bogart); as Quintain leads Dodd on a tour of the lot, we see with
the efficiency expert how "carpenters, electricians, artisans of all sorts" enable a studio to
operate. Dodd, however, has to learn that these are not "cogs" or "units" but people, three
thousand of whom will be unemployed if the sale goes through. (▶ Figure 2.16)
Eventually, that happens. "Sex and Satan" is an unfixable turkey due to Cherie's contractual control, and the bank completes the sale to Nassau behind Dodd's back. Fired by the
bank, Dodd schemes with Quintain to reverse the sale; they trick Cherie into breaking
her contract, which then gives them freedom to re-edit and shoot new scenes for the
troubled picture. But to complete this new cut, Quintain still needs forty-eight hours
inside the studio as well as help from the fired employees who are in the process of leaving
en masse as Nassau takes possession of the lot.

At this point *Stand-In* gets very interesting with regard to how it sees Hollywood
through the studio's infrastructure. Inspired by a radio account of steel strikers staging a
sit-down and defying all efforts to remove them for forty-eight hours, Dodd tries to stop
everyone at Colossal from leaving. "Fellow workers," he implores the crowd of three thousand, "I must talk to you." Calling him "white collar," crew members harass Dodd and
refuse to listen. Finally, he locks them inside the compound, tossing the key over the
fenced front gate. Earlier in the film, when first arriving at the studio by bus along with
other workers, Dodd was stopped at the gate because he did not have a pass. "I don't care
if you're the tax collector," the guard announced to him then, "nobody gets through
without a pass." Dodd applauded the guard's obedience to his duty as this man physically
led the efficiency expert away from the entrance and back to the street. In the conclusion
of *Stand-In*, by securing all the workers inside the studio compound, Dodd exploits the
authority as well as efficiency of that locked gate.

"Now you've got to listen to me," he shouts to the unruly crowd. "You regard me as
your enemy, don't you? I'm capital and you're labor, that's the way you see it, isn't it? But
it isn't as simple as all that." Explaining that "our stockholders" are similar blue-collar
workers, such as "a streetcar conductor, a bricklayer, a soldier's widow, a studio worker,"

he reminds his audience, "these are capitalists" whose "savings built this plant." Going on to insist, "There's no trouble here that a good picture won't cure," he asks the Colossal employees to work without pay for the weekend, helping Quintain to save "Sex and Satan." "Do as I ask, and I pledge you my word that I will convince the stockholders that we are entitled to an interest in this business that we saved." When someone challenges the legality of his proposal since Nassau technically has taken possession of the studio, Dodd rejoins, "There are three thousand of us and we won't let the law in." Staging a "lock-in," the cheering workers grab Nassau and toss him over the wall separating the studio from the street outside. (▶ Figure 2.17–2.18)

In its depiction of filmmaking *Stand-In* reflects upon a studio's operation in economic as well as industrial terms, and in doing so, it alludes to the potential power of organized labor in opposition to management, which was staunchly anti-union. Christopher Ames observes that the sit-down takeover of Colossal, which simulates a strike, is "the most remarkable example of how *Stand-In* reflects its historical context" (Ames 1997, 147). Yet, he points out, the conclusion's "imagery of worker rebellion (a mob of milling and angry laborers) is transformed into a comic resolution that preserves the studio and enshrines the banker as hero" (149). The legerdemain occurs as Dodd pledges to convince the stockholders to think of the workers as co-owners of Colossal, a radical idea of socialist entitlement on labor's part, to say the least—or at least that is how I interpret his promise to "convince the stockholders that we are entitled to an interest in this business that we saved." But Dodd is himself just an ex-employee of the bank holding the studio's debt, and he has no direct experience of or interest in filmmaking; he is the "stand-in" for an absent management, and this absence further obscures the relation between a studio head in Hollywood and the board of directors and their financial partners in New York. In speaking *for* all the regular people who own a share of Colossal as stockholders, Dodd speaks *to* the thousands of employees present on the lot who have their own stake in the picture business. Yet while vaguely pledging to support their right not just to work but to profit from their work, Dodd's speech does not legitimate the workers' collaboration with management and Wall Street. According to how he begins his speech, they remain "labor," hourly wage earners, and therefore not really entitled to "an interest in this business," in contrast with the shareholders' "capital," since their savings "built this plant." Consequently, despite his pledge, Dodd excludes from *financial* partnership the mob of workers he is organizing, all the while seeking their unpaid *industrial* cooperation to finish the new cut of "Sex and Satan."

Using his reference to those "little" shareholders to mediate what, his speech implies, is the agitated relation between management and labor occurring extrafilmically in real-life Hollywood, Dodd removes management from the rhetorical negotiation; by locking the workers in the studio and tossing away the key, he functions not only as a stand-in for management but also as a security guard who won't let anyone inside, or outside for that matter, so the studio then can operate as a law unto itself. Thus, while the lock-in preserves the studio's integrity, product, and labor from manipulation by *bad* capitalists like Nassau, this view of Hollywood as a gated compound reiterates its implications for those working "inside" of extralegal protection, spatial isolation, and private governance.

"Hollywood Is a State of Mind"

Though it appears literally as the sign of industrial Hollywood in so many backstudios, a studio's guarded entrance carries with it a symbolic value that has similarly become conventionalized over time. As *Stand-In* makes much of in its conclusion, the secured front gate keeps outsiders from entering while implicitly locking inside the compound the people working there. Thus, along with marking out the privileged position or "currency" of those allowed inside the studio, the front gate encloses them in an insulated environment that is also disciplined and hierarchical.

In ensuring this spatial containment, the guarded entrance symbolizes how and why Hollywood comes to be understood as a state of mind, even in "quickie" pictures like *Hollywood Boulevard*: As an ideology enveloping its citizens in a mode of thinking, desiring, and judging, Hollywood justifies the insider/outsider mentality and the attitudes arising from it. Hence Pat Blakeford's warning to Jay Wallace: "You're going to stay in Hollywood just as long as it wants you—and then you're going to stay longer. You love it. You love it because it's crazy and senseless and exciting." The still common perception of what happens to a person when he or she "goes Hollywood," as Dixie Dugan's boyfriend, Jimmy, accuses her of doing when her first starring role goes to her head, accounts for why Tinseltown and its inhabitants are so often criticized by mass-culture scholars, exploited by the tabloid press, and satirized by backstudio pictures for having inflated egos and a deluded sense of reality. As the basis of a singular if distorted state of mind, Hollywood determines who has experiential access to everything that makes it "crazy and senseless and exciting," starting with the front gate at the studio.

To imagine Hollywood as a state of mind is to understand how it operates as an ideological force enabling or preventing identification with everything the studio represents—and regulates. Recall in *Sunset Boulevard* the arrival of Norma Desmond (Gloria Swanson) at the Bronson Gate of Paramount Pictures, where a young guard first denies her entrance. "Norma *who*?" he asks. Deeply offended, Norma sees Jonesy, an older guard from her time at Paramount, and after calling him over to be recognized, she orders, "Now open that gate." "They can't drive on the lot without a pass," the young guard argues. But Jonesy informs his junior colleague, "Miss Desmond can," and the iron gate swings opens for her automobile to pass through. (▶ Figure 2.19)

Despite Jonesy's willingness to give her temporary entrance, Norma's presence on DeMille's set is not much different from that of a visiting columnist or dignitary, and it intensifies her sense of loss as someone who, in her youth, once belonged to and even dominated Hollywood. "I just didn't realize what it would be like to come back to the old studio," she confesses. "I had no idea how I'd missed it." This realization—that she can no

Norma Desmond (Gloria Swanson) arriving at the front gate of Paramount. (*Sunset Boulevard* ©1950 Paramount)

longer identify with Hollywood because she no longer belongs to "the old studio"—brings tears to her eyes and strengthens her desire to work again. Norma may own oil wells in Long Beach and retain all the glamorous supplements of 1920s stardom, such as the pet chimpanzee, the tile dance floor on which Valentino danced, the prints of her old films she runs in her private screening room as a means of reliving her youth, the narcissistic display of her photographs in every room, and her Isotta-Fraschini, that handmade automobile upholstered in leopard skin and with a gold-plated car phone, but she no longer is *in* Hollywood. To add insult to injury, it turns out all Hollywood wants from her is to borrow that car for a Bing Crosby picture.

Norma's return to her old studio firmly establishes that Hollywood no longer wants her, but it also shows that what she lost when Hollywood dropped her was its protective cocoon, which had in the past protected her from suffering the full consequence of her excessive, self-indulgent life as a big star. Hence DeMille's half-hearted instinct to protect Norma during her visit: He wants to keep from her the information that Paramount called only to rent her car and therefore orders Gordon Cole to find another one to use; he invites Norma to his set so she can see how filmmaking has changed since the days when they worked together, presumably to nudge her into forgetting her ill-advised comeback; he allows her to believe, as she departs and they say good-bye, that he has read her script of "Salome" and intends to direct her in it. However, since DeMille is not about to hire her in any capacity, he cannot undo Norma's exile nor dispel her conviction that she will work again and rejoin the studio community as their diva.

Norma's situation compares to that of other has-been stars in backstudios when they too have been dropped by their studios and consequently must face the outside world without the mediation personified by the security guard at the front gate. At one extreme is the example of Mary Evans (Constance Bennett) toward the end of *What Price Hollywood?* (1932). Once her stardom is rocked by scandal, the studio ceases to protect her, and, to prevent her ex-husband from taking custody of their son, she takes refuge in the French countryside until the studio and her ex-husband take her back with open arms in a contrived happy ending. Also happening outside the gate is the downfall of Norman Maine (Fredric March in 1937, James Mason in 1954) in both versions of *A Star Is Born*. As long as studio head Oliver Niles (Adolphe Menjou, Charles Bickford) keeps Norman under contract, the head of publicity, Matt Libby (Lionel Stander, Jack Carson), protects him from bad press, scandal, and possibly jail time for disturbing the peace. Once dropped by the studio and without the safety net formerly provided for him, Norman's downward trajectory begins. Although *The Star* (1951) ends more satisfactorily for has-been star Margaret Elliot (Bette Davis), she likewise finds a hostile outside world once she loses her sanctuary in Hollywood. Her possessions are auctioned off; in debt, she is evicted from her apartment; she is harassed by greedy relatives who still expect her financial support; she has to lie to her young daughter to save face; she is arrested for driving out of control while drunk; she irrationally steals a display bottle of perfume that turns out to contain water; she deigns to take a job clerking in a department store, only to walk out in a huff after insulting customers when they wonder how the store could hire her because of her notoriety.

Implicit in the gated entrance of a studio, furthermore, is its protection of stars from unruly fandom. In real-life Hollywood, fans would line up across the street from a studio's gated entrance in order to gawk at stars arriving or departing but not interfere with them. Most backstudios, though, usually depict fans as a much more ambiguous blessing for Hollywood. In *What Price Hollywood?* the studio head, Julius Saxe (Gregory Ratoff), warns Mary Evans, "You belong to the public. They make you and they break you." Director George Cukor visualizes this sentiment in montages encapsulating her rise and fall in popularity. True, Saxe's statement is somewhat disingenuous. After all, his studio creates Mary's extremely popular star image as "America's Pal," and later on his studio fails to support "America's Pal" due to outside pressure from women's groups when they brand Mary box-office poison on moral grounds because of the murky, scandalous circumstances surrounding her mentor's suicide. Before that happens, the public gets wildly out of hand as Mary's wedding party leaves the church. An unruly mob barely restrained by police, their maniacal faces and grasping hands shown in close-up, Mary's fans tear at her wedding dress, attacking her as if they were predatory animals trying to feed; this riotous crowd forces the wedding party to retreat to a back room of the church for refuge. Then an exultant Saxe exclaims triumphantly that this event has broken "all house records" for the church, and he informs the bride and groom that they must postpone their honeymoon for at least a week, well, maybe for two, because the studio needs Mary for retakes on her latest film. Further illustrating the couple's subjection to his authority, after Saxe leaves the room, a photographer appears in an open window to take a candid shot of a disappointed Mary and her new husband.

In *What Price Hollywood?* the studio's control of Mary's private life is accepted as the trade-off for the security it offers. Reminiscent of Mary's wedding, at the funeral of Norman Maine in *A Star Is Born* fans mob his widow, Esther Blodgett, who is now the big star Vicki Lester (Janet Gaynor in 1937, Judy Garland in 1954), again suggesting Hollywood's ambivalence toward fandom when outside the studio's direct control. Earlier in *A Star Is Born*, the audience's comments on preview cards and in the lobby announced the successful arrival of Vicki Lester as Oliver Niles's new star, one whose popularity quickly overshadows Norman's. At Norman's funeral, however, in both versions of the film it looks as if her fans are attacking Esther, pulling off the widow's veil to see her grief-stricken face, as a voice from the crowd tries to assure her that her late husband is not worth grieving over, causing Esther to scream helplessly in terror.

On screen, then, fans may be a necessary component of institutional Hollywood but only when they are controllable as a generalized "public" mentioned in dialogue, shown in an audience at a sneak preview or as adoring spectators watching stars attend a movie premiere, or represented as polite teenage girls trying to outwit a press agent, as in *The Youngest Profession* (1943). When outside the order imposed by the studio's institutional framework, on the other hand, fans pose more of a danger, as at Norman's funeral and Mary's wedding, because in these situations they elude studio discipline and begin to think a star is *their* property. In *Singin' in the Rain* (1952), while fans listen to and worship every word and toothy grin of Don Lockwood (Gene Kelly) at the premiere of *The Royal Rascal* which opens this film, when his car breaks down on Hollywood Boulevard afterward, other fans mob him and literally tear off pieces of his clothing for souvenirs.

These examples illustrate how Hollywood regulates the lives of those working within the studio system by noting moments when its protective hold either breaks down or disappears. To be sure, not every backstudio picture imagines the studio as a safe haven only to wrench it away from its protagonists, as happens in narratives about fallen stars. In *The Bad and the Beautiful* an unexpected studio career saves Georgia Lorrison from drunkenly worshipping and feeling inferior to her late father. Despite her momentary breakdown when she discovers the infidelity of her mentor and lover, Jonathan Shields (Kirk Douglas), all we see of her afterward is her successful embodiment of Hollywood stardom within the studio system. Not too differently, at the end of *The Goddess* (1958) the fictionalized Marilyn Monroe figure finds her version of a safe haven in her studio. Retreating from her real-life problems and relationships, Emily Ann Faulkner (Kim Stanley), who has become the emotionally unstable star Rita Shaw, suffers another breakdown at her mother's funeral and then retreats to the maternal ministrations of her studio-supplied secretary and companion (Elizabeth Wilson), who readily dispenses the pills that calm her down and enable her return to Hollywood.

Those two films are still critical of Hollywood and the narcissism it fosters. A more favorable treatment of how Hollywood fully and successfully envelops its stars in a protective bubble can be found in the earlier screwball comedy, *Bombshell* (1933). For star Lola Burns (Jean Harlow) there is no outside to her studio-controlled life. Everything that happens to her during the course of the film, whether at her home, the Coconut Grove nightclub, or a desert springs resort, is micromanaged by her studio's publicity man, Space Hanlon (Lee Tracy). Ironically, the one unmanaged event in *Bombshell* occurs *inside* the studio, when Lola goes there to reshoot a scene. Before filming begins, her phony marquis-fiancé, who has already been denied entrance at the front gate until Lola rescinds Space's instruction to the guard, and then her pompous father each invade the set, causing tumult with the director, an old flame of Lola's, who wants them taken away. Everyone starts arguing with each other until the director, Jim Brogen (Pat O'Brien), walks off the set in a huff. Never far from Lola, it seems, Space smooth-talks the interlopers into leaving so that filming can proceed, and his protective if exploitative manipulation of Lola continues apace for the remainder of *Bombshell*, even when she assumes otherwise.

Space Hanlon can successfully manipulate Lola and remain her primary love interest because Hollywood *is* her state of mind: it mediates whatever she thinks, says, feels, and experiences. At one point Brogen, her former lover and sometimes director, exclaims in exasperation, "You're just playing a scene with yourself!" Similarly, late in the film when she has fled to a desert spa with the intent of quitting acting for good, stardom remains her sole point of reference. Alone on horseback and admiring the view, she holds her body dramatically in ways that suggest she is still posing for an absent camera (thereby doubling our awareness that Harlow, the original of which Lola is but a copy, is herself posing for a real camera). For that matter, when she meets Gifford Middleton (Franchot Tone) from Boston at this spa, and he greatly impresses her with his dignity and politeness, Lola purrs to Space, who has followed her to the resort, "Not even Norma Shearer and Helen Hayes in their nicest pictures were spoken to like that." At this point, though, Lola has no idea that Space is stage-managing her short-lived romance with this Boston Brahmin as a means of getting her back to Hollywood so she can finish her picture, and his plot succeeds in delivering her to her studio.

Of all backstudio pictures, perhaps *Sullivan's Travels* (1941) most explicitly recognizes how Hollywood exerts an irresistible gravitational pull that not only keeps members of the industry firmly within its protective orbit but also shapes the way they think. Preston Sturges's protagonist, John L. Sullivan, aka "Sully" (Joel McCrae), comes from an elite background; educated at boarding school and a college graduate, he became a "boy genius" director in his twenties, making successful light comedies and musicals. Now he wants to make a serious film like the one he screens for his studio bosses in the opening of *Sullivan's Travels*. To research his new script, Sully decides to leave Hollywood, hitting the open road as a tramp, in order to discover what "real trouble" is like in Depression-era America. After some debate his studio agrees to let him go, but only with his studio ID sewn into the soles of his boots. In addition, the studio assigns a crew of professional and personal assistants (including a staff writer and photographer, a short-wave radio operator, a cook, and a doctor) to follow Sully in a land yacht, which essentially functions as a portable studio enclave charged with keeping him safe, albeit from a discreet distance.

Sully's efforts to seek out the real outside world take the form of several vignettes, each concluding with him back where he started, in some version of Hollywood. He first tries to outrace the land yacht by catching a ride on a thirteen-year-old's hot rod, resulting in a Keystone Cops–style chase through the countryside. He bargains with the crew to meet him in two to three weeks in Las Vegas and takes off again, now completely alone. Taken in by a lusty widow and her sister, Sully does some handyman work for the widow; later that evening, after accompanying her to the local movie theater, he makes a getaway from her amorous inclinations by climbing out a second-story window of her house. When Sully hitchhikes out of that small town, it turns out his ride is going back to Los Angeles. Dropped off at a diner somewhere in Hollywood, Sullivan meets the unnamed girl (Veronica Lake), who herself is trying to leave Hollywood after failing to get into pictures. Still dressed as the tramp and not yet revealing his identity, Sully offers to give the girl shelter in his Beverly Hills mansion, but when he retrieves his own car, he is arrested for car theft since his butler has reported it stolen. Once things are sorted out, he and the girl head to his well-appointed residence. "No matter where I start out for," he muses, "I always end up right back here in Hollywood." Finally, with the girl now accompanying him, Sully makes another effort to ride the rails as a tramp, but since he gets feverishly sick, they have to give up this plan too. When they reach a town, he says sarcastically, "I suppose it's Hollywood"; it turns out they have stopped at a roadside diner on the outskirts of Las Vegas and the land yacht is parked nearby, waiting for him as planned. While he recuperates in the land yacht as it returns to Hollywood, Sully philosophizes to the girl, "It's a funny thing how everything keeps shoving me back to Hollywood and Beverly Hills." Coughing, he continues, "Or this monstrosity we're riding in. Almost like gravity, as if some force were saying, 'Get back where you belong. You don't belong out here in real life, you phony, you.'" (▶ Figure 2.20)

After he has recovered, Sully makes one last attempt to experience real life outside of Hollywood. A montage shows Sully and the girl walking among the poor in a Hooverville; they stand in a food line, put up with lice, take public showers, find shelter in a rescue mission. Finally starvation forces them back home to Hollywood. Now that he feels he has experienced "real trouble," Sullivan decides to show his gratitude to the tramps he has met on this last venture; alone and still in tramp costume, he returns to the Hooverville to hand out five-dollar bills to two hundred tramps. As Sully distributes the money without realizing the greed or desperation it incites, a tramp who has previously stolen Sully's boots attacks the director to steal his cash. The tramp is then killed by a train and everyone assumes the corpse is Sully. In the meantime, suffering a concussion and temporary amnesia after being knocked unconscious by the tramp, Sully gets into a second fight when he belligerently if also confusedly refuses to obey a railroad agent ordering him away from the train tracks. Since he no longer has the boots with his identification secreted inside and he cannot remember who he is, Sully finally does get to pull away from Hollywood's orbit. He is tried, convicted, and sentenced to six years' hard labor on a chain gang, where he suffers every imaginable indignity: he is beaten, starved, confined to a sweat box, forbidden to speak. Once his memory returns, the only way he can get anyone to believe him is by confessing to be his own murderer, which puts his photograph in newspapers around the nation for Hollywood to see and reclaim him.

Obviously Sully's horrendous suffering in this final episode of his travels fulfills to the letter what he had initially claimed he sought, namely, to experience *real* trouble; more to the point of the backstudio genre, his state of abjection in the work camp leads him to realize that the light entertainments in which he and Hollywood specialize do matter greatly. After his rescue Sully decides to forgo directing his realistic film because he has seen firsthand that for some people, like the audience at the Sunday picture show—when his fellow convicts and poor African American churchgoers laugh together at a Walt Disney cartoon—all they have are the movies: "And there's a lot to be said for making people laugh."

With this maxim, *Sullivan's Travels* concludes by endorsing Hollywood through its product, reiterating the comparable closing viewpoints of earlier backstudios like *The Extra Girl* (1923), *Show People, Free and Easy, Movie Crazy* (1932), and *Make Me a Star*. In those pictures, the Hollywood hopeful arrives with an ambition to be a serious actor (or in the case of *Free and Easy* not to act but to manage actors), and either through accident or by trickery, they each become successful slapstick comedians even if against their will, proving the art required of such lightweight entertainment. The discovery that the Jerry Lewis character in *The Errand Boy* is a comic genius and "a gold mine" for Paramutual Pictures makes the same claim. *Sullivan's Travels* differs from these other backstudio pictures in the case it makes for comedy, which for Preston Sturges's narrative earns a redeeming social value through Sullivan's "real trouble." The 1930s backstudio pictures, by comparison, establish the entertainment value of a new comic star by undercutting this character's more serious yet unrealistic initial ambitions—and in the case of *The Extra Girl* and *Make Me a Star*, by refuting in dialogue that character's own lasting discomfort with being a success in what Merton calls degrading "cross-eyed comedies." John L. Sullivan, on the other hand, is a writer-director like his creator, Sturges, not a wannabe movie star like his companion, the girl; more to the point, Sturges places both Sully's efforts to experience "real trouble" and the concluding defense of entertaining the masses with laughter in a very recognizable contemporary social context that is clearly outside of Hollywood: from the widow's small town, to the diner outside Las Vegas, to the Hooverville, to the work camp somewhere in southern swamp country.

To earn that celebratory ending for Hollywood, though, *Sullivan's Travels* has to cheat. After all, regardless of the extenuating circumstances for Sully's arrest, he did attack the railroad agent. Nonetheless the revelation of Sully's true Hollywood identity treats his release from incarceration as if an innocent man had been wrongly imprisoned; we may perhaps infer that his sentence was commuted offscreen, but even so, he is not innocent of committing the crime. Ignoring this fact, the film abruptly segues from the girl's discovery of his photo on the front page to his reunion with her and the rest of his Hollywood cronies and bosses aboard a plane taking him back home. What this sleight of hand, achieved through narrative ellipses and judicious editing, lets slip is how Hollywood has all along been providing Sullivan with a desirable and flexible safety net. So long as he retains his Hollywood identity, the studio is there to rescue him, which is just another way to describe his complaint that some gravitational pull keeps "shoving" him back to Hollywood as if it were some inescapable force. Until the final act of Sully's story, Hollywood exerts such a powerful force, as made clear when he and the girl arrive at the diner and it turns out, as if by magical wish fulfillment, that the land yacht is parked outside, waiting for him. Only after he temporarily forgets his identity do Hollywood and Sully lose sight of each other, and without that safe haven pulling him back like a gravitational force, he falls into an abyss of "real trouble." Even then, as he ponders how to convince the world of his true identity, Sully thinks in Hollywood terms: "If ever a plot needed a twist, this one does," he mutters. For all his sincere determination to escape Hollywood and experience real people's troubles firsthand, Sully enacts the Hollywood mindset already shaping his view of "the outside"—which is ultimately why he cannot pull away from that gravitational force until he loses his memory.

"That's the Picture Business"

Sullivan's Travels crystalizes how "Hollywood" as the condensation of the film industry undergoes a morphing process in the backstudio genre: from a mappable place to a gated studio to an industrial mode of thinking and, finally, as John L. Sullivan articulates it, to an overwhelming and irresistible institutional force pulling some people in, pushing others out. That said, I should acknowledge that every example I have cited so far dates from the studio era. By the late 1960s the association of "Hollywood" with American filmmaking persisted, but the linkage had to overcome the namesake street's growing notoriety. The credit sequences of *The Legend of Lylah Clare* (1968) and *Myra Breckinridge* (1970) occur over footage of their main characters strolling along Hollywood Boulevard's Walk of Fame. For both cult films, the boulevard's shabby if overly commercialized condition, along with its reputation for drug dealing, prostitution, and runaway teens, signals the main characters' outsider status while reflecting Hollywood's own diminishment. In their openings both backstudios register, at least symptomatically, how the boulevard had become a liability for the Hollywood brand, which may account for the emergence at about this same time of the Hollywood sign as the new geographic marker symbolizing LA's status as the entertainment capital. Not coincidentally, too, at around this time *Fade-in*, aka *Iron Cowboy* (1968), the backstudio picture made during and about the location shoot of the western *Blue* (1968), may be the first time the genre refers to a difference between "Los Angeles," where the film crew lives, and "Hollywood," which is wherever they work.

This is not to say that backstudio pictures from this period forsake the later generic convention of locating Hollywood primarily inside a studio setting. However, most often this enclosed studio compound, along with the male characters forming its hierarchical power structure, functions onscreen to evoke nostalgia for an older Hollywood, as in glossy biopics like *Gable and Lombard* (1976), literary adaptations like *The Last Tycoon* (1976), origin stories like *Nickelodeon* (1976), or farces like *Under the Rainbow* (1981). By 1990, too, Hollywood was becoming a movable sign. In 1989 Disney-MGM Studios opened in Walt Disney World Resort in Orlando, and the following year Universal followed suit when its studio tour, more or less a replica of the one in southern California, opened as part of Universal Orlando Resort. Both still operate, although in 2008 Disney ended its licensing agreement with MGM and renamed its attraction Disney's Hollywood Studios. In signifying Hollywood, the studio image itself became something of an abstraction. The original Warner Bros. logo, used from 1923 to 1929, had a picture of its old studio in the top half of its shield, so to celebrate the company's seventy-fifth anniversary, for a short while Time-Warner added a photo of the Burbank studio that rippled into the famous shield logo as a few bars of "As Time Goes By" played.

But in backstudios made during this period that are set in their contemporary moment, a Hollywood studio still represents the mindset keeping filmmakers within (or outside) the industry's orbit. In *The Player* (1992) the activity of filmmaking comprises deal-making, pitching projects, and schmoozing at industry events or expensive restaurants, not actual filming or (save for two screenings) scenes of actors acting. True, this satire opens with an allusion to the making of a movie. We hear the sound of a clapper as voices mutter, "Quiet on the set," "Scene one, take ten," "And—action!" The voice-off dialogue at first suggests we are coming upon a scene being filmed inside a studio. But what is being filmed? The screen itself is filled with a painterly image of what looks like Cecil B. DeMille directing a young Gloria Swanson, possibly as Salome. However, with the cry "And—action!" an actress (Leah Ayres, playing a secretary) enters the frame to answer a ringing phone, and the image in question turns out to be the painting behind the executive assistant's desk in the front office: a painted backdrop turns into the real thing, which is to say, a prop in a backstudio scene. The camera then moves back to include the executive assistant, Celia (Dina Merrill), as she enters this room. (▶ Figures 2.21–2.22)

So begins, beneath the opening credits, director Robert Altman's famous eight-minute tracking shot around the rear of the studio's administrative buildings and its adjacent parking lot, where we see people milling about, getting in or out of their cars, engaged in conversations as they walk, and on occasion going inside an executive's office. Although we do see the exterior wall of Stage 9, with the painted slogan exclaiming, "Movies, Now More Than Ever!" (a play on the "Movies Are Better Than Ever" postwar industrial motto), the camera never goes inside to glimpse production taking place, nor does it extend its gaze onto the backlot. (▶ Figure 2.23) Rather, it wanders back and forth among men and women in suits giving orders to their assistants, gossiping about the future of executives, leading a group of Sony people on a tour, and meeting with Griffin Mill (Tim Robbins) to pitch stories. During this visually self-conscious opening, Walter Stuckel's (Fred Ward) dialogue as he strolls on the lot first with an assistant, then with the real-life writer Buck Henry, not only calls attention to the technical virtuosity—and artifice—of Altman on display here, but throughout Stuckel unknowingly but self-reflexively cites the shot's cinematic lineage. Repeatedly referencing Orson Welles's opening in *Touch of Evil* (1958)—a tracking shot that was compromised by Universal's superimposition of the credits in the trimmed release print—Stuckel claims ignorance of other examples, as his companion mentions *Absolute Beginners* (1986), *The Sheltering Sky* (1990), and possibly the most audacious use of the long tracking shot of all, *Rope* (1948).

Stuckel's extended self-referential commentary on what Altman himself is doing may draw attention away from what the extremely long take visualizes as a modern-day working film studio. Except for the interior of the front offices, where Griffin Mill hears story pitches, everything else in the studio compound is seen only from the outside, which is also to say that the importance of, let alone an interest in, production has been subordinated to that of the business or, as the Sony tour guide puts it, to "where all the greenlighting is done." Even so, *The Player*'s opening scene on a studio lot still takes for granted the presence of an enclosed, gated compound because Griffin calls attention to two crucial lapses in security. First, the real-life writer Adam Simon comes on the lot to pitch a science-fiction story. Angry at being taken by surprise, Griffin orders an assistant to "find out from studio security how Adam Simon got on the lot." During this long take, too, Griffin subsequently receives a phone call and we hear him say, "I want to know why security is lax." Ironically enough, the man musing about long takes and *Touch of Evil* throughout this opening, Walter Stuckel, *is* the head of security, but he is apparently indifferent to these tiny breaches. Second, at one point during this long take, the young man delivering mail has an accident with his cart, causing the mail bags to spill their contents onto the ground. As the traveling camera moves closer, it reveals one picture postcard with the printed slogan "Your Hollywood Is Dead." The long take concludes when this postcard is delivered to Griffin, who turns it over to read the angry message from the anonymous writer harassing him. (▶ Figure 2.24)

Although still iconically represented by the studio compound shown in the opening but now primarily focused on office buildings inhabited mostly by people interested in making money more than movies, Griffin's Hollywood has been condensed into the marketing slogan "Movies, Now More Than Ever." But more *what* than ever? The nonsensical slogan functions in *The Player* as an abstraction, an industrial brand that Griffin sells to donors at the black-tie celebrity banquet honoring Hollywood's past. Further, as a state of mind echoing if inverting the moral of *Sullivan's Travels*, Hollywood's gravitational force in *The Player* still protects Griffin and brings him his happy Hollywood ending: he gets away with murder, marries the victim's lover, becomes an expectant father, and runs the studio. Griffin's own Hollywood ending thus ironically if uncannily parallels the star-driven "Habeas Corpus," its originally intended hard-edged realism significantly effaced in response to audience testing, which demanded that Bruce Willis rescue Julia Roberts to deliver a happy ending. From this perspective, and despite its biting satiric edge, as the logic of Hollywood motivates and then resolves Griffin's own fate, *The Player* remystifies that imaginary and by now rather immaterial place signified by "Hollywood."

In comparison, *The Muse* (1999) views Hollywood from the writer's perspective. A Paramount exec like Griffin Mill terminates screenwriter Steven Phillips's (Albert Brooks) three-picture deal and evicts him from his office on the studio lot. (At film's end, this exec will himself be fired for stealing props.) Now without studio affiliation, Steven asks his agent to get him a meeting with Steven Spielberg, who was apparently a friend when both were young. What follows is a funny sequence that makes vivid Steven's low status through his inability to get close to Hollywood's inner circle of power.

We first see Steven driving to the front gate of Universal City Studios in the valley. The guard, however, tells him he does not have a drive-on and will need to make a U-turn, park across the street, and walk back. "I don't have a drive-on?" Steven insists. "No, sir, you have a walk-on." "Is that the worst a person can get," Steven returns, "or is there, like, a crawl-on?" Next we see Steven turning a corner by Stage 3, and a long shot reveals his tiny figure walking along the exterior of more soundstages as a Universal Tours tram goes by. The guide points out the soundstage where a popular Jim Carrey picture was filmed and adds, "On your left is a man who obviously did not get a drive-on." Then a sweaty, panting, and exhausted Steven can be seen trudging up a hilly street on his way to Spielberg's offices. Finally, wiping his brow with a handkerchief, Steven approaches the Universal Scene Dock and spies the Spielberg Building. (⏵ Clip 8)

As Steven Phillips (Albert Brooks) trudges onto the Universal lot, a tour guide points out that he must have gotten only a walk-on pass. (*The Muse* ©1999 USA Films)

Steven's trek inside Universal visualizes how outside the system he is, so that even as he gets inside, Hollywood still eludes him. Entering the office area of the Spielberg Building, where men in suits are chatting and phones ringing, Steven goes to the receptionist. "I'm here to see Mr. Spielberg," he tells one of the three women behind the wide desk. She checks a printout, going through pages of names until finally she finds Steven's. She sends him to the second floor, office 202. Still wiping his brow, he walks down the corridor—and learns his appointment is with *Stan* Spielberg, Steven's cousin (Stephen Wright). "Where's Steven?" Steven asks, the circularity of the two names becoming apparent, and Stan replies that he hasn't seen him in nearly a year. When asked about his role, Stan says he doesn't know what he does exactly. "Steven gave me the job and I never questioned it." Frustrated, Steven stands to leave, as Stan advises him, "Just remember. Make it in color. The people love color." Steven's encounter with Hollywood in this sequence, in sum, is with a faux Spielberg, a vacuous stand-in for the absent mogul, who is elusive, being elsewhere.

The corporate identity of a movie studio has changed since *The Player* and *The Muse*, as the vast industrial plants of the past that specialized in filmmaking have been fully absorbed by the multimedia conglomerates of today, but imagery of the studio compound in backstudios still symbolizes Hollywood in the face of its industrial abstraction as a movable sign. What stands out about contemporary backstudios, in fact, is how many continue to take place in the studio era as opposed to their own time, as if that older institutional system, its infrastructure, its enclosed property, and its historical setting are still necessary to signify "Hollywood" as a concrete place and identity for today's audiences. Alternatively, the few recent backstudios set in the present tend to go on location (*State and Main* 2000, *Tropic Thunder* 2008) or take a Hollywood personality away from LA (*Birdman* 2014, *Top Five* 2014). The handful of backstudios that make use of a contemporary studio setting in LA are often comedies like *The Muse*, which feature a hapless protagonist whose admission *into* Hollywood merely serves to indicate his isolation *from* Hollywood. Alternatively, as in *La La Land* (2016), a movie studio portrays Hollywood as a setting much like a theme park fantasy land, cut off from the real world.

In *La La Land* a Starbucks-like coffee shop serves as the portal through which Mia (Emma Stone), a wannabe movie star and barista, takes Seb (Ryan Gosling), a wannabe jazz club owner, on a tour of the Warners backlot after he "basically hauled ass past the guard gates." She points out "the window that Humphrey Bogart and Ingrid Bergman looked out of in *Casablanca*," adding, "I love being around this stuff, you know?" As the couple stroll down the street, an assistant stops them so an outdoor scene can begin shooting, its artifice contrasting with the realism of the actual studio location where Mia, who mutters that she loves the actress being filmed, and Seb continue to talk in whispers. (▶ Figure 2.25) This moment recalls a similar one in *Singin' in the Rain* as Don and his pal Cosmo pass by several silent movies filming on adjacent sets. When the director says, "Cut it there," Mia and Seb walk past the crew members and actors, who pay no attention to the couple. They next pass an open soundstage, pausing to look inside, and a reverse shot tinted in rose and gold shows a dozen or more people working on the set, an obviously painted backdrop of a city street and adjacent freeway lit by six klieg lights, which evokes the film's bravura opening musical number. (▶ Figure 2.26) The shot looks like a painted image in its own right until a woman in an evening dress walks from one side of the frame to the other. "I love it," Mia again murmurs. One cannot help sensing that Hollywood is not only her professional goal but also a source of movie memorabilia.

As they continue their tour of the Warners lot, their conversation about Mia's ambition to break into pictures now echoes the comparable scene in *Sunset Boulevard* when Joe Gillis (William Holden) listens to Betty Schafer (Nancy Olsen) talk about her failed plans to be an actress as this couple walks through the empty Paramount lot at night. More so than in that film, in *La La Land* the movie studio setting represents Hollywood as a privileged site for dreaming, so it epitomizes a utopian state of mind. The epilogue's fantasy revision of the film's ending, which has shown Mia becoming a film star yet married to someone other than Seb, harks back to studio-era Hollywood's manufacturing of romance through musicals. Not only does this fantasy evoke parallels with the big ballets in MGM musicals, but the set where Mia and Seb first dance with the ensemble is the very set they had looked at when they strolled around the Warners lot; furthermore, as Mia leaves this setting for her audition, in the corner of the frame we can see what looks like an old-time director with a megaphone. (▶ Figures 2.27–2.29)

No wonder that the opening title card of *La La Land* reproduces the original font from the 1950s to announce that it is "Presented in CinemaScope," that "The End" appears in a font resembling the final title card of studio-era Paramount features, and that beneath those two words *La La Land* repeats the old MGM slogan, "Made in Hollywood, USA." This contemporary backstudio evokes the wondrousness of the dream factory of yore as something still palpable and ongoing, as something historical yet unchanging, while disaggregating it from its plotting of romance and heartbreak, of ambitions and rejection, happening outside those studio gates.

3

Movie-Struck Hollywood

Even a cursory glance at the appended filmography ought to reveal the frequency with which female star narratives dominated the production of backstudios through the end of the 1960s. As mentioned in the introduction, this long trajectory of stories about female stars rising or falling in the industry began in the 1920s, flourished in the 1930s, but tapered off during the 1940s, and was reenergized as a vigorous but more cynical second cycle during the 1950s and 1960s. This chapter examines star narratives from the first cycle, and the next chapter takes up those from the second.

The two cycles view Hollywood stardom differently, to be sure, as I will be documenting, but they also reveal some illuminating continuities. First, both cycles represent stardom through backstudio narratives that portray female stars as, to borrow the phrasing of Robert Allen and Douglas Gomery, "actors 'with biographies'" (Allen and Gomery 1985, 172), which is also to say that these are narratives about the making or breaking of careers. As Richard Brody has recently pointed out, moreover, because there have been few female directors, women have been denied that platform for "self-revelation." "In classic Hollywood," he states, "there's an extra, and decisive, reason to pay attention to the lives of actresses in particular.... The stories of actresses' lives often provide our closest glimpse of the deepest substance of the art of women in the industry" (Brody 2017). This is as true of fictional star narratives, which trace the shifting yet always contradictory status of female stars as well-compensated and powerful Hollywood women working during the studio era.

Second, both cycles manifest the industry's understanding of the usefulness of backstudios in circulating while also manipulating the discursive excess that has always surrounded female stars—in accounts of their independence, their glamour, their sexuality, their consuming, their determination to control their own labor. A main difference between the two cycles, as one celebrates and the other damns Hollywood through stardom, resides in their own historical moment of production with regard to the studio system's dominance, the context for this chapter, or its dissolution, the context for the next one.

Specifically, then, this chapter examines how female star narratives from the 1920s and 1930s focus on the industrially charged figure of the ambitious "movie-struck" girl traveling to Hollywood in search of the economic prosperity, social mobility, and sexual license that stardom promised. A personification of female spectatorship of early cinema by the industry and popular press, this figure has been well documented by much recent feminist scholarship. Shelley Stamp, for instance, has explored how "the fan who confused her love of cinema with a desire to appear onscreen herself became a popular, if cautionary model of film enthusiasm in the teens" (Stamp 2000, 37). A target of mockery and object of condescension, the "movie-struck girl" was a site of contradiction, for, in being a diehard fan solicited by Hollywood, she was also "at once vital to the industry and a challenge to expected audience decorum" (39). Thus, as Lucy Fischer comments, whereas feminist scholars now focus on the "agency," "upward mobility," and "rejection of traditional female roles" in early fandom, the "cultural custodians of the day" emphasized the frivolity with which "juvenile, pathological, amorous naïfs…put their lives and moral stature at risk by leaving home" (Fischer 2016, 18).

The stereotype of the movie-struck fan girl reinforced the emergent star system, and both coincided with the social theorization of adolescence as a category describing unmarried people in their teens and early twenties (Anselmo-Sequeira 2015). Although the press characterized the movie-struck girl as a self-indulgent consumer of Hollywood fantasies, correspondence in magazines revealed these young fans to be identifying with the rags-to-riches biographies of the first wave of comparably adolescent female stars such as Mary Pickford and Marguerite Clark. Stardom in this respect targeted a cohort of "girl fans who dreamed of exchanging the dullness of schoolrooms and store counters for the exciting adventures of studio lots and on-location shootings"—and for the economic prosperity and social mobility that came with stardom (23).

Because the movie-struck girl was such a conflicted figuration of female spectatorship, she was made symptomatic of the labor issue arising from the industry's address to young female viewers through stardom. There was simply not enough work for the legions of girls traveling west. A 1921 editorial in a trade journal, *Camera!*, entitled "Pictures and the Girl Question," described a married couple from Spokane who came to Hollywood searching for their orphan niece. This young woman, the couple feared, "had, in our fair city, 'gone to the bad,' or…had, at least, 'joined the movies,' which was in their minds unquestionably one and the same procedure." While their attitude offended the editorial's female writer, the visit nonetheless gave her cause to ask her readers in the industry, "Whose problem after all is the salvation of these thousands of enchanted girls, who possessing more perseverance than talent, continually arrive at the film capital to commence startling careers?" (F.R. 1921, 3).

Still pondering this question, the next day the writer asked her "favorite waitress"—whose demeanor of "two rows of ridiculous peroxided little curls and a superfluity of messy mascara" imitated someone like Pickford—for her life story. Hailing from Wichita, the waitress had been in LA for a year, tried to get into pictures but couldn't get even a job as an extra, and "you hafta eat." The writer concludes, "The girls who wait on us over counters, wires, and tables are those who having learned much about the law of average are making the best of it." As for the film industry, it "must not be held responsible" for those "others who have been less sensible or weaker." The editorial closes with a paean to "the hard-working people whom we are." In short, with the industry absolved of blame, the burden of survival "in this most fascinating and consequently most overcrowded of professions" was dependent on the girl's own strength or weakness of character (F.R. 1921, 3).

The *Camera!* editorial may have been too complacent in opining that the fate of the movie-struck girl was just "worth a little thought" in 1921 (F.R. 1921, 3). That same year, due to the inflammatory press coverage of the death of Virginia Rappe in Fatty Arbuckle's San Francisco hotel suite and his several trials afterward, the "extra girl" or "studio girl"— two other terms for the young woman who traveled on her own to Hollywood in search of stardom, or at least some work in the movies, and "who went west in search of unparalleled opportunities for self-invention, artistic exploration, professional advancement, romantic adventures and just plain fun" (Hallett 2013, 17)—posed a serious public relations threat for the film studios because her potential economic, social, *and* sexual independence challenged conventional patriarchal mores. For by now "images of young women corrupted and destroyed by the stars in their eyes would blot out those of savvy, self-sufficient bohemians" (184). Later depictions of the movie-struck girl, as in *Hollywood Extra Girl*, a 1934 short featuring a paternal Cecil B. DeMille counselling hopeful Suzanne Emery (an extra in his *Crusades* who reminds him of his daughter), therefore needed to demonstrate that "passion for the movies did not threaten the authority of traditional institutions over young women's social and sexual conduct, and thus Hollywood could be maintained as a locus of fantasy and desire where anybody could become a star and reap the attendant economic and libidinal rewards" (Kenaga 2011, 88).

The contradictions raised by the movie-struck girl, in sum, were inherent in the institutionalization of female stardom and fandom from their beginnings, and these tensions structure many early star narratives. In these backstudios the mystique of Hollywood draws young women to Los Angeles in search of fame and fortune, and, if only implicitly, an escape from the social restrictions of small-town life. *A Girl's Folly* (1917), although never leaving the East Coast, may have originated this template to a certain extent, but its heroine's dreams of achieving wealth and avoiding her lot as a farmer's bride are inspired by books, not the movies, just as her possible fate of being a male star's mistress when she leaves home and fails her screen test owes as much to Thomas Hardy's novels as it does to any industrial concerns about movie-struck fan girls. In contrast, backstudio narratives in the 1920s and 1930s repeatedly dramatize female empowerment and independence through stardom. Additionally, what stands out in these backstudios is the frequency with which a wannabe star is herself a diehard movie fan at the start of her story. The first cycle of star narratives seeks to overcome the otherwise impassable gulf separating the manufacturers of Hollywood product from its avid consumers by imagining the continuity between fans and their objects of adoration and emulation; the determined fan girl Esther Blodgett is the inchoate star Vicki Lester just waiting to be born. But far from simply catering to fan girls as a means of reinforcing their investment in Hollywood stardom, these backstudio pictures feature strong, active, and desiring young women set in counterpoint to the manipulative or paternal-minded men running the industry and for whom female stars are commodities.

Movie-Struck Stardom

Befitting its title, *The Extra Girl* (1923) gives comic expression to those anxieties about female independence as personified by that figure of the movie-struck studio girl. It opens with Sue Graham (Mabel Normand), "would-be star of the silver screen," practicing her craft on "the willing victim of her endless rehearsals," the smitten Dave Giddings (Ralph Graves). Resisting her father's order to marry a more prosperous suitor, Aaron, yet refusing to elope with Dave because she will not leave her parents, Sue enters a contest promoted by the Golden State Film Company, which is looking for new faces. Before Dave can mail Sue's letter, though, the more seductively attractive Belle Brown, a "grass widow" with her eye on him, secretly substitutes her own photo for Sue's in order to get her rival out of town. Still insisting that she does not want to get married even though her father has arranged her wedding to Aaron, Sue is saved at the last minute by a telegram from Hollywood telling her to come at once. With Dave's help, the runaway bride races to the train station and makes a last-minute getaway from domesticity. Once in Hollywood, the studio manager immediately realizes that Sue does not match the photo sent in with her application; rather than go home in defeat, she takes a job in the costume shop, sweeping floors and preparing hats and clothes for the day actors. Dave soon makes his way to Hollywood, too, finding a job on a film crew. Eventually Sue does get to make a test, which she fumbles in a big slapstick scene; although her antics lead the director to realize she is "naturally funny," comedy is not the film career she has envisioned for herself. Dave, in turn, wants Sue to give up her career for marriage. A coda jumping ahead four years reveals her choice; it depicts a happily married Sue with a young son.

In some respects, *The Extra Girl* is a female version of the now lost *Merton of the Movies* (1924), which had already been a popular novel by Henry Leon Wilson and an equally successful stage adaptation by Marc Connelly and George S. Kaufman but would not reach the screen for another year. While trading on the already well-known template from *Merton* of the naïf who wants to be a serious actor but is "naturally funny" despite himself, *The Extra Girl* does not merely put its heroine in that character's place. After realizing that Hollywood does not want her, Sue's plucky spirit enables her to land honest work as a day laborer behind the scenes. By the time it ends, however, *The Extra Girl* belies the apparent attraction of Hollywood for extra girls like Sue, who has to choose between getting married to a nice guy like Dave, the fate she stubbornly refuses when the film begins, and entertaining people by being "naturally funny" (like Mabel Normand herself), thus forgoing her dream of becoming a serious dramatic actress in the movies. The coda makes clear that marriage *is* the better future for Sue, although at the same time the self-reflexive irony of the pleasure *The Extra Girl* affords viewers through Normand's own slapstick art is just as irrefutable.

Released the same year as *The Extra Girl*, *Souls for Sale* (1923) offers an alternative to that comic representation of the naïve movie-struck girl who never should have left home. Remember Steddon (Eleanor Boardman) escapes from her conniving, abusive husband, Owen Scudder (Lew Cody), who turns out to be a con artist and Bluebeard, and crashes into the movies by accident when she stumbles upon a desert location shoot. "Are you real or—a mirage?" she asks a man costumed as a sheik, and he replies, "Neither. I'm a movie actor." With nowhere to go, she travels back with the troupe to Hollywood, where she works hard to gain bit parts before hitting it big. Working in the movies preserves rather than spoils Mem's virtue, even while intertitles warn against the industry, thus overdetermining this film's view of stardom. "Mem had heard that the only way to succeed in the movies was to sell your soul," we learn. "She had nothing else left to sell." Likewise, a casting director tells her that she has to sell herself to the public, not to a director or producer—advice that intimates just the opposite. "I must have work," a hungry Mem claims. "I know I must pay 'the price.'"

Souls for Sale refutes the public image of Hollywood as Babylon while taking that image very seriously. Mem's greatest worry, reinforced by a bona fide concern in intertitle narration and the quoted dialogue, is that she will get caught up in a fatal scandal if her "unfortunate" marriage is revealed. *Souls for Sale* therefore takes great pains not only to show the folly of blaming "the screen" when actors get into trouble in their personal lives,

"Are you real or—a mirage?" Mem (Eleanor Boardman) asks a man looking like a sheik. "Neither. I'm a movie actor," he replies. (*Souls for Sale* ©1923 Goldwyn)

but to emphasize the hard work required of them by the industry. We are told, "To make their faces and bodies and souls interesting to the workaday world that buys them by the yards, the toilers of the screen endure every hardship, every hazard, night and day." Film work, in short, is far from glamorous or leisurely.

Through Mem's determination to harbor her secret and succeed in Hollywood, *Souls for Sale* further acknowledges the tension between her larger-than-life status as a star and her industrial position as a laborer. When the wicked Scudder discovers her fame and arrives to claim her riches, he hypocritically shouts at Mem, "Is there anything about you that *is* real—you actress!" His accusation points to the illusory basis of stardom, which does fabricate compelling personalities. Yet an intertitle also acknowledges the material commodification of stars by Hollywood, commenting that what *is* real about an actress is the money she "slaves" for. Thus, when Mem tries to buy off her husband, he accuses her of fooling her public into believing that she is as pure as the parts she plays. But she rebuts this charge, articulating the moral growth enabled by Hollywood: "I don't belong to you—or to anybody. I belong to myself." (▶ Figure 3.1)

Souls for Sale presents a fascinating portrait of stardom in 1920s Hollywood, in no small way because it raises questions about, while nonetheless disavowing, the public's perception of the price a female star has to pay to crash Hollywood—and then stay there. By contrast, the witty *Show People* from 1928 seems deceptively simpler in its sendup of Hollywood's pretenses as its means of endorsing the value of slapstick entertainment— and of movie stardom. Marion Davies's performance of Peggy Pepper's acting affectionately mocks Mabel Normand's miming in *The Extra Girl* just as it alludes to Gloria Swanson's beginnings with Mack Sennett as well as Swanson's later diva stardom and marriage to a titled European.

Accompanied by her father, Peggy arrives in Hollywood from Georgia dressed as if ready to audition for a Civil War epic—with her face shielded by a parasol, her hair arranged in long ringlets, her dress all ruffles and bows—but also resembling Normand's Sue Graham. Peggy's audition for the MGM casting director exaggerates Sue's rehearsing before Dave, which itself was an overly embellished dumbshow. To demonstrate her acting skills, Peggy mimes various moods, such as "contemplation," "anger," "sorrow," and "joy." Asked for photos, she brings out pictures of herself as a baby and as a child. The casting director thinks she's "very funny," although she herself aspires to the higher art of playing drama.

As their money runs out, Peggy and her father meet Billy Boone (William Haines), "a custard pie artist from the slapstick lots," who informs her that "crashing the movies is no cinch." Offering to help, Billy gets her a bit on his current picture, which requires Peggy to be doused by soda water. Not realizing it is a slapstick scene, her spontaneous performance delights the director, but afterward she needs to be persuaded to continue. Although she has no understanding of slapstick—the director declares, "I didn't think they made 'em that green!"—Peggy turns out to be a natural comedienne. At the completed film's preview, no less than Charlie Chaplin compliments Peggy on her performance outside the theater and asks for her autograph. After several successes with Billy for Comet Studios, High Arts Studio beckons. At this big-time studio she makes a screen test reminiscent of that earlier audition at MGM's casting office: told to enact "love," "hate," and "suffering," Peggy distorts her face grotesquely to mime these feelings but stops short at "sorrow." Despite many attempts, she finds herself unable to cry until the director repeats something that reminds her of her professional and personal separation from Billy, and the tears flow uncontrollably. "That's what I call good commercial crying," this director exclaims, not appreciating the authenticity of her sobbing.

Good commercial crying aside, stardom at High Arts Studio results in Peggy's being anything but her genuine self. The studio renames her Patricia Pepoire and pairs her with a new costar, the pretentious and dandified Andre d'Bergerac, le Comte d'Avignon (Paul Ralli). This new persona completely alters her. Under Andre's influence, she learns "the manner of the elite," perpetuates a fictionalized biography as a descendent of Robert E. Lee, turns her back on her friends and former colleagues at Comet Studios, condescends to Billy by disdainfully pointing out his "lowness, crudeness, and vulgarity," consorts at a studio banquet with numerous big-time stars like Douglas Fairbanks and Mae Murray, and accepts Andre's marriage proposal. "No one realized Patricia Pepoire's importance more than Peggy Pepper," an intertitle informs us. (▶ Figure 3.2)

Significantly, it is the self-important (and European) Andre, not the studio, who is most responsible for advising Peggy to take on her haughty, self-important alter ego. And just as notably, as Patricia Pepoire loses touch with the "greener" and more authentic Peggy Pepper, this transformation alienates her audience, causing the head of High Arts to think about firing her. "Peggy Pepper," he declares, "when I first signed you you were human—regular—full of ambition. You're not on the level with the public that made you—and from now on I want to see the *real* Peggy Pepper on the screen." Claiming she will not sacrifice her art even if the studio cancels her contract, Peggy lets her inflated ego threaten to derail her career. Only after Billy crashes her wedding day, restaging in the banquet room the slapstick scene they had filmed together on her first day at Comet, does Peggy fall "down to earth" to get "a clearer view of things worthwhile." With her wedding dress drenched in soda water and Andre's face covered in cream pie, she scornfully tells the prospective groom, "Look at yourself! Look at me! We're only fakes—just clowns." Billy, by contrast, "was the only real person" in her life, and now Peggy fears she has lost him. That fear, of course, proves false, and *Show People* closes with their reunion. Secretly arranging for him to be her costar in a serious drama with King Vidor directing (as he was actually doing off camera for *Show People*), Peggy surprises Billy on the first day of this new shoot. Their scripted kiss lasts beyond the duration of the take, to the exasperation of the director and his crew, who throw up their hands and take a break from filming.

As contrasted with Peggy and Billy, the pretentious "high-art" pairing of the naïve, self-deceived "Patricia" with the pretentious Andre absorbs the excesses of Peggy's ambition, evident in her declaration of being a great dramatic actress when she first arrives in Hollywood with her father, determined to succeed. All the same, despite the puncturing of Peggy's conceit as she reaches the big time, underscored by the toothy expression that Davies fixes in place as Patricia Pepoire's movie-star mask, the film's closure slyly acknowledges this female star's industrial authority once she returns "the *real* Peggy Pepper" to the screen. After all, High Art Studio was not interested in Billy, just another "custard pie artist," when the company initially signed Peggy. Only through her subsequent interference, as revealed in a conversation with director Vidor before Billy's appearance on set, does her lover get this new job and she get to reunite with him.

Furthermore, Peggy and Billy are not costarring in custard-pie slapstick but acting in a drama whose setting and costumes evoke Vidor's gigantic success for MGM, *The Big Parade* (1925). Their new film is exactly the kind of serious drama to which Peggy had aspired when she and Billy watched Vidor's *Bardeleys the Magnificent* (1926), the regular feature shown before the preview of her first comedy, which had so impressed Chaplin. "That's the kind of acting I'm going to do someday," she stated to Billy then. "That's real art." With a wink to its audience, *Show People* mocks the artifice of the Hollywood-made Patricia Pepoire and Andre d'Bergerac, while confirming Peggy's authenticity and, more to the point, her agency as a movie star who, in this final scene, looks more like Marion Davies than at any other time in the film, in contrast with the visible difference between actress and character shown earlier, when the naïve and unpretentious Peggy first arrives at High Art and crosses paths with the "real," more sophisticated and modern Davies. (▶ Figure 3.3)

Going Hollywood

According to Samantha Barbas, with so much evident public anxiety about the extra girl as a challenge to conventional femininity, Hollywood sought to manage representations of this figure through all its discursive venues, such as studio publicity, journalism, fan magazines, and films and short subjects. From this coverage, two paired figures came to epitomize "Hollywood's evils" in the 1920s: "the conniving actor and the naïve, desperate movie-struck girl" (Barbas 2001, 74), the very figures sent up by *Show People* in the figures of Andre and Peggy/Patricia.

The manipulative Andre's influence in creating the vain and pompous Patricia Pepoire exaggerates the hypocrisy of Hollywood, just as the naïve Peggy's desire for stardom enables it. Using these two complementary types as a structural device, *Show People* established something of a template for the star narratives in the subsequent decade. For much as *Souls for Sale* does with Mem, *Show People* dramatizes how a naïve movie-struck girl like Peggy Pepper is no simple stereotype created to reassure the public about Hollywood's morality. Anxious to crash Hollywood first with Billy's, then with Andre's assistance, Peggy is not only ambitious but as often as not conniving or at least opportunistic and arrogant, as her transformation into the conceited Patricia Pepoire reveals. Naïveté is not her sole character note: this studio girl welcomes the conniving actor's influence if it helps her career. Additionally, while the aspiring star may, again like Peggy, fall under the influence of a devious Hollywood type who exploits her for his own purposes, as often as not later backstudios forsake the conniving actor. Instead an older or established mentor unselfishly guides the young woman's career or helps to set her back on a less self-indulgent path to success. In *Show People* Billy serves both functions for Peggy.

We can see similar treatment of an aspiring young female star two years later in *Show Girl in Hollywood*, an early talkie from 1930 that also recounts the potentially disastrous influence of a vain, duplicitous mentor on an ambitious wannabe star. Dixie Dugan (Alice White) goes to Hollywood after director Frank Buelow (John Miljan) meets her in a Broadway nightclub and asks, "Have you ever thought of going into pictures?" Boasting about his unchallenged authority at Superb Studios, he promises Dixie a contract. Arriving there, however, she discovers that Buelow has no right to sign her, has done this many times before with beautiful young woman he has a yen for, and has just been fired by studio head Sam Otis (Ford Sterling). It later turns out that Buelow regularly goes to New York to attend Broadway shows in order to plagiarize their stories, as he has just tried to do at Superb with "Rainbow Girl," the short-lived musical by Dixie's boyfriend, Jimmie Doyle (Jack Mulhall). Selling the rights to Otis and hired to assist in the production, Jimmie follows Dixie to Hollywood and persuades the studio to cast her in the lead of "Rainbow Girl." Angry at being humiliated by the studio, Buelow interferes, secretly telling Dixie that she is too good for this film and instructing her how to act like a star. "The more trouble a star gives 'em, the more they want her," he advises.

Following his counsel, Dixie "goes Hollywood," as Jimmie accuses, when she insists on major rewrites to the script and a new director, telling Otis, "I'm demanding, not asking. And that's my last word." This behavior not only gets her fired; it also throws everyone out of work since, rather than capitulate, Otis shuts down production of "Rainbow Girl." At first Dixie does not care because Buelow has let her think he wants her for a more prestigious film that he plans to direct for another studio. But the scheming director has manipulated the unsuspecting Dixie in order to get "Rainbow Girl" canceled out of spite. "I put Dugan up to this," he boasts, "… and the poor little fool fell for it.…I hope it costs them a quarter of a million dollars. I'll teach Otis he can't fire me and get away with it!" Jimmie overhears Buelow's bragging, punches him for his arrogance, and tries to persuade Dixie to apologize to Otis. "Motion picture producers are businessmen," Jimmie tells her, delivering one message of this film to aspiring starlets everywhere; "making moving pictures is their business, not arguing with temperamental dames." Dixie, however, still believes "the studios always want real artists" and insists that real artists do not ask but make demands.

Show Girl in Hollywood, I should note before going any further, is not the first appearance of Dixie Dugan on screen. *Hollywood* is a follow-up to *Show Girl* (1928), which takes place on Broadway; both First National films were adaptations of serialized novels by J. P. McAvoy; and the character had already successfully migrated to the comic strip pages by 1929. Thus, even as an aspiring movie star in this film, the character of Dixie

Dugan was already a popular feminine stereotype of the Jazz Age, complete with her striking helmet haircut. And much like the youthful Joan Crawford of that era, Dixie is a flapper who displays an enthusiasm for nightclubbing and going to parties, a driving ambition and hunger for success, and a willingness to use her sexual attractiveness to her advantage. Yet she is not promiscuous. Dixie makes it perfectly clear to Buelow that she has only a professional interest in his mentorship and she remains steadfastly faithful to Jimmie, her fiancé, although she will not stand down once she starts making trouble on the set of "Rainbow Girl."

Along with having good-bad mentors in those two men, Dixie finds a female mentor in her new friend Donny Harris (Blanche Sweet), who lives out a cautionary tale about the Hollywood careers of women, one somewhat predictive of Norma Desmond two decades later. A former star herself—Dixie, in fact, was a fan of hers before traveling to Hollywood—Donny gives the aspiring star (who at this point does not have a job, let alone a contract) several important lessons about Hollywood's tinsel and ageism, although Dixie does not listen closely enough. As mentioned in chapter 2, Donny declares that Hollywood is nothing more than "a land of make-believe," in which "everybody is making believe for everybody else," much as Donny herself is doing since, simply out of a false sense of pride, she still lives in her large mansion even though she can no longer afford its upkeep. Hollywood, Donny also points out, is a place where fresh, young faces like Dixie's are everywhere to be had. This is the reason why Donny, only thirty-two yet already washed up in pictures, feels "older than the hills up there." Further intensifying her damaged pride, Donny is Buelow's estranged wife. The womanizing director has apparently betrayed her many times already and now forbids his assistants to take her phone calls. (▶ Figure 3.4)

Becoming fast friends with Donny before falling under Buelow's influence a second time after "Rainbow Girl" begins shooting, Dixie facilitates the former star's comeback by getting her a supporting part in the film. Thus, when Dixie "goes Hollywood" under Buelow's influence, causing her first picture to be canceled on the spot, her actions have repercussions for Donny's comeback. Jimmie scolds, "This was Donny's last chance, Dixie, and it meant everything in the world for that girl. And you lost it for her." Despondent, Donny attempts suicide, calling Dixie before the pills take their full effect: "I'm in terrible pain. I'm not coming back. I'm too much of a coward to go on living. I've had my chance. I lost it." Accepting her responsibility, Dixie vows to speak to Otis: "I'll crawl back on my knees. I'll do anything to make him start the picture again and give Donny another chance." Donny's function as a mentor for this showgirl in Hollywood, then, is to correct Dixie's diva-like behavior so that she can be assimilated into the motion picture business as productive labor—just as Jimmie had told Dixie that she needed to do in order to stay working in Hollywood as a star. *Show Girl in Hollywood* confirms Dixie's subordination to patriarchal Hollywood when she announces her intent to marry Jimmie after the premiere showing of "Rainbow Girl" but has to cut her planned honeymoon by half when, from the audience, Otis demands that his new star return to work after a week.

In *Show People* and *Show Girl in Hollywood* female stars are at once naïve and conniving when their careers go to their heads, and this ambivalent portrayal results from how their films also depict them as ambitious, professionally minded young women fully and publicly engaged in work, thereby reducing the importance for them of domesticity, marriage, and motherhood. Along with *The Extra Girl* and *Souls for Sale*, these early star narratives draw attention to the conflicted status of female performers since these women are at once industrial laborers empowered by their eventual stardom and single women whose agency is still severely restricted by an institution that reinforces patriarchy, as the closures insist upon underscoring.

But any backstudio dealing with female stardom has to reckon in some way with what these early films suggest is already a highly ambivalent viewpoint toward the women working in Hollywood. Molly Haskell notes about the 1930s and 1940s woman's film more generally, "In no more than one out of a thousand movies was a woman allowed to sacrifice love for career rather than the other way around. Yet, in real life, the stars did it all the time, either by choice or by default—the result of devoting so much time and energy to a career and of achieving such fame that marriage suffered and the home fell apart.... And yet, what was the 'star' but a woman supremely driven to survive, a barely clothed ego on display for all the world to see" (Haskell 1974, 5). While Haskell's observation may now seem to go without saying, the point she makes is central to understanding *how* as well as *why* the female star narrative so successfully branded Hollywood throughout the studio era. As Emily Carman comments in her study of major actresses without long-term studio contracts, during the first decade of sound "female stars truly did rule Hollywood screens as top box-office attractions" (Carman 2016, 8). Consequently female stardom served as "the economic underpinning of the larger industrial apparatus of Hollywood during the classical era, and as the major studios consolidated their monopoly over the American film industry after the transition to sound cinema" (14). The centrality of female stardom for the industry pretty much went unchallenged until the mid-1940s, in no small way aided during the early years of that decade by the absence from Hollywood of male stars serving in the armed forces.

Drawing on Haskell's observation about the dichotomy between movie plots and actual careers, Allen Larson points out that, in disavowing its challenge to patriarchy, Hollywood's discourses of stardom in the 1930s constructed the idea of the female star, onscreen and off-, by means of the central contradiction we have seen operating to varying degrees within these early backstudio pictures. On one hand, Larson notes, the charismatic female performer exhibits " 'star quality' as a state of preexisting traits simply discovered by the cinematic machine and carried to the masses." But on the other hand, coverage by both the popular press and fan magazines reiterated how her stardom derived from genuine talent and the "drive and determination," not to say discipline and training, to make great use of that talent (Larson 2007, 188–89). Backstudios in the first cycle typically bring out this contradiction, stressing a young actress's innate yet passive "star quality" while letting her ambition and determination drive the story. In the backstudio genre, as in Hollywood itself, female stardom is ideologically riven simply by definition.

Working in Pictures

That conflicted view of female stardom is more pronounced in the two most famous backstudio pictures released prior to *A Star Is Born* (1937): *What Price Hollywood?* from 1932 and *Bombshell* from 1933. While tonally and narratively different from each other— the former veers toward the woman's film, the latter is screwball comedy—each was in- spired by the biography of Clara Bow, whose career was characterized by success, scandal, and the public's amnesia as soon as her stardom had faded (Smyth 2006, 251–63). Perhaps because of that heavily rewritten source, the implicit contradiction inhering within filmic representations of female stardom explicitly drives both narratives despite their generic differences. Both backstudios assume stardom is a natural resource nurtured and har- vested by Hollywood, yet both recognize stardom as a goal a woman labors against all odds to reach, as a rare professional achievement that offers her sexual and economic independence in exchange for the patriarchal oversight of the studio system.

What Price Hollywood? begins by deferring the expected facial close-up of star Constance Bennett in order to establish immediately the Hollywood aspirations of her character, Mary Evans, through Mary's movie fandom. (▶ Figures 3.5–3.12) Focusing on her legs, torso, and mouth, the opening sequence fragments Mary's body, visualizing her interpellation by Hollywood as a movie-struck fan. Mary models her appearance on the stars, imaginatively treating them as a kind of composite alter ego: hence the rather long delay before finally revealing Bennett's face. A montage alternates between shots of a movie magazine, with a woman's fingers flipping through the issue but stopping at partic- ular pages, and shots of her following the examples that catch her eye. To start with, after she studies an ad that exclaims, "Glinda Golden, Frolic Beauty and Screen Star, Wears Sheer Silk," we see only her headless body as she sits on a bed in a lacy slip and slides ho- siery up her legs. A two-page feature, "Follow Hollywood Star Styles," precedes another headless shot of her pulling one of the very dresses pictured in that article over her shoul- ders and down her shapely figure. Finally, she stops at a page advertising makeup— "Hollywood Stars Prefer . . . Kissable Lipstick"—and a tight close-up on the lower half of her face shows her applying lipstick, presumably the same kind being advertised.

Only now does the camera pull back to reveal the full face of Bennett's Mary Evans. She scrutinizes herself in a hand mirror as she puts the finishing touch to her kissable lips, glances back to the folded magazine page, checks the mirror again with a smile, purses her mouth, demurely looks back at the magazine once more; satisfied, she straightens her neck and holds her chin in an obviously studied pose for the mirror, a stand-in for an imaginary camera. Lowering the mirror toward her dressing table, Mary's gesture signals a dissolve to a medium close-up of her contemplating an article in the magazine. As an indication of her strong interest, she brings the page closer, and the page folded behind the one she is reading—a photo of Greta Garbo and Clark Gable in a romantic clinch—covers her face. Turning the magazine over to look at the photo, Mary mutters, "Oh, boy," bends the magazine in half so that Gable's cheek rests on hers, and imitates Garbo's accented lovemaking. After this elaborate preparation, the camera pulls back to reveal Mary's single-room living space. Realizing the time, she closes her Murphy bed, puts on her hat and goes to the door, turns back to bid good-bye to Gable, and rushes out. A fade to the exterior of the Brown Derby restaurant reveals Mary's destination: her job waiting on tables at the famous Hollywood watering hole. This opening sequence, in sum, establishes an initial disconnect between Mary's fantasized self-image, derived from being a movie fan who models herself on the stars, and her actual status as a Hollywood wannabe peering in on stardom from the outside.

At the Brown Derby, whose clientele apparently comprises, along with a few elderly tourists, producers, agents, and actors making deals on the telephone, Mary establishes her determination to make her own luck. After proving to be adept at dismissing the attentions of salacious producers while unsuccessfully trying to finagle her way into real film work, she persuades a fellow waitress to switch stations so she can wait on the director Max Carey (Lowell Sherman), who arrives, greatly and loudly inebriated. (⊙ Figure 3.13) Mary tells her hesitant coworker, "Oh, you can have the tip. I'm not interested in that. I'm looking for a break. And I'm going to get it." Impressed with her cleverness

Mary Evans (Constance Bennett) makes love to a photo of Clark Gable in a fan magazine. (*What Price Hollywood?* ©1932 RKO)

and directness, Carey invites Mary to accompany him to the premiere of his new picture at Grauman's Chinese Theatre. There she follows his lead in mocking Hollywood's elitist pretensions. "You know the motto of Hollywood: 'It's all in fun,'" he tells her, although his behavior, which includes his blowing a raspberry into the radio microphone, implies more derision and even self-loathing than joviality. Mary's performance as his guest, the faux "Duchess of Derby," expresses her comparable ironic detachment from celebrity, indicating a realistic assessment of Hollywood's exclusivity which the opening sequence did not hint at, although her jaded attitude when working at the restaurant surely implied it. "Mr. Carey is waiting," she says to the microphone in a phony British accent, "and there is nothing so exasperating as waiting on people," adding as an aside in her own voice and with a look back at Carey, "I oughta know."

Her impromptu act at the premiere catches the eye of a gossip columnist, who asks in the next morning's newspaper, "Who was the devastating blonde with Max Carey who knocked 'em cold over the radio at the Chinese opening?" That inserted newspaper shot segues to Mary awakening in Carey's living room; we quickly learn that he does not remember much of the previous evening, that Mary slept alone on the couch, and that she quit her job at the Derby to leave with him for the premiere. After she jogs his memory about who she is ("I bought you from another waitress"), she begs for a part in his picture: "I'm no wise guy. But I believe in myself. All I need is a break." Requiring some persuasion, Carey reluctantly agrees to give her a small part. "Let me give you a tip about Hollywood," he advises before sending her home after she refuses any financial assistance from him as compensation for her quitting her job. "Always keep your sense of humor and you can't miss."

Her sense of humor, however, does not help Mary nail her minor role, for she seems incapable of following Carey's direction. Overhearing him order a replacement for the next day, she rehearses tirelessly in her boarding house in order to get the right mix of acting technique and effortless naturalism. Carey agrees to see her do the bit again, and needless to say, her rehearsing pays off in spades. More to the point, Mary was surely right about needing only that one break. When the studio head, Julius Saxe (Gregory Ratoff), screens footage of her scene he sees a *nova stella*: "Who is that gorgeous creature?... Sign her up immediately.... Maybe she's a great discovery." Carey agrees: "She's got something." Saxe offers Mary a seven-year contract, and, though he first sees her as a possible "great discovery," he is quickly calling her "a new star." "We must make her a typical American girl," he tells the department heads seated near him in the screening room. "I got it! We make her 'America's Pal.'" Still dazed by having gotten her break at last, Mary mutters to herself, "I'm in pictures!"

I have spent so much time on the first several sequences in *What Price Hollywood?* because Mary's trajectory from movie-struck fan (the opening) to the wannabe laboring on the margins of Hollywood (at the Brown Derby) to her bit part (which she first loses but then regains due to her hard work in mastering Carey's direction) to stardom (in the screening room where the blueprint for taking her from bit part to stardom is laid out) confirms how her ambition and determination reward her; in fact, retrospectively we might even consider the initial sequence when she models herself on stardom as much a part of her game plan as evidence of her own movie fandom. On the other hand, once Mary hits big in pictures, the narrative shifts from that emphasis on her doggedly getting work in pictures by hook or crook (and learning what good work entails) to showing her working hard at being a star—and "being a star" means having an interesting romantic life offscreen. Thus a montage detailing Mary's starry rise from featured to costarring to over-the-title billing leads to a shift in time and place from Hollywood to Santa Barbara, where, now an established star for Saxe, she is on location for a new film. Here she meets-cute her future husband, the socialite Lonnie Borden (Neil Hamilton). (▶ Clip 9)

Stardom in Hollywood gives Mary license to freely express her sexual desire. First, spotting Lonnie on the polo field and struck by his good looks and hard body, she ogles him openly, acknowledging the attraction to her maid. (▶ Figure 3.14) Later, when the couple meet off the field, Mary seductively antagonizes him because Saxe has told her that Lonny claims to have no use for Hollywood blondes. Similarly, when Mary later stands him up for their arranged private supper, Lonny pays her back in kind, hinting at a mutual class hostility underlying (and motivating) their obvious sexual attraction to each other. But attraction it is, and as outward hostility turns to passion, an engagement and then marriage follow in short order.

Still, Santa Barbara and Hollywood make for an uneasy social alliance according to *What Price Hollywood?* Lonny tutors Mary in proper etiquette and fashion sense, and he tries to tolerate her studio friends and stifle his boredom when they gather at their house for script conferences or he visits a movie set; but he also looks down on her colleagues for being "cheap and vulgar," just as he hates the publicity and glare of the "Hollywood spotlight" on everything his wife does. At the same time, Mary stays loyal to Carey, whose artistic decline as a director due to his alcoholism and, more implicitly, to his loathing of Hollywood inversely parallels her success; their professional bond threatens Lonny, even though it is clearly not sexual but an expression of her gratitude to his mentoring and affection for him personally. After Saxe fires Carey because the director's alcoholism has gotten out of control and diminished his talent, Mary's kindness in tolerating his drunken, self-destructive behavior eventually causes Lonny to depart for Reno.

With the ink on the divorce decree barely dry, Mary discovers she is pregnant. The gossip mavens turn against her, speculating that Carey may be the reason for her divorce and then, after the birth, asking, "Is 'America's Pal' Becoming High Hat?" since Mary refuses to let her child be photographed by the press. To make matters worse for Mary, Carey shoots himself in her house after she bails him out of jail because, in despair at his self-degradation and apathy, he does not want to cause her any more pain or trouble. His selfless act backfires, however, since committing suicide in her home results in a scandal that ruins Mary's career when she refuses to say anything to the press about their relationship. At this point a montage reverses the one that had recounted her rise; it shows Mary's star fizzling out as a series of newspaper front pages keep the scandal aflame with headlines about the suicide at her home, the inquest where she testifies, the funeral where she breaks down, and the banning of her pictures by women's groups. It ends with dirt thrown on the newspapers. (▶ Clip 10)

As *What Price Hollywood?* unfolds, then, Mary Evans's stardom gives way to romance; her career and her loyalty to Carey conflict with her marriage; but motherhood trumps everything. This star narrative redirects its opening section, which was driven by Mary's determination and ambition to get her big break, into the more melodramatic form of a 1930s woman's film. Fearing that scandal will give Lonny license to claim custody of their son, Mary forsakes her career and flees to France with her child. A very rushed ending—during which Lonny tracks Mary down in the French countryside to beg for a reconciliation while also bringing her word from Saxe that he has a comeback picture to revive her career—wants us to see that motherhood, marriage, and a life in the movies are fully compatible for a woman in Hollywood. But this closure only adds to the film's conflicted view of female stardom. *What Price Hollywood?* refrains from blaming Hollywood itself for turning its back on a female star when she bucks its will. Although her buildup as "America's Pal" and her wedding typify how Mary's public and private personae are adeptly managed by Saxe's studio, he disclaims responsibility for her success or her fall, stating that she belongs to the public, which can make and break her.

No surprise, then, that the film's depiction of Mary Evans's star persona is incoherent. Although promoted as "America's Pal," a nickname that stays attached to her and calls to mind someone like Janet Gaynor, references to Mary's pictures indicate a different, more sexualized and suggestively transgressive feminine persona. She is no "pal," with the word's tomboy or asexual implication, but instead plays an unwed mother in weepie after weepie. Shortly after her wedding, when her Hollywood friends gather around the pool, much to Lonny's discomfort, Mary asks Saxe, "Do I have to have a baby in every picture?," and he replies, "This baby is different. You are getting married first." The titles representing Mary's rise to stardom in the first montage, each displayed on a movie theater marquee, capture this impression of her incoherent star image: first America's Pal is a featured player in "Loves Holiday," then a costar sharing billing with her male lead in "Revenge Is Sweet," and finally solo-billed, with her name in letters even larger than her film's title: "Mary Evans—America's Pal—in—Playing Around." After the successive assortment of fallen women pictures that Mary alludes to, the comeback vehicle that Saxe has in mind for her offers still another variation on this role of suffering female victim: "You go to prison for the man you love."

"America's Pal," in short, starring in one pre-Code fallen woman picture after another, divides Mary's screen personality in much the same way that the narrative of *What Price Hollywood?* splits its protagonist. Mary remains professionally driven, shown to be concerned about her scripts, her pictures, her director, even when Lonny's presence on the set or at a meeting distracts her; by the same token, while the nickname strips her of her femaleness by giving her a gender-neutral identity as the nation's "pal," it does allude to her unwavering loyalty to and friendship with Carey, a nonsexual male-female relation that the press and the moviegoing public cannot understand except in scandalous terms. At the same time, when imagining her movie roles, the film registers how Mary's ambition and sexuality, the forces behind her stardom more than her innate screen presence (which is what Saxe sees at the screening), disturb the patriarchal regulation of women in Hollywood. As a result, the narrative seeks to contain those female energies even while remystifying Mary's stardom. After he reads aloud Saxe's letter inviting her back to Hollywood, Lonny makes his extemporaneous appeal for reconciliation as if it were the postscript to the studio head's missive. The personal plea disavows the economic imperative of Saxe's investment in reviving America's Pal, but Mary's comeback is still narratively designed to serve a double ideological imperative as a means of putting this female star back in her proper place: as the implied condition of her return to Hollywood, she will display contrition on screen (the premise of the proposed film) and resume her former life offscreen as Lonny's wife and his son's mother.

Like the other star narratives I have discussed so far, *What Price Hollywood?* plays to wider cultural anxieties about Hollywood women, so it would be remiss to discount the material basis of these tensions in the institution of filmmaking. All these early star narratives register anxieties about the industry's empowerment of women. Onscreen and off-, these women are sexually and economically independent yet also laboring in and for a patriarchal institution, which is why a male mentor often plays an important role in guiding their careers, why the studio heads are typically characterized as benevolent father figures enveloping the women in a protective all-male institutional environment, and why domesticity or romantic coupling is usually a female star's destiny at the fade-out. Christopher Ames observes that backstudio stories of this era often reflect "an anxiety built into the male-female relationships of the studio system, in which the biggest stars were female and all the other powerful figures (director, producer, production chief) were male" (Ames 1997, 146). To be sure, this anxiety resonates throughout most Hollywood product of the 1930s and 1940s featuring strong female protagonists, as in women's films or romantic comedies, but it becomes more transparent whenever a backstudio from this period centers its story on a female star. Then it becomes the explicit *thematic* problem the backstudio narrative is openly working out.

This same institutional ambivalence about female stardom informs the narrative of Lola Burns (Jean Harlow) in *Bombshell*. Unlike *What Price Hollywood?* or any of the backstudios I have looked at so far in this chapter, *Bombshell* begins with its fictional star already a fixture of the Hollywood pantheon. Yet not unlike the initial sequence in *What Price Hollywood?*, an opening montage immediately establishes her stature by identifying Lola as the alter ego of her portrayer, Jean Harlow, and doing so through movie fandom. (⊙ Figures 3.15–3.16) A cannon explodes and a smiling, glamorous Lola emerges in a cloud of smoke, her pose evoking Lady Liberty as she moves toward the camera until there is a cut to her close-up. Newspaper pages fly in the air, one settling down to display a partial ad for a new film exclaiming, "Here she is! Lola Burns." This image dissolves into spinning film projectors. Then various fan magazine such as *Modern Screen* and *Photoplay* roll off the presses with Lola on their covers and stories like "The Love Life of Lola Burns." Eager readers of both genders snatch up these magazines at newsstands. Newspaper headers follow, recording Lola's romances and scandals as well as publicity events staged by her studio; these apparently have the same wide readership as those fan magazines. Additionally, testimonials in ads for hosiery, face powder, and perfume reinforce Lola's star wattage, the ads cut into shots of female consumers using the products. Finally, Lola's name blazes electronically across theater marquees as coins spill across the frame to indicate her box-office appeal. These theater signs dissolve to the faces of enrapt spectators watching Lola and Clark Gable kiss. Moving away from that space, a camera somewhat incongruously pans into an apartment window where a young woman stares into space dreamily, a copy of *Photoplay* on her chest. Back in the auditorium, a close-up of a male audience member cuts to another excerpt of a Lola Burns film.

Following the montage, and contrasting with its initial divine-like grounding of her stardom in Harlow's, Lola's home life is pure chaos. The butler brings her sauerkraut juice instead of orange. Before she can even get out of bed, studio personnel arrive to prepare her makeup and hair for the day's shoot, bickering, getting in each other's way, and making a mess of blankets. Lola's personal assistant (Una Merkel), who takes every advantage of her, quarrels with her personal maid (Louise Beavers), Lola's confidante. Lola's father (Frank Morgan), a pompous braggart entrusted with managing her finances and pretending to be a horse breeder, arrives home from being out all night. Her chauffeur has gone to bed after driving the father around town; she therefore wants to drive her roadster to work herself, but her brother has it in Tijuana while the cook has taken the stationwagon to visit a pregnant sister. Lola exclaims, "I don't know why I go on putting up with this! I do all the work, and everyone uses my automobiles except for me!" Miss Carroll from *Photoplay* arrives for a breakfast interview set up by the studio's public relations maven, Space Hanlon (Lee Tracy). Complaining to her father that Space won't give her a minute to herself and has lies printed about her, Lola nonetheless cooperates, making up a biography with "a new slant" for *Photoplay* in collaboration with her father. Close-ups of the journalist's notepad show her translating Lola's pretentious version into less glamorous and more prosaic facts. Before Lola can finish, her assistant learns that rain has forced a postponement of the planned location shoot, so the star has to go to the studio instead, where she will have to memorize new pages of script since the Hays Office has required retakes for a picture already in the can and set to open. Pushing back her three wild sheepdogs, Lola heads for the door and a waiting studio car. As she departs, she moans, "Well, here goes another day's work, and I'm dead on my feet already!"

From this point on, every scene in *Bombshell* dramatizes how Lola has no control over her career, her publicity, or her personal life. To be sure, the chaos surrounding her appears circumstantial, primarily the result of Space's manipulations to keep her name on the front page and to sustain her blond "bombshell" star image, but it also defines Lola Burns's stardom on the basis solely of her looks, making her a valuable commodity for the studio. "I dubbed you 'The Hollywood Bombshell,' and that's the way they love you,"

Space states about her fans, as the montage has previously shown. From this perspective, Lola Burns is the opposite of Mary Evans, "America's Pal." A star whose appeal lies solely in her onscreen charismatic appeal and offscreen mercurial personality, Lola is valuable to Hollywood solely for her "to-be-looked-at-ness," in Laura Mulvey's famous phrase— an "innate" star quality that also gives Lola license to be sexually adventurous even with men attached to other women, as evident in the dialogue's allusions to her former affairs with Space and director Jim Brogan (Pat O'Brien), not to mention in the montage's headlines about her sexual dalliances.

Space's interventions in Lola's private life as a means of keeping her in the news and perpetuating the bombshell image render her without agency since he manipulates her at every turn, and he does so with the studio's blessing. "Lola makes great copy," Space proclaims, "because she doesn't know what she wants and she wants something different every day." *Bombshell* continually derives its comic energy from Lola's mercurial personality; every change in what she wants reinforces her illusion of being an independent and empowered woman. Space is the master at bending Lola to his will, however, and his will is always in line with what most benefits the studio. Furthermore, as its plotting moves Lola from one screwball situation to the next, narratively speaking *Bombshell* makes just as clear that her conventionally feminine desires are nothing more than Hollywood-inspired performances. Nevertheless, and somewhat paradoxically as far as studio thinking might go, each performance turns Lola into a potentially disruptive female figure.

Following the montage and opening sequence at her home, the narrative places Lola in situations that reveal her inability to conform to patriarchal expectations of femininity simply by virtue of her being a movie star. First, she believes she is in love with her fiancé of the moment, a dandyish marquis named Hugo. To break up the couple, Space arranges for Hugo to be arrested and possibly deported, the repercussions of which confirm that the man's interest in Lola is primarily for her money. Second, almost immediately following the demise of that romance, Lola abruptly wants to satisfy a suddenly emergent maternal longing by adopting a child as a single parent. When two matrons arrive from the orphanage to interview her, Lola's drunken brother and father embarrass her. Meanwhile Hugo wants to serve Lola papers in a trumped-up lawsuit, and Space tricks him into racing to her house, where reporters are waiting to record the expected fireworks. Needless to say, between Hugo, Space, the reporters, and the shenanigans of her brother and father, the interview is a disaster, ending Lola's plan to adopt a child. Third, furious at Space for spoiling her dream of motherhood, Lola walks away from Hollywood, retreating to a desert spa. Ordered by the studio to get Lola back so she can finish the picture she is shooting, Space follows her there. At the spa she meets Gifford Middleton (Franchot Tone), scion of a Boston Brahmin family, and hopes to marry him. However, when her brother and father arrive seeking cash, the two families bristle due to their class differences, and finally Gifford explains that he cannot go against his parents' wishes, which gets Lola's back up, causing her to leave the spa and head home. All of this goes according to Space's plan, as it turns out. Back on the studio lot, Lola accidentally learns that Gifford and his parents were out-of-work stage actors whose snobby "characters" at the spa were part of Space's scheme to return her to work. In the same vein, a running gag concerns a stalker claiming to be the husband Lola has deserted along with their children, who increase in number every time the bogus spouse harasses the star, and this man also turns out to be in Space Hanlon's employ.

Romance, marriage, and motherhood, in sum, are all Hollywood fabrications as Lola experiences them, fabrications not that different from the bombshell roles she plays on screen. Her failure to perform those roles satisfactorily indicates what makes female stardom dangerous to patriarchal culture: she can flout the rules because she is sexually independent and financially well-off. Especially important in this regard is how the maternal urge is just another star turn for Lola, challenging the cultural presumption that motherhood is by default the natural goal of every woman. Lola's longing for a child is prompted by a female reporter's queries. Interviewing Lola in her kitchen as the star is photographed at the stove to illustrate her domestic skills, the reporter asks Lola if she doesn't want children. Lola at first replies, as if by rote, "Our life is dedicated to our public." The reporter persists with her inquiry, citing "the right of all womanhood," referring wistfully to "the patter of little feet," and invoking "the call of motherhood." Now enthralled by the idea of becoming a mother, Lola decides, "An American must be the father of my child." So she proposes to Brogan, who wants only to resume their affair. Speaking for Hollywood, he insists, "You can't have a family and make five pictures a year." As a way for her to sidestep the leave of absence required of a pregnancy, he suggests adopting from an orphanage, an idea Lola takes to with great gusto.

Always the brash pragmatist, Space Hanlon likewise speaks the truth for women working in Hollywood, reminding Lola that her apparent freedom from sexual convention is simply a condition of her employment, and it has its limits: "Lola Burns can't have a baby....It's not in her contract." Even more than her publicized and often scandalous love life, if Lola were to succeed in becoming a single working mother, she would not only bypass the marriage contract but would also shatter her star image. "You think I want my bombshell turned into a rubber nipple?" Space rhetorically asks the reporters gathered outside her home when they press him for the truth behind rumors that Lola may be pregnant.

The priority of maintaining her bombshell stardom may trump domestic ideology according to Space, but it does not necessarily give Lola total free rein. As an employee of Hollywood, even one making scads of money, taking on numerous lovers, and enjoying luxuries that Depression audiences could not imagine on their own without MGM's help, Lola mistakes those economic perks for genuine independence. In fact, one might conclude that she internalizes the mercurial, dumb blonde, bombshell persona created for her to avoid seeing that she is so regularly manipulated by Space in his capacity as the representative of her studio. "I'm the only one who has anything to do with it," she shouts to him when he tries to talk her out of the adoption. Of course, she is wrong; each of those

Lola Burns (Jean Harlow) discovers her repressed maternal longing. (*Bombshell* ©1933 Metro-Goldwyn-Mayer)

three major segments of the narrative concludes with her learning otherwise—with her realizing that the press agent is always pulling her strings. (▶ Figure 3.17)

The finale of *Bombshell* ensures that Lola remains securely within Hollywood's orbit. Before she discovers that Gifford and his parents are just actors, the star defends the movie business to them. "What's wrong with pictures?" she asks the stuffy Gifford, who expresses distaste for such entertainment. "It's perfectly honest work, isn't it?" Likewise, when several fans approach her in the resort's restaurant, she explains to his parents, who are shocked at this breach of decorum and privacy, "These people are my friends." After praising Hollywood and returning there, Lola reconciles with Space, whom the film puts forward as her proper mate to achieve closure. Immediately after they reunite in her dressing room, though, she learns of his trickery at the spa and retreats to her car in a huff. Running alongside her auto, Space pushes his way inside; after first explaining that it was all done for publicity, he finally declares, "I love you," and they kiss. At that moment the phony husband sticks his head in the car window and says hello to Space, confirming that his pestering of the star has also been orchestrated for publicity, which causes an outraged Lola to begin screaming again at her on-and-off lover. *Bombshell* concludes with the two engaged in another shouting match. Their "ending cute" may mark them as a screwball couple, but it also confirms Lola's domination by a lover who not only master-minds her star image but also thinks and speaks faster.

Throughout this chapter I have been emphasizing the tensions inhering in these star narratives around, on one hand, the actress's achieving or maintaining a career and, on the other hand, her submitting to the cultural imperatives of romance, marriage, and/or motherhood—in no small way in order to depict her submission to the studio and its industrial mode of production. In their closures, *Bombshell* and *What Price Hollywood?* both try to imagine some means of containing, minimizing, or effacing the female star's authoritative position in the movie business, a result of her being such a reliable source of revenue, as those stacks of coins and theater marquees in the opening montage of *Bombshell* confirm. But along with the requisite domestication or romantic coupling, before "The End" appears these star narratives seek to remystify the female star's value *as* a star, reiterating her contradictory status.

Cinderella in the Movies

Possibly the most famous fictional Hollywood star of this era, Esther Blodgett (Janet Gaynor) in *A Star Is Born* (1937), is also introduced as a movie fan. Returning home after seeing a Norman Maine (Fredric March) film, Esther ignores her aunt's complaint that all she thinks about is going to Hollywood when she picks up a movie magazine to read. "You'd better think about getting a good husband and stop mooning about Hollywood," the aunt advises. Esther's granny, however, supports those dreams, calling Hollywood her granddaughter's "wilderness" and comparing it to the Dakota frontier that the older woman had helped to settle in the previous century. The grandmother sends Esther off to Hollywood, now imagined as the modern-day American frontier, with the pioneering spirit of conquering the movies. As Esther later says in the Central Casting office, she believes in herself and has faith that she may be "the one" to reach stardom, alone among the thousands who fail. (⏵ Figure 3.18)

Central Casting was established in 1926 to register seekers of extra work as another means of managing what was otherwise an ad hoc female labor force for the industry at large. Its presence also meant to discourage too many movie-struck fans from venturing to Los Angeles with unrealistic expectations about finding studio work. Esther's visit to Central Casting delivers this message plainly: "We haven't put anyone in our books for over two years," she is told. Despite the explicit discouragement, it turns out Esther does have what it takes to be singled out: native talent, screen charisma, good luck, but most of all the mediation of someone powerful and already inside the industry, namely, Norman Maine, her future husband.

Even with her pioneer spirit and Norman's influence, Esther never seems as scheming as, say, Mary Evans at the Brown Derby or Dixie Dugan under Buelow's influence. But when she arrives in Los Angeles, the first thing Esther does is to see if she can fill Norman's footprints at Grauman's Chinese Theatre. Given how the narrative makes Esther his successor as well as his costar and spouse, her tourist gesture implies more than her movie fandom and adoration of this one star: it predicts how she will succeed him as a new and different generation of Hollywood stardom. Thus, when she first sights her idol in the flesh at the Hollywood Bowl, she criticizes his behavior, bringing this celestial being down to earth in her imagination. Watching him fight with photographers who are disturbing his privacy, a disillusioned and disapproving Esther asks her companion, Danny Maguire (Andy Devine), "Is he always like that? . . . And he's so wonderful on the screen." In the following scenes, after pounding the pavement, Esther finally gets work serving at an industry party, and she hopes to turn the occasion to her advantage. As she circulates among the partygoers with finger food, she impersonates big stars like Dietrich, Hepburn, and West but fails to make an impression. Although her ploy is not successful, this party is where she meets Norman face to face. Afterward he instigates the chain of events that result in her stardom.

The trailer for *A Star Is Born* promises that it will not be another "Cinderella story or a glorification of motion pictures," but that assurance is a bit misleading: once Fairy Godfather Norman takes Esther in hand, the newly named Vicki Lester has an easier time attaining stardom than do most of her fictional predecessors. Norman arranges for the screen test, acts in it with Esther, and talks the studio head, Oliver Niles (Adolphe Menjou), into casting her in his film. But as crucial to this film's tracing of her birth as a new type of star, and despite her fierce determination to succeed in Hollywood against all odds, Esther has an uncomplicated sweetness that her predecessors lack, in part due to Gaynor's performance and star persona and in part due to the script. "She's got that sincerity and honesty that make great actresses," Norman tells Niles in a drunken phone call after meeting Esther at that industry party. Similarly, Niles later sees her star potential, acknowledging that "tastes are going back to the natural." Thus, unlike Mary Evans, Esther does not have to prove her acting mettle. Given her naturalness, the antithesis of the glamorous film stars who were already going out of fashion (Jurca 2012, 125), Esther just has "to be," which is the lesson the makeup department learns when trying to redo her face. "Does she have to look surprised all the time?" one cosmetician asks. Drawing for inspiration on Joan Crawford's smear of a mouth and Marlene Dietrich's contoured cheeks, the makeup artists commit the same error Esther had made at the industry party with her bid to get the attention of producers: they only need to let her be "herself" as she was with Norman when they met face to face. (▶ Figure 3.19)

Paradoxically, though, in order to sell her naturalness the Niles studio still has to make Esther Blodgett into a Hollywood artifact, giving her instruction in diction and posture and inventing a new name and biography for her so that "Esther Victoria Blodgett" becomes "Vicki Lester." This name change is important for how *A Star Is Born* depicts female stardom in its industrial context—and successfully tames it. "Vicki Lester" is more docile, more manageable than the quietly but still fiercely determined Esther Blodgett of the film's opening sequences. Stardom domesticates her pioneering spirit, which may be why, unlike Norman, Niles calls her "Vicki" rather than "Esther." In contrast not only with the likes of Lola Burns and Mary Evans but also with the impression of powerful, desiring 1930s female stars on- and offscreen that Jeanne Basinger and Molly

Haskell both examine at length, "Vicki Lester" is a more tractable personality. The symmetry of her rise to stardom as set against Norman's fall is thus more than simply a formal structuring device. This double trajectory reveals how the errant male star absorbs the disruptive energy of his female counterpart, which is to say that *he* functions as the means through which *she* can, in turn, personify a "sweeter" expression of stardom as carefully nurtured and protected by Hollywood.

Her sweet, unthreatening persona accounts for the ease with which Vicki Lester displaces Norman Maine from the studio's roster of big stars. J. E. Smyth argues that, by the close of the film, "[Esther as Vicki] may eclipse [Norman's] career and inadvertently cause his despair and his death, yet his footprints [at the Chinese] are too big for her; she cannot fill them. By implication, no modern star can fill the shoes of those [silent] stars who loomed larger than life and dominated, however, briefly, a more intimidating, exotic era" (Smyth 2006, 277). However, the case can be made that Esther *does* fill Norman's shoes once she hits big as Vicki Lester. To illustrate her star rising as his plummets, an inserted shot displays "Vicki Lester" being pasted over "Norman Maine" as the only above-the-title star on a billboard for her debut film, "The Enchanted Hour."

Later, albeit with great sincerity and pathos, Esther appropriates Norman's name when she addresses the radio audience in the famous final moment, declaring, "This is Mrs. Norman Maine." Ames shrewdly observes that, during the course of *A Star Is Born*, Esther "moves through four names and identities," shifting from her birth name to her star name to the name on her marriage license ("Mrs. Albert Henkel") to the widow's name (Ames 1997, 37). Esther's multiple identities mark her progressive incorporation by Hollywood while also tracing Norman's disgrace and banishment. After he leaves the Niles studio, he falls off the wagon when a deliveryman calls him "Mr. Lester." Spiraling downward and without work, his drinking results in his accidentally striking Esther at the Academy Awards banquet when he shows up late, interrupts her acceptance speech, and begs the industry for a job. (⊙ Figure 3.20)

A short while later, following Norman's release from a rest cure at a sanitarium, Matt Libby (Lionel Stander), Niles's publicity man and formerly the guardian of Norman's public image, goads the sober ex-star into a fistfight that leads to another long drinking binge and subsequent arrest. At this lowest of low points, Norman is arraigned under his birth name. "You're nothing but an irresponsible drunk," the judge admonishes him when handing down a jail sentence, only to be stopped by Esther's plea for leniency under her watch. (⊙ Figure 3.21) Norman is then publicly emasculated by being released to the guardianship of his loyal, self-sacrificing wife, who, significantly, is "Vicki Lester" in the courtroom to her husband's "Alfred Henkel." Once she decides to give up her career to tend to him, Esther tells Niles, "There'll be no more Vicki Lester." The studio head replies sadly but with understanding, "Good-bye, Vicki Lester. You were a grand girl. Good luck, Mrs. Norman Maine." Norman's suicide means to free Esther to continue her career as Vicki Lester without his weighing her down in further heartbreak and bad publicity.

As a star narrative, in sum, *A Star Is Born* recounts the birth of a docile female star, a highly manageable counterpoint to her unruly male consort, who then personifies all the implicitly disturbing energies of stardom, in Norman's case as reflected not only by his alcoholism but also by his vanity, womanizing, aggression, and violence. Like Max Carey, Norman has no backstory to account for his self-destructive alcoholism, so one has to blame Hollywood, either inferring that the self-indulgence afforded him by stardom eradicates his self-respect or, more in keeping with his character (and Carey's too), that his disillusionment with the movie industry causes self-loathing, perhaps even boredom with his work since he feels trapped by the business until he sees what he calls the "purity" of Esther, the one bright spot in his otherwise tarnished life.

Additionally, the more docile Esther becomes as Vicki Lester, the more Norman resists studio authority over his private life, so his drunken outbursts do more than offer evidence of an unpredictable and ungovernable temperament: they appear to be his means of fighting back, causing momentary ruptures in the studio's authorship of and authority over his identity. His relationship with Esther, in fact, tracks the studio's inability to manage him. Their meeting face to face occurs in the kitchen of that industry party; not only do Norman and then Esther break the dishware she is supposed to be washing and putting away, but he also entices her to walk away from her first paying job in Hollywood. Similarly, after the sneak preview of their film and her debut, Norman leads Esther toward a rear exit in order to avoid Niles and his entourage, who are awaiting the new star to congratulate her publicly in the theater lobby. The couple's elopement foils Libby's plan for a publicized event like Mary Evans's wedding, and the ceremony itself occurs in an out-of-the-way town without their Hollywood names.

Finally, after their marriage, Norman wants their estate to offer a refuge from work. When in their secluded "castle," he tells Esther, "we'll never use ugly words like 'contracts' and 'pictures' and 'careers.'... When we come through those gates, we'll check the studio outside." Almost as soon as Norman finishes this last sentence, however, Libby arrives with a photographer in tow to take pictures meant to record how the couple's "honeymoon never ends." (▶ Figures 3.22–3.24) Obviously the studio cannot be checked at the gate. Niles's entrance occurs moments afterward with more bad news for Norman: "You're not slipping. You've slipped." (▶ Figure 3.25) Once cut by the studio, Norman becomes a loose cannon and a threat to his wife's career, as when he makes that humiliating spectacle of himself at the Oscars. How fitting, then, that his funeral turns out to be the big Hollywood event that he had prevented his wedding from becoming with their elopement.

Esther's self-identification as "Mrs. Norman Maine" in the finale *is* a well-earned moment of grand pathos, to be sure, worthy of its legendary status in crystallizing the price one pays—namely, heartbreak—for Hollywood stardom. But that moment also concludes the institutional containment of Norman Maine, effacing his presence as an unruly male movie star by turning him into a tearful memory and transferring his name to her new identity as his grieving widow; the show must go on, and the star must keep her commitments despite her grief. As Vicki Lester's new alter ego, moreover, "Mrs. Norman Maine" is a willing stand-in for the studio system at large: the institution that gives birth to, nurtures, and protects its obedient female progeny.

The Girl in the Picture

As the backstudios of this era brand Hollywood through their portrayals of young female stars, they characterize stardom itself as the opportunity for economic prosperity, social mobility, and sexual independence for ambitious young women everywhere. So despite industrial anxiety about the extra or studio girl in the 1920s and the resulting campaign to discourage movie-struck fan girls from making their way to Hollywood in hopes of becoming stars like their idols, backstudios tracing the rise to stardom of that very type of movie-crazed girl persisted throughout the 1930s. Even the supposedly demystifying *A Star Is Born* voices caution to potential studio girls and fans like Esther Blodgett, all the while insisting to those same viewers that Esther is indeed the one among thousands whose star is born—which implicitly encourages viewers like Esther to continue to hope.

Bombshell may be the major exception to the many "star is born" narratives being produced during this period, but Lola Burns's stardom is still defined through fandom just as it crystallizes the lure driving those many fictional wannabe stars like Esther migrating to Hollywood with stars in their eyes. This pattern dominated backstudios about stardom made during the early 1940s as well.

Warners' twenty-two-minute short, *Alice in Movieland* (1940), for instance, recycles bits and pieces of *A Star Is Born*. "Our story begins in any city, town, or village from Maine to California," a card reads as *Alice in Movieland* opens. Then a newspaper header announces, "Win a Trip to Hollywood—Local Girls Will Have a Chance for Fame in Hollywood!" Alice Purdee (fifteen-year-old Joan Brodel shortly before she became Warners' star Joan Leslie) wins a beauty contest that sends her to Hollywood. (▶ Figures 3.26–3.27) While friends, neighbors, and relatives expect Alice to be a star, her grandmother gives her a letter with an instruction not to open it until she is discouraged enough to want to return home; from what Grandma says, one assumes that the envelope contains money for her return ticket. Once settled on the train, as the rhythmic sound of wheels on the tracks morphs into the enticing phrase "Hollywood, Hollywood," Alice falls asleep and dreams of her arrival in a city where, as a neon sign exclaims, "All Roads Lead to Hollywood." A montage of LA sights, much like the one in *A Star Is Born*, follows. However, rather than finding a straight road to stardom, Alice experiences setback after setback, although she is buoyed up at every low point. Waiting three weeks only to learn that her screen test did not pass muster, she opens the envelope from her grandmother and finds inside a letter telling her not to return home until she becomes a star. After being sent away from various casting agencies, Alice enters a nightclub talent show where second-tier Warners contract players are in attendance. However, the emcee insists that Alice dance rather than sing, which is her talent; as she gamely tries to perform, the audience shows no interest in her, and she runs off the stage in tears. In the dressing room an attendant, a former star herself, gives Alice a pep talk, telling her, "Keep fighting, dear."

When Alice finally gets a call for work as an extra on a costume picture, the cast and crew make fun of her for her unselfconscious excitement at finally being inside a studio. "She is kind of fascinated with herself," the assistant director comments even before the cast watch Alice pretend to perform with an imaginary male costar on a deserted set. He decides to exploit her greenness and make her the butt of a gag for everyone's amusement. However, when she tells him off afterward, Alice tearfully adds that she *will* succeed because she does not share their cynicism. Watching her emotional and spontaneous outburst, the director quickly decides to record it on film and declares, with words every girl arriving in Hollywood waits to hear, "I'm going to make a star out of you!" And indeed he does. Alice awakens from her dream after a gala premiere and winning an Oscar. (▶ Figure 3.28)

Alice in Movieland closes on a promissory note, with Alice arriving at a set-bound replica of Union Station and, after conversing with the redcap about whether wishes do come true, bravely marches up a long staircase to the street. Despite her determination, this featurette goes to great lengths to keep deferring stardom in her dream, so it sends a conflicted message to similar star-struck Alices "in any town, city, or village from Maine to California." On one hand, each setback teaches Alice that her persistence and innocence will be her means to eventual stardom. On the other hand, as the director of her first unsuccessful screen test states in her dream, Alice is "just another small-town kid who won a contest." Adding to this ambivalence, whereas Alice was played by Joan Brodel, an actual fifteen-year-old who herself had yet to achieve stardom and was essentially an "unknown," in 1947 Warners reissued the short with a new title card using Joan Leslie's by-then more familiar star name, thereby giving extrafilmic credibility to Alice's dream.

Alice Pardee is cut from the same cloth as Sue Graham, Peggy Pepper, Dixie Dugan, Mary Evans, and Esther Blodgett, despite their variations in age. And so apparently was 1940s star Linda Darnell. Her third film, *Star Dust* (1940), made when she was seventeen and had been at Twentieth Century-Fox for just a year, builds on her own experience as a studio girl who, in traveling to Hollywood as an adolescent, was initially sent home when it became apparent that she was even younger than she claimed to be.

In *Star Dust* former silent screen star Thomas Brooke (Roland Young) works for Amalgamated Studios as a talent scout, traveling across the United States in search of new faces. As casting director Sam Wellman (Donald Meek) informs three such hopefuls when they arrive in Hollywood, their train tickets paid for by the studio, "If you have what we're looking for, we'll be very happy. If not, we're sorry, you'll be sent home." In factory-like fashion, one cohort of young women and men depart at the same time as another arrives. With the studio seeming to function like a prep school for youthful talent, the new group receives coaching from Lola Langland (Charlotte Greenwood) for their screen tests, which determine whether they stay or go. Except for Amalgamated's revolving door, the studio's representation as a pedagogical institution of sorts evokes knowledge of MGM's publicized cohort of underage actors like Mickey Rooney, Freddie Bartholomew, and Judy Garland attending school together on the Culver City lot, just at it harks back to Paramount's Astoria school for young talent in 1925 and 1926, which produced future stars like Buddy Rogers and Thelma Todd (Kaufman 1990).

Star Dust opens at Grauman's Chinese Theatre, where a preview of "Dancing Debutante" reveals Brooke's new discovery, Lorraine Lorey. With another new star secured for Amalgamated Studios, Brooke sets out to find more young talent, this time traveling south. On the campus of Randolph College in Rockville, Alabama, he meets Carolyn Sayres (Linda Darnell), who works in her aunt's soda shop. She tricks Brooke into watching her perform on an empty stage, and he recognizes her potential, but since she is not quite seventeen, he decides not to send her to Hollywood. (▶ Figure 3.29) However, Carolyn is undaunted. She forges a letter in Brooke's name that asks studio head Dane Wharton (William Gargan) to give her special attention. Arriving in Hollywood for her test, Carolyn apologizes to her would-be mentor, explaining, "I simply had to get here somehow."

Despite a successful screen test, Carolyn falls victim to Hollywood politics. Wellman has his own protégée, Carolyn's hotel neighbor June Lawrence (Mary Beth Hughes), whom he is grooming for stardom. Furthermore, he greatly resents Brooke's track record of finding new stars for the studio. "Of course she has talent," Wellman tells his assistant about Carolyn's test. "So have lots of girls. For the time being Brooke has discovered enough people. The next one that goes over I'll have the credit for." In order to eliminate her as a competitor for June's roles, Wellman refuses to show Wharton the test and sends Carolyn home, telling her that his decision is in her best interest since she is at "that in-between age that's difficult to cast." Dejected, Carolyn boards the train leaving Los Angeles, but upon reaching San Bernardino she changes her mind and cashes in her ticket.

Back in the hotel, Carolyn discovers a script left for June along with Wellman's instructions about what scene to prepare for an upcoming test. Brooke still tries to persuade Carolyn to return home, but when he learns that his rival, grooming June for stardom, has canceled all other tests for this upcoming big movie, Brooke decides that Carolyn will test for the part, doing it covertly with Lola's tutelage while June is away in Malibu for the weekend. However, secrets are not well kept at the studio, and Wellman learns about Brooke's scheme before the test even gets to the lab. Accusing Carolyn of stealing the script, Wellman gets Wharton to bury her screen test. "Your little girlfriend is out," Wellman smugly tells Brooke, who promptly quits. With no hope of succeeding, Carolyn departs for home with her new beau, Bud Borden (John Payne), not knowing that Brooke and Lola intend to show the test to Wharton, come hell or high water. Lola gets around the ban on printing it, has it inserted in a Movietone News short subject, and smuggles the reel into the projection booth of the Chinese theater. As Wharton, Wellman, and Brooke watch, the Movietone News shifts from a spot on aviation to this header: "HOLLYWOOD—School Girl Creates Sensation in Film Test. Eyes of Cinema City on

Rising New Star." What follows is Carolyn's screen test. The audience's excited response confirms that she has star quality, so Wharton fires Wellman for his deception and rehires Brooke. A coda shows Carolyn back in Hollywood, her stardom burnished and bright as she places her footprints in the forecourt of the Chinese theater. (▶ Figure 3.30)

Star Dust may be a minor effort but, much like *Alice in Movieland*, it encapsulates what earlier star narratives do in using the figure of the ambitious movie-struck girl to epitomize the film industry as "Hollywood" for like-minded young women in the audience. To be sure, in contrast with other backstudios that I have discussed in this chapter, most of which trace a young woman's career from discovery to full-fledged stardom, *Star Dust*, again like *Alice in Movieland*, focuses solely on the process of discovery, and the studio's catch is explicitly characterized *as* a teenager. While young men like Bud and Ronnie (George Montgomery) are of college age and sent packing, the characters who pass studio muster are all very young women: Carolyn, June, Lorraine, and Mary Healy (Mary Andrews), another of Brooke's discoveries. Significantly, too, with Wellman's "mentorship" of June and his offhand remark about Brooke's "girlfriend," *Star Dust* even seems to recognize that these young women are not just Hollywood's prized commodity, as evident in the characters' comments about Lorraine Lorey in the opening, but its sexual currency as well.

Furthermore, since it is a backstudio coming out several years after *A Star Is Born* and that film's many predecessors, the somewhat anachronistic tone of *Star Dust* cannot be ignored. Carolyn is exactly like the movie-struck studio girls whom the industry had publicly worried about in the late teens and twenties. Just about to turn seventeen, Carolyn is an adolescent by the standards of her time. Her youth does not stop her from being ambitious; on the contrary, eager to get out of her small southern town, she is pushy, deceptive, and manipulative—all the while being characterized by the script as sweet and innocent. The men who surround her are sources of comic relief like Bud or paternalism like Brooke or villainy like Wellman. Indeed detracting from Carolyn's own scheming, the egos of Brooke and Wellman create the most conflict for the narrative; the older men, not her youthfulness or her own dishonesty or, for that matter, her rivalry with the patronizing June Lawrence, pose the greater obstacle to Carolyn's success in Hollywood.

Perhaps it was because Hollywood in its own right was still a young industry during the teens and twenties that the association of stardom with ambitious movie-struck girls onscreen and off- seemed so axiomatic for early backstudios like *The Extra Girl* and *Show People*; the association nonetheless persisted in the 1940s with *Star Dust* at the start of the decade and a virtual remake of that star narrative from Fox, *Dancing in the Dark* (1949), at the end. The on-film association of stardom with girlhood may have still seemed unremarkable in this decade because, going back to its beginnings, female stardom in Hollywood had fostered what Gaylyn Studlar terms the "juvenation" of young women. Major stars like Mary Pickford, Shirley Temple, and Deanna Durbin began their careers as child performers and still elicited "fascination with girls and girlhood" as they matured, regardless of their actual age (Studlar 2015, 7). In the 1940s Joan Leslie's career followed this model, and despite her youth—or, rather, emphasizing it—she was cast opposite much older male stars such as James Cagney and Gary Cooper (Cohan 2010, 88–90). Just as the cultural category of "adolescence" had a wider age span that it does today, so too "girlhood" was a variable and fluctuating onscreen category that overlaid qualities suggestive of a female's teen years upon a somewhat older star body.

Furthermore, the declining popularity of glamorous stars like Joan Crawford and Marlene Dietrich in the latter part of the 1930s in favor of more "natural-looking" actresses like Andrea Leeds (who stars as an ordinary moviegoer advising a studio head in a 1938 backstudio, *The Goldwyn Follies*) no doubt kept in play the value of "the girl" as a central figure for this period's star narratives (Jurca 2012, 101–12). Janet Gaynor's appealing girlish qualities as Esther in *A Star Is Born* sustained a screen persona that had crystallized in the late 1920s, which made the character's youthfulness convincing, the actress's own age at the time notwithstanding (Gaynor was thirty-one in 1937). The scenes in which Esther does a bad imitation of glamorous stars and the cosmeticians unsuccessfully try to give her a glamorous look simply confirm the lack of pretense and sophistication that her girlishness connotes. During the 1930s and 1940s, moreover, major female stars—Gaynor, Constance Bennett, Barbara Stanwyck, Carole Lombard, and Irene Dunne—migrated from studio to studio on short-term contracts, often working for two companies concurrently, and some even getting a percentage of profits, thereby taking charge of their careers (Carman 2016). The backstudios' depiction of the fictional star as girlish also responded to the threat these independent women posed to patriarchal Hollywood by ignoring their professional examples as inspiration for characters.

Despite the few other backstudios focusing on male stars, such as *Hollywood Boulevard* (1936), or on male writers, such as *Boy Meets Girl* (1938), or the inclusion of compelling male characters like Max Carey, Space Hanlon, and Norman Maine, narratively speaking at least, in this cycle of backstudios Hollywood was mostly being branded on film through its identification with youthful female stars and the empowerment that their stardom, while contained by the studio system, imagined for their fans. Although the ambitious girl's personification of Hollywood's appeal distorted the realities of the film business and was still a site of institutional anxiety in her numerous portrayals, the figure reiterated how working in the movies offered young women everywhere the opportunity for escaping the many restrictions of ordinary life outside of the movies. At the same time, these narratives registered the institutional need to manage female agency in onscreen representations of Hollywood, subordinating to the studios' authority the power implied by women's labor and made evident in fan magazines as stardom; in branding Hollywood, these backstudios work out of and try to reconcile the tensions between the mystique of stardom and its basis as labor in a male-dominated system. Hence the presence of those compelling male figures who mentor the young women and of paternal studio heads like Saxe and Niles who claim to sire and protect them. In turn, the star's girlishness appears to warrant that male authority even as her ambition challenges it.

Isn't it fitting, then, that the Veronica Lake character in *Sullivan's Travels* (1941), who finally does not have to return home because she finds work in Hollywood with the help of John L. Sullivan (Joel McCrea), has no name but is simply referred to as "the girl," even in the cast list? This association of Hollywood success with female youth lasted pretty much until *Sunset Boulevard* (1950) changed course for the genre by replacing the figure of the ambitious girl with the specter of the aging star abandoned by the system that had previously nurtured her back when she herself had been a movie-struck studio girl.

4

Monstrous Hollywood

Following widespread reporting in 1950 of MGM's dismissal of Judy Garland from *Royal Wedding* and her subsequent suicide attempt, Hollywood's exploitation of its dysfunctional female stars was covered by the press and fan magazines and became material for backstudio pictures about stardom. The pathos with which studio-era female stars were considered Hollywood's victims was intensified in 1962 with news of Twentieth Century-Fox's firing of Marilyn Monroe and, shortly after she was hired back, the shock of her unexpected death, and then of Garland's passing seven years later. Both fatalities were officially reported as accidental drug overdoses, but Monroe's may have been a suicide (or, as conspiracy theorists have speculated for the past fifty years, an assassination due to her involvement with the Kennedys). The Garland and Monroe stories were flagship moments in a new era of scandalous revelations and gossipy half-truths about stars' infidelities, addictions, alcoholism, and other peccadillos that were published in *Confidential* magazine and its imitators (Desjardins 2015, 99–141).

The star narratives made during this period respond to that greater public awareness of older, established stars as Hollywood's victims, addicts, and tramps. Whereas earlier backstudios generally take as their protagonists ambitious young women crashing Hollywood in search of stardom, the second cycle of star narratives, beginning with *Sunset Boulevard* (1950), focuses more directly on fictional (and in a few cases real-life) female stars, most of them abandoned or abused by the studio system. In playing to the public's altered perception of female stardom as a site of excess, indulgence, and pathos, the entire second cycle of star narratives addressed dramatic changes occurring in Hollywood. The shift in narrative focus from ambitious girls to narcissistic, self-destructive older women reflected the maturation of the star system and the film industry alike, chronicling how the past hovers over the present.

Not every critic writing on the genre entirely agrees with this last statement. In one of his final essays, the late Robert Sklar claims that the "movies about the movies" genre is ahistorical. Much as in Hollywood biopics, he states, "the past hardly plays a role, in any historical sense. Characters, of course, experience change—nobodies become somebodies, and vice versa—but institutions and social relations appear fixed and immutable" (Sklar 2012, 71). Sklar singles out three backstudios from the early 1950s—*Sunset*

Boulevard, The Bad and the Beautiful (1952), and *A Star Is Born* (1954)—as the rare exceptions depicting institutional changes. "They introduced temporality into the Hollywood story, not just for individuals but also for the institution as a whole. They viewed their subject in multiple time frames, the present actively regarding the past, the past in turn shedding light on the present" (72). However, while those three canonical films justifiably stand out and deserve my close and repeated attention in this book, they are not alone in responding to and representing the industry's instability and mutability.

The backstudio picture is historical when it sets stories in Hollywood's past, but it is just as historically minded when it recognizes how the past weighs heavily on the industry's present, as star narratives in the second cycle illustrate. Emblematic of this historical sensibility is the anachronistic setting of the Oscar ceremony in the remake of *A Star Is Born*. By 1954 the venue for the awards had long been held in a movie theater on Hollywood Boulevard, and in 1953, the same year as the introduction of CinemaScope, the ceremony was televised for the first time, with a pickup in New York supplementing the main show in Hollywood's Pantages Theatre. Critics have speculated about why director George Cukor and screenwriter Moss Hart retained the nightclub setting of the original 1937 version. At the time of the film's release it was assumed "the room was deemed better suited to [James] Mason's drunken dramatic entrance and speech than the stage of a theater like the RKO Pantages" (Scheuer 1954).

The scene itself as presented in widescreen, however, still fascinates. As Hollywood types appear on stage at the Ambassador Hotel's Cocoanut Grove to present and receive acting awards, those huge palm trees on each side of the stage frame the area to give the impression of a proscenium theater; more striking, to the right of the stage is a supersized television screen on which those small human figures are magnified and projected for better viewing by the attendees seated at their tables in the nightclub. Sklar believes that the mise en scène "functions as a sign of television's emerging dominance" (Sklar 2012, 90). I think the set design may be even more historically dense than that. While perhaps

The Academy Awards ceremony in *A Star Is Born*. Note the shape of the frame and the shape of the TV screen to the right. (*A Star Is Born* ©1954 Warner Bros.)

not Cukor's or Hart's deliberate intent, the CinemaScope imagery of Esther Blodgett (Judy Garland) accepting her Academy Award on stage and on a television screen visualizes the overlaying of past and present, of an older era when the Oscar ceremony took place as a private industry dinner in a nightclub during the 1930s, juxtaposed with both its relocation to a theater in the 1940s and its contemporary transmission on television in 1953. Furthermore, the TV screen at the right side of the frame effectively represents the older Academy screen ratio that had been the standard before the industry began its conversion to widescreen processes, yet that smaller screen size is located inside and so enveloped by the much larger CinemaScope rectangular frame, the new screen size of the 1950s introduced to compete with television.

Obviously with this minor example I am calling attention to a striking image of the film industry's historicity that is achieved with framing and special effects (the superimposition of the televised image in postproduction). As this chapter unfolds, I will be more concerned with how star narratives of the 1950s and 1960s acknowledge the setting of stardom in an industrial history that encompasses the past's relation to the present in a way just suggested by the anachronistic setting of the Academy ceremony in *A Star Is Born*. The historicity of these backstudios is evident in the texturing of their narratives, which depict the institution's awareness that Hollywood's past is discontinuous with if not yet transformative of its present because the conditions of filmmaking flow through the currents of history. The star narratives discussed in chapter 3 shared this awareness, too, but they did not have as full a weight of the industry's history pressing upon them. Nonetheless they still registered anxieties about female labor in Hollywood through the figure of the ambitious movie-struck girl who desires stardom, and those anxieties were historical, as I argued, specific to the film industry at that time. By comparison, the backstudios distinguishing the second cycle locate the figure of an older female star in narrative situations that address the postwar industry's more uncertain continuity with its past. These films recount cautionary tales of uncontrollable female ambition, making the older star herself the focal point for depicting an industry starting to spin out of control.

In commenting on *Sunset Boulevard*, Sklar notes in passing that "the need to control and regulate the behavior of female stars" is a "persistent" trope of the backstudio genre (Sklar 2012, 80). As is apparent in chapter 3, I agree. I now want to emphasize that, while the figure of the ambitious girl in the first cycle *historicizes* this trope, this second cycle of star narratives represents unruly female stardom as a *historical problem* for the industry. The backstudios of this later period position mature stars outside of studio control, and it is the lack of male regulation that enables these women to become excessive in their oversized egos, intense passions, and driving ambitions. This characterization, moreover, strips a star of the agency she formerly possessed as a major player in Hollywood. Journalistic and biographical accounts of Garland and Monroe have tended to portray these two troubled stars as victims of an indifferent, abusive institution. The backstudios of this period, on the other hand, shift blame to a star's psychology in order "to focus our attention on individuals rather than institutions," as Sklar notes about the three backstudios he admires (90). Those three films are studio product, so obviously, like the others I discuss in this chapter, they conform to the Classic Hollywood paradigm, which mediates historical change through a personal perspective, typically that of the leading characters. Additionally the prevalence of a popularized version of Freudian analysis during the postwar period supplied a recognizable discourse for understanding personality, supplying a subtext for characterizations. However, while a star's excessive behavior may be psychologized, in this era's backstudios her "monstrousness" is made symptomatic of the many insecurities and delusions caused by stardom as a Hollywood institution.

Viewed in this light the second cycle's star narratives justify the female star's waning importance as valuable labor for the studio system, rationalizing in narrative terms her economic marginalization by the industry, a marginalization that would become more pronounced in successive eras. The female star centering this second cycle bears the weight of the studio system's institutional disarray and the industry's alienation from its mass audience, whether she functions for a given backstudio picture as the cause of that disorder or its symptom.

The Studio Girl Grows Up

Although *Sunset Boulevard* is deservedly taken as the starting point for the backstudio picture's turn to a more critical, unquestionably cynical, and sometime hostile treatment of Hollywood, I want to continue with the Judy Garland remake of *A Star Is Born* for a while longer. Like its 1937 source, *A Star Is Born* in its 1954 incarnation is exemplary of its historical moment, as indicated by the anachronistic setting of the Oscar ceremony. Put simply, in this second cycle the unruly connotations of Norman Maine's stardom in 1937, successfully contained by its antithesis in Esther's stardom in that original film, gets transferred to the female star, who no longer crashes Hollywood so much as crashes in it. The 1954 remake performs this transference openly and complexly, which is my reason for not yet turning to this cycle's beginning and *Sunset Boulevard*.

Major differences between the two versions of *A Star Is Born* stand out right away. First, no longer does a fan girl like the 1937 Esther personify the ambitions or costs of stardom. In order to accommodate Garland's post-MGM star persona and real-life biography, her Esther is older to start with, apparently in her early thirties like Garland herself, and a singer with the Glenn Williams Orchestra when she meets Norman (James Mason). Unlike Janet Gaynor's Esther, Garland's is already a trouper, a working performer. Thus, whereas the first version hardly mentions Esther's talent, let alone cites any evidence of her having been trained to act, here Norman almost instantly recognizes that her talent is precisely what gives her genuine star quality, "that little something extra," so he mentors her in dreaming bigger than the Hit Parade. "He gave me a look at myself I never had before," Esther tells Danny Maguire (Tom Noonan) when she takes Norman's advice and quits the band. "He saw something in me nobody else ever did. And he made me see it too. . . . He made me believe it." So much so that, when the studio kidnaps a sleeping Norman for a location shoot, preventing him from arranging the promised screen test, Esther does not return to the band but persists in trying to find Hollywood jobs.

Esther consequently walks the pavement like her 1937 predecessor but only *after* bonding with Norman over her voice. Since in this second version Norman substitutes for the grandmother in inciting Esther's ambition, her drive and determination are not equated with the American pioneer spirit but with her dreaming big enough to imagine a career in professional terms. "A career is a curious thing," Norman tells her. "Talent isn't always enough. You need a sense of timing. An eye for seeing the turning point. Or recognizing the big chance when it comes along and grabbing it." Clearly stardom for this film means *movie* stardom: records, radio, and live performing are in second position to Hollywood.

Once Norman returns from location and reunites with her, the makeup scene before Esther's screen test, while following the original, makes a somewhat different point than it did with Gaynor in the hot seat. As before, the cosmetologists insist Esther's face is all wrong, but now, instead of letting her just be herself, they try to disguise her features, adding a blonde wig, filling out her nose, altering her eyebrows, applying bright lipstick, thick foundation, and blush—making her unrecognizable even to Norman. (▶ Figures 4.1–4.3) Esther asks why her voice matters if she doesn't look "right," and Norman astutely replies, "Your face is just dandy," so he supervises her return to a more "natural" look. Regardless, what then sells Oliver Niles (Charles Bickford) on using the untried Esther in the big-budget musical that has stalled due to casting problems is not her "look" in the screen test but her vocal track, which Norman arranges for the studio head to hear.

A second set of differences occurs from how densely Garland's own star text informs both Esther's and Norman's characters so that together they signify the highs and lows of her movie career. As almost everyone recognizes by now, the remake revived Garland's former MGM star image through Esther's talent and humility as she rises from band singer to movie stardom; however, it also encouraged Garland's offscreen biography to be refracted through the addictive personality and suicide of the obsolete star Norman Maine. Recognition that Garland was an implicit referent for both Esther and Norman built upon what was already, with her record-breaking Palace engagement behind her, the comeback motif of her post-MGM stardom.

This double relevance was immediately attached to Garland's remake of *A Star Is Born*. Press coverage emphasized the production's numerous delays and budget overruns, usually blamed on her tardiness or absences (though initial uncertainty about what screen ratio to use, which required expensive retakes, was also responsible for the long shoot). For its part, Warners' publicity department encouraged the film's identification with Garland's career. The trailer begins with the studio's announcement of Garland's triumphant return to the screen as a great artist, and the premiere program featured a rundown of her famous MGM roles, all leading up to this revival of her movie stardom by another studio. (▶ Clip 11) Within the film itself, the Palace comeback is specifically referenced through the long "Born in a Truck" segment, which is Esther's "star is born" moment on screen, though paradoxically the number itself takes the opposite view, that stardom is not "born" but requires persistence, hard work, some luck, and paying one's dues. Along with the intricate self-reflexivity of the musical numbers, references to Esther's not being glamorous enough and the corollary view, namely, that her talent is the more genuine form of beauty, bring Garland's MGM past further into *A Star Is Born* as a means of substantiating Esther's characterization. The makeup scene may have originated with the 1937 version, but it already resonated in 1954 (and then more strongly in years to follow) with accounts of MGM's many efforts to similarly "fix" Garland's looks during her tenure at the studio. Likewise her comment that she is "pretty girlish" in "Somewhere at Last" echoes the many times MGM scripts cast doubts on her prettiness.

Due to such self-reflexivity, Norman's fall from stardom somewhat uncannily repeats Garland's firing by MGM, even though he is male and his storyline follows the original. Norman's characterization certainly differs from what by 1954 had been reports of Garland's nervous breakdowns, illnesses, and recurring absences from studio sets. This version's Matt Libby (Jack Carson) compares Norman to "a child with a blow torch." While he also apparently causes production delays, as Garland had done in her final years at MGM—early on Niles is glad to hear that his star has temporarily brought the location shoot of his current action film to a halt due to genuine illness and not a binge or tantrum—Norman is more violent and infantile than the 1937 character, qualities Mason's nuanced performance skillfully brings out. Rather than starting a fistfight with photographers, as Fredric March's Norman does at the Hollywood Bowl, here a drunken Norman throws Libby through a full-length mirror in one of the Shrine Auditorium's dressing rooms and then goes backstage to harass the performers. When Esther resists his first invitation to take supper with him, Norman growls to her companion, Danny Maguire, "I know myself extremely well. I'm just near the fighting stage at the moment. If I don't get my way, I begin to break up people and things at this moment."

New speeches given to Libby emphasize that Norman's self-destructive behavior causes his loss of popularity, thereby denying that his failing career has anything to do with Hollywood. After Norman and Vicki successfully elope, Libby complains that they had no right to get married quietly: "He knows better than that. Mr. Public Nuisance can stand some decent publicity for a change, believe me. I've spent ten years covering up for him, killing bad stories, sucking up to the columnists to smooth away his insults." Libby is doing his job in shielding Norman from bad press; his complaint puts the blame entirely on the star's bad behavior, not on the institution. In the opening sequence at the Shrine, Libby tries to keep the inebriated star from going on stage as scheduled because Niles ordered him to do so. As Libby tries to keep Norman from leaving by trading him drinks for interviews and photo ops, Norman mutters, "Why do you disgust me? Why do I hate you so?" Those rhetorical questions give the lie to Norman's later befuddlement at the race track when he protests Libby's verbal abuse because he doesn't want to forget they are still friends. In both versions, Libby insists, "I got you out of jams because I had to. It was my job"—which never meant that they were friends or that Libby ever liked him.

Norman's "star biography," then, marks a third significant difference between the two versions of *A Star Is Born*. In the 1937 version, although well aware of Norman's outrageous public behavior as a reason why the press laughs "when I even try to get a decent mention of Maine," Libby (Lionel Stander) does not blame the studio for either creating or encouraging the situation, instead proclaiming, "The exhibitors don't like him, the critics don't like him, the public don't like him, and I don't like him. Who likes him?" When the time comes for Niles (Adolphe Menjou) to talk to Norman about his slipping popularity, the studio head delivers the bad news with velvet gloves and only puts the errant star on probation. In fact, Norman initiates this conversation almost as soon as Niles arrives at his and Esther's estate, their putative escape from the studio. "You remember I told you I'd be ready for the curtains when the time came," Norman reminds his old friend. Niles, however, thinks that Norman's popularity can return, and he has a "swell script" for him, although he also plans to cast Esther opposite a rising male star in her next film instead of Norman. "All right, Oliver," Norman agrees, "we'll make a try at it. Let's hope it's not too late."

That it *is* too late is signaled moments later on a billboard by the substitution of Vicki Lester's name for Norman's as the sole top-billed star of "The Enchanted Hour." Following that shot, the exhibitor's manual for Niles's lineup of upcoming productions features three films starring Vicki, "the screen's newest sensation," and a faceless exhibitor comments, "No arguments. I'll buy those." The next page announces only two pictures with Norman, "the screen's most finished actor," and the same exhibitor remarks, "I'll say he's finished. He keeps them away in droves." Norman's banishment from the screen in the 1937 version, then, occurs for reasons external to Hollywood insofar as the benevolent studio head tries to keep Norman despite the bad press, exhibitor resistance, and public disapproval.

In the 1954 remake, by contrast, both Norman and the film industry share the blame. Probably the impression one takes away from a first viewing is determined by what Niles says about Norman's self-destructive behavior after the studio head and Esther bring the chastened ex-star home from the drunk tank. In response to Esther's decision to quit pictures, cure Norman, and give him a second chance at work in Europe, where his reputation has not yet fully preceded him, Niles tells her the hard truth: "There's nothing left any more. It happened long before last night. Long before we let him out of the studio. Twenty years of steady and quiet drinking do something to a man. Long before it showed in his face it showed in his acting, little by little, more and more, with each picture. That's why he slipped. It wasn't just bad pictures. It was him." This account of Norman's fall blames the star more than Hollywood, much as Libby does in the 1937 source.

Yet that verdict of why Norman himself is to blame for turning into "just a shell of what he once was" does not entirely jibe with a previous scene when he parts ways with the studio. The two men steal away from a party at his Malibu house. Sensing that his friend and employer has something on his mind, Norman presses until Niles finally comes clean. "The, uh, New York boys have been out here this past week," Niles says. Norman tries to fill in the blanks. "They want me to take a salary cut?" he asks. Actually, they want Niles to buy up the rest of his contract and pay him off. Norman protests that although his pictures have not done as well as in the past, this is the present state of affairs for everyone. But this decision is "not about picture grosses." No, the reason is much what Dore Schary would be saying years later in documentary footage about why he had to fire Judy Garland in 1950. "They can't afford you any more, Norman. You're too big a risk. Those big fat flush days when a star could get drunk and disappear and hold up production for two weeks are over. Even if you hadn't slipped a little, they still wouldn't take the chance. Your record's too bad. No one can afford it anymore. Things are too tough. I tried, Norman. I tried very hard." (▶ Figure 4.4)

Sklar also refers to this conversation to underscore that "things were tough and getting tougher," a sign of this film's historical awareness of changes occurring in the economics of the industry and its reliance on pampered stars (Sklar 2012, 88). The film's awareness goes deeper than that. In comparison with the 1937 source, the 1954 remake of *A Star Is Born* makes Norman even more of a symptomatic outburst of unruly male stardom disrupting the otherwise safer story of Esther's incorporation by Hollywood as the docile Vicki Lester. However, awareness of the "unruly" Garland, dropped by MGM when she became "too big a risk," uneasily complicates the neater symmetry of the 1937 version. The historical specificity with which the 1954 script recognizes that the movie studios can no longer tolerate let alone nurture the kind of larger-than-life stardom previously celebrated in star narratives like *What Price Hollywood?* (1932) and *Bombshell* (1933) is ultimately why the association of Norman with Garland seemed so axiomatic at the time of the film's release. That identification, moreover, "feminizes" his characterization as a fallen star insofar as it attaches Garland and obsolete, out-of-control female stardom in general to the fictional Norman Maine as an unstated yet recognizable historical referent, despite the obvious gender difference.

To note this "feminization" is simply to recognize that Norman's characterization in 1954 as a doomed and addicted Hollywood star, victimized by the system that created and then dropped him, needs to be placed not as fictionalized versions of real-life out-of-control male stars like Errol Flynn but rather alongside the fictional depiction of unruly female stars that increasingly came to dominate the second cycle of backstudio pictures. These portray female stars as dysfunctional and "crazy" due to their narcissism and excessive or addictive personalities. In contrast to how the studio's publicity maven in *Bombshell* watches over Lola Burns, in these postwar backstudios female stars suffer a fate like Norman's. Film after film confirms Niles's explanation to Norman in 1954 about the New York money men no longer willing to indulge star behavior like his. Consequently, Norman's implications in 1937 of a male star's resistance to studio control, which his suicide and then his widow's tribute successfully manage, are now more explicitly and pretty exclusively transferred to unruly female stars whom backstudios depict as figuratively and even sometimes literally "monstrous." This pejorative characterization makes the star's uncontrollable agency seem not only symptomatic of the industry's postwar disarray but also implicitly if illogically responsible for it.

The Studio Girl Grows Old

Sunset Boulevard's Norma Desmond anticipates the Norman Maine of 1954 even though, starting with their gender and extending to the accounts of their private lives, the two figures seem to bear little resemblance to each other. But it is useful to recall that Norma's situation in 1950 as a forgotten silent star already had a few fictional antecedents from the 1930s, including Donny Harris (Blanche Sweet) in *Show Girl in Hollywood* (1930). However, more often than not the cast-off figures were former *male* stars like Norman Maine. In *Hollywood Boulevard* (1936), the forgotten John Blakeford (John Halliday) had been "a big star" in 1929 but now is without work until his scandalous memoirs renew the public's interest; in *It Happened in Hollywood* (1937), silent cowboy star Tim Bart (Richard Dix) falls victim to the talkies until his offscreen heroics revive his career. After the 1937 *A Star Is Born*, *Star Dust* (1940) features Thomas Brooke (Roland Young), a former silent screen star now working for Amalgamated Studios as their national talent scout. And shortly before *Sunset Boulevard* premiered, *Dancing in the Dark* (1949) recycled the plot of *Star Dust* with its lead character, Emory Slade (William Powell), first shown "joining the immortals" in the forecourt of Grauman's Chinese in 1932. Cut to the film's present-day setting seventeen years later and, because of his vain, temperamental, and mean personality, Slade is justifiably forgotten by the industry until he, too, gets the call to interview new talent. Implicit in this list of has-been male stars is nevertheless the longevity of Hollywood careers for men. With the exception of Norman Maine, the male characters in these films all get a second chance, whether before the cameras or in some other capacity. The 1937 Norman Maine is already like Norma Desmond in *Sunset Boulevard*; she also does not get her second chance but instead achieves notoriety before the newsreel cameras as the crazy, forgotten star who murdered her gigolo lover.

Without real employment as a movie star to account for her narcissism and blindness to the transience of fame, from her entrance to her final mad scene on the staircase, Norma acts *out* her rage by acting *like* the mad woman in a gothic mansion; she is unbalanced and delusional, but also angry at being cast adrift by Hollywood. Reinforcing this impression, Gloria Swanson's acting seems all over-the-top histrionics, with her bulging eyes, talon-like hand gestures, and snapping, even snarling delivery of her lines, all mannerisms that Carol Burnett parodied so well for her TV show in the 1970s. Additionally, the deck seems stacked in favor of Joe Gillis, a self-aware wordsmith, according to his voice-over—surely the characteristic most befitting a writer, even a hack like him. William Holden establishes his character's greater modernity and authenticity through his naturalistic acting and spoken delivery. Joe dominates our narrative perspective of Norma through his voice-over, which is at once that of a cynical, often caustic observer of the passing Hollywood parade and eerily spectral since he is speaking to us from the afterlife. By contrast, through her deployment of silent film's obsolete repertoire of signifying gestures and expressions Swanson is performing Norma in the style of old-fashioned silent-era melodrama. (⏵ Figures 4.5–4.7)

Norma, then, is performing "performing." As Aaron Taylor points out, "Norma dramatizes each moment, turning everyday interactions into star turns....Each gesture is played as if to an adoring audience from her heyday as a silent deity" (Taylor 2007, 20). Yet as Taylor also observes, *Sunset Boulevard* carefully uses Swanson's stylized performance "as an element in its critique of an industrial art that does not revere its past" (21). This critique is part of the film's remystification of an obsolete form of female stardom as well as its indictment of corporate indifference and insecurity by postwar Hollywood, and it supplies the terms of the ongoing fascination with *Sunset Boulevard* as a canonical backstudio and with Norma Desmond's character as well.

Norma's gothic mansion, with its overpowering staircase, ornate furniture, ominous shadows, leaky roofs, rat-infested swimming pool, and wheezing organ, similarly determines an unflattering view of her as the reclusive has-been star caught up in her delusions of ageless beauty and timeless fame. She is most villainous as a film noir spider woman in this house. Joe is, in turn, most victimized as a film noir hero when inside the secluded house on Sunset Boulevard. He thinks he determines events in his favor, using the deluded former star to hide his car and make a quick buck, but he loses control of his scheme and, reduced to Norma's gigolo, becomes a bad imitation of a Valentino-like character in her melodramatic scenario. The only power he entertains once he accepts his position as "screenwriter-as-prostitute" (Ames 1997, 210) is his posthumous voice-over; his narration tries to control how we see Norma by mediating her dominance of him through his acerbic commentary about her. (⊙ Figure 4.8)

Beyond Norma's house, however—that is, in Hollywood itself—it is another story. Both characters have been pushed out of the postwar film industry, chewed up and forgotten. Furthermore, if, as his posthumous voice-over wittily reminds us, Joe literally as well as figuratively functions as Norma's ghostwriter, we ought to remember that she is not the only actress-turned-writer with whom he collaborates. Betty Schaefer (Nancy Olson) wants to partner with Joe on the screenplay she has pitched to the producer Sheldrake (Fred Clark) because, she declares, "I don't want to be a reader all my life. I want to write." Joe's nightly writing sessions with her—his secret life away from Norma and her mansion—take place within the bounded studio lot of Paramount Pictures, where he engages in his illusion of independence and empowerment through his work. On her part, Betty is obedient studio labor, a third-generation industry worker who, though groomed for an acting career, failed to make the grade even after fixing her nose. A studio girl who lost her shot at stardom, she has since settled for rank-and-file work in the story department, although she hungers for a screenplay credit. "What's wrong with being on the other side of the cameras?" she asks Joe on one of their nighttime walks through the deserted studio backlot. "It's really more fun."

As for Norma, Joe's other collaborator and the antithesis of Betty, remember that the time elapsed between the end of her film career and the present day of *Sunset Boulevard* is over a decade, at least twenty years or even more. Although "thirty million fans have given her the brush," so her former mentor Cecil B. DeMille laments, apparently nothing can be done to help her return to the screen (in contrast with the real-life Gloria Swanson). It is significant that the famous director does not even make a token effort to find Norma a role in his own picture—or "on the other side of the camera," as he did for real-life Henry Wilcoxon, formerly a leading man in several DeMille epics who successfully transitioned to playing character parts and then served as the director's associate producer in the mid-1950s. Apparently, because of Hollywood's ageism and her narcissism, DeMille, like Norma herself, axiomatically views her stardom as a fixed entity, envisioning it as an unchangeable if by now obsolete image; this view may have once suited her glorious and iconic standing as a great star of silent film, but it now reduces her legendary status to the hundreds of photographs turning her mansion into a shrine to her past.

Norma's own self-image appears affixed to the face of the seductive ingénue she watches repeatedly and rapturously in her private screening room, but she herself is not frozen in time. Rather, *Sunset Boulevard* stresses, she is victimized by the institution of stardom. While stardom may be transcendent, as she believes, Norma herself does not transcend stardom. Her Hollywood career inscribes how "a plucky young little girl of seventeen," to recall DeMille's comments to his assistant when Norma returns to Paramount, got to be "a terror to work with" later on because "a dozen press agents working overtime can do terrible things to the human spirit." Here the director anticipates the *Star Is Born* remake some four years later. Much like that conversation between DeMille and his assistant, Niles tells Libby, "You missed a lot not knowing Norman Maine" as he himself did when both men were younger. When the publicity maven objects, saying he spent his life knowing Maine and predicting what he would do before he did it, Niles reiterates, "You didn't know him at all. He was quite a guy."

DeMille's remembrance of Norma as the overwrought diva makes sense of her predicament in 1950, just as Niles's depiction for Esther of a burnt-out Norman does in 1954. However, that is not the only reason either film offers for why a star falls. Like *A Star Is Born*, from the anecdotal account of Norma's career, her outrage at what the talkies did to the great faces of silent film, and the example of her fellow bridge players, the "waxworks," *Sunset Boulevard* puts forward an industrial reason. For also like Lina Lamont in *Singin' in the Rain* (1952), as Alan Nadel notes, albeit in a different context (Nadel 2017, 19, 70), *Sunset Boulevard* intimates that Norma could not survive the transition to sound because of new demands placed on the voice and the corresponding alteration of performance styles inaugurated by the microphone.

In this regard, Norma's return to the Paramount studio lot offers a crucial industrial backdrop to her obsolete stardom in 1950. I discussed in chapter 2 how the front gate where Norma is initially refused entrance functions to define both the studio's purpose as safe haven and her expulsion from it. I now want to consider further what this sequence indicates about Norma's outdated relation to studio work as a star. Significantly, Joe and his voice-over do not follow Norma onto the soundstage; he remains outside in the automobile with Max Von Mayerling (Erich Von Stroheim), her former director and husband and now her butler, so this scene is not mediated and shaped by Joe's commentary

(Sklar 2012, 76). The excursion to Paramount establishes Norma's tense relation to the film industry in ways that her secluded mansion does not because the sequence resituates her in the daytime industrial setting of present-day Hollywood and its below-the-line labor. By contrast, the mansion obscures that relation by tonally representing it as perverse film noir melodrama, with Norma in the role of the spider woman trapping Joe in her web while he ensnares her in his narration.

At Paramount the pathos of Norma's predicament as a washed-up star is brought out by the fact that all her contemporaries, from DeMille to Hog-eye and the other old-timers working on set with the director, are still employed there, whereas she, the once great star, is unemployed—and unemployable. In fact, DeMille is older than Norma, yet shown directing *Samson and Delilah* (1949), the film he was actually making at Paramount while Billy Wilder filmed *Sunset Boulevard*. As the crowd gathers around Norma to pay homage and Hog-eye illuminates her with a spotlight, she basks in their worshipful reception, yet their respectful adoration only emphasizes all the more her banishment and isolation from working Hollywood. DeMille's comments to his assistant—when he recalls what Norma was like as a spirited, engaging young woman before a dozen press agents worked her over—indicate that her studio once nourished, protected, and then spoiled her. Now, however, Hollywood treats her as a pariah who has been discarded and forgotten or, as here on the set, scrutinizes her as an exotic animal assumed to have been extinct. It's not a happenstance image when Norma's feathered hat gets in the way of the boom microphone and, visibly irritated, she pushes the annoying instrument from her face with an angry shove. The Paramount sequence offers a more sympathetic understanding of Norma's delusions than she otherwise elicits in the seclusion of her mansion, where she imagines time has stopped. (⊙ Figure 4.9)

Additionally, the studio setting establishes why Hollywood, which cast her aside with the advent of sound technology, may actually have something to fear from an ambitious star like Norma Desmond. As Sklar points out, while older backstudios usually regulate a female star through an authority figure identified with the industry, "no male can exercise that authority—not DeMille, not Max, not Joe—which may be equally a symptom of her craziness or a lack that drives her crazy" (Sklar 2012, 80). Indeed viewing her from that perspective, it may be safer for Hollywood to imagine Norma through her deranged remembrance of things past and thus to see her as a female monster. Believing that DeMille wants to direct her screenplay of *Salome*, Norma confesses to her former director that she might even be prepared to pay for such an expensive project. "I just want to work again, I don't care about the money," she tearfully tells DeMille on the Paramount soundstage. Yet this desire does not prevent Norma from issuing her usual demands as a great star: "But remember, darling—I don't work before ten in the morning, and never after four-thirty in the afternoon."

While glossing Norma as a diva, this rather abrupt shift in her tone—first she plaintively confesses to missing the work, then she haughtily sets her own hours—establishes the threat she poses as a star with an unrealistic sense of entitlement that Hollywood had

Norma Desmond (Gloria Swanson) surrounded by extras and crew members during her visit to Paramount. (*Sunset Boulevard* ©1950 Paramount)

once nurtured. Certainly that she refuses to act her age and is deluded by the mystique of her own stardom makes Norma a "monster" in the eyes of the insecure postwar studio system. But that is not all. Starting with her late arrivals and early departures, Norma's egoism threatens to take over Paramount Pictures should she return to work. She even dares to imagine herself as a female Orson Welles: "He's a shrewd old fox. He can smell box office. Only I'm going to outfox him a little," she boasts to Joe about DeMille as they leave Paramount. "This isn't going to be C. B. DeMille's 'Salome.' It's going to be Norma Desmond's 'Salome,' a Norma Desmond Production, starring Norma Desmond."

As it happens, these lines are from the shooting script (Wilder 1999, 88) and not from the release version of *Sunset Boulevard*, which cuts from DeMille watching Norma drive away to Joe's voice-over and the montage of her rigorous beauty treatments as she prepares with great discipline for her presumed return to the screen. Yet despite this omission, a careful viewer like Sklar still senses the institutional threat Norma poses to male authority figures like DeMille. Furthermore, even though Joe's voice-over reclaims the narrative following this scene, *Sunset Boulevard* gives Norma the last word, literally so, since her final speech comes immediately after his voice-over ceases. As she mistakes the newsreel cameras for DeMille's directing her comeback as Salome, she expresses her unadulterated joy at returning to work. "I just want to tell you how happy I am to be back in the studio making a picture again. You don't know how much I've missed all of you.... You see, this is my life. It always will be. There is nothing else—just us and the cameras and those wonderful people out there in the dark." After a beat she then delivers the film's most repeated line: "All right Mr. DeMille. I'm ready for my close-up." (▶ Figures 4.10, 4.11)

This conclusion is laden with ironies. Her speech is heartfelt yet also an expression of her descent into madness and notoriety, just as her sincerity is tempered by her moving toward the camera afterward as if to devour it. But Norma's sentiment also bespeaks a certain historical truth about the intimacy of the movies with its audience through female stardom. Her final speech is the moment she breaks entirely free of Joe's mediating voice-over and, visually and vocally, addresses the film's audience most directly. In these final moments Norma laments and personifies the imminent breakdown of the studio system, the female stardom it nurtured, and the mass audience that kept it going.

Inaugurated by *Sunset Boulevard*, the second cycle of backstudio pictures produced during the 1950s and 1960s equates the star diva with the moribund studio system, identifying Hollywood's excesses, insularity, and obsolescence through her figure: hence the implicit comparison of Judy Garland with Norman Maine in the minds of audiences and columnists when watching the 1954 remake of *A Star Is Born*. In earlier backstudios the new female star, like Esther Blodgett in the first version of *A Star Is Born*, personifies Hollywood through her characterization as an ambitious young woman toiling within the system as a docile laborer, albeit a well-paid and glamorized one. The second cycle of films, by comparison, tends to feature an older female star who is cast off or destroyed by Hollywood; victimized by the studio system, she is also vilified for her ambition and her unhealthy, excessive, and hence "monstrous" desires. Yet as the Garland remake and *Sunset Boulevard* both indicate, this changed understanding of stardom reflects the institution's inability to sustain the industrial system it once celebrated through its star narratives: "Those big fat flush days...are over." In a film's end, the recalcitrant star is either banished, like Swanson's Norma as she takes over the screen with her final close-up, or tamed, like Garland's Vicki Lester when she makes herself a memorial to her late husband by identifying herself as "Mrs. Norman Maine," her tiny figure dwarfed by the final extreme long shot looking down at the Shrine Auditorium stage and her voice drowned out by an offscreen heavenly chorus.

Unruly Stardom

Comparable apprehensions about uncontained female star power can be felt in several backstudios that follow *Sunset Boulevard*. Two years later Lina Lamont (Jean Hagen) causes no end of trouble for Monumental Pictures in *Singin' in the Rain*. Of course, Lina is not the protagonist of this backstudio musical but functions primarily as its comic villain: the inept silent screen star replaced by the more talented ingénue, Kathy Selden (Debbie Reynolds), as costar Don Lockwood (Gene Kelly) makes his modernizing transition from hamming it up in grand historical melodramas to singing and dancing in film musicals. Nonetheless, as Nadel reminds us, one can easily view *Singin' in the Rain* as the story of Lina's "abjection." (Nadel 2017, 51).

Amplifying Lina's unattractive speaking voice and dimwittedness, not to mention the hilarious malapropisms that pepper her lines, she is called a "triple threat," unable to act, sing, or dance. When, according to *Singin' in the Rain*, the smash success of *The Jazz Singer* (1927) abruptly changes the industry almost overnight, Lina fails to make the smooth transition to talkies, while Don does so more effortlessly, especially once he realizes that musicals are the future of the movies. She is simply incompetent with the new technology, unable to remember all the instructions of her vocal coach when delivering lines and forgetting where the microphone has been placed, so half the time it records her heartbeat, muffling her voice. To exaggerate both her ineptitude and the artifice of her stardom, much of the film's physical comedy comes at Lina's expense.

The comedy deflects attention away from how Lina dares to challenge studio authority when she discovers that, in order to save Don's career but not hers by converting their first talkie to a musical, the studio has had Kathy secretly dub her speech and singing. What is more, Monumental intends to acknowledge Kathy's role as Lina's voice double with a screen credit and publicity campaign. At this point the dumb blonde is as dumb as the proverbial fox. For with her career on the line and fearful of being made a laughingstock by her own studio, an outraged Lina goes behind the backs of the publicity department by telling every columnist in town about studio head R. F. Simpson's (Millard Mitchell) enthusiasm for "her singing pipes and dancing stems." More impressively, after wisely consulting her lawyers, Lina makes full use of her contract's fine print, which discloses that she, not the studio, controls her publicity—although Monumental Pictures is still responsible for every word about her that sees print. Lina defiantly warns Simpson that if the studio exposes her as a liar and gives Kathy screen credit, it will be "detrimental and deleterious" to her career, and reason enough to "syoo" Monumental for everything it's worth. Simpson backs down, agreeing to Lina's demands, first that Kathy's screen credit be removed, and second, that she will be Lina's secret voice double on all subsequent pictures. "You'll be taking her career away from her," Simpson charges. "People don't do things like that." "*People*?" Lina asks incredulously. "I ain't *people*." And she goes on to quote from that morning's newspaper, which calls her "a shimmering, glowing star in the cinema firmament." (⊚ Figure 4.12)

This scene when Lina threatens to "syoo" is obviously funny, preparing the way for her deserved humiliation at Grauman's Chinese Theatre, when Don reveals that Kathy is the true star speaking and singing for Lina's image—at which point Lina magically disappears from *Singin' in the Rain*. More to the point, that scene with Simpson enables her arrogant and by this point threatening figure to absorb blame for everything troubling the industry, which resonates throughout *Singin' in the Rain*: not only the uncertainty besetting Hollywood in 1927 due to the changes wrought by the introduction of sound technology, but also the instability affecting the industry that was already perceivable in 1952 as a result of rapidly falling attendance, the majors' loss of their profitable theater chains, the emergence of television as a rival, suburban migration, and the musical genre's beginning decline in popularity. If nothing else, the polished style of the musical numbers keeps bringing present-day film production, with all the modern bells and whistles serving the choreography as staged for the camera, into historical contact with the narrative's representation of the 1920s, even when those numbers mean to satirize the period setting.

Narratively speaking, Lina functions as the primary obstacle in the plot of *Singin' in the Rain*, blocking progressive movement with respect to the studio's future and Don's career, as well as stalling and then interrupting his romance with Kathy. Lina's inability to adjust to talkies, in contrast with everyone one else at Monumental, it seems, stands in the way of cinema's modernity, just as the "birth" of Kathy Seldon as a new, talented, and more docile kind of female star, especially in her relation with the much older Don, significantly tames the kind of stardom formerly personified by the likes of Jean Harlow or her alter ego, Lola Burns, two figures from those "big, fat, flush days" who partly inspired the creation of Lina Lamont. Finally, without talent of any kind to give it heft, Lina's stardom is all smoke and mirrors. Her villainy, all of this is to say, is overdetermined: Lina gets the custard pie in the kisser in every respect since *Singin' in the Rain* makes fun of her from beginning to end, all the while letting her serve as the agent of much discord and delay. When Lina stands up to Simpson and threatens to "syoo," her audacity in challenging the patriarchal system oversteps the privileges of her stardom as it never does for her male counterpart, Don Lockwood, who essentially takes over his films, writing dialogue, telling Simpson how to turn "Dueling Cavalier" into a musical, arranging for the dubbing of Lina without her knowledge or consent, and apparently choreographing and staging his numbers, just like Gene Kelly in the present day. Lina's threat to take over Monumental Pictures, not unlike Norma Desmond's deleted intent to take over the production of *Salome* from DeMille, explains why Lina's character takes the hit for the industry's problems.

In *The Star*, also from 1952, Bette Davis's character, Margaret Elliot, is another out-of-work star. After three years of unemployment, she now cannot make the rent on her small apartment and, to pay her other debts, must auction off all her possessions, save for her drinking companion, her Oscar. (▶ Figures 4.13–4.14) Margaret's decline, while symptomatically evident in her arrest for drunk driving and her kleptomania, is linked to her attempt at controlling her career. Desperately hoping for a comeback in the film adaptation of a novel she had previously optioned but was unable to get off the ground, Margaret finagles a screen test for a secondary role. Then, against all advice to respect her young director's authority, she disregards the script's characterization, rearranges her costume and makeup to look more glamorous, ignores how she is told to perform line readings, shows off her familiarity with the crew, and relights the set to show her face more attractively, all in a misguided effort to prove that she can still play the much younger lead character. The test is, predictably, a disaster—"It's horrible, it's horrible," Margaret mutters as she watches it—and the secondary role goes to a more appreciative character actress. (▶ Figures 4.15–4.16)

Margaret's plight as a has-been star, supposedly modeled on Joan Crawford's initial efforts to maintain her glamorous image when starting *Mildred Pierce* (1945), until she and director Michael Curtiz reached a degree of mutual trust (Considine 2017, 192–94, 279), obviously resembles Norma Desmond's—but not only because everyone blames her decline on her age and her ego. At one low point Margaret reveals that, frustrated with the tripe her studio was dishing out to her as starring vehicles, she had put her own money into "three wonderful pictures," but the film companies would not give them a "decent" release; their failure due to studio indifference consequently depleted her financial holdings and established her unpopularity at the box office, which now explains her inability to find work and to pay her rent. Indeed when Jim Johnson (Sterling Hayden), a studly boat repairer whom Margaret had once made her costar, asks if she wasn't to blame for their failure, the former star, clutching her Oscar, accuses the studios of juggling the books and labeling her independent films "flops."

As a pointed contrast to this account of a female star using her own money to take charge of her career but finding the studio system an obstacle to that independence, the producer-friend who arranges for the screen test believes, "Stars are so naughty, like children. At the same time, they're so appealing, also like children." *The Star* puts Jim forward as the patriarchal authority who will help Margaret grow up and be able to leave Hollywood and its falseness behind her. When she steals from a drugstore the sample bottle of her favorite and very expensive perfume, "Desire Me," it turns out to be only colored water. "When you grabbed it, you thought it was real," Jim comments. "Story of your life, isn't it?" A short while later, after starting to work at the May Company, Margaret indignantly puts down two older customers who make snide remarks about her notoriety due to her arrest. Walking off the floor, she exclaims, "I am Margaret Elliot. And I intend to stay Margaret Eliot." The screen test proves otherwise, of course.

Not until a writer, Richard Stanley (Paul Frees), holds that proverbial mirror to her face does Margaret believe what Jim has been telling her. At a party Stanley pitches to Margaret a screenplay, "a Hollywood story" about a movie star—here, the implied referent to Crawford is obvious—who has "been on a sleigh ride but she can't face the fact that it's over, like half the people in this town." Instead she still plays being a movie star "twenty-four hours a day," thinking only of what kind of impression she is making and being "demanding, driving, ambitious," but "for what?" "Power," he replies. "To stay on the top" because she "can't look down." Asked how he will create sympathy for the protagonist of the film he calls "Falling Star," Stanley replies, "Not sympathy, Miss Elliot. Pity. Profound pity." After telling Margaret he aims for pathos, he adds, "My character is denied her birthright, the privilege and the glory of just being a woman." Hearing that, Margaret abruptly leaves the party and, with her young daughter in tow, returns to Jim on his houseboat.

The Star is not critiquing Hollywood, then, so much as wringing its drama from Margaret's inability as a fallen star and older woman to recognize, first, the inauthenticity, ephemerality, and impermanence of stardom and, second, the folly of disrespecting the patriarchal authority of producers, her agent, and her lover. In contrast with *Bombshell*, say, which draws comedy from Lola Burns's sudden maternal craving, *The Star* asks us to take that writer's comment about a woman's "birthright" with all the gravity implied by his sententious tone. (Ironically enough, if Margaret's character is indeed based on Crawford, the latter would go on to have another of her career resurgences in 1953 with the success of *Sudden Fear*, belying the message of *The Star*.)

The Star's view of stars as children who, not knowing their own minds, are controlled by their desires and fears, typifies the characterization of female stardom throughout much of this second cycle. MGM's other backstudio picture from 1952, *The Bad and the Beautiful*, is itself not a star narrative since its focal point is the producer Jonathan Shields (Kirk Douglas), so it more rightly belongs in chapter 5. One of the film's three major plot lines, however, does feature a woman's rise to stardom under Jonathan's tutelage, and it also psychologizes the troubled actress as childlike in her father fixation and dependence on Jonathan as he becomes her mentor and lover.

The narrative framework of *The Bad and the Beautiful* is a series of flashback narratives told from the viewpoints of three people whom Jonathan has nurtured but then betrayed: a director, a writer, and a star, Georgia Lorrison (Lana Turner). Her flashback outwardly reverses the downward pattern of *The Star*. While in the present day Georgia is a *grande dame* of the silver screen—perfectly coiffed, costumed, composed, and "the best actress, the best box office," as another character states—she first appears in the story as a drunk and a tramp "playing the doomed daughter of The Great Man," as Jonathan berates her. (Any resemblance to the late John Barrymore and his alcoholic daughter, Diana, the subjects of the later *Too Much, Too Soon* [1958], was apparently not coincidental; see Harvey 1989, 211; Naremore 1993, 119.) Georgia's Oedipal love-hate obsession with her father and later Jonathan feeds her insecurity and vulnerability, making her unmanageable because of her excessiveness—her excessive drinking, her excessive promiscuity, her excessive emotionality. This characterization makes an arrested adolescent out of the grown woman, but not to depict her as a girl like those many heroines in earlier star narratives; rather, this view of Georgia attributes the appeal of and ground for female stardom in a woman's childlike psyche, echoing how the producer in *The Star* describes stars as "naughty" yet "appealing" children. Indeed, James Naremore's impression of Georgia in her flashback emphasizes the childlike quality of her emotional makeup. During her affair with Jonathan after he decides to make her a star, Naremore observes, "She behaves like a child, wearing his big overcoat, sitting on his lap, gazing at him adoringly" (Naremore 1993, 121). (▶ Figure 4.17)

While Georgia's star narrative starts rather than ends with her on the skids, for most of *The Bad and the Beautiful* she is an overly emotional, unpredictable, and unmanageable woman in Hollywood, first as her dead father's alcoholic, promiscuous daughter, later as Jonathan's high-strung protégée. Georgia's stardom depends upon Jonathan since he channels her otherwise excessive and immature passions into the performance he wants, which transforms her from bit player to major star. He does not teach her how to act so much as how to act like a star: how to walk, speak, hold a cigarette as a meaningful prop, wear a historical costume as if it were made of the flimsiest material, and so forth. She does not need to master technique because, as Jonathan comments, her onscreen presence is palpable. Georgia's hatred of him in the present sustains her high-profile stardom with a diva's chilly, imperious air and glamorous appearance, reflecting how well she has learned her lessons. (▶ Figure 4.18)

The contrast between the two personalities—the insecure, volatile, and alcoholic child-woman versus the glamorous movie star with a perfectly calm and composed demeanor, her face veiled and her body draped in black clothes, fur piece, and glittering jewels—is evident in the histrionic conclusion to her flashback. Realizing that the way to manage his new star is to sustain her infatuation with him, Jonathan has gotten the performance from her that he wanted by playing the attentive lover throughout the fourteen-week duration of her film's shoot. But with the picture edited and in the can, Jonathan cuts Georgia loose the night of its premiere, betraying her with a bit player who is making the rounds on his studio's casting couch. Angry and hysterical after discovering his perfidy, Georgia drives off during a torrential rainstorm.

This climactic scene is now famous for teetering between pathos and camp. For as Georgia loses control of her car and the storm whips the automobile back and forth, director Vincente Minnelli's visualization of her histrionic breakdown utilizes "his showiest celluloid fakery—flashing lights and buckets of fake rain glorify[ing] this shrieking blur of rhinestones and ermine" (Harvey 1989, 213). Georgia's unrestrained breakdown here ends her flashback portion of *The Bad and the Beautiful*. Minnelli dissolves from the crazed Georgia—who is still screaming and sobbing as the automobile comes to a stop, the pouring rain still whirling around her—to movie star Georgia in the present day. The emotional wreck has become the perfect screen mannequin, "preternaturally poised, absurdly glamorous" (215). With her face composed, she calmly reiterates that she will never work with Jonathan again. "I know how you feel about Jonathan," Harry Pebbel (Walter Pidgeon), Jonathan's business manager, had stated before Georgia's flashback begins. "After all. You're a woman. And an actress." The two make for an uncontrollable combination in this picture, it seems: the bad and the beautiful. (▶ Figures 4.19–4.20) (▶ Clip 12)

Similarly *The Barefoot Contessa* (1954) depicts Maria Vargas (Ava Gardner), a Spanish dancer turned into a Hollywood star evocative of Rita Hayworth, as another sexualized child-woman, innocent yet promiscuous with her various male "cousins" because she just wants to be loved yet fears being vulnerable. "Emotionally she's a child," her confidante and director, Harry Dawes (Humphrey Bogart), comments. "She's lived her whole life as a fairy tale." At other times Maria is said to be "not a woman," to inhabit the "body of an animal," and to live "half in dirt, half out." The trailer casts her in the same light, describing her as "the world's most beautiful animal," while delineating multiple personae that splinter her identity and subject her solely to her desiring: "Spanish Gypsy! Café Society! Dancer! Great Hollywood Star!"

The potentially unmanageable child-woman stars in *The Bad and the Beautiful* and *The Barefoot Contessa* may resonate with echoes of the girl figure of earlier backstudios, not to mention young girls like Elizabeth Taylor, who had grown up to become a major adult movie star by the early 1950s, but the figure here is a highly sexualized adult, not a girl by any stretch of the imagination. Nor are Georgia and Maria anything like the virginal and boyish child-woman personified by Audrey Hepburn, one of the big new stars to emerge at the start of the 1950s. Rather, even though each fictional star has her real-life counterpart in Diana Barrymore and Rita Hayworth, respectively, the two characters associate female stardom with the sexualized and voluptuous child-woman personified by Marilyn Monroe, the other big new star of the period, who came to prominence at the time both backstudios were released.

The Goddess (1958) makes this connection explicit. It recounts the transformation of Emily Ann Faulkner (Kim Stanley) into movie star Rita Shaw, a character modeled on Monroe, who remains arrested in her childhood trauma of loss and abandonment. Desperate for affection yet driving away her two husbands and rejecting her daughter just as her mother had rejected her, Emily Ann becomes dependent on the kindness of alcohol, sleeping pills, and the ministrations of her maternal secretary, Harding (Elizabeth Wilson). Much more disruptive to the system of production, which otherwise seems able to handle neurotic, addicted female personalities with the help of pills and assistants like Harding, this star has a nervous breakdown on the set, causing her latest film to be shut down for ten days, at considerable expense to her producer. Characterizing Rita Shaw as the still emotionally hungry girl of Emily Ann's childhood, *The Goddess* erases her agency as a performer: we never see her at work but only in episodes of unpredictable and violent emotional outbursts that increase in severity and occur off-set in the privacy of her homes or hotel rooms.

Nearly a decade later the eponymous heroine of *Inside Daisy Clover* (1965), possibly modeled on Judy Garland, is not only a child-woman but a girl-boy: "Miss Huckleberry Finn," according to the studio promoting her; her husband, bisexual movie star Wade Lewis (Robert Redford), likewise describes her as "a crazy, monstrous child." Seduced and betrayed by Hollywood, Daisy (Natalie Wood) also dares to walk away, but to do so she has to fake her death. That same year, the highly fictionalized *Harlow* with Carroll Baker views its title character as a comparable child-woman. I include this biopic alongside these invented star narratives because characters describe Harlow as if she were more Monroe (and Emily Ann) than Harlow. "She has the body of a woman, the emotions of a child," says her agent, who uses this insight to establish her screen persona. "She's scared of her own sexuality—afraid to trust herself…the girl next door on fire inside." (I doubt anyone at MGM ever made that claim about Harlow or her alter ego in *Bombshell*.)

The pop psychology in these various backstudios seeks to "explain" the female star's unruliness, which extends from her private demons to her defiance of the studio's patriarchal hierarchies, and then to justify the studio's or a producer's parental supervision. The female star as child-woman depicts her as the personification of excess—an excess of

Jane Hudson (Bette Davis) and her sister, Blanche (Joan Crawford): washed-up and monstrous former stars of Old Hollywood. (*What Ever Happened to Baby Jane?* ©1962 Warner Bros.)

desire, ambition, dependency, neuroses, depression, and hence an excess of financial instability for her studio's balance sheets. This figuration of stardom as feminine excess easily becomes glossed as "monstrous" because of her abject state of mind, unruly desiring, and, in the case of older stars like Norma and Margaret, her aging body. As the most grotesque exaggeration of the star as child-woman, Bette Davis's Baby Jane Hudson in *What Ever Happened to Baby Jane?* (1962) exemplifies what is to be most dreaded—and hence what is rendered onscreen as most dreadful—about the monstrous has-been female star during this second cycle: her assertion of star power in an industry that no longer has the economy to support her demands or to tolerate her agency. Though Jane and her sister, Blanche (Joan Crawford), seem like two B-picture Norma Desmonds, shut up in their secluded house and driving each other crazy with their pent-up rivalries, their backstory locates their present-day abjection (which actually takes place "yesterday," a title card informs us) in 1930s Hollywood.

The Hudson sisters' story starts with them as children. A first pretitle prologue occurring in 1917 shows Baby Jane's vaudeville act. This sequence reveals the child star adored by other little girls and doted on by her daddy; offstage Baby Jane is spoiled and mean-spirited. That the child star's sweet demeanor onstage is a mask that she does not wear offstage predicts the older Jane's deluded mental state as she tries to re-create that lost youthful persona in the present, getting more violent and more lost in time as the film progresses. A second prologue happening in 1935 reveals Jane to be an alcoholic and promiscuous woman without much talent who is flailing about in Hollywood films, some of which are so terrible they do not even get released in the States. "Boy, what a no-talent broad that Baby Jane is," a projectionist complains after screening footage. "Why can't she stay sober?" his co-worker asks, no doubt rhetorically. As Ben Golden (Burt Freed), a studio producer, complains to Marty (Wesley Addy), Blanche's agent, even before that just-screened picture finished production Jane had already "guzzled her way through six cases of Scotch and slugged two studio cops, not to mention one or two other less savory items of publicity." Jane is unruly but also intolerable because her films repeatedly cost the studio in bad publicity and delays as well as red ink.

The studio cannot fire Jane, however, because Blanche, who selflessly stood in the shadows of Baby Jane's stardom in their vaudeville days, is now queen of the lot, "the biggest thing in movies today. She can write her own ticket. She's got script approval." Since her contract also requires the studio to make a picture with Jane for every one of hers, at first we may simply assume that Blanche acts as her dysfunctional sister's caretaker. After all, catching sight of a sullen Blanche in the wings of the vaudeville theater, her mother had said, "Someday it's going to be you that's getting all the attention. And when that happens, I—I want you to try to be kinder to Jane and your father than they are to you now." "I won't forget," young Blanche had vowed with a look of fierce determination. (▶ Figure 4.22)

Presumably that promise dictates the terms of Blanche's studio contract, although why it does so is not made immediately clear. It could simply be her misguided effort to make Jane a star again, or so Golden assumes when wondering why Blanche cannot be persuaded to remove the clause. On the other hand, her agent explains to him that Blanche is simply "a fine person" and, remembering what her sister did for her in the old days, is now paying her back. Paying her back indeed! In the film's big revelation we learn that Blanche had tried to run down her sister, causing the car accident that left herself paralyzed and dependent on Jane's ministrations, while letting Jane, who was too drunk after the accident even to remember she was not driving, become mentally unbalanced from years of built-up guilt and resentment. Therefore the contractual obligation to keep her sister working in films could as easily have been a form of revenge since it assures Jane's humiliation in picture after picture while Blanche herself basks in the spotlight of bona fide stardom. For that matter, in the years following this prologue, despite her confinement Blanche may still have been getting satisfaction from watching her sister slowly turn into a horrific and grotesque parody of the once famous Baby Jane Hudson, child star, while she herself is confined to her bedroom but enveloped there in reminders of her youthful beauty and film career, not to mention her enjoyment of the second life of her old films on afternoon television. (▶ Figures 4.22–4.23)

The car accident, of course, ends the sisters' Hollywood careers prematurely and sets up the main horror narrative by laying the groundwork of their present-day abjection. The 1935 prologue links their physical monstrousness as aged former movie stars to their figural monstrousness as working actresses in Old Hollywood who resisted studio control. The Baby Jane clause is the major sticking point with Blanche's studio since it has to bend to her will legally. The clause essentially gives Jane license to misbehave on the set, drinking and brawling with the gusto of a Norman Maine but without fear of termination. No doubt, like Lina, Blanche could "syoo" if the clause were in any way breached, and from Golden's comments, the studio's lawyers have been unable to break the contract, which is why he asks Marty to speak to Blanche again at the party she is throwing that evening at the Grove.

The two prologues establish the basis for why the Hudson sisters' present-day transformation into nightmarish likenesses of their youthful selves seems inevitable, possibly even justified given their past behavior. At the end of the 1935 prologue, Golden stops at an expensive-looking convertible—the car that will shortly figure into the accident that leaves one Hudson sister crippled for life—and asks, "What do they make monsters like this for?" "For Blanche Hudson," Marty replies, as if the outsized car were one of the perquisites and necessities of movie stardom. Slapping him on the shoulder, Golden replies, "That's our problem." The "problem" Golden likely has in mind is Blanche's sister, whose monstrousness in his eyes is enabled by that contractual clause keeping the untalented and soused Baby Jane in pictures despite the cost to the studio. Or possibly Golden means that monsters like Jane are a problem, but one with the residual effect of testing Blanche's greatness, her compassion and beneficence. By the time the film concludes, however, the phrase resonates beyond either meaning to make Blanche the Dr. Frankenstein to her sister's hapless, victimized monster.

The motivation for Jane's abusive treatment of Blanche years later has at least two sources in what we see happening in the present day: Jane's resentment at learning that Blanche secretly plans to sell their house and confine her to some sort of benign institution, and Jane's jealousy at watching the revival of Blanche's stardom through a local television station's broadcasting of her sister's films in order to cash in on the nostalgia craze for old Hollywood just starting to take shape in the early 1960s. The Hollywood backstory thus never stays confined to just the beginning of *What Ever Happened to Baby Jane?* for it permeates the main narrative.

Like the portrait of Blanche on her bedroom wall, the film never lets us forget that, no less than the two stars portraying them, the Hudson sisters are not only old but Old Hollywood as well. Hence the recurring impression throughout the film's Grand Guignol storyline that what survives the wreckage of Old Hollywood are monstrous versions of its once ageless, glamorous female stars. As survivors, Jane/Davis and Blanche/Crawford simultaneously bear witness to the system's demise and implicitly bear responsibility for it; their abject images as not only faded stars but older women evoke "the big, fat, flush days" that supported their type of stardom but that Hollywood could no longer afford by the early 1960s. This thinking greatly accounts for why female star narratives in the second cycle repeatedly include at least one crucial scene when the star challenges or openly defies studio authority. That such unruliness on her part is something to be dreaded is signaled by the way her age, sexuality, and ambition tend to be troped as something "monstrous" and "dreadful." As figures in a horror film, the two Hudson sisters in *What Ever Happened to Baby Jane?* seem the logical conclusion of this institutional myth.

Fatal Stardom

Most of these fading star narratives call attention to their historical moment of production because they either feature big female stars past their prime (Swanson, Garland, Davis, Crawford), as far as concerned the industry suits, or model their fictional characters on recognizable real-life stars personifying excessive behavior (Garland, Monroe, Hayworth), according to the press and the public imagination. *The Legend of Lylah Clare* (1968), director Robert Aldrich's follow-up of sorts to his *Baby Jane*, is an exception insofar as it lacks such an extrafilmic context. Furthermore, because the story *Lylah Clare* concocts is never fully comprehensible in terms of plot, style, or performance, it can easily be written off—as indeed it was at the time by MGM (who did not know how to market it and took a loss) and also by star Kim Novak (who never made another picture in Hollywood). However, even without a legible informing context in "real-life" Hollywood, *Lylah Clare* brings out the same implications about the monstrousness of female stardom that I have been discussing.

In this backstudio, meek Elsa Campbell née Brinkman may or may not be possessed by the ghost of her famous double: the Garbo-like, sexually perverse, assertive, mannish yet erotic, beloved, and very dead star she is playing in the biopic we watch being filmed, "Lylah Clare, Film Star." (▶ Figure 4.24) With Kim Novak at times dubbed with a deep, guttural Germanic accent to indicate this "possession," Elsa is a monstrous hybrid embodying past and present Hollywood. The mysterious, inexplicable fusion of Elsa Brinkman aka Campbell with Lylah Clare reaches the point where Elsa herself can no longer tell if a publicity photograph is of her or Lylah. As this fusion of Elsa with Lylah happens, observers of her within the film similarly cannot decide if the neophyte star's uncanny impersonation is a ghostly possession or Elsa's own instincts (and research) as an actress, making her perfect casting for the biopic. "I could swear that's Lylah," someone remarks after viewing a nearly completed rough cut of the biopic. Before then, as Elsa is increasingly held in thrall to her famous predecessor, she goes into trance-like states wherein she suddenly speaks in Lylah's guttural voice and tells off Hollywood studio heads and gossip columnists who matter, insulting their authority; furthermore, the actress's identification with her role appears so strong that she not only internalizes Lylah to the point of losing herself entirely but also appears to repeat Lylah's life, although I will want to qualify this statement momentarily. By the film's end, when Elsa gives up her own voice and speaks just as Lylah, she apparently even knows secrets about the dead star that only Lylah, her widower, and her confidante, Rossella (Rossella Falk), could know.

Without any sort of mythology explaining how it could happen, Lylah's possession of Elsa is frankly preposterous, so Elsa's conflict with her director makes *The Legend of Lylah Clare* perhaps more interesting than it has any right to be. For just as Elsa loses her identity to Lylah, so too does her director and lover, and Lylah's widower and mentor, Lewis Zarken (Peter Finch), demand that Elsa lose her identity as an actress to his direction. "I want someone who can walk, talk like I taught Lylah," he declares at the start of their venture.

Once on set, as Elsa has trouble understanding her motivation for driving a car, Lewis publicly berates her for being unable to follow his orders and for demanding further direction about what she is supposed to feel. "You stupid cow," he screams at her. "All you've got to do is do as I say and then your feeling will be up on the screen. All I need is your face."

As "Lylah Clare, Film Star" nears completion, Elsa's resistance begins to make itself felt more forcefully. After thirty-three takes, she still fumbles the final scene, re-creating Lylah's fatal fall from the open staircase in Lewis's mansion. Deciding that Elsa instinctively senses the falseness of this scene despite its fidelity to known facts, Lewis crafts an entirely fictional version of his dead wife's accidental death. "Without an ending you have no picture," he tells the producer, who balks at this revision and (functioning as Elsa's agent as well) refuses to let his star go on. Elsa herself defiantly reminds Lewis, "Without an *actress* you have no picture." Shortly thereafter, however, she is shown seductively waiting for him in his bed. After they make love, he puts her back in her place as his mannequin, ordering, "You be on the set at nine o'clock in the morning and do exactly as I say. Because you're an illusion. Without me, you don't exist. You're nothing! Do you understand? Nothing!"

The next day, as if in retaliation, Lylah appears to have taken over Elsa's consciousness entirely. As she and Lewis again quarrel in her dressing room, Elsa states in Lylah's distinctive voice, while holding a hand mirror to his face, "I am what you made, Lewis. Look. Look. Look. You're a god. I am created in your image." Not at all taken aback by her sarcasm, he rejoins, "You've taken on a life of your own, haven't you? You don't need me. A director's just somebody to keep the technicians happy." Yet she is wrong, he insists, just wrong. "Without a director you're just a vulgar little exhibitionist." Taking his bait, Elsa/Lylah exclaims, "All right, little man. I'll show you. We'll see who's number one." She decides "to put Lewis in his place" by directing the final death scene herself and acting in it without benefit of her stunt double. "No one stops me until I say cut," she orders in Lylah's voice. Lewis asks, "You are the boss?," and she taunts back, "All right, Lewis, we will see if I'm an illusion." After two successfully completed single takes, with her fall from a trapeze into a hidden net meant to simulate this newly invented account of Lylah's death, Lewis goads Elsa into looking down on the crowd below, and she falls for real, breaking her neck—which still does not stop the director from filming her death scene in close-up. "Play it!" he shouts to the stunned cast, demanding that they complete the scene while his camera records the real-life event. (▶ Figure 4.25)

Elsa's fatal fall uncannily yet unfaithfully mirrors Lylah's death; furthermore, in offering a representation that bears witness to its own factuality, this made-up ending for the biopic suggests how much Elsa drives the legend of Lylah Clare as opposed to the other way around. There is, to begin with, a good deal of inconsistency as to the circumstances of Lylah's own fatal fall twenty years earlier. The film offers three different accounts of what happened, each based in fragmented revelations of Lylah's perverse sexuality, but all three versions still show her falling from the second-floor landing in Lewis's home, and not from a trapeze in a circus setting, as in the biopic's revised finale. Since he declares that Elsa could not perform the original ending convincingly because she knew it was not "true," the emotional if not factual veracity of what we have seen in those three luridly framed and hazy flashbacks is further called into question.

When justifying his newly fictionalized ending for "Lylah Clare, Film Star," the director borrows the already famous line from *The Man Who Shot Liberty Valence* (1962): "We make the legend," he claims. "The legend becomes truth." On one hand, his statement confirms as a truism the illusory basis of stardom as manufactured by Hollywood. Though his producer reminds him that people think they know how Lylah died and so will instantly question the biopic's fidelity to facts, Lewis insists that his fictional ending will displace "facts," since ten years hence that ending will be the basis of how people believe Lylah died. From Lewis's perspective, then, his highly contrived account of her death means to prove that the female star is always just an illusion created by her director, who controls not only her face and feelings but also her biography.

On the other hand, since Elsa *really* dies, the death scene as filmed *is* authentic, more so than anything else in the biopic, and it is in this sense that Elsa and Lylah merge personae and share biographies, just as it suggests how "the legend of Lylah Clare" takes over the biopic's production, superseding Lewis's control. Thus by the end of *The Legend of Lylah Clare* one finds oneself mired in the proverbial chicken-and-egg dilemma, for it is unclear whether Elsa simply repeats Lylah's story or re-creates it in her own image, as happens with her death scene. Increasingly throughout the course of the narrative, what happens to Elsa has its source in the movie she stars in and not in Lylah's actual life story—to the point where, by the time of the premiere, Elsa, not Lylah, becomes the real-life referent and guarantor of the authenticity of "Lylah Clare, Film Star." At that point everyone in the theater audience knows that the representation of Lylah's death is a record of her portrayer's actual death; in this sense, the biopic *does* alter what people now know about Lylah.

This is the haunting sense in which Elsa is not living out so much as determining the legend of Lylah Clare in the film's present day. When the finished black-and-white biopic premieres at Grauman's Chinese, we see how exactly it reproduces Elsa's death as we previously witnessed it, including the shot of the empty swinging trapeze that marked the end of that scene as it happened. There is one notable difference, however. In her own death scene Elsa's final words, "I love you, Lewis," were heard in Lylah's dubbed voice, but when the biopic is shown at Grauman's that voice is Elsa's (that is, Novak's own)—although since the statement is delivered as a voice-off cut to a close-up of Lewis as he watches, it is not clear if the diegetic audience hears Elsa or if he recalls her voice internally as he relives the scene. (▶ Figure 4.26) In any event, *The Legend of Lylah Clare* never makes clear exactly what we are meant to take away from its convoluted backstudio plot, especially given how Aldrich finally ends the film with a dog food commercial that blows a raspberry at Hollywood. Nonetheless, however one views *Lylah Clare*, it is impossible to ignore its basic premise: what Lylah's legend obscures is the monstrousness of female stardom, which takes over Elsa's life and ends up destroying her.

Fake Stardom

Troped as "monstrous" images of abjection, postwar figurations of female stardom from *Sunset Boulevard* to *The Legend of Lylah Clare* depict women challenging the male power structure organizing Hollywood, even though, at this same time, that system of production was economically imploding. And just as telling of how this second cycle of backstudios then appears to blame this defiant female star figure for the studio system's dissolution, additional challenges to Hollywood's institutional identity, which were already clearly evident at that time, are barely noticed by the backstudio genre except indirectly, as in the European setting of *The Barefoot Contessa* or the Jennifer North (Sharon Tate) plot line of *Valley of the Dolls* (1967) when, her Hollywood career behind her, she goes to Europe to make sexploitation films. I am thinking of runaway production to Britain and Europe, due to postwar currency restrictions and cheaper labor, and the simultaneous phenomenon of the internationally cofinanced blockbuster that cast European names alongside American; the repudiation of the well-made studio-made picture implicit in the emergence of foreign language films (Italian neorealism, French new wave, British kitchen sink dramas), which were regularly endorsed by the New York critics and found an informed, alternative audience in big cities and college towns; and the emergence of auteurism as a means of canonizing certain Hollywood directors for their apparent transcendence of studio restrictions, elevating them over other above-the-line creatives like writers and producers—and movie stars.

Having for so long carried the weight of Hollywood's self-mythification, by the end of the 1960s the fictional star narrative ceased to dominate the backstudio genre. A series of biopics in the 1970s traded on that era's nostalgia boom (e.g., *Gable and Lombard* and *W. C. Fields and Me*, both in 1976), and a few exploited a recently deceased star's renewed notoriety (e.g., Joan Crawford and *Mommie Dearest* in 1981). Displaced by backstudios revolving around male directors, writers, and producers, star biopics centering on women migrated to the small screen as made-for-TV movies (e.g., *The Jayne Mansfield Story* in 1980 and *White Hot: The Mysterious Murder of Thelma Todd* in 1990, both starring Loni Anderson). This move corresponded to a significant hierarchical shift within the Hollywood star system itself, as male stars increasingly dominated box-office polls and studio output, and the industry pretty much lost interest in female audiences, reinforcing the view that the primary market for most theatrical movies are young males. By the turn of this century, broadcast and cable had become the prime medium for recounting the lives of real-life stars such as Dorothy Dandridge (1999), Audrey Hepburn (2000), and Judy Garland (2001). As I shall be discussing further in chapter 6, Marilyn Monroe's biography in particular has supplied material for repeated treatments. The few recent theatrical films about fictional stars occurring in the present, like *Notting Hill* (1999) and *American Sweethearts* (2001), focus less on their careers as professionals in Hollywood and more on their being flamboyant celebrities who live out their lives in public. In this context, before I close this chapter, *S1m0ne* (2002), a rare star narrative from the turn of this century, deserves a close look, for in many respects it can be viewed as a millennial updating of *The Legend of Lylah Clare*.

A fitting twenty-first-century retort to the studio-era female star narrative, *S1m0ne* imagines how computer software can digitally create a compliant animated female star beloved by both Hollywood and its unsuspecting public, yet this virtual star still acts on desires and ambitions beyond her director-creator's control. To be sure, this audacious conceit initially derives from both a misogynist and contradictory anxiety about powerful, unregulated women in present-day Hollywood and a yearning for the old days of the studio-era star system, but its satiric viewpoint ultimately turns the tables on a narcissistic auteur, Viktor Taransky (Al Pacino).

As the film opens Viktor is trying to placate his diva star, Nicola Anders (Winona Ryder), a petulant, self-indulgent, talentless, and emasculating "supermodel with a SAG card," as the director calls her. Nicola's contractual demands drive Viktor crazy. For instance, she requires seven packs of cigarettes waiting for her in any room she enters (with three packs already opened), a first-class seat for her nanny whenever she has to travel (yet she has no children), and all cherry Mike-and-Ikes removed from a glass candy bowl. Viktor, in fact, is frantically picking out red candies as Nicola storms off his picture for good, claiming that he has breached her contract and shown her no respect because her dressing room trailer, parked next to one that is slightly higher because of overinflated tires, is not the largest on the lot. In this opening the star is a Lola Burns gone berserk with her whims and the director is a deflated Space Hanlon. Nonetheless, for all this star's outlandish behavior, given the artistic pretenses of Viktor's film in the absurd pseudo-arty footage shown, there may be some truth to Nicola's complaint as she departs that she does not understand Viktor's script, and, she adds, neither will an audience, although that does not turn out to be the case within the diegesis.

Viktor has already shot almost everything he needs and can finish the film without his lead actress, but her attorney threatens to sue if the director uses even a single frame in which she appears. The alternative is to recast, but since no actress with a following will now take on the role, studio head Elaine Christian (Catherine Keener)—who also happens to be Viktor's ex-wife—fires him and claims she has to shelve the picture "if we ever want to be in the Nicola Anders business again." On his part, Viktor blames the system that caters to freakish personalities like Nicola's. "Don't you see? They're mocking us, Elaine. We're at their mercy." He goes on to evoke a memory of the old studio system when the proverbial inmates were not running the asylum: "What happened? We always had movie stars, but they used to be *our* stars, remember? We were the ones who would tell them what to do, what to wear, who to date.... When they were under contract to us we could change their names if we wanted to. Yeah, more than once." Elaine rightly points out in response, "Viktor, you realize you're nostalgic for an era you weren't even born in."

Not stopped by her just observation, Viktor further claims that he still remembers what attracted the two of them to this business in "the old days," namely, a desire to "illuminate hearts and minds with a ray of truth" in the indie manner of John Cassavetes and their other New York contemporaries. But since Viktor rhetorically identifies with the studio mavens who formerly created and controlled movie stars, he mistakenly assumes that he, a B-list director whose fame rests on two Oscar-nominated short subjects and whose previous three pictures "tanked," would have had any more authority over his work under the old regime or in New York than he does under Elaine's management. Underscoring his self-interested and self-deceiving impression, his heated accusation that they have lost their way from their Big Apple days diegetically occurs before frontage of brownstone apartments on the New York street set of the studio's backlot. (▶ Figure 4.27)

When "Simulation One," an innovative software program for creating "vactors," or virtual actors, falls in his lap unexpectedly, Viktor realizes that he can trump the will of his studio and of high-priced, egomaniacal superstars like Nicola by inserting in her place his own "discovery," the obedient yet charismatic Simone (a computer-enhanced Rachel Roberts). "This is a classic case of technology in search of an artist," Viktor's reasoning goes. "Someone with integrity, someone with vision...someone who can see that if a performance is genuine it doesn't matter if the actor's real or not." Similarly, while he may be guilty of a crime, as he reminds himself, as if addressing a jury while the revised film is previewed, "it was committed with the purest of intentions" because he wanted to send "a message to the acting community who put themselves above the work"—and, he adds under his breath, "who put themselves above me."

Simone, a condensation of the software's name, is herself a condensation of female stardom in Hollywood. After Viktor's revised film opens, a reviewer comments that she has "the voice of a young Jane Fonda, the body of Sophia Loren, the grace of, well, Grace Kelly, and the face of Audrey Hepburn combined with an angel." "Almost right," Viktor comments with disguised irony after Elaine reads the praise aloud to him. Afterward, alone with his computer on a locked and guarded studio soundstage, he continues to tweak his creation. "Simone, a star is digitized," he solemnly announces to her visage on the computer monitor before adjusting her appearance further. Fittingly, his reanimation of Simone's screen personality here evokes the makeup room scene in both versions of *A Star Is Born*. "Too much Meryl Streep," he observes as he scrolls a menu of famous Hollywood faces, deciding upon "a little less Streep and a little more Bacall," and then, after hearing Simone's deeper voice, adding "that thing Audrey Hepburn does in *Breakfast at Tiffany's*." Finally, he observes that Simone is just too perfect, "too beautiful," so to "fix that" he places a beauty mark on her cheek, copying the moles on Harlow's and Monroe's faces. (▶ Figure 4.28) (▶ Clip 13)

With his film a huge success due to Simone's incandescent, unworldly performance, Viktor not only believes that he controls every aspect of his work but enjoys his many ruses for keeping Elaine and her lackeys as well as the rest of his cast and the press away from his creation as the two embark on a second project. "I know my process is an unusual way to work," Simone tells her costars from a monitor at the first table reading of Viktor's new script, "but I just have found that I relate better to people when they're not actually here." More to the point of his scheme, Viktor succeeds in making Simone the

A star is digitized. (*S1m0ne* ©2002 New Line)

kind of passive, malleable actress that Lewis wanted Elsa to be in *Lylah Clare*. Simone considers herself merely "an instrument" of her director, instructs her costars to "always do what Mr. Taransky says," and on a remote camera pickup for a talk show interview, explains her shyness by confessing, "I guess I think actors talk too much."

However, much to his shock, Viktor's discovery soon eclipses him in value as a brand, merchandising a fragrance, becoming a music star at sellout arena concerts, and accepting her two Oscars (she ties with herself for best actress) via another remote pickup, this time from her goodwill tour of the world. At the Academy ceremony, Simone neglects to thank her director. "How could I forget?" he asks himself rhetorically. "I wrote it." This moment marks the point at which the simulated star takes over from Viktor, despite his subsequent efforts to put her in her place by ruining her popularity: on talk shows he has her endorse smoking and the wearing of fur, and then lets her direct herself in an artsy movie that, even though ending with her crawling and eating in a pig sty, still receives thunderous applause. When Viktor finally tries to confess the truth about his fraudulent creation to Elaine, she assumes he speaks metaphorically because every actor is, in a manner of speaking, a director's invention. But then Elaine points out *his* debt to Simone's stardom: "You made Simone, Viktor? She made you."

Simone's usurpation of Viktor's authority is inevitable because she is his double, the projection of his desire to control every aspect of his film, to be artistically cutting-edge yet still critically acclaimed and wildly popular. Clicking the "mimic" button on his computer screen, Viktor ventriloquizes Simone's speech so that we frequently hear his voice beneath hers when she speaks from the monitor in the secluded soundstage where he performs her. "I'm so relaxed around you. I'm so myself," he confesses to her in that early scene when he tweaks her voice and visage, confirming, as does the entire history of her success, that she is no more than a literal image radiating "to-be-looked-at-ness." "Mr. Taransky, we both know I was nothing without you," Simone replies. "I was computer code. I was ones and zeros. I was nothing." He likewise performs Simone at every one of her "remote" public appearances and concerts. This doubling does not mean to suggest that Simone reflects Viktor's "feminine" nature as an artist; far from it, since her very existence means to address his suspicion of women who, in his mind, have taken over the business. He blames the entire acting community, but at least as far as we can tell, his problems are with an actress whom he cannot control and a female studio head who keeps him on only for the sake of their daughter but then fires him as soon it comes down to "investment and return." Simone's compliant example encourages Nicola's later come-uppance; inspired by Viktor's creation, Nicola fires her entourage, takes acting lessons, and begs for a part playing Simone's sister in his next picture. Similarly, jealousy of Simone eventually reawakens Elaine's feelings for her former husband and drives away her present, younger spouse.

As Simone becomes more dominant and Viktor comes to realize that "she's taken on a life of her own," this third-act development is wryly funny and consistent with paranoiac fears about artificial intelligence in sci-fi yet also, given this film's verisimilitude in estab-lishing its premise about a software able to create vactors, as illogical as Elsa's possession by Lylah Clare. Simone neglects to mention her director when accepting her two Oscars, but Viktor himself supplied that speech beforehand; she is, after all, no more than a CGI Charlie McCarthy to his Edgar Bergen. Yet this turn in the narrative does force Viktor to confront his own narcissism as a director. "Here I was trying to convince the world that you existed," he mutters as her fame eclipses his. "But what I was really trying to do was convince them that *I* existed." After failing to ruin her career by making her unpopular, Viktor's solution is to infect Simulation One with a virus that effectively eliminates Simone, but with her disappearance comes his arrest for her murder—she was *too* well-liked and *too* real for anyone to believe his confession of fraud. Viktor's computer-savvy daughter, Lainie (Evan Rachel Wood), rescues him by curing the software of its virus in order to revive the star and vindicate her father. "She's indestructible," he mutters when he sees Simone's reemergence on TV. With a tongue-in-cheek sight gag, the film's conclusion fully domesticates Simone in the manner of earlier star narratives. Although Viktor and Elaine reconcile behind the scenes, a radiant Simone announces her political ambitions, as the resigned director poses with his revived star and their new son, baby Chip. The image dis-solves to a shot of Viktor seated by himself in front of a green screen. It appears he will now forever be in thrall to the indestructible Simone. (▶ Figures 4.29–4.30)

No moral repulsion at the deceit behind his virtual creation bothers the characters in *S1m0ne*. When Viktor apologizes to Lainey for tricking her, she informs him, "The mistake wasn't making something fake, Dad. We're fine with fake. As long as you don't lie about it." Elaine goes even further in accepting Viktor's fraud. "You know what you have to do now," she states right after Simone's resurrection and Viktor's release from the police station. At first Elaine seems to be suggesting he must make a public confession. But she continues, "Why stop at one character when you can have a whole cast? You have to finish what you started. We can do it together." When applied to the history of stardom, as sug-gested by Viktor's evocation of the old days when "we" controlled the lives and behavior of "our" stars, the digitization of Simone reiterates the myth of studio-era Hollywood, albeit updated for the era of CGI manipulation of the digital image. As Viktor explains to his creation, "Our ability to manufacture fraud now exceeds our ability to detect it."

S1m0ne revels in its clever depiction of stardom as a fraud perpetuated on an unsuspecting and gullible public. As important, although it takes its title from its female star figure, *S1m0ne* follows Viktor's male perspective, registering Hollywood's growing disregard for female audiences along with its suspicion of female stardom. By the time of *The Legend of Lylah Clare* in 1968 such disregard and suspicion were already inspiring backstudio pictures to pay more attention to the creative psyches of Hollywood men like Lewis Zarken; by the time of *S1m0ne* in 2002 that masculinist bias was simply accepted by the genre as a matter of fact.

5

Masculine Hollywood

Many people forget that *King Kong* (1933) is another backstudio from the early 1930s. Filmmaker Carl Denham (Robert Armstrong) makes what he calls "outdoor pictures" in remote locations. Since both critics and exhibitors agree that his films would double their grosses if they had a romance plot, this time out he is adding that ingredient. He concedes that he does so begrudgingly, however, and only "because the public, bless 'em, must have a pretty face to look at." Still, given Denham's reputation for secrecy and recklessness, no professional actress will board his boat the *Venture* to work with him. This is the problem that leads him to penniless Ann Darrow (Fay Wray) and the two of them to Skull Island and Kong.

King Kong portrays Denham as a filmmaker in several ways worth pointing out. He is a multi-hyphenate: he produces, he directs, he writes, he even cranks the camera. He is the one-man show, "Carl Denham Pictures," as it states on the equipment. A real-life inspiration for this character seems to have been Frank Buck, the wild animal hunter and collector and author of bestselling books like *Bring 'Em Back Alive* (1930). The 1932 film version of that book began Buck's other career as a narrator of and sometimes actor in jungle-adventure documentaries. When complaining about the illegal dynamite and gas bombs being stored aboard his ship, the skipper of the *Venture* agrees with Denham that, despite the danger, "you always bring back a picture. And everyone says there's only one Carl Denham." Similarly, when Weston (Sam Hardy), the talent agent, explains to Denham why his reputation has prevented him from finding any actress willing to travel with him to parts unknown in the South Pacific, the filmmaker comments, "You talk as if I never brought anyone back alive." In addition to being all aspects of "Carl Denham Pictures," then, Denham's filmmaking is characterized as a dangerous adventure, and a robustly masculine one at that. However, *King Kong* gives very few clues as to what constitutes Denham's moving picture enterprise. One can infer that he makes up a good deal of his plot on the fly, depending on what he finds in the secret and remote locations to which he travels with his crew. Nonetheless filmmaking receives the most attention until Denham and company reach Skull Island, lose all the equipment and footage, and ultimately bring Kong back alive to New York City for theatrical exhibition. At that point Denham appears to leave behind his filmmaking career.

From the very opening of *King Kong* until the giant ape appears, moreover, people near him think Denham is "crazy." In the first scene, the night watchman asks Weston, "Are you going on this crazy voyage?" The watchman does not know exactly what is "crazy" about the "moving picture ship" except that "everybody is talking about that crazy fella running it." At this point, Jack Driscoll (Bruce Cabot) calls out to Weston, informing him that "Denham's getting wild" waiting to hear if the talent agent has found an actress. A short while later, Driscoll asks the skipper if he thinks Denham is "crazy," and the skipper replies, "Just enthusiastic." Once the *Venture* embarks and the "crazy" filmmaking adventure begins, Ann tells Driscoll she would do anything for Denham, and he replies, "I'd say he's crazy enough to try anything." This running commentary keeps equating Denham's filmmaking with his "craziness" to indicate that the man knows no limits because of his passion for filmmaking.

Peter Jackson's remake of *King Kong* (2005) follows the original rather closely in its storyline but refrains from ever calling Carl Denham (Jack Black) "crazy." Rather, this version characterizes Denham as a hustler working within the Hollywood system, at least to start with, and out to make money from his jungle-adventure films. The only indication that this filmmaker may be "crazy" comes from Black's wild, pop-eyed facial expressions, though his acting as easily signifies the filmmaker's insincerity and determination when lying, which he does very easily, or his self-delusion in believing what he says without regard for its truthfulness or falsity.

Additionally, although this 2005 *King Kong* is, like the original, set in the early 1930s, Denham's filmmaking here reflects awareness of the industry's standard practices for commercial pictures. Denham has hired a screenwriter, the well-known playwright Jack Driscoll (Adrien Brody), who is shanghaied aboard the *Venture* in order to finish the script while they travel. Carl the cameraman at least holds the tripod while Denham cranks the camera when on the island. The filmmaker has a major Hollywood actor, Bruce Baxter (Kyle Chandler), in place for the romantic scenes and now just needs to find a willing actress. With a screenwriter and male and female leads, it appears Denham is making not a documentary but a more conventional Hollywood romantic adventure.

Reinforcing this impression, Denham depends upon studio men to back his film, which is why his first appearance is not on the ship, as in the 1933 original, but in a screening room where the suits are watching his footage. They now have to approve Denham's budget overruns as well as his intent to move out of a soundstage for location shooting with his actors, but are reluctant to do so, calling Denham not crazy but "a preening self-promoter" who has made several "near hits." They own the footage Denham has already shot and decide to sell it to Universal for stock in order to cover their losses. To prevent his film project from being aborted, Denham steals the footage. The theft motivates his need to find a new, unsuspecting actress immediately, which he does when he comes upon a very hungry Ann Darrow (Naomi Watts), and then to embark with his cast, writer, and crew before he gets arrested. The theft also positions him not as a maverick like 1933's Denham but as an outlaw on the run from Hollywood.

Taken together, these two versions of *King Kong* sketch the terms by which backstudio pictures represent the creative side of filmmaking. On one hand, like the Denham of 1933, the filmmaker may be movie-crazy, which is to say he seems crazed to others because of his intense passion for making movies; he will do anything and everything to realize his vision, despite the human cost. Bucking the system quixotically, this filmmaker tends to be characterized as out of control, driven to excess or neurosis or delusions by both his passion for filmmaking and his egoism. On the other hand, like the Denham of 2005, the filmmaker may not be Frank Buck but out to make a buck. As a talented Hollywood professional, in order to survive in Hollywood he has to be a hustler or self-promoter who sometimes tries to game the system. Either way, the filmmaker narrative is typically concerned with exploring who holds power within the industry since *power* is central to Hollywood's appeal in these backstudios. Whether maverick or outlaw, artist or hack, dreamer or hustler, the filmmaker may stand up to studio bosses, but he usually cannot defeat their overriding concern with the bottom line. His resistance, like his creative energy, nonetheless makes the filmmaker a glamorous figure, the new personification of Hollywood's mystique since the end of the studio era. Indeed, just as the female star narrative dominated the genre until the 1970s, the filmmaker narrative with a male protagonist became more prominent as the Hollywood mode of production and financing changed with the purchase of studios by nonmedia corporations. Since then the filmmaker narrative has served to masculinize the backstudio genre along with the Hollywood brand.

Unlike the previous two chapters, which traced the historical trajectory of female star narratives from the 1920s to the 1960s, in this one I follow exemplary figurations of the male filmmaker in backstudios that focus on the creative side of making movies: the producer, writer, director. In each case comparing a studio-era film with two more recent ones, my aim is to examine how the backstudio picture locates "creativity" in both the business and the art of filmmaking, and how the genre subsequently equates a masculinized—and white—view of cinema with the cultural aura of "Hollywood."

The Producer

With the exception of Stanley Shriner Hoff (Rod Steiger), the ruthless studio head in *The Big Knife* (1955)—who in his actions resembles a mob boss and in his appearance, David O. Selznick—producers may be mocked in backstudios, but rarely during the studio era or even afterward does their folly turn into something truly corrupt or sinister. Absent as a protagonist is an amoral and unredeemable producer like Sammy Glick, the title character of Budd Schulberg's novel *What Makes Sammy Run?* After its publication in 1941 the name Sammy Glick became generic for the film industry heel who thinks only of his career and is willing to step over everyone and anyone as he speedily makes his way up the ranks to run a studio. Still considered the granddaddy of the Hollywood novel about the inner workings of power within the industry, *What Makes Sammy Run?* has never made its way to the big screen, although it was adapted for television, first in 1949 as an hour version by Paddy Chayefsky and then as a full-scale treatment in 1959 by Schulberg and his brother Stuart. A few years later the pair wrote the book of a musical version for Broadway. Schulberg's novel found a large readership when first published, but the studios considered it too anti-Hollywood, possibly too pro-union, and definitely if mistakenly too anti-Semitic for filming because of its unsympathetic Jewish main character.

According to Schulberg, in 1950 MGM tested the waters, but he mistrusted the studio's intent to make a faithful adaptation of *What Makes Sammy Run?* When a deal stalled, MGM produced *The Bad and the Beautiful* (1952) instead, which Schulberg saw as "kind of a rip-off," as if the men at Metro "definitely got together and said, 'Well, screw him if he doesn't want to do it, we'll do our own Sammy'" (Melton 1998). With its allusions to their lives and careers *The Bad and the Beautiful* draws on David O. Selznick and Orson Welles as sources for the main character, producer Jonathan Shields (Kirk Douglas) (Harvey 1989, 211; Naremore 1993, 118; Sklar 2012, 81). However, as Schulberg suspects, the character seems to have been equally inspired by his novel's Sammy Glick.

It probably always went without saying that MGM's stylish treatment of a Hollywood heel would turn out to be more romanticized than *What Makes Sammy Run?* The narrative of *The Bad and the Beautiful* covers the eighteen years in which Jonathan, himself the son of a disgraced and much reviled motion picture mogul, becomes an acclaimed independent producer with his own studio, Shields Pictures Inc. In the wake of his success he leaves behind three protégés—director Fred Amiel (Barry Sullivan), star Georgia Lorrison (Lana Turner), and writer James Lee Bartlow (Dick Powell)—whose careers he mentored. In the present day, however, due to his hubris the studio is bankrupt and Jonathan himself cannot raise a dime on his own signature. Through his business manager, Harry Pebbel (Walter Pidgeon), he now hopes to inspire these three bankable names to join him on his comeback film, although each has vowed never to work again on a Shields picture. (▶ Figure 5.1)

Jonathan's career is recounted in three long flashback sequences, as Fred, Georgia, and James Lee recall in succession how he drew them in with his passion for filmmaking, only to end their close professional relation with a shocking betrayal of their trust. After learning his craft on B movies alongside Fred, Jonathan successfully pitches Fred's dream project to producer Pebbel, then Jonathan's employer, but replaces his friend with a more experienced director. (▶ Figure 5.2) After taking a chance on Georgia because of her undeniable screen presence, Jonathan exploits her infatuation with him to get the performance he wants but rejects her on the night of her film's premiere. After hiring James Lee to adapt his historical novel for the screen but finding Rosemary Bartlow (Gloria Graham) a distraction, Jonathan secretly arranges for Latin film star "Gaucho" Ribero (Gilbert Roland) to romance her, freeing the writer to focus on his work, but the adulterous couple die in a plane crash while en route to Mexico. After each flashback, Pebbel points out how Jonathan had sold them out for their own good. Having had to stand on his own two feet, Fred is now a distinguished, Oscar-winning director. Having had to overcome her dependence first on her late father and then on Jonathan, Georgia is now one of Hollywood's biggest stars. Having been freed of a confining domestic relationship, James Lee is now a successful screenwriter and author of a much lauded, Pulitzer Prize–winning novel based on his late wife, whom he did not really know while she lived.

What Pebbel points out is indisputable insofar as all three figures have achieved career heights since becoming independent of Jonathan. But does their success redeem Jonathan's abusive treatment? As the flashbacks progress his betrayals get crueler, more selfish, and less morally justifiable. In terms of the human cost, there is considerable difference between Jonathan's deciding that Fred is too inexperienced a director for a big-budget, A-list picture that will make or break his own career and Jonathan's callously arranging, however indirectly, an affair between Rosemary and Gaucho just so James Lee can finish a screenplay.

Discouraging any suspicion that Jonathan may be of the same amoral bent as the opportunistic Sammy Glick, the thread connecting the flashbacks and apparently redeeming his behavior is Jonathan's charisma as a producer. Sammy has no talent or imagination of his own when it comes to filmmaking, but he has a keen sense of how to get credit for the work of others, just as he gets mileage from his own mediocrity, as when he sells a treatment for a "sarong picture" by asking friends for a synopsis of *Rain* and reversing the plot to feature a female missionary and a male racketeer. By contrast, the European director Von Ellstein, who replaces Fred on "The Faraway Mountain," praises Jonathan's screenplay for being "a script prepared by a producer who thinks like a director." Afterward, as success piles upon success, "the Shields Touch" accounts for the shelf of Oscars in Jonathan's office and the placement of "two or three of his [films]" on every list of the ten best pictures ever made, says Pebbel.

Whereas Sammy Glick climbs over people in his race to the top and displays little evidence of his own creativity or much interest in filmmaking as an artistic process, what makes Jonathan Shields run, and run *over* those closest to him, is his cinematic imagination. In his rather conventional statements about the effect of lighting or subtle use of a prop or value of a silent close-up, Jonathan speaks what is instantly recognizable to everyone watching as "the language of cinema." He is a great producer because he inspires and instructs. Thus he is shown working closely with Fred in executing and elevating a B horror picture, with Georgia in guiding her line readings, and with James Lee in editing his screenplay. (⏵ Figure 5.3) For much the same reason, Jonathan's one fit of hubris occurs when he steps out of the producer's role. After quarreling with Van Ellstein and disrespecting the director's expertise, Jonathan takes over "The Proud Land," the adaptation of James Lee's novel that has brought the writer to Hollywood, but he makes a terrible picture with "no timing, no pace, nothing," just as the fired director had cautioned him against doing. Though in hock to the banks and against Pebbel's advice, Jonathan refuses to release "a picture of mine that I know is bad."

Jonathan's artistic integrity means to trump any lack of emotional or personal integrity on his part because his passion for making a movie, not his opportunism or cruelty, justifies his hurtful actions. "When he was in love with a scene money meant nothing to him," Georgia recalls. "Fatigue even less, his or anyone else's. We did it over and over until we could hardly stand." The excitement Jonathan feels on set becomes palpable enough for others to experience it alongside him. Director Vincente Minnelli distinguishes *The Bad and the Beautiful* by the specificity with which he himself films filmmaking to render his characters' sense of "experience[ing] moments of unalienated labor and liberating, imaginative play" (Naremore 1993, 126). What draws these three protégés to Jonathan, then, is the man's ability to personify for each how filmmaking can be a utopian experience. (▶ Figure 5.4)

Still, the condition enabling a utopian experience of filmmaking is another form of alienation since Hollywood in *The Bad and the Beautiful* is a hermetically sealed world where friends or lovers matter only as collaborators, their lives mirror their art, and the act of making a movie together substitutes for any form of intimacy that goes beyond professional collaboration. Jonathan declares to Fred, "When I work on a picture it's like romancing a girl. You see her. You want her. You go after her. The Big Moment. Then the letdown. Every time, every picture. The after-picture blues." His speech draws out the equivalence of his creativity and his heterosexuality, especially as Fred replies, "Don't worry. Some day you'll learn to love 'em, leave 'em." The sexual metaphor invests Jonathan's passion for making a movie with his libidinal energy, indicating that producing makes him feel alive with an excitement akin to heterosexual desire, but at the same time it underscores an emotional void, his failure to experience desire except when making a picture.

Jonathan's rejection of Georgia is another expression of "the after-picture blues." He tries to explain to her, "I need to be alone tonight. After a picture is finished something happens to me. A feeling of letdown, of emptiness." As Georgia pleads with her erstwhile lover not to shut her out, Lila's (Elaine Stewart) revelation of her presence in Jonathan's mansion is signaled by a shadow falling across Georgia's face. Jonathan's aggression at this point seems crueler and more self-serving than necessary, as he screams, "Who gave you the right to dig into me and turn me outside and decide what I'm like?" Furiously adding that Georgia has no right to know how he feels about her, and comparing intimacy to being owned, he grabs her by the shoulders and forcefully throws her out of his house, resulting in her breakdown as she drives away, a scene discussed in chapter 4. (▶ Figure 5.5)

Jonathan's professional collaboration with his two male protégés differs considerably from his handling of Georgia and the brutality with which he ends their professional and personal relationship. As Christopher Ames observes, "In the world of Jonathan Shields, real affection is built in masculine relationships within the industry; women threaten the ultimate goal of getting the Shields name on a great picture" (Ames 1997, 161). Jonathan showers paternal attention on Fred to start with: he gives the tongue-tied director confidence to express his creative ideas, and he has to tell Fred to propose to his girlfriend, Kay, even supplying the ring to use on the occasion. Nonetheless the scenes in

154 | Hollywood by Hollywood

which they work together, learning their craft on B pictures, show the two men on equal footing, enjoying and excited by the give-and-take of collaboration.

James Lee, on the other hand, arrives in Hollywood impervious to Jonathan's charm, but the producer beats back that hostility and the two develop a collaborative partnership that similarly displays great warmth and companionship. Given the close bond that develops, it is not surprising that, however hypocritically, Jonathan helps the writer get through his grief after Rosemary's death. Likewise, when he sees how dejected his friend is after the decision to shelve "The Proud Land," James Lee invites Jonathan to accompany him to Lake Tahoe. This is the moment when Jonathan, his spirit revived by his friendship with James Lee, lets slip that he had known about Gaucho and Rosemary all along. "Whether you like it or not, you're better off," Jonathan declares. "She was a fool. She got in your way. She wasted your time. She wasted you. You're better off without her." These words are not only harsh and unfeeling; they're presumptuous in their rationalization of his god-like interference in James Lee's marriage, which disturbingly rhymes with Jonathan's earlier masterminding of Fred and Kay's engagement. Certainly the contempt for Rosemary that Jonathan spews reiterates his fear that women possess men by getting inside their heads and discovering what they are really like. However, the cruelty of his speech betrays what may be inarticulate jealously on Jonathan's part; after all, he had arranged for Gaucho to squire Rosemary around so that he and James Lee could be alone to work full time on their script and without the hindrance of a woman.

And then there is Syd Murphy (Paul Stewart). An enigmatic figure, Syd first shows up, nameless and unaccounted for, as Jonathan's companion when the pair attends a Hollywood party with Fred and Kay. A short while later, to explain why he happens to have an engagement ring in his pocket for Fred to use, Jonathan mutters, "Syd Murphy knows a friend who knows a jeweler." At the sneak preview of "Doom of the Cat Men," Syd reviews the audience response cards with Pebbel. Though his job is not yet specified, Syd then sits with Jonathan to evaluate screen tests for the lead of "The Faraway Mountain," and that evening he accompanies Jonathan and Fred to a nightclub as they attempt to lure Gaucho with women and liquor into accepting the part. By the time of Georgia's flashback, Syd has moved on to Shields productions just as Pebbel has done. Syd, like Pebbel, advises Jonathan not to sign Georgia and then has the thankless task of searching for her when she fails to show up on the first day of shooting. In James Lee's flashback, Syd puts the Bartlows up in the Beverly Hills Hotel. His occupation as a press agent is finally revealed when Syd protects James Lee from reporters at the crash site after Gaucho's plane goes down. And Jonathan learns that when his company's funds and credit dried up, Syd and Pebbel used their own funds to keep "The Proud Land" going during its final week of production. (⏵ Figure 5.6)

James Naremore proposes that the actor playing Syd, Paul Stewart, "in a minor but memorable role," is one of the many allusions to *Citizen Kane*, in which Stewart played the publisher's major domo at Xanadu (Naremore 1993, 118). I think the character's recurring yet never fully explained presence, which begins when he accompanies Jonathan to that

Hollywood party, may also be resonant with just how densely *The Bad and the Beautiful* imagines the creative energy driving filmmaking as an expression of homosocial masculinity. Jonathan sublimates his heterosexuality in his creativity—hence the equivalence drawn between his "after-picture blues" and postcoital letdown—but while sublimated, the creativity exceeds its psychosexual origin in the aesthetic pleasure it yields and the male companionships it offers him. Such a depiction of cinematic creativity as a heteromasculine activity of a homosocial man has the added effect of psychologizing the contradiction Jonathan embodies as a filmmaker in Hollywood, namely, "that the qualities that make him a great producer also make him a 'bad' or 'evil' man" (Ames 1997, 152).

The Bad and the Beautiful leaves it up to the viewer to decide if that contradiction implicates the institution in the "dehumanization and disloyalty" that success requires (Ames 1997, 152) or if a critique of Hollywood is confined to Jonathan alone because the three narrators have thriving careers with their scruples apparently intact (Sklar 2012, 83). The three narrators blame the person, but that man himself is also Jonathan Shields Inc. An inability to disaggregate the person from the business is made evident at the beginning, when Georgia draws the disfiguring moustache on the Shields logo at the entrance to the company's corporate offices, imitating what Jonathan does in her flashback to the face of her father on a caricature hanging in her studio apartment. (▶ Figure 5.7) Moreover the individual always defending Jonathan and worrying about the company's balance sheets is the man most identified with Hollywood as a business, Harry Pebbel, whose motto would otherwise appear to be the antithesis of Jonathan's aesthetic goal in making movies: "Give me pictures that end with a kiss and black ink on the books."

Pebbel's goal is also the mantra of the world of *The Player* (1992). By now it is practically a truism that this backstudio is a satiric indictment of late twentieth-century Hollywood's amorality and, worse, its lack of creativity and artistic courage. As Jack Boozer points out, the long-take opening sequence "announces the film as a reflective commentary on the entire world of Hollywood studio existence rather than merely a focus on one producer and the uncertainty of his position" (Boozer 2013, 79). But this is also to say that Griffin Mill (Tim Robbins) personifies the "Hollywood studio existence." The anonymous postcard addressed to Griffin by a disgruntled writer announcing the death of "Your Hollywood" begins the narrative action, which recounts Griffin's effort to discover the identity of the sender, his causing and then covering up the death of David Kahane (Vincent D'Onofrio), his surveillance by the police, and his ultimate if unjustified vindication by the ministrations of the studio's head of security and its lawyer.

As a Hollywood player, Griffin is neither crazy about making movies nor interested in what lies outside the Hollywood bubble; all he cares about is the status his position brings him as a power broker. As he explains to June Gudmundsdottir (Greta Scacchi), who was living with Kahane, "I listen to stories and decide if they'll make good movies or not. I get a hundred twenty-five phone calls a day, and if I let that slip to a hundred I know I'm not doing my job.... The problem is I can only say yes, my studio can only say yes, twelve times a year. And collectively we have about fifty thousand stories a year, so it's hard. And I guess sometimes I'm not nice and make enemies." Griffin reduces his role in crafting his studio's product to his greenlighting a dozen projects annually, just as the pitches he hears condenses the classic Hollywood narrative form to the mashed-up concepts tossed out to him during his brief meetings with writers in late twentieth-century Hollywood's version of speed dating. What Griffin looks for, he explains to June, are the "certain elements" that David Kahane's script lacked, namely, "suspense, laughter, violence, hope, nudity, sex, happy endings. Mainly happy endings." But "what about reality?" June asks in reply, and Griffin changes the subject.

At the close of *The Player*, Griffin has achieved everything he wants: he gets away with killing Kahane, becomes the studio head over his rival, Larry Levy (Peter Gallagher), and has his Hollywood ending with June, who is pregnant with his child. If the studio era of Shields Inc. was about manufacturing dreams and glamour while making good pictures, by the time of *The Player* the film industry had repudiated the edginess of New Hollywood and was content with "pictures that end with a kiss and black ink on the books," as the revision of "Habeas Corpus" illustrates. The director, Tom Oakley (Richard E. Grant), initially wanted a downbeat conclusion and a cast without stars. His film was going to be "an American tragedy in which an innocent woman dies. Because that's reality." He therefore demanded "no Hollywood ending," for the heroine had to be executed for a crime she did not commit. However, the version ultimately screened for the studio's executives stars real-life Bruce Willis and Julia Roberts, and the former saves the latter from her execution at the last minute. "What about truth? What about reality?" asks Bonnie Sherow (Cynthia Stevenson) after the screening, repeating June's earlier question to Griffin. "What about the way the old ending tested in Canoga Park? Everybody hated it," responds the director. "We reshot it and now everybody loves it. *That's* reality." Because she complained, Bonnie, who was Griffin's assistant and his lover until June came into the picture, is made Hollywood's scapegoat and loses her job.

As a producer, Griffin's behavior with his creatives is much like that of micromanagers Barry Diller and Michael Eisner at Paramount in the early 1980s. These two men were "notorious for micromanaging writers with notes and memos. Executives would agree on script notes before a meeting, presenting a united front and giving writers little option but to accept most of the notes if they wanted to stay on projects" (Hoxter 2014, 107). The ending of *The Player* reverses the earlier scene when Griffin, thinking he is setting up his rival Larry Levy to take the fall for a bad idea, has him listen on a car phone to the pitch for the original "Habeas Corpus." Now Griffin is driving home when Larry transfers a call to his car phone. It turns out that Griffin created the happy ending for "Habeas Corpus." This is somewhat unexpected news insofar as his original scheme was to trick Larry into buying the script with the downbeat ending in order to discredit his rival's judgment. But once Griffin became head of the studio, Larry is no longer a threat and the new ending "worked like gangbusters," as Larry tells him. "That's why you get the big bucks."

More ominously, the purpose of the call is for Griffin to hear a pitch, which Larry thinks is hot, "a winner." Joining Larry on a speaker phone, an unnamed writer alludes to the threatening postcards he has been sending Griffin and then makes his pitch, which, in summarizing the plot of *The Player*, functions as a veiled threat. "It's a Hollywood story, Griff, a real thriller," the writer states. His story is about a "shitbag producer studio exec" who kills a writer he thinks has been harassing him, but it turns out he killed the wrong writer and now has to deal with blackmail and the cops. "But here's the switch. The son of a bitch, he gets away with it." Realizing the deal being extorted from him, Griffin asks for a guarantee of how the writer's new story will end: "He gets away with it?" "Absolutely," the writer replies. "It's a Hollywood ending, Griffin." Griffin makes the deal, of course, and asks for the title. The pitched movie is called "The Player." This filmmaker narrative therefore concludes on an ironically self-reflexive note, with the anonymous writer pitching a script that we have in effect just watched. There is no outside to the inside, diegetically or extrafilmically. (⊙ Figures 5.8–5.9)

What Just Happened (2008) is in many respects an update of both *The Bad and the Beautiful* and *The Player* for twentieth-first-century conglomerate Hollywood. If Jonathan Shields has "the touch" guiding his director, actress, and writer to their Oscars, and Griffin Mill approves a dozen pitches annually and gets his Hollywood ending by playing the game just right, then in *What Just Happened* we see a producer whose objective is simply to get the film in the can. The framing device for this backstudio is a *Vanity Fair* photo shoot of "the thirty most powerful producers in the business," where, pushed to the far left side of the P in the block letters P-O-W-E-R, Ben (Robert De Niro) reflects how, during the past two weeks, "my power credentials were on the line." "Power is an elusive term," he states in voice-over, "but in Hollywood it's everything. I don't care what they say. You either have it, want it, or are afraid of losing it."

Ben is the kind of producer characteristic of present-day Hollywood. "Producers in this era are no longer industry players per se, but talented middle men who view movie production as just one iteration (one format, one aspect) in a complex engagement and agreement struck between media conglomerates and their subsidiaries and partners in parallel industries in the United States and overseas" (Lewis 2016, 6). During the two-week period covered by *What Just Happened* Ben's power as a Hollywood producer is

The "thirty most powerful producers in the business" posing for a *Vanity Fair* cover. (*What Just Happened* ©2009 Magnolia)

tested and shown to be lacking on several fronts simultaneously: by his infantile auteur director, Jeremy Brunell (Michael Wincott), who delivers an edgy stinker starring Sean Penn; by a spoiled Bruce Willis, Ben's star on his next project, who stubbornly refuses to shave his Grizzly Adams beard or lose the weight he has gained; by Willis's neurotic, dyspeptic agent, Dick Bell (John Turturro), who is afraid to confront his client; and by a mild-mannered but persistent screenwriter, Scott Solomon (Stanley Tucci), who Ben believes is having an affair with his ex-wife, Kelly (Robin Wright Penn) but who has a script about a florist with Brad Pitt attached to it that he wants Ben to produce. Most of all, Ben has to cater to the wishes of studio heads like Lou Tarnow (Catherine Keener). "If the preview cards stink," Ben states in voice-over during the preview of Jeremy's "Fiercely," which begins the two-week period of his narrative, "let's just say many people will suffer. She'll make sure of it."

"Fiercely" tests poorly at the preview in Costa Mesa because of Jeremy's ending. Not only does the leading man die, but his faithful dog is shot in the head, an action that was not in the script and that causes the audience uniformly to gasp in shock and disbelief as it happens. At the conference in her office the day after the preview, Lou says she already knows they are going to lose money, "a lot of money," so she wants Ben and his director to recut the film and eliminate the dog's shooting. Ben stands there passively, agreeing with Lou while trying to mollify his angry director. "Do the right thing," she instructs Jeremy, or she will cancel his "big evening in Cannes," where *Fiercely* is set to premiere, and will cut the movie herself. Jeremy, however, continues to insist, "The dog dies!" He then has a tantrum, kicking and punching the table in front of him and causing candies to spill all over the floor. Ben asserts that Jeremy will come around. "I'll take care of it," he promises Lou. As the director leaves, sobbing like a child, a close-up shows his feet crunching the candy he had spilled. The next day, with the help of three Vicodins and a bottle of whiskey, a sedated Jeremy capitulates and the dog lives. However, at Cannes, where Lou offers Ben a ride back to LA on the company jet, Jeremy substitutes the original cut, the audience reacts much as they did at Costa Mesa, and Lou's plane takes off without Ben. (▶ Figure 5.10)

If *What Just Happened* appears to be riffing on *The Player* with its fictional director who, unlike that earlier film's Tom Oakley, refuses to capitulate to Hollywood yet acts self-righteously and childishly, it also seems to be doing so with its use of Bruce Willis, who plays himself in both films. In *The Player* Willis is the muscular leading man who, in the revised conclusion of "Habeas Corpus," at the very last minute rescues an unjustly convicted Julia Roberts from the gas chamber. By contrast, in *What Just Happened* Willis has tantrums much like Jeremy's. He throws down carts of costumes and screams about his "fucking artistic integrity" as his reason for not shaving his full bushy beard. When Ben boasts that he will compare his last three pictures against his star's last three, Willis replies, "You don't have any pictures. You know why? You're a fucking producer." Nonetheless the studio head on this project, an unseen Sidney Voss, tells Ben on the phone, "I'm not Lou. I like to be direct." He threatens not only to shut the movie down but to sue Willis for damages and Ben for misrepresentation. In this cat-and-mouse game, the petulant star keeps Ben dangling until the last minute. As the crew, director, and Voss's assistant (along with his assistant) wait with Ben to see if the picture is a go or not, Willis takes his time coming out of his trailer. After the usually soft-spoken Ben screams, "Come on!," the star appears in the doorway in profile, fully bearded and smoking a cigar, causing momentary consternation; but when Willis turns to face his audience, they see that he has shaved half his face. "Hey, how 'bout we get this fucker on the road, huh?" Willis playfully asks. (▶ Figure 5.11)

As Ben and Voss's assistant wait to see if "the status is quo" regarding Willis's beard, the assistant mutters, "They say, you know, we're measured by how we handle adversity," and Ben stops him short, declaring of his teasing, "You're going to have to stop it!" Ben's third challenge during this two-week period confirms that old adage. The stresses of his domestic life further test his masculinity, making more vivid his emasculation as a producer at the hands of the industry. All the while dealing with Willis's stubbornness and getting Jeremy to agree to an approved cut of "Fiercely," Ben's personal life is spinning out of control yet he does not seem fully to realize his alienation from his family. His two ex-wives each inhabit spacious, well-appointed houses while he lives in an apartment. Although he drives his children to school, he does not know them very well. For instance, Zoe (Kristin Stewart), his underage daughter by his first wife, has been having an affair with the much older screenwriter Jack McDonagh, whose suicide occurs early in the film.

As important, although divorced from his second wife, Kelly, for eighteen months and attending reverse couple therapy together ("how to let go"), Ben just cannot let go. After they have sex—a holiday from their therapy that causes Kelly finally to be entirely fed up because he interrupts their lovemaking to take a business call about Willis—he finds a man's argyle sock in her bedroom. Deducing it is Scott Solomon's simply because the latter wears argyle socks, he spies on Kelly, twice witnessing someone resembling her having a tryst, although he cannot make out facial details. When he later asks her point blank if someone else has been sleeping in their bed, Kelly angrily tells him that he has lost the privilege of asking that question and that he needs to get help. In retaliation, Ben lets himself be picked up by an aggressive young woman who announces her interest when she follows him into the men's room while the two are at a meeting with Israeli investors. The next morning we learn that the couple had taken ecstasy and had sex. After the woman departs, Ben exercises furiously and colors the gray on his head, beard, and chest to look younger. (▶ Figure 5.12)

Ben's personal and professional turmoil comes to a head the next day at Jack's funeral. There Ben finds out about Zoe's affair with the dead man and overhears men gossiping about Jack's taste for young girls, and Willis, looking "even thicker and harrier than yesterday," delivers a eulogy that self-consciously mocks Hollywood. Taking a Klonopin from Dick Bell, Ben has a momentary fantasy outburst: Scott is talking to him about his screenplay while Ben thinks he is negotiating with him about Kelly. Outraged, Ben pushes the writer's head through the window of a limousine and smothers him. Then, just as suddenly, the two men are back to conversing about the florist script. At the gravesite Ben stands next to Willis, each taunting the other as they toss dirt onto the casket. Ben then hits Dick in the groin, causing the agent to fall on top of the casket, as Willis watches and then walks away.

The film's title asks "What just happened?" because in the two weeks covered by the narrative Ben goes from being promised by *Vanity Fair* that he would stand by the O and the W to his ultimate placement "inches away from being completely out of the business." The bigger question, though, is "*How* did that happen?" How did an apparently successful producer like Ben lose his position in Hollywood? (▶ Figure 5.13)

Ben's emasculation is no delusion on his part, nor does it result from those failures in his private life; the personal failures register rather than cause his paralysis when confronting the actor, director, and studio head. In Lou's office, Ben sees a poster with the image of an animal's orange eye and the dollar amount of $810,000,00. "In the end," he comments to Jeremy, "no director, no stars, not even a title, just a number, a big number." (▶ Figure 5.14) According to this film, twentieth-first-century Hollywood is now simply about money; controlling the numbers translates to who has power and who does not. In conglomerate Hollywood a producer like Ben may juggle several projects at once, with one finishing as another starts up, but while he may arrange the financing he is the portal for other people's money—like that of Johnny the Israeli dry-cleaner who helped to finance "Fiercely" and walks the red carpet at Cannes with sixteen-year-old twins. The producer in *What Just Happened* is simply a manager of people, smoothing ruffled feathers and making sure that everyone on set, in the editing room, and in Lou's office is happy. He is subject to the whims of a childish director and actor and to the authority of a female studio head and the independence of his ex-wives and teenage daughter. What kind of power does that give him in Hollywood? "You're just a producer," Willis shouts at Ben at the funeral. "You're just the fucking mayonnaise in a bad sandwich." Touché.

The Writer

During the studio era, "and I am talking about the late thirties, forties, into the fifties, the producer was much more important, particularly at some studios, than the director," the screenwriter Daniel Taradash has stated. "The writer, of course, except occasionally, was not as important as either of them" (qtd. in Banks 2015, 161). Reflecting the emergence of superstar writers decades later, in *The Player* Larry Levy speculates at a meeting of the firm's executives that they might do away with writers altogether. He says, "I've yet to meet a writer who can change water into wine, and we have a tendency to treat them like that.... A million, a million and a half for these scripts. It's nuts." After a short pause, he adds, "And I think avoidable." He proposes instead, "A lot of time and money is to be saved if we came up with these stories on our own." For an example, he tells people at the conference table to pick a story from the newspaper. After one man reads the headline "Immigrants Protest Budget Cuts in Literacy Program," Larry pitches it as "Human spirit overcoming economic adversity. Sounds like Horatio Alger in the barrio. Put Jimmy Smits in it and you've got a sexy *Stand and Deliver*." After another reads "Mudslide Kills Sixty in Slums of Chile," Larry turns it into "Triumph over tragedy. Sounds like a John Boorman picture. You slap a happy ending on it and the script will write itself."

To be sure, as already implied by Taradash's comments, until the relatively new Screen Writers Guild secured its first contract with the studios, which was signed in 1941, according to industry logic films *did* seem to write themselves. Producers decided on who was put to work on a given film, could change writers at any stage of the scripting process, and determined which ones received credit on the finished product; oftentimes writers did not know if they were being credited until they saw the movie in a theater. Moreover writers were salaried employees, not the credited "authors" of what they wrote; copyright of films belonged to the studios, and scripters did not receive royalties, a fact that allowed them to unionize in the mid-1930s but that also cast a shadow on their occupation as far as the industry was concerned. Today the possessory credit ("a film by" or a name with an apostrophe *s*) still belongs to directors for the most part (Banks 2015, 27–65, 160–65).

As for fictional representations of the screenwriter, Lucy Fischer observes, "Almost always, the scenarist is male—and either a cad, a neurotic, a miscreant, or a womanizer (and sometimes all five) who is generally cynical about his profession" (Fischer 2013, 60). Her comment certainly applies to the character of Joe Gillis (William Holden) in Billy Wilder's *Sunset Boulevard* (1950).

Given that he is little more than a broke and unemployed Hollywood hack who willingly becomes an older woman's lover, *Sunset Boulevard* makes an effort to redeem Joe through his collaboration with Betty Schaefer (Nancy Olsen) on a script. Their collaboration takes some doing, however. In one of the first scenes of the film Joe pitches generic stories at Paramount to Sheldrake (Fred Clark), including a baseball plot that the producer for a moment thinks might be transformed into a Betty Hutton vehicle. (⏵ Figure 5.15) Feeling guilty for trashing Joe's script to Sheldrake, Betty later looks through the writer's rejected output and retrieves a six-page flashback about schoolteachers from "Dark Windows," a trial picture. She initially pitches the idea of making the flashback a script of its own to Joe at her fiancé Artie's New Year's Eve party. In a moment of candor Joe reveals that he had a teacher like that once. "Maybe that's why it's good," Betty replies. "It's true. It's moving." Her response causes Joe to ask sharply, "Who wants true? Who wants moving?" She tells him to drop that attitude because "here is something truly worthwhile." He defensively causes their conversation to become a parody of imperial romances, but learning of Norma's attempted suicide when he calls her house, Joe departs from the party in a rush, leaving Betty bewildered. (⏵ Figure 5.16)

They run into each other again at Schwab's drug store when Joe goes to fetch cigarettes for Norma. This time Betty tells Joe that she has half-sold Sheldrake on the idea for a script about schoolteachers by bluffing; with twenty pages of notes, she wants to work out the story with him. Joe declines, saying he has given up writing on spec, adding, "As a matter of fact, I've given up writing altogether." Somewhat ironically Joe thanks Betty for her interest in his career, and she reveals that it is *her* career too she is interested in. "I kinda hoped to get in on this deal," she admits, declaring her intention of becoming a writer by working with him.

At Paramount, while waiting for Norma, who has gone there to meet DeMille, Joe sees Betty and follows her to her cubicle. He invites her to use anything she wants from his trial script, and she confesses, "I'm not good enough to do it all by myself." When asked about the ideas she had, Betty advises him to "throw out all that psychological mess, exploring a killer's sick mind." Although Joe states his belief that "psychopaths sell like hotcakes," she counters with a more realistic angle. "This is a story about teachers," Betty explains, "their threadbare lives. Their struggles. Here are people doing the most important job in the world, and they have to worry about getting enough money to resole their shoes. To me it can be as exciting as any chase, any gunplay."

Betty implores Joe to work with her on this story, but he still refuses. Yet her new take on his old story "kept going through [his] head like a dozen locomotives," he states in voice-over, so he ultimately does begin sneaking out every evening to work with her on the script in her cubicle on the Paramount lot. Their collaboration proceeds apace, and he admits, "It's fun writing with you," as they work together on their "untitled love story"— until they fall in love. (▶ Figure 5.17) In voice-over Joe assesses his duplicity with her, that he is a heel and she a fool for not suspecting "there was something phony in my setup"; yet he also wonders, "Maybe I can get away with it, get away from Norma. Maybe I could wipe the whole nasty mess right out of my life." As Joe enters the mansion following this voice-over statement, Norma is telephoning Betty to inform her about the kind of man Joe really is, and he takes the phone to tell Betty to come out and see for herself. Once there, Betty tries to get Joe to leave with her, but he forces her to see his "setup" for what it is: "Older woman who's well-to-do. Younger man who's not doing too well." Betty refuses to listen, so Joe sends her, along with their nearly completed script, back to Artie with the intent of returning to his dull newspaper job in Dayton, Ohio. His sentimentality in giving up Betty notwithstanding, it is Norma who ruins Joe's chance of "maybe" getting away from his "phony" setup to be with Betty: Norma makes the phone call, which forces Joe's hand, and then she shoots him to prevent his leaving her.

In many respects, Joe never overcomes his hack instincts, which automatically go for what he thinks will "sell like hotcakes," although his writing turns out to be too formulaic, just as it apparently arrives too late to catch a trend. As Alan Nadel points out, Joe pitches his script's "generic qualities" to Sheldrake in that early scene, saying little about its "actual content" (Nadel 2017, 72), just as he turns to dialogue from the imperial romance genre when conversing with Betty at the New Year's Eve party, demonstrating the ease with which they know how to speak in Hollywood clichés (70). By the same token, for all the originality of *Sunset Boulevard* itself, Joe's life and death could have been the basis of one of those generic scripts he churns out from hunger—certainly his relationship with Norma and her eventual trial will be more like the story about the trial of the psychopath that Betty rejects; it will be nothing like the "untitled love story" the pair has been writing. Betty's comments about their script indicate that she envisions a more realistic drama that goes against the grain of standard movie genres to be "truly worthwhile"; what is more, she thinks the combination of the "important job" of teaching and the teachers' dire need for money can be just "as exciting as any chase, any gunplay" in a western or crime plot.

Is it just coincidence, then, that the extended flashback of *Sunset Boulevard* pretty much opens with a chase as the repo men spot Joe and pursue him, and ends with gunplay when Norma shoots Joe? By contrast, Joe's collaboration with Betty is the utopian moment of *Sunset Boulevard* that lets him regress to his feelings of childhood escapism through the movies. "It made me think of when I was twelve and used to sneak out on the folks to see a gangster picture," he remembers. "This time it wasn't to see a picture. It was to try and write one." What gives writing with Betty its utopian spin is that she pushes him to craft something "moving" and "true," and *that* is the pleasure we see him experience as the antithesis of being Norma's consort.

Sunset Boulevard depicts the screenwriter excitedly at work, with Joe and Betty collaborating at night on the deserted Paramount studio lot. But Wilder's backstudio also makes this activity secondary to the star narrative of Norma Desmond and its noir plotting of Joe's demise once caught in that spider woman's web. *The Muse* (1999) and *Adaptation* (2002), two millennial filmmaker narratives that return the backstudio genre's attention to the scripting process, focus not only on the independent screenwriter but also and more specifically on his writer's block.

In *The Muse*, Steven Phillips (Albert Brooks) does not know he is blocked until his producer and agent tell him that he has lost his "edge" and may be past his prime. An ordinary enough middle-aged man, Steven lives with his wife, Laura (Andie MacDowell), and their two daughters in Pacific Palisades, west of Hollywood, so he is understandably worried when Josh Martin (Mark Feuerstein) at Paramount not only rejects his latest script for an action movie but also cancels his three-picture deal. His best friend, Jack (Jeff Bridges), another screenwriter but who is much more successful, finally relents and tells Steven his secret: he uses a real-life muse, who goes by the name of Sarah Little (Sharon Stone). "They still exist," Jack assures Steven. "If you're lucky enough to be with her, you write better than you've ever written in your whole life." When Steven inquires about the process of collaboration, Jack informs him, "She doesn't actually write; she inspires."

The muse inspires while filmmakers shower her with expensive gifts and her newest client picks up the tab for all her expenses. "You need to think of this as an investment," Sarah advises Steven when he balks at the cost of renting her a top-floor suite in the ritzy Four Seasons Hotel and complains about being at her beck and call all hours of the day or night. "Inspiration can take a week to six months. It depends on you." Eventually Sarah moves into Steven's house, first displacing him from his office and then taking over the master bedroom. At the same time, as she inspires Laura to go into the cookie business, Sarah's interest in his wife's newfound career pushes Steven and his screenplay to the sidelines. Additionally, as Jack and other filmmakers, including the real-life Martin Scorsese and James Cameron, arrive at his home to consult Sarah, Steven has even greater difficulty getting her alone to benefit from her inspiration. (⏵ Figure 5.18)

The Muse discloses toward the end that the self-indulgent, childish, manipulative, and mercurial Sarah suffers from multiple personalities, that without her drugs she tends to act out, and that she has a history of escaping from the Briarton Institute in Ohio. "But the muse part is correct, yes?" Steven asks the doctor and nurse who have tracked Sarah to his house. "This is Hollywood," the nurse replies. "People here believe anything." But Sarah in fact *does* inspire Steven to write something different, a big summer comedy with Jim Carrey inheriting an aquarium. This happens when Sarah takes him to the Aquarium of the Pacific in Long Beach, where he gets the idea for his comedy after the two run into Rob Reiner, who thanks the muse for his recent hit. Later on, when Steven complains that he is stuck for his third act, Sarah, preoccupied with Laura and other clients, suggests he return alone to the aquarium; not knowing why, he goes anyway and, after he learns that a show has been canceled due to the illness of a sea lion, realizes how to end his film— with sick fish. (⏵ Figure 5.19)

His agent thinks the new script is hysterical, the best Steven has written, but when he returns to Paramount, Steven learns that it has been plagiarized; apparently the muse has also inspired Reiner to write "the same exact movie" for Carrey, and Universal is weeks away from shooting it. "The muse stole my idea," Steven complains as he hears the bad news, and Josh Martin thinks the writer has cracked from the strain of losing his edge. It's why writers don't live long, Josh explains. (⏵ Figure 5.20) Dejected because he is again without a studio deal for his script, in the film's conclusion Steven is working at his wife's new bakery, arguing with a child who wants more free samples, when his agent calls to tell him that Universal has pulled the plug on Reiner's script and Paramount is going ahead with Steven's. Arriving back at the Melrose lot, Steven learns that Josh has been fired and Christine, his successor, is a brunette double of Sarah in looks and personality (and perhaps the same woman?). "I just loved your script," she exclaims, as she leads him to a lunch that he will have to pay for because she left her purse at home. "Of course, it does have a few problems. That aquarium thing doesn't really work. But we'll fix that." (⏵ Figure 5.21)

The Muse offers a funny, whimsical, and original take on creativity and inspiration, on the writer's anxiety and insecurity in the Hollywood setting, and on the screenwriter's trade in crafting scripts for hire according to genre. Steven's scripts are anything but original, for they are consistent with the industry's commitment to genres as its means of churning out a standardized product. He sticks to writing what he knows the studios want to buy, as he himself states. In this respect, his instincts are like Joe Gillis's, although he has a more successful track record. Early in *The Muse*, at his first meeting with Josh, the executive tells Steven that his script is "flat," that "it feels like it's been done before." "It's an action movie," the writer replies. "It's been done a million times. But you guys keep making them, so here's a good one." At their second meeting, toward the end of the film, the talk has shifted to the "big summer comedy" genre. After calling his script "brilliant," Josh points out that it is also identical to Reiner's, which Steven cannot understand since, as he explains, he just wrote it. As well as blaming the muse for stealing his idea and giving it to Reiner, Steven tries to make Josh see how genres work. "I mean, there are lots of movies that feel like the same but they're not. Remember *Big*? You know, the Tom Hanks? Well, I mean, there were like nine of those but they were all different, so that's the case here. Remember one guy got high, and the other was small. And they all made money. And this one's gonna make money too." Ironically enough, when Universal puts the Reiner script in turnaround and Paramount greenlights Steven's, the new executive at Paramount—Sarah's double, remember—likes everything *but* the script's central and presumably original idea about the aquarium, which Reiner's shared and which she assures Steven is fixable.

All of this makes one wonder if writing for Hollywood can ever be truly inspired or original since the industry relies on genres, which good mainstream writers like Steven turn out, so all that changes from picture to picture within a genre are local details, such as the setting. Even the cast remains the same since these are star vehicles. Within this economy, the writer's work is still subject either to rejection by a studio executive like Josh or to interference by one like Christine—or to inspiration from a mercurial female like Sarah.

Adaptation ratchets up its take on the screenwriter and Hollywood's overreliance on genres to the nth degree. Charlie Kaufman (Nicholas Cage), a highly fictionalized version of the film's actual writer, cannot figure out how to lick the problem of adapting for the screen *The Orchid Thief* by Susan Orlean (Meryl Streep), a nonfiction book with no story and hence no filmic structure. Until its jolting last act *Adaptation* is simultaneously a meditation on adaptation as mutation with regard to evolution, human behavior, *and* turning a book into a film, and a self-reflexive series of fitfully false openings for Charlie's troubled screenplay. As we see on the screen what he describes in his head or writes, his prose and its imagery alternate with him or Orlean reading her contemplative passages on orchids in voice-over or with scenes involving her and the orchid thief, John Laroche (Chris Cooper), which happened in Florida three years prior to the film's present day.

Furthermore, in his self-conscious and self-deprecating voice-over, Charlie describes himself as fat, bald, pathetic, repulsive, and old; he says that he sweats too much and is a walking cliché. He masturbates to a fantasy of Orlean or the young woman who serves him pie in a coffee shop yet cannot express his feelings for the woman he is dating, Amelia (Cara Seymour). In counterpoint to this unflattering self-portrait is his identical twin brother, Donald (also Cage). Whereas Charlie is a furrow-browed intellectual, Donald is a wide-eyed lightweight. Whereas Charlie is asked to leave the soundstage of *Being John Malkovich* (1999), which he wrote, because he gets in the way of the camera's eyeline, Donald makes himself right at home, chatting with the craftspeople and eating off the craft table. Whereas Charlie is shy around women, Donald has no trouble hooking up with Caroline (Maggie Gyllenhaal) from the movie set or becoming friends with the real-life actress Catherine Keener. Whereas Charlie is a screenwriter with a career, Donald has a bad back and lives off his brother's beneficence. Whereas Charlie wants to do something original with his innovative, plotless script to express the wonder and beauty of flowers, Donald borrows the tuition from his brother in order to take Robert McKee's screenwriting seminar and apparently will be able to sell his harebrained script for a bundle.

Finally, when Charlie freaks at the thought of interviewing Susan Orlean, Donald stands in for him, doing the interview in New York City without embarrassing his brother (which was Charlie's worry). "I admire you, Donald, you know?" Charlie states late in the film. "I spent my whole life paralyzed, worrying about what people think of me, and you, you're just oblivious." Charlie means that as a compliment, but Donald takes umbrage. Charlie recalls his brother in high school when he seemed unmindful that a girl he loved would smile as he flirted but would make fun of him behind his back, yet it turns out that Donald was not oblivious and knew what she was doing all along. "It was mine, that love," Donald says. "I owned it." Her thinking he was pathetic "was her business, not mine," he continues. "You are what you love, not what loves you. That's what I decided a long time ago."

At his meeting with his producer, Valerie (Tilda Swinton), Charlie states his intent in adapting *The Orchid Thief*: "I just don't want to ruin it by making it a Hollywood thing.... I don't want to cram in sex or guns or car chases. You know? Or characters learning profound life lessons." However, while Charlie just wants to write "a movie simply about flowers," sex, guns, car chases, and life lessons like Donald's epiphany eventually and rather abruptly occur in *Adaptation* and hence will reappear in Charlie's script (and vice versa, given the film's layers of self-reflexivity; somewhat like *The Player*, we may be watching the filmization of his finished script as opposed to watching him actually struggle to write it, or we may be doing both simultaneously).

The turn in *Adaptation* to aggressively plotted action follows Charlie's decision to take McKee's seminar while in New York City. "He's all about originality, just like you," Donald says to his brother when describing what he has learned from the screenwriting course. "But he says we have to realize that we all write in a genre, and we must find our originality within that genre." Donald's own genre is the thriller. He has written a screenplay about a cop hunting a serial killer. Although the cop has never met the woman the killer has kidnapped, he falls in love with her. Since the killer has multiple personalities, all three characters are in reality the same person—that is the big twist of his screenplay. Besides calling the premise overused and clichéd, Charlie asks, "How could you have somebody held prisoner in a basement and working in a police station at the same time?" Not understanding why that would be a problem, Donald blankly replies, "Trick photography?" Charlie gives up and says, like one of the writers making pitches in *The Player*, "Very taut. Like *Sybil* meets, I don't know, *Dressed to Kill*." "Cool," Donald replies. "I really liked *Dressed to Kill*," adding but mispronouncing the key word, "until the third act *denouement*." Charlie's agent nonetheless considers Donald's script "a smart, edgy thriller," going so far as to suggest that Donald might help with the Orlean adaptation because "he's really goddam amazing at structure."

Charlie replies, "Don't say that," but the suggestion leads him to take McKee's course. Charlie's voice-over describes his sense of inadequacy, panic, and failure at having sold out as McKee (Brian Cox) lectures to a crowded auditorium about the linearity of story via the protagonist's pursuit of an object of conscious or unconscious desire "within the limits established by setting and character." (▶ Figures 5.22–5.23) Later that day Charlie asks McKee, "What if a writer is attempting to create a story where nothing much happens," since "nothing is resolved" as "a reflection of the real world." In a booming voice, McKee tears into him on several fronts, insisting first that such a screenplay, "without conflict or crisis," would bore an audience, and second that things *do* happen in the real world—some sad, some horrific, some violent, some tender. "If you can't find that stuff in life, then you, my friend, don't know crap about life!" Afterward a much-shaken Charlie seeks out McKee, and the two go for drinks. Charlie reads the end of Orlean's book to him, and McKee responds, "You gotta go back, put in the drama." He then shares a secret: "The last act makes the film. Wow them in the end and you got a hit."

McKee's advice changes the course of *Adaptation* according to his paradigm: "Your characters must change. And the change must come from them. Do that and you'll be fine." Accordingly, whereas Charlie told McKee, "I wanted to show that Orlean never saw the blooming ghost orchid," it turns out that she has lied in her book: the Susan Orlean of *Adaptation* did see the orchid; she and Laroche got high on the drug extracted from the plant, and they became secret lovers. After being interviewed by Donald, who thinks she is lying when she denies having more than a professional relationship with Laroche, Susan flies to Florida and the two brothers follow her there. Charlie is discovered at the window of Laroche's place when he unintentionally watches the two lovers getting stoned, and Susan recognizes Charlie but declares they have to kill him to protect their secret.

A shaken Charlie Kaufman (Nicholas Cage) seeks out screenwriting guru Robert McKee (Brian Cox). *Adaptation* ©2002 Columbia)

With Donald hiding in the car, Charlie drives a gun-wielding Susan to the swamp with Laroche leading the way in his van, but the brothers escape their captors, hiding out until morning. (▶ Figure 5.24)

This is the point where Charlie tells Donald he has always admired his obliviousness and Donald shares his epiphany about love. (▶ Figure 5.25) As they make an effort to leave, Laroche sees them, shoots Donald, but is ravaged by an alligator. The brothers make their way to the car and leave in a fury as a sobbing Susan screams at them, but when they reach the road they crash into another vehicle; Donald is thrown and dies. The coda has Charlie listening to his notes that recall Donald's epiphany and then meeting with Amelia. He finally confesses his love, albeit too late since she is with someone else now, and he realizes how to end his script: with a fictionalized version of this fictional Charlie driving home after meeting with Amelia. Whereas McKee denounced voice-overs as "flaccid, sloppy writing," Charlie concludes with more voice-over. "McKee would not approve. How else can I tell his thoughts?" his voice asks. "I don't know. Well, who cares what McKee says?"

Charlie wants to write independently of "the industry"—a term he denounces to Donald when Donald uses it—but, much like Steven Phillips, ends up in thrall to Hollywood in terms of his script's last act, which in a manner of speaking reveals his genre, the action movie, what with the sex, chase, guns, and life lessons that pepper the film's last act. When Valerie met with Susan to option her book, the writer says she has never written a script, but the producer reassures her, "Oh, don't worry about that. We have screenwriters to write the screenplay," as if the scripter were simply hired help, though in a very real sense they are just that—at least according to Hollywood's power dynamics. It turns out that the independent and innovative Charlie is no exception. At his meeting with Valerie, when Charlie explains that he does not want to write "a Hollywood thing," she replies, "Definitely," but adds, "I guess we thought that maybe Susan Orlean and Laroche could fall in love," and indeed in the last act of *Adaptation* they do just that.

"I wanted to want something as much as people wanted these plants," Susan states in voice-over before the last act begins. "But it isn't part of my constitution. I suppose I do have one unembarrassed passion. I want to know what it feels like to care about something passionately." Following Charlie's erotic fantasy of having sex with her, an imaginary Susan advises him, "Just find the one thing that you care passionately about. Then write about that." Charlie is himself deeply passionate about his subject matter, flowers, and is frustrated because he wants to do them justice with his screenplay, as he states throughout, so *Adaptation* fittingly ends with imagery of morning glories opening and closing as day turns to night. Charlie is just as passionate about doing right by Susan, moreover; she functions as both his muse and his antagonist. In the last act Charlie thus attributes passions to Susan—for the ghost orchid, its extracted drug, her secret lover Laroche—as signs of *her* mutation and adaptation in responding to the swampy, Floridian setting far away from her home and husband in New York City. "What I came to understand is that change is not a choice," she says in voice-over after purchasing her plane ticket for her final trip to Florida. "Not for a species of plant, and not for me. It happens, and you are different." The same applies to a script in relation to its source. While the account of Susan's change into a drug-addicted adulteress who wants to shoot Charlie may be as preposterous as the twist that cop, killer, and victim are one and the same person, this change is consistent with McKee's advice: "Your characters must change, and the change must come from them. Do that and you'll be fine."

Finally, with Donald's death Charlie sorely misses his identical twin brother, as he tells Amelia in the coda, though the fatal accident enables him to complete the screenplay, which is to say that in *Adaptation* the two siblings together constitute the film's depiction of the Hollywood writer. The screenwriting credit for *Adaptation* is therefore shared by the real Charlie Kaufman and the fictitious Donald Kaufman. Their joint authorship is consistent with the epitaph taken from Donald's supposed screenplay, which muses that "we are all one thing" but don't realize it, so "we envy each other. Hurt each other. Hate each other. How silly is that?" The dual signatures express the script's originality (Charlie's talent) within the system and its need for structure (Donald's) that defines how screenwriting occurs for and within the industry as a "Hollywood thing."

The Director

I have already discussed *S1m0ne* (2002) as a star narrative, but it just as richly satirizes the mix of egoism and narcissism, sexism and misogyny characterizing modern-day Hollywood's understanding of what makes a director create: hence the film's outrageous conceit in giving Viktor Taransky (Al Pacino) a new female star who is a CGI special effect that he manipulates—until she resists his control. Many backstudios similarly show that a woman places the operations of Hollywood at great risk whenever she is the filmmaker's muse. Although girls and women in star narratives were often objectified, appreciated for their charismatic appeal on screen and for their fans, in filmmaker narratives female figures are primarily fantasy objects inspiring or impeding the creative process of a male auteur. Ultimately, backstudios about directors are just as deeply concerned with the question of who wields the most power in a male-dominated industry as they are with exploring what constitutes an auteur's creation of cinema. In this respect, a female figure typically symbolizes his authority/authorship *and* his cinema.

While those twinned issues of a director's authority and his cinema are central to more contemporary films, we can see them already informing Preston Sturges's studio-era *Sullivan's Travels* (1941). As discussed in earlier chapters, John L. Sullivan (Joel McCrea), a writer-director like his creator, who works within the studio system, wants to change genres, shifting from the comedies that made him famous to a more somber dramatic picture that will, he proclaims, be "a commentary on modern conditions. Stark realism. The problems that confront the average man." Although Sully repeatedly comments, "These are troublesome times," both his studio and his staff at home remind him that he does not know what "trouble" really is. Consequently the director takes off dressed as a hobo in order to experience "trouble" firsthand, but, until he loses his memory, each time he sets out he is drawn back into Hollywood's orbit. In the prison camp Sully finally learns what "trouble" really is and, more to the point, how laughter with the type of movies he has formerly made equalizes audiences by leveling the considerable differences between imprisoned criminals, poor African Americans, and ordinary white moviegoers. But this revelation that his comedies are a form of democracy raises a problematic implication: "Like the prisoners chortling at their existence played back to them as a joke, *Sullivan's Travels* invites us, its audience, to laugh at the replay of our own enthrallment to Hollywood" (Moran and Rogin 2000, 126).

As also previously noted, Sully wryly observes to a police officer early on that there is "a girl in the picture," as there always is in Hollywood entertainments. (⊙ Figure 5.26) Sully meets the generically named "girl" (Veronica Lake), a Hollywood hopeful locked out of her room for overdue rent and planning to return to her hometown, when he finds himself back on the outskirts of Hollywood after his first slapstick attempt to go out on his own. Thereafter the girl accompanies him on his travels, and the most poignant sequence in *Sullivan's Travels* is the wordless montage when they cohabit day and night with homeless people in Kansas City. While the girl serves as Sully's sounding board about "trouble" after they meet, she serves as a safety net for him too: he gets into what the film considers *real* trouble when he goes alone to pass out money. More to the point, she represents his product, "the movies." When Sully tells the policeman, "There's always a girl in the picture," he adds, making the double meaning of "the picture" apparent, "Haven't you been to the movies?" Later on, after Sully's supposed demise, the studio head, LeBrand, tells her, "You were his last discovery. His last discovery. We'll take care of you always." Receiving this beneficence, the girl is on a film set in period costume when she sees Sully's photograph in the newspaper and rushes from the set to inform LeBrand and others that he is still alive.

Whereas the girl is "the movies," Sully himself is not the "average man," however much he tries to identify with average men on his travels. To be sure, the closure of *Sullivan's Travels* endorses his viewpoint about the democratic value of laughter, justifying writer-director Sturges's own hilarious screwball comedies. Sturges nonetheless views the privileged position of Hollywood people like John L. Sullivan from a more sharply critical distance. Sully may sympathize with the downtrodden, but, as his butler tells him, he is also blindsided by his wealth, which is why he keeps getting pulled back to Hollywood until the film's final act. (⊙ Clip 14) Hollywood—in the person of studio executives, the various and sundry people in the land yacht (publicity maven, doctor, cook, secretary, etc.), his valet and butler—looks out for Sullivan and allows him to think about "trouble" intellectually as an abstract concept; only when Hollywood thinks he is dead and abandons him does he learn what "trouble" really is. Yet the "trouble" Sully genuinely experiences is not starvation or privation but incarceration.

Furthermore, after being stripped of everything in the prison camp, including his identity, Sully still insists on freedoms, such as speaking before being spoken to by the warden, that imply his sense of classed and implicitly white privilege even while in the setting of the chain gang. After his memory returns, Sully informs Trusty, the wizened guard who has paid him kindnesses, "Look, they don't sentence motion picture directors to a place like this just for a disagreement with a yard bull, do they?" (▶ Figure 5.27) Sully is correct insofar as once Hollywood learns he is alive, he does go free; one can therefore assume from his happy Hollywood ending that Sully's ability to make people laugh with his comedies may justify his privileged stance (and enable others to evade for two hours or more their own miserable conditions through the movies' escapism), but it also greatly depends upon his occupying that stance.

Woody Allen's *Stardust Memories* (1980) alludes to *Sullivan's Travels* with its premise of a famous director of comedies who likewise wants to make a serious film. *Stardust Memories* opens with Allen on a train, seated with motionless passengers, their non-Hollywood faces frozen in one striking black-and-white close-up after another. He is the only person in the car who moves, and as he looks out the window, a reverse shot shows another train with an energized assortment of people partying. Allen acts as if he is on the wrong train but cannot get out. Dissolve to numerous seagulls flying overhead. He and his fellow passengers walk along the edge of a large garbage dumpsite as the people from the other train approach. (▶ Figure 5.28)

Much like the opening of *Sullivan's Travels*, with its clip of Capital and Labor fighting each other on top of a speeding train, it turns out that this scene is the closing moment of the most recent film that Sandy Bates (played by Allen) has written and directed as well as starred in, and it receives a good deal of criticism from studio execs for its morbid viewpoint. One person declares that it is "terrible, absolutely terrible," another that "this man is sick," a third that "he is out of his mind," and a fourth that "he's not funny anymore." The harsh critiques of his new work in this opening keep turning from the cinematic object to concerns about Sandy and his mental health.

The primary storyline of *Stardust Memories* takes place at the Stardust Hotel during a weekend-long tribute to Sandy, much likes ones organized around the work of real-life filmmakers during the 1970s. Throughout the weekend diehard fans repeatedly demand Sandy's attention (one woman's husband even drives her to the hotel so she can sleep with her idol), and other attendees keep asking for his support of various charity events and causes. At the Stardust, he meets Daisy (Jessica Harper), a classical musician who attends the weekend tribute to Sandy's work with Jack, a screenwriting instructor at Columbia. Sandy is drawn to Daisy because she reminds him of his past live-in lover, Dorrie (Charlotte Rampling), a hysteric who has starred in some of his films, was institutionalized, and is now married to someone else in Hawaii. While at the Stardust, too, Sandy asks his present lover, Isobel (Marie-Christine Barrault), to meet him at the hotel for the weekend; she arrives by train, announcing that she has left her husband, and her two young children follow her to the Stardust the next day. The main narrative connects the two crises that Sandy has to face during the weekend: if he wants to marry Isobel and if he can resist his studio's alternate "happy" ending for his latest film. At one point midway through *Stardust Memories*, the studio people show Sandy a recut version of his ending in which the passengers end up not in that waste site but in jazz heaven. "Too much reality is not what the people want," his producer informs him. (▶ Figure 5.29)

Sandy is known for his comedies but, much like the protagonist of *Sullivan's Travels*, he tells his agent, lawyer, and producer, "I don't want to make funny movies anymore." However, whereas Sully wants to be a social critic, declaring his intent to realize "the potentialities of film as the sociological and artistic medium that it is," Sandy argues for the merits of more abstract ideas when he and Daisy debate the significance of *The Bicycle Thief* (1948). Daisy says, "You can't divorce it from its social roots," while Sandy believes, "It's much more profound than that." He tells Daisy to forget about the social problem of starvation in postwar Italy in order to ponder "what happens if you're living in a more affluent society and you're lucky enough to not have to worry about that." With more than thirty years' distance from the time of *The Bicycle Thief*'s release, Sandy interprets Vittorio De Sica's neorealistic film by abstracting from it the more existential, if also more bourgeois problems of one's falling in love or not, or of pondering one's mortality.

Along with its references to *Sullivan's Travels*, with its complex layering of fantasy upon fantasy upon a film-within-the-film, *Stardust Memories* is just as immediately reminiscent of Federico Fellini's $8\frac{1}{2}$ (1963), paralleling and parodying "many of that well-known work's key images" (Siegal 1985, 78). As in $8\frac{1}{2}$, multiple levels of reality and fantasy are threaded together by Sandy's relation with women, who inspire, stall, or trouble his creativity.

Intercut with the main narrative are film clips of Sandy's oeuvre, genre parodies much like Allen's earlier output, which are usually motivated by and at first indistinguishable from something that happens to him in the main narrative. "The reality cuts are so numerous," Christopher Ames comments about *Stardust Memories*, "that the distinction between framed film and framing film…becomes obscured" (Ames 2013, 219–20). Paralleling the clips are two sets of recurring flashbacks, the first a running account of Sandy's tumultuous relationship with Dorrie, and the second returning him to episodes, some possibly fantasies, of his childhood. Then there are outright fantasies that fork out from the main narrative, such as Sandy's encounter with aliens and his death when a fan shoots him, after which the organizer of the weekend presents him with a posthumous award. Stylistically the fantasies are not that different from the main narrative, the flashbacks, or even the film clips, so they call into question the film's "reality." On a first viewing especially it is often hard to disentangle what is "real" and happening in the main narrative from what Sandy is imagining or remembering or showing to the audience assembled at the Stardust for the weekend. Despite the layering of film clips, fantasies, and flashbacks, "too much reality" intrudes upon Sandy's weekend in the form of persistent fans and their demands, his running anxiety about the final cut of his new film, and his relationship with Isobel. The difference between reality and fantasy does not greatly matter in the long run, however. In the final minutes, everything we have seen while watching *Stardust Memories* turns out to be a film within the film, with all the characters impersonated by actors attending a screening and chatting with each other afterward.

Before then, when Sandy asks the aliens, echoing his abstractions of meaning from *The Bicycle Thief*, "Why is there suffering? Is there a god?," the aliens reply that he asks the wrong questions. For, like those Hollywood executives, they prefer his comedies. "You wanna do mankind a service," they advise him, "tell funnier jokes." (▶ Figure 5.30) The aliens also inform Sandy that they prefer Isobel over Dorrie. Their partiality is not simply a gag line but sage advice. Dorrie, his actress lover, is a troubled muse and a fleeting ideal, repeatedly subject to screaming fits and bouts of jealousy. In one flashback she is too insecure to perform a scene. Already quite thin, she worries about being too fat and takes speed to kill her appetite. "Now my skin hurts," she complains. "I'm getting depressed." Daisy, also a pill popper, is a more manageable surrogate for Dorrie, but she is also linked to Sandy's fantasy life. Following their discussion of *The Bicycle Thief*, his car stalls and, walking back to the hotel, the two come upon a crowd of strange people waiting for UFOs; although it is not clear exactly when this fantasy sequence begins, in it he performs magic and levitates Daisy, and she is with him when aliens arrive.

This final extended fantasy sequence illuminates Sandy's precarious mental state. He declares he wants to give up everything and run away with Daisy, who tries to convince him that she's nothing but trouble and that Jack, the teacher of screenwriting, keeps her grounded. As Sandy and Daisy kiss, Isobel and others from the hotel arrive, shouting at and shaming him. Insisting to Isobel that he is tired of all the demands being put on him, Sandy adds that he does not want to get married, for the last thing he needs now is to have a family and make a commitment. As Isobel leaves and Sandy calls out to her, a fan approaches, announcing, "You know, you are my hero," and shoots him. Then, when receiving the posthumous award for his art, Sandy narrates for his audience the "stardust memory" that flashed through his mind as he lay on the operating table, dying. He remembered experiencing a perfect day with Dorrie: after a walk in the park, she sat on the floor reading as Sandy ate ice cream and felt the summer breeze wafting through his apartment window, while the Louis Armstrong syncopated version of Hoagy Carmichael's "Stardust" played. Sandy explains that this blissful memory of spending a perfect day with Dorrie offers "something to hang on to," the best one can hope for amid a world of death, despair, suffering, and helplessness.

This extended sequence blurs fantasy (the aliens, the shooting, the posthumous award) and reality (the crowd, his declaration to Isobel that he does not want to get married) and makes them inextricable from each other (his memory of a perfect day with Dorrie, which may or may not have happened). This long sequence, furthermore, may well be indicating that Sandy is having a nervous breakdown because, as his analyst states within the fantasy, "he saw reality too clearly." But then reality dispels this fantasy when a doctor tells Isobel that Sandy had fainted after having a hallucination that he had been shot. Still lying on the hospital gurney, Sandy calls Isobel "Dorrie," and she leaves for the train station with her two children.

The aliens are right to like Isobel best, for she turns out to be the woman in the picture, "the movies," so to speak. After she leaves the hospital, Sandy eventually pursues her to the railroad station, where he tells her that "a lot of strange thoughts" and "unusual things" have gone through his head during the weekend, but he feels lighter now and real- izes how much she loves him despite his floundering. Moreover he has come up with "a very, very remarkable idea for a new ending for my movie." He proceeds to describe the opening of *Stardust Memories* but adds, "It's not as terrible as I originally thought it was because, because we like each other." Isobel replies, "I don't think it's realistic," and he complains about her bringing up realism at this late point—whether he means at this point in their relationship or in *Stardust Memories* does not matter since they amount to the same thing. "A huge, big wet kiss will go a long way to selling this idea," he states. "I think this is a big finish." They kiss and, surprisingly, an audience applauds. The house lights go up, and we see that their kiss is the Hollywood ending to Sandy's film (and Woody Allen's), and that all the "characters" within this fictional backstudio are really actors in a movie. This movie concludes on the train with Sandy and Isobel in a clinch, paralleling the opening of *Stardust Memories* with something like the "jazz heaven" alter- native proposed by Sandy's producers: a swing score plays as the couple kiss and the train pulls away from the station. (▶ Figure 5.31)

With its self-reflexive commingling of fantasy and reality, *Stardust Memories* views its hero's emotional turmoil with ambivalence. Sandy says, "I don't want to make funny movies anymore," but he continually cracks one-liners when speaking to the weekend audience and in passing conversations with the people he encounters. Furthermore, his reunion with Isobel is colored by his narcissism; when telling her about his new ending, he not only describes the character based on her as "warm and giving" but, instead of professing *his* feelings for her, goes on to say *she* is "crazy" about him. As his dialogue slips from the character to Isobel he states that *she* thinks he is "the most wonderful thing in the world" and that *she* is "in love" with him despite his fool- ishness. That is when Isobel brings up the lack of realism, complaining of his sentimen- tality, and he proposes the big kiss to sell the idea. Given the audience's response when the scene turns out to be the end of his movie, the kiss confirms what Sandy says since it apparently seals the deal.

What are we to make of Sandy's theorization of cinematic meaning in relation to this film's conclusion, its Hollywood ending? Are we to take seriously his repudiation of Hollywood entertainment since there is so much comedy in *Stardust Memories*, from the dialogue to the film clips? Sandy abstracts universal questions of love and mortality from the sociohistorical context of *The Bicycle Thief* that mirror his own depressed preoccupa- tions; nonetheless, however lightened by the multiple flashbacks, fantasies, clips, and one-liners, these issues do make up much of *Stardust Memories*, just as the self-reflexivity of its ending invites viewers to abstract the kind of big themes Sandy argues for in his conversation with Daisy. In fact, audience members in the final scene comment about the "heavy, original" things about life and love that Sandy has communicated through his film. By the same token, other viewers discuss what the director's Rolls Royce symbolized ("His car," a man replies), the actress playing Dorrie still complains she is fat, and the women impersonating Daisy and Isobel compare how Sandy kissed them with insistent tongue. So does this closing revelation that everything has been a film within the film pull the rug out from Sandy Bates's artistic pretenses or not? Has he again sold out to Hollywood his ambition to make serious art cinema in the manner of Fellini? Or is the final revelation of a film within a film a sign of Allen's own artful disengagement from Sandy's breakdown and his happy ending? *Stardust Memories* does not give a direct answer. The last shot is of Sandy Bates (or Woody Allen?) in the empty auditorium, where he finds a pair of dark glasses on the floor, puts them on, looks back at the empty screen, and, walking toward the camera, leaves the room as the screen goes dark prior to the end credits. (▶ Figures 5.32–5.33)

Clint Eastwood's *White Hunter, Black Heart* (1990) similarly does not take place in Hollywood. Rather, this backstudio travels to Africa in a fictionalized account of the pre-production of *The African Queen* (1951), where the filmmaker is completely if unofficially in charge despite the producer's frustrations and the scripter's growing alienation. This film likewise indirectly reflects Eastwood's own auteurism while representing another and somewhat different type of auteur filmmaker. Director John Wilson (Eastwood), the fictionalized John Huston, and script doctor Peter Verill (Jeff Fahey), the fictionalized Peter Viertel who authored the roman à clef source novel, are rewriting the script of "The African Trader" and arguing about retaining (Wilson) or revising (Verill) a bleak, un-happy ending in which the two leads die with all the Germans when the ship explodes. Mostly, though, Wilson wants to shoot a bull elephant, "the biggest tusker in all of Africa," and thus "a risk well worth taking." Aside from the pleasure he takes in aggravating his producer—European-born producer Paul Landers (George Dzundza) of Sunrise Films, the fictionalized Sam Spiegel of Horizon Pictures—Wilson's primary motive for doing the film and for insisting on the African location is the safari.

Even after the cast and the rest of the crew arrive in Africa from Hollywood via London, Wilson's obsession determines everything that happens. He refuses to start shooting until he has shot his elephant, frustrating Landers and causing his two stars, facsimiles of Humphrey Bogart and Katharine Hepburn, to wait with little else to do as the start of production gets delayed while their director takes off into the savanna every time an elephant herd is sighted. With the hired white hunter's refusal to continue guid-ing the search for the big tusker because of the danger, Wilson employs an experienced African, Kivu (Boy Mathias Chuma), and moves cast and crew to the man's village for filming, though nothing is shot, putting the company a week behind schedule before they have begun. Finally, Wilson gets his best shot at the massive elephant when the bull is sighted with a herd of cows. Kivu intervenes to protect Wilson when the tusker charges to protect a calf, and the African is killed. As drums spread news of Kivu's death and the villagers chant, "White hunter, black heart," Wilson tells Verill, "You were right, the ending is all wrong." The shoot begins with the director intoning "Action" in a soft voice as *White Hunter, Black Heart* dissolves to a black screen before the end credits appear against footage of an orange African landscape.

Wilson is a compelling yet contradictory and at times unsympathetic figure. When the film opens he is broke—so he desperately needs the job of directing "The African Trader"—yet living in an English country house lent to him by a high-society friend. Verill's opening voice-over describes the director, shown galloping on a horse in full English riding costume, as "a violent man given to violent action." (▶ Figure 5.34) Wilson is also arrogant, condescending, insulting, and cruel to the people he works with, especially to the perpetually frustrated and anxious Landers and the production manager, Ralph Lockheart (Alun Armstrong), but at times even to his friend Verill, who receives the brunt of the director's macho posturing. When Verill arrives in England from Switzerland, he tells Wilson that he finally had gotten his new book going when he "hooked up with a dame." Afterward, when he couldn't write and didn't get much skiing done either because of her, Verill states that he couldn't figure out "why it all seemed so important" at the time. "There's nothing tougher than trying to remember why you've chased a dame once you've had her," Wilson replies, his misogyny not concealed. The evening of Verill's arrival, Irene Sanders (Catherine Neilson) shows up dressed for a dinner date that Wilson has forgotten. The couple and Verill dine together, after which Irene pitches her screenplay, a silly story about a dog with a female lookalike in heat. "Isn't that something," Wilson says as he leads Irene up to his bedroom, leaving Verill as an observer of his apparent prowess.

In Africa, as his macho posture is potentially jeopardized by his failure to bag the elephant, the director maintains his brash self-esteem by emasculating and so feminizing Verill in his speech, calling him "kid" and Paul's "boy." Remarking about Verill's impatience to get the film rolling, he describes the writer "sitting around stewing like a dame who's just been kicked out of bed." Verill retorts to this last charge by accusing the director of being "either crazy or the most egocentric, irresponsible son of a bitch that I've ever met." But Verill also knows that "romantic futility" is Wilson's "one true love." We see this in Wilson's behavior at several points throughout *White Hunter, Black Heart*: when he insults and berates the anti-Semitic woman with whom he has been flirting at the African hotel; when he challenges to a duel that he cannot win the younger and huskier white maître d'hôtel, Harry (Clive Mantle), who has kicked a black waiter for dropping a tray; and when he performs the role of colonial Anglo gentleman in the hunting lodge, viewing his role with some measure of distance, even irony, while using the pose to aggravate Landers. More brazenly, to rebut Verill's charge that he is blowing the whole picture to commit the crime of killing a rare and noble creature, Wilson explains that it's not a crime but "a sin. It's the only sin you can buy a license and go out and commit."

Wilson's "romantic futility" extends to Hollywood as well. In his opening voice-over Verill also describes the director as "a brilliant, screw-you-all type filmmaker who continually violated all the unwritten laws of the motion picture business yet had the magical, almost divine ability to always land on his feet." Later in Africa, as Lockheart refers to Wilson and Verill as "the hunters from Hollywood" and mentions sarcastically, "No Hollywood safaris for me," Wilson stops the man short, accusing him of using the word

John Wilson (Clint Eastwood) defends Hollywood. (*White Hunter, Black Heart* ©1990 Warner Bros.)

"Hollywood" as an insult. Lockheart denies doing so, but Wilson states that he has heard it before, "in the army, in New York, in the theater. Hell, I've heard it everywhere. People say 'Hollywood' when they want to insult you. But really 'Hollywood' is just a place where they make a product." He goes on to blame the insulting connotation on "the cheap element from there," not the people who "try to do something different," but "the whores who sell words and ideas and melodies" and who "put 'Hollywood' up as a big target." Wilson knows what he is talking about: "I've done a little hustling in my time. A helluva lot more than I'd like to admit to. But what I sold when I was whoring I'll never get back. What I'm trying to say, Ralph, is that the whores put Hollywood up as a big target." After hearing this speech, Verill comments, "John, I didn't realize you were such a hometown boy," to which the director replies, "Well, I am, kid. I am when I'm in Africa.... Oh, I'm serious. It took Africa to bring all this out of me. Africa and, uh, the smell of my first wild elephant."

Wilson's mocking and derisive treatment of his producer, the wheeler-dealer Paul Landers, follows from what the director also explains to Verill is his maxim of how to survive in Hollywood. Rather than sign long-term contracts, saving every cent only to die of a stroke at fifty, Wilson prefers "to let the chips fall where they may, refuse to sign their contracts and tell off the guy who can cut your throat and flatter the little guy who's hanging by a thread that you hold." Thus he does not care if "The African Trader" is filmed in color or black-and-white so long as it is filmed on location in Africa for authenticity but also so he can hunt big game, and he is furious at Landers for discussing with the film's backers the option of shooting it in London to cut down on costs.

As for the script, when defending the unhappy ending that kills the two leads, Wilson explains his reasoning: "You see, we're gods, Pete, lousy little gods who control the lives of the people we create. We sit up in some heavenly place and decide whether they live or die. On the merits of what happens to them in reel one, two, three, et cetera, and then we decide if they have the right to live. And that's how we arrive at our ending." When Verill opines that he considers himself "a swell god and thinks the couple should live because of all that they have gone through," Wilson tells him that is why he will never be a good screenwriter. (⊙ Figure 5.35) "You let eighty-five million popcorn eaters pull you this way and that way. To write a movie you must forget that anyone is ever going to see it." As Verill works on the script, much as Jonathan Shields does with James Lee Bartlow, Wilson instructs the writer about the cinematic virtue of "simplicity." Later on, shortly before the tusker and his herd are sighted in the fatal confrontation, the production is poised to start when we learn that when Wilson directs he does not look at the script, fearful he will lose his artistic spontaneity. *White Hunter, Black Heart* represents Wilson as a true auteur, shaping his film by virtue of his artistry and personality and evading Hollywood whoredom.

Why, then, after Kivu's death, as the villagers chant, "White hunter, black heart," does the director agree with Verill that "the ending is all wrong"? And how does this decision indicate the film's (and possibly Eastwood's own personal) attitude toward Wilson's larger-than-life expressions of his virility as the condition of his creativity? Much depends upon how one views Wilson's call of "Action" to start filming in relation to the disastrous hunt and Kivu's death. For surely, as my own discourse has already shown, the double meaning of "shoot" for killing with a gun and filming with a camera suggests that each action functions as a reflection of the other. Dennis Bingham, for instance, sees Wilson's whispering of the word "action" as a retreat from his "ill-fated 'action'" as hunter to the fantasy of Hollywood moviemaking (Bingham 1994, 229). Paul Smith reads the gesture as the irresponsible director's accepting responsibility for both Kivu's death and "making his film" (Smith 1993, 260). Additionally, Smith sees Wilson's acceptance of the script's revised ending as a turn "back to Hollywood, to its tradition and its history," drawing upon the image of John Wilson/John Huston "as auteur" in order to consolidate that of filmmaker Clint Eastwood as a comparable auteur (261). By comparison, Luis Miguel García Mainar views the ending as a critique of the men's movement of the late 1980s, with Kivu's death showing up "the inappropriateness of Wilson's notion of masculinity, and therefore of his turning to nature for self-discovery" (Mainar 2002, 26). Yet the turn to filmmaking in the closing moments also "lacks the potency to dissipate the vividness of Kivu's death," and from this perspective the film ends with the director finally accepting his moral responsibility for others, which he has tried to repress (27). (⊙ Figure 5.36)

Whether we understand filmmaking as escapism or accomplishment, and view Wilson's virility as authentic or performative, this hunter—and his Hollywood—are still white, privileged, and patriarchal. Before Wilson and Verill depart London for Uganda, they go to a nightclub with the Hepburn, Bogart, and Lauren Bacall surrogates, Wilson's companion Irene, and Landers and his British backers. After a sincere toast by Landers and a mocking one by Wilson, the room darkens, drums roll; a seminaked black man comes out in native costume, beating a bongo in ritualistic fashion; a blonde white woman screams and begins to spin on the dance floor; and someone in a gorilla costume appears, chases the woman, and begins to rip off her flimsy dress, a layer of cloth at a time, as she continues to dance back and forth across the floor, her arms outstretched. "Now, doesn't that make you long for the Dark Continent?" Wilson whispers to Irene, and next we see the gorilla twirling as he holds the supine woman over his head. After he puts her down, there are cuts to the faces of the native drummer, the vulnerable blonde, and the gorilla staring down at her; the implication, of course, is bestial rape in the primitive setting of the Dark Continent, and the imagery is evocative of Kong and Ann Darrow. With another shot of the drummer, the camera moves in on his hands beating the bongo, and the image dissolves to an animated map, with a red line tracing the route from England to Uganda, and the sound of the drum morphs into the roar of a plane's propellers. (⏵ Figure 5.37) (⏵ Clip 15)

This nightclub entertainment, while ironically heightened by director Eastwood and his protagonist Wilson, reminds us that *White Hunter, Black Heart* implicitly travels into the territory of the 1933 *King Kong*. John Wilson is like Carl Denham, an adventurer-filmmaker with a heart of darkness, Wilson for daring to commit the sin of shooting the big elephant and Denham for bringing the giant ape back to America in chains for theatrical exhibition. Filmmaking is a highly masculinized enterprise for both "crazy" men, one that tests their virility, which is why both *White Hunter* and *King Kong* draw the equivalence of going on location for a movie shoot with hunting for big game. That the hunt stalls the filmmaking process in *White Hunter, Black Heart* gives more space for director Eastwood to be self-reflexive and critical about Wilson's performances of masculinity, resulting in the ambiguity beclouding the final word, "action." Pete Verill's viewpoint is important since his growing alienation from Wilson helps to control our perspective of the director's excessive behavior even if at times we feel sympathetic toward him, as when Wilson challenges Harry for the man's racist treatment of a waiter or shames the woman in the African hotel for her anti-Semitic views. Although set in the studio era and not in Eastwood's own Hollywood, the elephant hunt in Africa brings to the forefront of *White Hunter* the racism of white male privilege in Hollywood that, in this instance, affords Wilson the luxury of such romantic gestures as a means of inflating his masculine self-image.

The Outsider

In contrast with the filmmaker narratives focusing on the travails of writers and produc-ers, backstudios about directors characterize them as auteurs who are "crazy" because they are single-minded and obsessed about their work (or, in Wilson's case, a substitute for the work that is viewable as a metaphor of that work). Moreover my examples have themselves been directed by auteurs working *for* Hollywood even when they are not *in* Hollywood: Sturges, Allen, Eastwood. By contrast, Mario Van Peebles's *Baadasssss!* (2003) is an auteur backstudio shot on digital video for a million dollars about an independent auteur going rogue to make a film, his father Melvin's *Sweet Sweetback's Baadasssss Song*

(1971). Unlike his father's film, *Baadasssss!* premiered at Sundance and Toronto and was released by Sony Pictures Classics; moreover, while made on a small budget and reaching only a tiny theatrical audience, its content speaks *of* Hollywood of the late 1960s and, at least implicitly, *to* Hollywood of the 2000s and the resistance of both past and contemporary industries to minority casting, crews, and demographics.

Sweet Sweetback's Baadasssss Song inspired the blaxploitation genre of the early 1970s and encouraged Hollywood for a short while (before the advent of the multiracial buddy film) to market action films like *Shaft* (1971) specifically for black audiences, offering a temporary bright spot for fading downtown movie palaces. Melvin Van Peebles, one of the few black directors working in the industry when he wrote *Sweetback* in 1970, made his "revolutionary" film outside the Hollywood system while always cognizant of both its financial hold on filmmaking and its institutional racism (Wiggins 2012). To locate the production historically three decades later, *Baadasssss!* is punctuated by news footage of white and black activists resisting or fighting with police, along with talking-head shots that feature Mario's actors speaking in character about the tumultuous yet exciting shoot (imitating *Reds* [1981], itself following the example of numerous documentaries).

Melvin Van Peebles (played by director, coscripter, and coproducer Mario) has just finished *Watermelon Man* (1970) for Columbia Pictures, and the studio wants to sign him to a three-picture deal. His agent (Saul Rubinek) advises Melvin to come up with a safe, funny follow-up in case *Watermelon Man*, a comedy about a white man who one morning wakes up black, opens poorly and the studio gets cold feet. However, in statements voiced at the start of *Baadasssss!* over that footage of rioting or protesting students and black activists, Melvin knows full well that black America "wasn't in a laughing mood." "Times were changing," he explains. "The Panthers knew it. The students knew it." Over a shot of the entrance to Paramount, he adds, "Hollywood was ignoring it." Or as the B cameraman, José Garcia (Paul Rodriguez), states in a later talking-head shot, "The truth is, if you weren't white you were the joke. And we weren't laughing." Instead of another comedy with stereotypical black characters, Melvin wants to make "a film about a real brother," "a street brother who turns revolutionary. . . . The Man comes after him . . . and he gets away." His agent warns, "Even Cagney didn't get away with killing cops, dirty or otherwise," but Melvin is undaunted. Before starting, he lists the four principles that will guide his production: there will be "no cop-out" for he will elevate rather than denigrate black people; his film will be entertaining because "if folks get bored it's over"; it has "to be a moneymaker" because "the Man ain't gonna carry no messages for you for free"; and it will "star the community . . . the faces that Norman Rockwell never painted."

Baadasssss! follows the process of making *Sweet Sweetback's Baadasssss Song* from inspiration to exhibition, during which an increasingly stressed Melvin does not waver from his four principles. Following a montage of him writing the script, with more and more pages taped to his bedroom wall as he frantically scribbles, Melvin walks away from a meeting with his agent and studio executives on the Columbia lot after he watches a black actor play a Stepin Fetchit–type character. With recommendations from his friend

Melvin Van Peebles (Mario Van Peebles) writing his screenplay. (*Baadasssss!* ©2004 Sony Pictures Classics)

Bill Harris (Rainn Wilson), a white hippy who initially confers with Melvin in a hot tub and will assist him on the production of *Sweetback*, Melvin seeks "independent money" since "nothing truly revolutionary is gonna come from the studio machine." Several leads from Harris go nowhere, mainly due to the cigar-smoking Melvin's machismo: a rich former cowboy star, who now finances European art films, makes a pass, and Melvin angrily departs; then Melvin embarrasses a competitive pudgy financier in front of their children by showing off his own physical strength instead of downplaying it to appease the man's ego. Finally, at a loud, crowded party with flashing lights, painted nude bodies, and drugs, Melvin gets a commitment from a dealer to be a silent producer; only the man gets busted as filming is about to start.

With shooting three days away and his financing up in smoke, Melvin learns he cannot use any SAG actors, so he decides to play the lead role himself. Using what money he has and borrowing from loan sharks for the rest, Melvin bankrolls production and pares the shooting schedule to the bone. To supplement the few professionals willing to work for him, he gathers together a ragtag crew; for example, Big T (Terry Crews), a big, hulking black guy hired for "ghetto muscle," doubles on the sound boom, although he knows nothing about sound. Avoiding the "lily white" closed shops of the craft unions and their higher rates, Melvin arranges for porn filmmaker Clyde Houston (David Alan Grier) to come on board. With Clyde on the set as a producer, Melvin at first shoots the explicit brothel scenes of *Sweetback* for the union watchdogs to observe; they leave Melvin alone for the remainder of filming since "the unions don't bother with smut films."

Once production begins, Melvin becomes ruthless about making his revolutionary movie *his* way. He will not listen to criticism or tolerate opposition. The script supervisor warns him that he has only sixty-five minutes of film, so Melvin, declaring he is editing in his head, fires him and adds this job to his several others while cutting more days from the schedule. Melvin refuses to back down on using (for free) his adolescent son, Mario (Khelo Thomas), as young Sweetback in an explicit sex scene, and relents only partially when, pressured by his girlfriend, Sandra (Nia Long), he agrees to use a skin wig to preserve the boy's proud Afro. Key members of the crew get arrested returning from a location simply for "being black" and in possession of what the police automatically assume must be stolen camera and sound equipment. After borrowing money from Bill Cosby (T. K. Carter) for bail and to wrap filming, Melvin argues with Bill Harris about going to see the jailed men during the weekend to boost their morale; knowing the racism of the police, he intends to let the white man, posing as the "Dutch" Mr. Van Peebles, get them released on Monday when bail court will be back in session. He fires Clyde when the latter buys four instead of six magazines of film in order to pay for a stunt man, as Melvin declares he needs that extra film to finish and can do the stunt himself.

When the shoot is complete, more problems overwhelm Melvin. During postproduction, the loan sharks threaten his life if he does not pay up. Worse, Melvin loses vision in his left eye from stress and has to wear a patch to save his sight. His cutter, who has been working for just the credit, quits to take a paying job, and, desperate to finish, a furious Melvin hits the young man in the face and prevents him from leaving. When the film is in the can, potential buyers are invited to see it at a screening for cast and crew, but they cannot get out fast enough. Even his agent, a close friend but also a white man, finds *Sweetback* threatening. Finally, after getting an X rating from the Motion Picture Association of America, Melvin makes a distribution deal with Cinemation, a low-rent distributor with a huge load of debt, which can open *Sweet Sweetback's Baadasssss Song* only in two cities because, as Melvin is told, "black folks don't own theaters in America, white folks do." Traveling to Detroit, where *Sweetback* is booked to premiere on a triple bill in an old downtown palace, Melvin fast-talks the twin Jewish theater owners to single-book his film; since the X rating prevents newspaper advertising, he goes on radio to promote his film and the soundtrack music by the new group Earth, Wind, and Fire. During what starts out as an extremely slow opening day, word of mouth spreads, and by evening the cavernous Grand Circus Theater is sold out. Prior to one more sequence of talking heads, which includes a shot of the real Melvin Van Peebles, we see the vocal black crowd being hugely entertained, just as Melvin intended, and he says in voice-over, "Folks started calling me 'Mel baby' again." (⊙ Figure 5.38)

Like his character, Sweetback, the Melvin Van Peebles of *Baadasssss!* is a revolutionary outlaw, bucking the Hollywood system at every turn. And like some other filmmakers discussed in this chapter, he is considered "crazy" because of his single-mindedness in making a revolutionary film, despite the personal cost to his crew, friends, children, girlfriend, and ultimately himself. Still, as depicted by *Baadasssss!*, Melvin's revolutionary black film culture is a rigorously masculine world. With Melvin at the center, a thread organizing Mario's account of the shoot is the building of interracial male camaraderie. Melvin was their leader and they followed him, José Garcia comments in one of the talking-head shots: "If he was crazy, we were fucking lunatics." Big T, for instance, is at first resistant to working with Tommy David (Ralph Martin), the A camera operator who is a short white man, but after the cameraman is arrested along with Garcia and the other African American crew members, Big T considers Tommy an honorary black man. The two men develop mutual respect for each other by working on the film, and at the first screening, Big T tells Melvin that Tommy is taking him along as his assistant on his next project to teach him his craft.

Women, on the other hand, have little place in the production of *Sweetback* or the diegesis of *Baadasssss!* except to serve as objects of pleasure for men. Sandra knows about Melvin's other women but looks the other way; as Melvin makes his film she takes care of his two children, who have come to live with him for the summer, and she looks out for their welfare, buying them meals, for instance, when their father forgets. Aside from a fleeting glimpse of the hooker who seduces young Sweetback, as played by Melvin's young son, the only female of consequence we see in *Sweetback* is the black prostitute in the brothel scene who goes topless. Melvin's secretary, Priscilla (Joy Bryant), hungry to act, is cast in the role until her boyfriend—who turns out to be Maurice of Earth, Wind, and Fire—objects to what Melvin wants her to do and she quits the role at the last minute. To replace her, Melvin phones Ginnie (Karimah Westbrook), a woman he slept with after the drug party in a four-way with Bill Harris; he invites her on a "special date" early the next morning that turns out to be the shoot's first day. She assumes Melvin is making a black porno and wants no part of it, but he talks her into staying "because it will be totally revolutionary." Melvin then clinches the deal when he promises Ginnie that she will be "the first soul sister sex goddess"—but she still insists on being paid in cash up front. Bathed in red light and wearing a transparent negligee, Ginnie dances before Melvin, playing Sweetback, as the crew, Melvin's father, and some extras watch, their aroused or shocked faces shown in one close-up after another. "Bet you've never seen no shit like this before," Big T says to a visibly stunned Tommy. Facing each other, Ginnie and Melvin slowly strip off their clothes, one item at a time; we see his bare chest, then hers, as the watchers' catcalls compete in the diegesis with the musical soundtrack playing over it. (▶ Figure 5.39)

Mario Van Peebles partly edits this scene to include shots that achieve a measure of critical distance from Ginnie's nudity for twenty-first-century viewers. For instance, at one point her nude dancing is obscured, shown as a red screen through the viewfinder of the camera. (▶ Figure 5.40) So it is never entirely clear if the excitement visible on the faces of men like Bill Harris and Clyde Houston, which are cut into the sexual action, is erotic or due to the thrill of seeing Melvin actually getting his film off the ground. Nevertheless, just a short while before this scene we have seen Ginnie wake up in bed with Melvin, Bill, and a white woman. In that scene Ginnie's painted bare breasts clearly registered her sexual objectification, as Bill goes down on her while Melvin continues to chatter to him about his revolutionary motion picture. Now, in the brothel shoot, despite those distancing moments, Mario at times foregrounds her eroticization. Ginnie displays her bare breasts as she shimmies and gyrates, and because of the cuts to men watching her we are well aware that she has a live audience as she is being filmed. By comparison, in the few reverse shots of Melvin, he stands monumental and phallic-like, retaining his wide-brimmed gambler hat and signature cigar: he is never shown nude below his chest. The brothel shoot concludes with a cut to Melvin's production team screening the dailies from this scene, framed shots of Melvin and Ginnie continuing their mutual strip tease. Then on a larger framed screen we get the full-frontal body shot of Ginnie, followed by a reverse shot to the projection booth that reveals two union guys asking Bill Harris what everyone is watching. "Some kind of black porn thing," he replies.

Baadasssss! is itself not a revolutionary film, but in the context of the backstudio genre this independent production is a rare representation of black filmmaking on the margins of Hollywood. It is no coincidence but a reflection of Hollywood's institutional racialization of moviemaking, both in 1970 and the present century, that the films I have been discussing here as well as in other chapters are all about white Hollywood. Nonetheless, even when challenging "the Man," African American filmmaking in *Baadasssss!* is still a man's club.

6

Historical Hollywood

For most casual viewers of backstudio pictures the quintessential example of Hollywood historicizing itself is probably MGM's *Singin' in the Rain* (1952), which affectionately satirizes the transition from silent films to the talkies while condensing this period to a few months during 1927. Given the film's popularity and endurance over the years, many consider the conversion to sound to have been *the* epochal event in Hollywood's history, more so than the introduction of color or 3-D or the many new technologies developed over the past several decades.

The more recent and Oscar-winning *The Artist* (2011) also attests to the significance of sound's debut, ostensibly to warn "modern-day filmmakers," facing the "death" of celluloid at the hands of digitization, "that pride, an unwillingness to change, threatens to destroy us. Transition in this film is inevitable; join or disappear" (Gilbert 2012). The opening of *The Artist* at the Hollywood premiere of silent screen star George Valentin's (Jean Dujardin) new espionage picture deliberately evokes the premiere that begins *Singin' in the Rain*, complete with the male star's hammy bowing to the audience. However, unlike the musical's Don Lockwood, George is resistant, even hostile, to the arrival of sound. "I'm the one people come to see. They never needed to hear me!" he exclaims in 1929 to studio head Al Zimmer (John Goodman) when the latter shuts down Kinograph Studios to convert the plant to talkies. Events prove George disastrously wrong, however. A proud yet narcissistic and vain star whose strongest relation is apparently with his costarring dog, a Jack Russell terrier (Uggie), George decides to write, direct, produce, and finance his own silent jungle epic, which not only bombs but opens on October 25, 1929, the day after the stock market crash on Black Thursday and the same day that Peppy Miller's (Bérénice Bejo) new talkie, "Beauty Spot," premieres to long lines.

Peppy is a dancer whom George initially helped to get started in bit parts at Kinograph and who has been infatuated with him ever since. She is now Kinograph's biggest star in talkies, a modern Joan Crawford type who accounts for her popularity by declaring at an interview (in George's hearing, unfortunately), "People are tired of old actors mugging at the camera to be understood." With his silent jungle epic playing to empty houses and the stock market collapse breaking him financially, George's wife gives him two weeks to vacate their mansion. After the auction of his possessions,

George loses himself in drink. A few years pass, and it is now 1932. Angry at himself for his pride and stupidity, which has cost him his career, George nearly dies in a house fire when he lights a match to his films but is rescued by his dog's vigilance. George then recovers at Peppy's mansion, while she strong-arms Zimmer into signing George as her costar in a musical. Thus, just like Don Lockwood, this silent star gets reborn as a song-and-dance man—at which point *The Artist* itself becomes a full-fledged talkie. As George and Peppy move into a spirited tap number with a hot swing beat, sound and image, body and voice finally come together. The first word spoken on set after their dance number concludes is "Cut," and the final word after Zimmer asks the couple to do their duet a second time is "Action."

Singin' in the Rain and *The Artist* each treat the coming of sound as proof of the industry's greater modernity As both films depict it, the addition of sound to the image gives a fuller, more realistic sense of presence to the body and the space it occupies. Both films, moreover, view the advent of the talkies from the vantage point of their own present day. *Singin' in the Rain* makes this deliriously if self-reflexively evident with "The Broadway Ballet." While meant to be a visualization of what Don describes in 1927 as a number yet to be shot for "The Dancing Cavalier," in the use of Technicolor, prerecorded dubbing and sound recording, editing and camera work, the number as shown takes full advantage of every technology available to Gene Kelly, Stanley Donen, and the rest of the Freed unit in 1952. Given the MGM musical's decline as the 1950s came to an end, in retrospect the number seems like a last great hurrah. Similarly, *The Artist* came out when the studios were about to make their full conversion to digital delivery and exhibition. Postproduction digitization slightly increased the speed for its projection in theaters to re-create the look of silent pictures and to make Dujardin's dancing look more "brilliant," giving the "message" about moving with the times an even greater if subliminal sense of urgency (Cohen 2012, 2).

Singin' in the Rain was not the first Hollywood backstudio to recount the momentous marriage of sound and image. Two earlier films from Twentieth Century-Fox, *Hollywood Cavalcade* (1939) and *You're My Everything* (1949), cover much the same ground to show how sound transformed filmmaking and audiences. Each of these backstudios, moreover, was produced when the filmgoing audience had begun to retrench—*Hollywood Cavalcade* after the lackluster promotion of 1938 as the Movies' Greatest Year campaign failed to get the hoped-for footing with moviegoers, and *You're My Everything* at the start of the postwar decline in theater attendance.

In their recounting of Hollywood's past, these stories about the coming of sound are not unique. Historical backstudios have been produced ever since Hollywood has had histories to tell. This chapter singles out accounts of three eras that have preoccupied the genre: 1929, the year Hollywood undertook its conversion to all-talking pictures; 1951, the year the U.S. House Un-American Activities Committee (HUAC) renewed its investigation of the motion picture industry; and 1962, the year of Marilyn Monroe's death, signaling to many the end of Hollywood's Golden Age, as illustrated by the numerous biopics about that star. This year is central as well to a recent cable series covering the legendary feud between Bette Davis and Joan Crawford.

1929: (Un)solved Mysteries

Three backstudios produced at different moments in Hollywood's real-time history fictionalize notorious scandals from the early 1920s, yet as it turned out none saw much box-office success. *Hollywood Story* (1951) takes place in the present day, but its lead character solves a murder from 1929 that in broad outline is very much like what happened in 1922 to film director William Desmond Taylor, a case that was never solved. *The Wild Party* (1975) is an adaptation of Joseph Moncure March's long narrative poem that received only a limited publication in 1928 due to its erotic content. However, the film relocates the setting from Greenwich Village to Hollywood and Beverly Hills in 1929, and it remodels the poem's main character to remind audiences of Fatty Arbuckle, whose film career ended after the 1921 death of Virginia Rappe in his San Francisco hotel suite and three subsequent trials (two hung juries and finally an acquittal in 1922). The climax of *Sunset* (1988) occurs during the first Academy Awards ceremony in 1929 and leads to a revelation that evokes well-known insider gossip that producer Thomas Ince did not die from a heart attack in 1924 but was mistakenly shot by William Randolph Hearst during a party on his yacht, the *Oneida*. Hearst allegedly mistook Ince for Charles Chaplin, whom he suspected was consorting with Marion Davies, a story recounted by *The Cat's Meow* (2002).

In *Hollywood Story* producer Larry O'Brien (Richard Conte) becomes fascinated with the unsolved murder of silent film director Franklin Ferrara (the surrogate of Taylor), which he believes will make a compelling film. "He had walked in on an old hunk of Hollywood history and already he could hear the cameras grinding in his head," his agent and boyhood friend, Mitch Davis (Jim Backus), remarks in voice-over. At the same time, Mitch tries to dissuade Larry from taking on this story because old Hollywood history has no sales potential. "Backstage stories are okay," he explains. "Backcamera stories are absolutely no good."

In due course Larry encounters the leading suspects in Ferrara's murder: Roland Paul (Paul Cavanagh), a John Barrymore type of leading man ruined by the scandal and now playing bit parts in westerns; Vincent St. Clair (Henry Hull), an unemployed, derelict screenwriter fired by Ferrara at the time of the murder, whom Larry hires to write his screenplay; and Sam Collyer (Fred Clark), Ferrara's business manager who is now Larry's producing partner. Not only is each man the possible killer of Ferrara back in 1929 but, in the present day, each may also have murdered the late director's secretary and putative brother, the formerly missing Charles Rodeo, after he made an appointment with Larry to "break the Ferraro case wide open." Additionally, Sally Rousseau (Julie Adams), the daughter of Roland Paul and Amanda Rousseau—a composite of Mabel Normand and Mary Miles Minter, two stars linked to Taylor's murder by the press and for a while by police—tries to stop Larry from making his film to protect her mother from further scandal. It seems that Amanda, though married at the time, was infatuated with Ferrara much as Minter was with Taylor; furthermore, reflecting an early theory that a love triangle was the motive for Taylor's murder, Sam carried a torch for Amanda, feelings she did not return, and at the time he wondered if she might have been the killer.

Before the film's brisk seventy-six-minute running time concludes, Larry discovers that St. Clair is the real Ferrara sibling and the double murderer who tried to frame Sam for both deaths as retaliation for telling his brother (who wrote the scenarios he directed with St. Clair's name attached) that he had no writing talent and deserved to be fired. To protect himself when he found the dying Ferrara and realized he was being framed, Sam had covered up that crime to make it look like a burglary gone wrong, much as people working for Famous Players–Lasky (shortly to become Paramount Pictures) collected and later destroyed numerous papers from Taylor's bungalow right before police declared it a crime scene. A shootout with St. Clair on a studio set duplicating the Ferrara murder scene repeats the details of the old crime exactly; however, in voice-over Mitch assures us that Larry's film modifies this coincidental ending since "audiences couldn't believe it happened the same way twice." (▶ Figures 6.1–6.2)

Made to cash in on the success of *Sunset Boulevard* the previous year, *Hollywood Story* arouses memories of silent-era filmmaking and includes in cameos several famous silent stars: Francis X. Bushman, Betty Blythe, William Farnum, and Helen Gibson. In addition, *Hollywood Story* came out at a moment when the studio system was being dismantled as a result of the government's successful antitrust suit against the majors and HUAC had returned to Los Angeles to revive its witch-hunt. Even more specifically, Universal-International, which produced and distributed *Hollywood Story*, was floundering, about to be taken over by Decca Records in 1952 (itself to be absorbed into MCA a decade later). By 1951 the industry-wide audience decline for movies had been countered by the rise of television as radio's successor, indirectly evident in this film's opening titles, which begins at the famous intersection of Hollywood and Vine, travels to Ciro's nightclub on Sunset, then dissolves to signage for the radio stations of ABC, NBC, and CBS, and returns to the Roosevelt Hotel on Hollywood before ending at LaBrea and Sunset and the old Charlie Chaplin studios, which by 1953 would be where several CBS TV series were being filmed.

What follows the montage is a sudden if ghostly echo of Hollywood history. A player piano sounds out a melody, the keys moving on their own; a gun, aimed directly at the camera, is fired; a body falls in silhouette, as the piano continues to play. Mitch states in voice-over, "A deserted motion picture studio. A shot. And a corpse. The year: 1929." (▶ Clip 16) This studio, renamed the National Artists Studio, has, until Larry rents it, been deserted since that murder happened; as Larry reopens the case the ghosts of 1929 become alive again. In its fictionalized account of Hollywood's most notorious and still unsolved murder, *Hollywood Story* could have distracted audiences from the industrial tumult in 1951 with its nostalgic evocation of Hollywood's scandalous days, but the film did not make much of an impression in its premiere engagements in Chicago and New York. Its account of 1929 is therefore more revealing of an institutional viewpoint toward the past than it is of audience tastes at the very start of the 1950s, the success (and greater cynicism) of *Sunset Boulevard* notwithstanding.

The Wild Party was also not a success and subject to as much corporate disorganization and more studio interference. Its producer-distributor, American-International Pictures, cut twenty minutes from director James Merchant's longer version (which was restored in a limited theatrical release in 1981 and is now the edit on DVD). In the mid-1970s AIP was going through an identity crisis of its own, relying on blaxploitation, gangster, and Kung Fu films to compensate for the waning appeal of its signature genres, horror and beach party pictures, while releasing a few mainstream films such as *The Wild Party*. By the end of the decade the company would be sold to Filmways, which was sold to Orion Pictures a few years later.

The Fatty Arbuckle–like protagonist of *The Wild Party* is the overweight Jolly Grimm (James Coco), a "funny man in the movies" and a rival of Chaplin and Buster Keaton. Absent from the screen for five years, Jolly is preoccupied with making a comeback to show the industry that he has not lost his touch, as everyone presumes. The titular party is meant to be the occasion where Jolly will screen his new self-financed picture, "Brother Jasper," for studio heads in the hope of getting a distributor, but a rival party at Picfair has attracted most of the influential people who were invited.

Additionally, it *is* 1929 and Jolly *has* lost his touch as a comic filmmaker. To start with, his film is silent. As one studio chief, Murchison, tells him as he leaves the party for Picfair, "We're going to sound now. The public wants it." Kreutzer, another studio head, who arrives late but has come because Jolly promised him two redheads, expounds, "No sound? What are you, in the Dark Ages?" Second, Jolly refuses to adjust his slapstick humor to the more sophisticated tastes of movie audiences, as James Morrison (David Dukes)—who has helped to write the title cards, doesn't think Jolly needs sound, and appreciates the pathos in the film—advises him to do. Rather than cut a corny cannibal scene, Jolly declares, "What's funny is always funny," and tells Jimmy to leave the editing room. From the scenes shown, "Brother Jasper" appears to be tonally inconsistent, its narrative ranges all over the place, and the humor is self-indulgent. During the screening at the party the audience laughs politely at the physical humor but gets restless during scenes of Jasper and a young girl that aim for pathos in imitation of Chaplin and *The Kid* (1921). Third, for all his arrogance and egoism, Jolly can barely conceal his desperation. "Brother Jasper" reeks of Jolly's hunger for approval. After Kreutzer tells Jolly that audiences now want action and gangsters, and although "Brother Jasper" takes place in the eighteenth century, Jolly invents a gangster scene on the spot to add to his film for Kreutzer's benefit. However, both studio heads put Jolly off, unwilling to pick up his film. (▶ Figure 6.3)

The year of Jolly's last Hollywood film for a major studio, 1924, may also not be an arbitrary date. Ince's suspicious death in that year marked the finale of a series of major

Hollywood scandals in the early 1920s, all exploited by sensational journalism and most recently well documented in William J. Mann's *Tinseltown: Murder, Morphine, and Madness at the Dawn of Hollywood*. As already noted, there were Rappe's death and the subsequent three Arbuckle trials in 1921 and 1922 as well as his banishment from pictures. Taylor's unsolved murder in 1922 revealed his numerous aliases and the wife and daughter he had abandoned, ruined Minter's career and tarnished Normand's, and the police investigation, which ultimately went cold after several years, may have been obstructed by Paramount to conceal the director's homosexuality, for which he was possibly being blackmailed. There were several publicized drug-related deaths, such as Olive Thomas's in 1920 and Wallace Reid's in 1923, not to mention Robert Harron's fatal self-inflicted gunshot wound in 1920. Mary Pickford's divorce from Owen Moore in 1920 to marry Douglas Fairbanks generated much press too. By 1922 church and women's groups were clamoring for censorship of motion pictures, and the Arbuckle trials and Taylor's murder only intensified their efforts. Now in 1929 Jolly's party gets progressively wilder to evoke silent Hollywood's reputation, fomented by those scandals, as a wanton Babylon. Jolly's guests get drunk, use soft and hard drugs, and form homosexual, lesbian, and bisexual as well as heterosexual couples and groups for orgiastic sex, all the while a voice-over performer sings, "Ain't nothing bad about feeling good."

Possibly as another allusion to the Arbuckle scandal, as the partygoers retreat to various bedrooms in Jolly's mansion, Nadine, an underage girl who has come to the party uninvited at her sister's suggestion with the hope of getting into pictures, dances seductively for the very drunk host. As the two kiss in the kitchen, the sister's boyfriend attacks Jolly for taking advantage of the young girl and a fight breaks out. (⏵ Figure 6.4) Dale Sword (Perry King), a smooth and confident rising star who has made a sexual conquest during the party of Jolly's live-in mistress, Queenie (Raquel Welch), beats up the boyfriend, but then an enraged Jolly verbally attacks Queenie, reiterating the vicious streak that has been in evidence since the film began. The drunken host soon grabs a gun and shoots James, Queenie, and Dale, injuring James and killing the other two on the grand staircase of the mansion. This wild party marks the end of Jolly's career and, in its diegesis, closes the 1920s with another major Hollywood scandal.

Unlike *Hollywood Story*, *The Wild Party* does not appeal to nostalgic feelings about the silent era but, with an unsympathetic protagonist and sexually free-for-all party, exploits the new freedom of the screen in an effort to attract a hip, cynical, and young audience jaded by Watergate and the Vietnam War and gravitating away from traditional big-budget Hollywood fare. *The Wild Party* thus seeks to illuminate the dark underside of the liberated sensibility of silent-era Hollywood. In its fuller form, however, *The Wild Party* is a motley hybrid, reflecting the uncertainty of both its studio and its director. It is sensationalistic in the Hollywood milieu it portrays yet apparently serious in its thematic and artistic intentions; a drama that wants to be a musical with more than half a dozen songs, most sung in voice-over; and an adaptation of an infamous poem, with "sometimes poet" James Morrison, acting as a surrogate for March, quoting lines from the source in his hospital bed to function as a narrator. In its abbreviated form when released to theaters in 1975, *The Wild Party* could not compete with productions from the majors that also came out just as New Hollywood was in its last hurrah: somewhat cynical, critically acclaimed, and yet popular films such as *Chinatown* (1974), *The Godfather, Part Two* (1974), *The Conversation* (1974), *Nashville* (1975), *Dog Day Afternoon* (1975), and *One Flew over the Cuckoo's Nest* (1975). Moreover 1975 was the year of *Jaws* and the beginning of the practice in which big blockbusters opened in thousands of cinemas nationally, the current pattern of exhibition and the mentality governing conglomerate Hollywood as studios plan their annual schedules around four quadrant tentpoles.

Blake Edwards's *Sunset*, made at the very start of the conglomerate era, is more circumspect in its allusions to the mysterious death at its core, namely, the murky circumstances of Ince's death as gossiped about within the film industry. The Hearst figure here is Alfie Alperin (Malcolm McDonnell), who rose to fame as a silent-era star, nicknamed "the Happy Hobo," and now runs a major film studio. (⊙ Figure 6.5) According to Alfie, while Fox and Chaplin are betting on sound, he is gambling on a big silent western, "Lawman," with star Tom Mix (Bruce Willis) as Wyatt Earp and Earp himself (James Garner) hired as technical adviser. The two men bond when Alfie's abused second wife, Christina (Patricia Hodge), asks Wyatt—a former lover, apparently—to investigate a charge that her son, Michael (Dermot Mulroney), whom Alfie has adopted, beat up a woman at the Candy Store, a Hollywood brothel where the prostitutes all look like famous movie stars. However, Wyatt and Tom discover the club's owner, Candy Gerard, beaten and dead in her guest cottage. Michael is there with the body, drunk and incoherent. Believing Michael to be innocent and the victim of a frame, the lawman and his portrayer keep him hidden from police (until the young man himself runs away and gets arrested) while they begin an investigation of their own. Wyatt and Tom befriend Candy's daughter, Cheryl King (Mariel Hemingway), and eventually the trio obtain Candy's little black book with all the names of her high-powered clients.

Wyatt Earp (James Garner) and Tom Mix (Bruce Willis) on the first day of filming "Lawman." (*Sunset* ©1988 Tri-Star)

Suspicion keeps falling on Alfie, whose brutality toward his wife and employees becomes increasingly more visible, and his equally violent bisexual sister, Victoria (Jennifer Edwards). Alfie has in his pocket the corrupt chief of police, Captain Blackworth (Richard Bradford), and the town's leading gangster, Dutch Kiefer (Joe Dellesandro), who is Victoria's consort and was with her when *she* killed Candy. It turns out that in 1916 Candy had watched Alfie beat his first wife and throw her overboard from his yacht. He then beat and raped Candy but said if she kept her mouth shut, he would set her up in business; hence the Candy Store. Now, thirteen years later, Alfie has beaten Candy again and Victoria has killed her to prevent the woman from revealing the truth about the first wife's murder in retaliation. Moreover, unable to have a son of his own, Alfie has grown to hate Michael, who with his own perverse sexual history at the Candy Store is a prime patsy for Candy's murder. Christina later overhears Alfie plot with Kiefer to kidnap Tom's girlfriend, Nancy (Kathleen Quinlan), for leverage in obtaining Candy's little black book and warns Tom on the phone, a call that Alfie overhears. As punishment he beats and throws her down the staircase in their house, resulting in her death in the hospital shortly thereafter. All of this comes out on the night of the first Academy Awards, where Alfie performs his Happy Hobo act to a delighted industry audience before attempting to make his getaway on his yacht.

In contrast with *Hollywood Story*, which follows the basic template of what was then known about Taylor's murder, or *The Wild Party*, which uses the portly James Coco and his character Jolly Grimm to create a physically credible version of Fatty Arbuckle and his wild parties while forgoing the trials and banning of Arbuckle's films, the "secret" revealed as the center of *Sunset*'s mystery alludes only in very broad strokes to the circumstance of Hearst's purported killing of Ince on his yacht. That story may be censored in *Sunset*, but it returns in the way that Alfie, the Happy Hobo, is deliberately modeled on Chaplin; after all, the Little Tramp, who eventually ran the studio used in *Hollywood Story*, was purportedly Hearst's intended target when the publishing magnate unintentionally shot Ince. Furthermore Candy has witnessed what Alfie did to his wife on his yacht and received the Candy Store as her payout, mirroring how the shooting by Hearst was supposedly witnessed by Louella Parsons, who, it was believed, received her lifetime contract at his newspaper syndicate in exchange for her silence about Ince. Yet just as the real-life Earp died on January 13, 1929, several months before the first Academy Award dinner, so too Parsons reportedly received her contract to be Hearst's main Hollywood correspondent a short time before Ince's death. For that matter, while Earp and Tom Mix knew each other in real life, by 1929 Earp was already much older than his impersonator, James Garner; and whereas in the film Earp arrives in Hollywood to work for Alfie, in real life he had already been living in Los Angeles for a while at the time of his death.

But what Wyatt and subsequently Tom keep repeating throughout *Sunset* applies to how this backstudio represents Hollywood history: "That's the truth, give or take a lie or two." This refrain indicates how Hollywood history functions as fable for *Sunset*. There is enough grounding in the re-created look of 1929 studio shooting and LA locales, in location filming at the western ranch in nearby Santa Susana, and in allusions to the gossip regarding how Ince died to give this account of historical Hollywood a sense of truthfulness. At the same time, *Sunset* spins out that history as a lighthearted tall tale.

The jaunty air of Tom and Wyatt's investigation of Candy's murder belies the sense of menace and corruption that Alfie and his cohort personify. For in addition to abusing his wives, Alfie beats his chauffeur and bodyguard for not stopping Wyatt from meeting with Christina, and he blackmails the man so that he has to withstand repeated beatings. Likewise Alfie savagely beats his sister to give credence to her false claim that Tom has raped her. She herself is a comparable piece of work; in addition to killing Candy, she orders her bodyguard to beat up Tom when he pays a visit to her home, where she and several ladies of the evening are entertaining themselves. As Victoria screams curses at Tom, he shows what he learned from Jack Dempsey by cutting the arrogant bodyguard down to size. As for Kiefer, he has Wyatt pistol-whipped and "tied up like a calf" when he is caught checking out on his own the gangster's Kit Kat Club. While Kiefer summons the crooked Captain Blackworth, Wyatt is rescued by Cheryl, who bashes Blackworth's nose with a frying pan. A Mexican stand-off between Wyatt and Cheryl on one side and Kiefer and Blackworth on the other is settled by Tom, who arrives unexpectedly and trumps the police captain's ankle pistol with the barrel of a shotgun that turns out to be the pole on a mop. (⏵ Figures 6.6–6.7)

"In an actor's world things are seldom what they seem," Tom states as he leaves with Wyatt and Cheryl. "A pauper is a prince. Or a shotgun is a mop." Although Tom has had real cowboy experience, as a movie star he is a dandy, a rhinestone cowboy in all-white duds who likes to show off his virility as a movie star with great bravado, as when he greets Wyatt's arrival by train on his horse and sends him off the same way at the film's end, or when he boasts about the number of automobiles he owns, or when he condescendingly mocks Blackworth and Kiefer with his departing statement about an actor's world in pictures. (⏵ Figure 6.9) The illusionism of film as shown in *Sunset* appears to blur the difference between the fictional world's "reality" and the lightheartedness of the film we are watching, in which Tom and Wyatt act just like larger-than-life movie heroes. For instance, Tom charters a plane for Wyatt and him to rescue Nancy from Kiefer's thugs; he gets in the pilot's seat without ever having flown before, yet his inexperience does not prevent the plane from staying in the air for most of the journey. (⏵ Figure 6.8) Similarly, Wyatt does not know how to drive yet takes the wheel without much difficulty as he and Tom elude the cops following the two men's discovery of Candy's body. And although Tom is arrested on Victoria's accusation that he raped her, the charge goes nowhere in the plot; moments later he is sprung in time to attend the first Academy Awards banquet. The lighthearted shenanigans of the dandy cowboy movie star and the taciturn, retired marshal from Tombstone establish a tonal counterpoint to the sinister undercurrent of Alfie's corrupt Hollywood that does not efface the inescapable brutality of his power as a movie mogul or the violence that follows Tom and Wyatt in the wake of their investigation, including the men they kill when rescuing Nancy.

Early in *Sunset*, after watching Tom perform a bar fight for "Lawman," Wyatt applauds but states, "Well, I thought it was real thrillin' but, uh, I've never been in a fight like
that in my whole life." By the same token, Wyatt senses that Tom is not entirely comfortable being a movie star. Tom mentions his past as a bronco buster before he entered pictures, which suggests to Wyatt the similarity between the two men: they are "a whole lot
alike. Part fact and just enough fiction to sell newspapers." Tom replies that he guesses
"nobody's entirely comfortable bein' anything," and Wyatt responds, "I think the trick is
to know the fact and don't believe the fiction." This conversation occurs as the two men
stroll through the studio with scenes being acted and filmed behind them. An air of play-
acting as well as mystification characterizes both the banter between the two friends and
their behavior as they follow clues, deal with Alfie's and Blackworth's threats, and transform what could be construed as fiction into "fact," give or take a lie or two. (▶ Figure 6.10)

Like *Hollywood Story* and *The Wild Party*, *Sunset* did not have much traction at the
box office and its critical reception was not favorable. Like those two films as well, *Sunset*
was made by a troubled studio, in this case Tristar, part of the Columbia Pictures complex,
which at the time was owned by Coca-Cola, although the two jointly owned film studios,
a financial drain on Coke, would be sold to Sony the following year. With the purchase by
Sony in 1989, film became software for that company's hardware. Coke's sale to Sony,
moreover, was the start of what would become a conglomerate and globalized Hollywood
in the following two decades as other film studios were absorbed into massive international corporations with holdings in all fields of entertainment and with control of various
distribution portals (broadcast, cable, theaters, home video, streaming, and the like).

These three historical backstudios each came out at a moment of significant transition for the film industry: 1951 with the return of HUAC and the dismantling of the
majors' oligopoly; 1975 with the end of New Hollywood, first studio takeovers, and beginning of the blockbuster era; and 1988 with the start of the studios' absorption into multimedia corporations. Yet the year in which the films' narratives occur, which deviates from
when the scandals that provide their sources happened, seems to disavow any relation to
their present moment of production. The question that each film raises, then, is this: Why
so emphatically redate the scandal narrative to 1929? *Hollywood Story* announces in its
opening voice-over that the year is 1929; *The Wild Party* does this with an opening title
card; and *Sunset* identifies this year with its climax at the first Oscars.

On the surface, 1929 seems simply to work as shorthand for a historical moment that
is discontinuous with 1951, 1974, or 1988. In *Hollywood Story* Mitch comments that 1929
was the year he started high school, and Larry remarks, "That's the year my father finished
in Wall Street." When coming clean to Larry about his role in the Ferrara murder, Sam
mentions that "movies started to talk" in 1929, and he wanted to salvage a few silent pictures while he could. *The Wild Party* recognizes the datedness of Jolly's film as the public
wants sound and implies the coming Depression with a song played on the soundtrack as
partygoers do a sexualized two-step, "The Herbert Hoover Drag." (▶ Figure 6.11) In
Sunset, the actual date of May 16 for the first Academy Awards indicates the time frame, so

its mystery unfolds just as all-talking pictures were taking off following the gigantic suc-cess of *The Singing Fool* (1928), which turned Hollywood upside down. (▶ Figure 6.12) The first Best Picture winner in 1929 was the silent *Wings* (1927), but the second year the prize went to the "all-talking, all-singing, all-dancing" *Broadway Melody* (1929), which premiered about three weeks after the first Oscar ceremony and climax of *Sunset*.

In addition to marking the full conversion to talkies, 1929 was an undeniably pivotal year for the film industry. "The coming of sound," as Douglas Gomery explains, "ought to be remembered for the consolidation of economic power we now call the studio system" (Gomery 2005, 138). Taking the lead with their initial use of sound, Warner Bros., Fox, and the newly formed RKO-Radio began to compete with Famous Players–Lasky/ Paramount and Loew's/MGM as vertically integrated companies. These five major stu-dios would dominate filmmaking in the United States for the next four decades. In addi-tion, the studios' full conversion to sound recording transformed the infrastructure of daily production, technology, and labor. Along with the coming of talkies and the coales-cence of the studio system, the stock market crash in 1929 initiated the eventual receiver-ship during the 1930s of firms that had overexpanded, like Paramount and Fox, and the Academy of Motion Picture Arts and Sciences was created by the studios to serve initially as a labor organization, mediating and minimizing the emergent union movement in Hollywood. In these three fictionalized Hollywood histories, 1929 signifies *the* major transitional moment for the film industry that further displaces, yet symptomatically in-dicates, what were more immediate and pressing, but at the time more incoherent, trans-formations occurring in the present, signaling in each case the crumbling of what was then the present mode of production and exhibition—as exemplified by the economic uncertainty of Universal-International in 1951, AIP in 1974, and Columbia Tristar in 1988.

1951: Rites of Confession

This is by now a familiar story but one worth recapitulating. In 1947 the House Un-American Activities Committee singled out nineteen established writers, directors, and producers for a public interrogation of their past affiliations with the Communist Party of the USA. The ten who were subpoenaed to testify in Washington, DC, refused to answer the Committee's questions; citing them for contempt, the Committee refused to let the witnesses read their statements in defense of the First Amendment—although they let declared anti-Communists like Adolphe Menjou, Robert Montgomery, Gary Cooper, and Walt Disney speak freely. Hollywood studio heads responded to the hearings, which had devolved into a public spectacle of bullying and baiting by the Committee and bellig-erence and open hostility by the ten subpoenaed witnesses, with what amounted to a blacklist of anyone connected with the Communist Party. At first the studios canceled the contracts of the Hollywood Ten, as those "unfriendly witnesses" were called, but an in-dustry-wide blacklist later applied to an indeterminate cohort of political "unfriendlies" unless they cleansed themselves of their radical past by naming names. The Hollywood

Ten appealed their convictions for contempt of Congress, but the Supreme Court ruled against them, and they began their brief prison terms in 1950.

Although the actions of HUAC beyond Hollywood are usually viewed through the lens of Cold War ideology and the postwar formation of the national security state, it is equally important, as Dennis Broe argues in his book about film noir, to remember how the expulsion of the radical left from the film industry, which began in 1947, targeted labor activism both nationally and locally in the Los Angeles region. The period of left hegemony was short, 1945–50, "at a moment when working-class consciousness was heightened by a series of strikes, both in the nation as a whole and in Hollywood in particular, and when middle-class anxiety over increasing corporatization was acute" (Broe 2009, 30). Broe considers HUAC a strike-breaking tool, arguing that it combined with the anti-Communist mandate in section 9h of the Taft-Hartley Act to function as a two-pronged assault on what had been a progressive vision of organized labor, resulting, for instance, in the Congress of Industrial Organization's expulsion of its most radical unions in 1949 and 1950 (Broe 2009, 34). In his book on political activism and the union movement in Hollywood, Gerald Horne similarly observes, "The hearings on Taft-Hartley legislation had sent a clear signal that militant trade unionism would henceforth be viewed as equivalent to Communism" (Horne 2001, 213).

Prior to Taft-Hartley and the HUAC hearings, the film industry saw "a feverish pitch of union activity" organized in early 1945 by the Conference of Studio Unions (CSU), which voiced "a collaborative vision of craft and creative unions joining together against the studios" (Broe 2009, 35). The CSU had 10,500 members, compared with the 16,000 members in the studio- (and mob-) controlled International Association of Theatrical and Stage Employees (IATSE). In a two-year period, from 1945 through 1947, the CSU held three major disruptive, combative, and bloody strikes against the studios, targeting Warner Bros., MGM, and Disney. In anticipation of the first strike, which lasted from March through October in 1945, the studios had stockpiled a nine-month supply of films (Horne 2001, 167). Eventually the studios collaborated with the Screen Actors Guild, the Teamsters, and IATSE to break the CSU. The militant labor leaders were investigated as Communists, and more than 3,500 former CSU members were blacklisted.

With the CSU dismantled, the only remaining oppositional union in town was the Screen Writers Guild, which had always been the most vocal ally of the CSU, had remained critical of Taft-Hartley, and was an opponent of the anti-Communist loyalty oath. One Hollywood Ten member, Dalton Trumbo, considered the destruction of the trade union movement to be as important a reason for HUAC's investigation of Hollywood as its declared intent of removing leftish content from the screen and its implied goal of paralyzing "anti-fascist political action" (Broe 2009, 37). The HUAC investigation of Hollywood "was anti-labor in the guise of being anti-Communist" (38), as evident in the typical linkage of two opening questions of witnesses that joined the threat of Communism with that of militant organized labor: "Are you a member of the Screen Writers Guild?," followed by "Are you a member of the Communist Party?" With the Committee's return to Hollywood in 1951 with more subpoenas, the blacklist was reinforced by right-wing organizations such as the American Legion and the Motion Picture Alliance for the Preservation of American Ideals, and the ritual of confession—of naming names before members of HUAC or private groups like the Legion or Alliance in a humiliating purging—was quickly established as the means of being cleared to work again in Hollywood.

Andrew Paul argues that subsequent historical and fictional narratives about the Red Scare have "avoided dwelling on the politics of the blacklist, choosing instead to emphasize the moral crime of implicating others to save one's own career" (Paul 2013, 210). This was the context for industry-wide and at times vociferous objections to Elia Kazan's Lifetime Achievement Award at the 1999 Oscars. Specifically, Paul mentions how, in the few Hollywood features about the Red Scare, "the blacklist's racial and ethnic dimensions, its largely Jewish base of victims and its anti-Semitic tone, its antagonism toward social democratic thought, and its insistence that those allied with civil rights movements must be 'un-American' are overlooked" (210). Instead, he argues, "American popular memory of the blacklist is subject to a lasting consensus ideology," which leaves out "race, ethnicity, and radical politics" in order to reiterate that "most Americans, or at least those whose ideas exemplify normative American thought, can agree on a set of postracial, civil libertarian principles" (210–11).

In Paul's account, HUAC and the blacklist made the Red Scare a question of "who or what was an 'American' and who was not," whereas the rare Hollywood backstudios depicting this period—*Guilty by Suspicion* (1991) and *The Majestic* (2001)—take as their protagonist a politically naïve liberal faced with the dilemma of naming names or losing his career (Paul 2013, 211). (The third film Paul discusses is *The Front* [1976], about the television blacklist in New York City.) *Guilty by Suspicion* and *The Majestic* each take place in 1951; each explains that its lead character attended a CP meeting when much younger and then only to pursue a girl; each concludes with his refusal to name names; and each applauds his defiance, effecting a utopian revision of the real history that each film claims to be recounting. In both films, the witch-hunt arising from the Red Scare is led by bullies seeking to get their names and photos in newspapers by hounding Hollywood celebrities, and the blacklisted hero stands up to them with a speech that proves he, not they, is the true American.

To be sure, both films are crafted according to traditional Hollywood formulas, which subordinate a professional plot (progressing from the character's thwarted desire to work in Hollywood) to a personal one (instructing him in the virtues of love, family, honor, etc.) and view history through the lens of the beleaguered protagonist. As Jeanne Hall observes of David Merrill (Robert De Niro), the blacklisted director in *Guilty by Suspicion*, a renewed commitment to his home life motivates his finally agreeing to testify before HUAC, but those same personal reasons eventually lead him to defy the Committee. In his refusal to testify against others, David is therefore "maintaining his rugged individualism while simultaneously undergoing a tortured retreat to the nuclear family" (Hall 2001, 22), albeit with the possibility of imprisonment given the end title card mentioning the many real jailed "unfriendlies." (⊙ Figure 6.13)

David Merrill (Robert De Niro) refusing to testify in an open HUAC hearing. (*Guilty by Suspicion* ©1991 Warner Bros.)

Similarly, Peter Appleton (Jim Carrey), the blacklisted writer in *The Majestic*, loses his memory and gets mistaken for a dead war hero in a Capraesque town that lost scores of young men in World War II. After helping to restore the eponymous movie theater, when his memory returns and the FBI catches up with him, Peter not only becomes a bona fide patriot by refusing to name names, but he also leaves Hollywood afterward to return to that small town, run the movie theater, and marry the fiancée of the man whose identity he had (innocently) assumed and whose memory had finally inspired him not to testify. When questioned at his hearing, Peter invokes the First Amendment, declaring, "This is a bigger issue than whether or not I am a Communist." He explains to the Committee that the contracts enumerated in the Bill of Rights "are the only contracts not subject to renegotiation." Then he adds, "Too many people have paid for this contract in blood." As he walks away, the packed audience, which had initially laughed at him when he dithered about naming names, stands and applauds. The Committee lets him off the hook on the technicality that he has named someone, the girl he mentioned when he explained why he had attended a CP meeting during his college years. But he is no stool pigeon since, ironically, she had named him to the Committee in the first place! A coda depicts his subsequent life as husband and father, testifying to his normality as an American. (▶ Figures 6.14–6.16)

Whereas *The Majestic* places the amnesiac Peter in a small town that is hungry to embrace a returning war hero and is the picture of white Americana, *Guilty by Suspicion* makes more of an effort to depict what happened in 1951 with characters whose situations recall real-life models. It opens with the interrogation of Larry Nolan (Chris Cooper), read Larry Parks, who begs, "Please don't make me do this," because he knows that the Committee already knows the Hollywood Reds they want him to name. (▶ Figure 6.17)

This scene makes clear that the testimony being exacted from him is a ritual of purging through confession, and to underscore the power play at work here, the interlocutor calls Larry "son." Larry squirms and sobs and does name names, which enables him to work but alienates him from his friends and his wife, the actress Dorothy Nolan (Patricia Wettig). She loses custody of her son to Larry, much as in real life Dorothy Comingore lost custody of her children to her ex-husband, a CP member who named names. Comingore was blacklisted in 1951, but the status of the fictional Dorothy is less straightforward; she is an emotionally unbalanced alcoholic who kills herself out of despair over losing her son to her ex-husband, so her drinking and outbursts may be reasons for her unemployment, since the one time we see her on set she has barricaded herself in her dressing room, where she is hysterical about not getting to be with her child, and she never receives a subpoena. (⏵ Figure 6.18) We also get a fleeting glimpse of a Jules Dassin/Joseph Losey figure in Joe Lesser (Martin Scorsese), who cheerfully departs for Europe in the dead of night to evade a subpoena.

Guilty by Suspicion sprinkles a few real people and a real studio, Twentieth Century-Fox, into its mix. In a slight anachronism, David's childhood friend Bunny Baxter (George Wendt) is doing rewrites for Gentlemen Prefer Blondes (1953), which did not begin production until the middle of November 1952. David visits Bunny, who will later be subpoenaed, on the set of Blondes, where we get a glimpse of Marilyn Monroe's backside as "Diamonds Are a Girl's Best Friend" is being shot. While on the phone with Howard Hawks, Darryl F. Zanuck (Ben Piazza) watches clips of Monroe performing another number. (⏵ Figure 6.19) Like his real-life counterpart who was opposed to the blacklist but capitulated to the New York office (Lev 2013, 110, 163–64), the film's Zanuck wants to protect his people, but his hands are tied, given David's behavior. The wonder-boy director, called home from location scouting in France by Zanuck, is apparently ignorant of HUAC and the blacklist occurring in his absence. He takes umbrage when meeting with a lawyer hired by the studio to clear him through private testimony and refuses to name names.

In the original script by Abraham Polonsky, David was a former Communist and not the naïve liberal who had been kicked out of a CP meeting for arguing too much; but with revisions written by director Irwin Winkler, like Dorothy's and Bunny's, David's past was depoliticized so as to avoid giving the impression that the film was about Communists. This revision makes him an innocent victim, unjustly accused as he is hounded off a job directing on Poverty Row, followed coast to coast by the FBI, and finally bullied by sinister congressmen at the hearings. Polonsky ended up withdrawing his name from the script because of Winkler's revisions (Navasky 1991; Paul 2013, 214).

The Way We Were (1973), an earlier backstudio that recounts a wider history of radical politics, concluding with the blacklist, likewise suffered from censorship of a sort from its director, Sydney Pollack, who cut scenes pertaining to his heroine's politics after a preview showed that they stalled the conclusion of the film's love story, which was its big selling point. The Way We Were follows Katie Morosky (Barbra Streisand), a Jewish working-class radical, and Hubbell Gardiner (Robert Redford), a WASP Golden Boy, from their college years in the late 1930s through their reunion during wartime in the early 1940s and their married life in Hollywood at the end of that decade, where he is adapting his novel for the screen. The tensions in their relationship are due to Katie's politics, which makes her push too hard, in Hubbell's view, especially when she gets argumentative and hostile with his wealthy friends, in contrast to his more laissez-faire attitude, which finds humor in everything, including the ideals that she believes in so strongly, if also so stridently.

The couple's final breakup begins when, disregarding Hubbell's wishes, Katie goes to Washington to support the Hollywood Ten as a member of the Hollywood Committee for the First Amendment. In the tumult at Union Station that occurs when the group returns, Katie and Hubbell retreat to an empty restaurant, where he claims that people are more important than principles, and she retorts, "Hubbell, people *are* their principles." But while the film is most sympathetic to Katie's perspective, Hubbell gets to speak with the advantage of screenwriter Arthur Laurent's historical hindsight. "People will get hurt and nothing will change," Hubbell angrily tells Katie. "And after five or six years, when it's practical," some "fascist producer" will hire "a Commie writer" to save his troubled movie, so the writer's going to jail will all have been for naught. (▶ Figure 6.20)

Like her Jewishness, Katie's radical politics, which include her presidency of the Young Communists League while in college and her later defense of the Ten, remain in the final version of *The Way We Were*. (▶ Figure 6.21) During its development, though, Pollock was not happy with Laurents's original screenplay and at different points hired other writers to revise or add scenes. His dissatisfaction had nothing to do with the script's political content but, rather, was due to his desire to build up Hubbell for Redford to play, giving more heft to the otherwise politically passive character. Pollock even hired Dalton Trumbo, one of the Ten, to script scenes of Hubbell testifying before HUAC as an informer. In a letter to Trumbo, Pollock explained that having Hubbell inform "moves the blacklist dead centre to the drama" and "fulfills the metaphor of 'Hubbell' as 'America'" (Tieber 2010, 57). Trumbo delivered two scenes. In the first, Hubbell refuses to name names or to testify about his wife's Party membership yet lies under oath about having lent his name to a blacklisted friend's screenplay. Because he has committed perjury and the Committee knows it, if word gets out about his fronting that script then no one in Hollywood will believe he writes any of his own pictures; another scene thus shows a resigned Hubbell naming names (60–61). Together, these two scenes deepen and add pathos to Hubbell's characteristic sense of earnestness and privilege; the situation before HUAC, which begins with his "unrealistic sense of his own possibilities," forces him to confront that "his options are now limited" (63).

As far as I know, the Trumbo scenes were not filmed and almost all of Laurents's screenplay was used in the end, including one of the scenes eventually cut following the preview. (It is now excerpted in the "making of" documentary on the DVD and Blu-ray disc.) In it, after Hubbell tells Katie that a friend from college has named her and she will be called to testify before HUAC, she realizes that so long as *she* won't name names, *he* "won't get a job in this town." However, if they divorced, she comments, he "wouldn't have a subversive wife. That would solve everything, wouldn't it?" Although Hubbell replies "No," reminding us of the opposing views regarding people versus principles that have always caused rifts between them, she asks him to stay until their baby is born. That Katie feels compelled to leave her husband—so as not to sacrifice her principles or force him to give up what he loves doing—dramatizes how the political does intersect with the personal. The couple divorces and he has a successful Hollywood career, while she moves east and continues her activism. (▶ Clips 17–18)

With the political context of their divorce effaced by the cut, why Katie later asks her husband to stay with her until their baby is born (and why he subsequently has never seen his child) is more ambiguous. To be sure, the cut straightens out the condensed timeline that otherwise occurs due to the additional scene. For with that scene intact the time frame seems puzzling to me. Katie is pregnant when she goes to Washington in 1947, but as she says in the scene, she is "a nobody," so I doubt HUAC would have been interested in her then. On the other hand, in 1951 they would have been looking for informers in Hollywood and vilifying anyone, even nobodies like Katie, with a radical past who did not inform. In any event, the direct threat to Hubbell's career from the blacklist is now mainly implicit in the theatrical version. In a scene that occurs just before they decide to separate, Katie declares that she hates how Hubbell has sold out to Hollywood, but she also discloses that she knows he recently slept with his old college girlfriend, who is now the estranged wife of his best friend. The adultery is a slap in the face to Katie since she has always felt inferior to the woman's Upper East Side bearing. When Hubbell asks Katie who told her, she says, "A friend." "Some friend," he replies. "Well," Katie continues, making a deliberate comparison with the political witch-hunt, "it's a friendly town if you don't mind having your friends inform on you." Without the deleted scene, which would make clearer how the couple is directly affected by the HUAC hearings and that Katie consequently leaves Hubbell for the sake of his career, the immediate takeaway from The Way We Were is that, while political disagreements cause tensions in their marriage, Hubbell's infidelity ends it. Yet whereas the cut scene states that Katie herself was named by a former friend and will be subpoenaed to name names, the way she contextualizes how she has learned about Hubbell's adultery, as well as her comment about Hollywood's "friendliness" as a town, at least suggests the parallelism of the personal and the political.

Jeanne Hall notes "two flurries of blacklist 'nostalgia' which occurred in the mid-1970s and the early 1990s," with the first wave of documentaries, books, articles, and op-ed columns taking a sympathetic view of the blacklisted writers, and the second wave, reflecting a different political climate, taking a more critical stance toward Party members' own ideological rigidity. She attributes Winkler's skittishness about having a Communist protagonist in Guilty by Suspicion to the conservative backdrop of that second "flurry" (Hall 2001, 16). As for The Majestic, its conservative view of Americanism can be attributed to millennial anxiety that was further enhanced by the events of

September 11, 2001, and all the flag-waving following in their wake, which happened just a few months before the film's release at Christmastime.

The liberal political perspective that informs *The Way We Were*, on the other hand, dates from that first period of "blacklist 'nostalgia,'" when many Hollywood films advanced social criticism through traditional formats. In a subsequent essay, Hall critiques *The Way We Were* for overdetermining "the central conflict" that defines the couple, noting that every time the script raises a political issue it immediately backs away and turns to the personal (Hall 2006, 159, 161–62). The theatrical cut of *The Way We Were* blurs what otherwise could be a sharper and more irreconcilable divide between Katie's radical politics and Hubbell's laissez-faire liberalism. This may be why the ending is still so fondly remembered for Katie's approving comment about Hubbell's new "girl" and her touching of his hair, and not for the disclosure that he has never seen his own child and presumably never will. Because of Katie's political past, in order to safeguard his career Hubbell has had to excise her and their daughter from his life. In this respect, the dissolution of their marriage and his declining the invitation to meet his daughter and Katie's new husband may be reenacting how postwar liberals were complicit in purging the radical left from American political life during the Red Scare.

I therefore agree that *The Way We Were* is confused or at least uncertain in its final stretch insofar as the political thrust depends primarily on the argument in the train station, which occurs several scenes before Katie and Hubbell split up. The personal and the political are then made to seem two sides of a single coin. It is nonetheless worth noting that, in contrast with *Guilty by Suspicion* and *The Majestic*, *The Way We Were* still tries to view American cultural front politics of the decades before, during, and after World War II. Katie's character foregrounds a history of American activism that found its way to Hollywood, while also registering the negative impact of HUAC's anti-Semitic bias, its constriction of the democratic process, and its inflexible determination of what counts as true American values.

1951 Redux: Welcome to Capitol Pictures

Joel and Ethan Coen handle the Red Scare and HUAC much more offhandedly in *Barton Fink* (1991) and *Hail, Caesar!* (2016). Along with the twenty-five-year gap between them, their two historical backstudios differ in style and tone: the first is a surrealistic nightmare arising from the protagonist's writer's block and the second, a pastiche of old Hollywood gossip and genres. But the two films are connected at least superficially by their taking place at the same fictional movie studio, Capitol Pictures.

Barton Fink is set in 1941, not 1951, so at first glance, and even a second and third look, it may seem to have nothing to do with HUAC and the blacklist. The title character (John Turturro) is a New York City Jewish playwright, modeled on playwright Clifford Odets. Barton wants to write "a new living theater for the common man" but accepts a job in Hollywood writing scripts at Capitol Pictures. There, studio head Jack Lipnick's

(Michael Lerner) fast-talking, narcissistic, bombastic, and patronizing figure, a composite of Jack Warner, Harry Cohn, and Louis B. Mayer (Allen 2006, 48), sends up the stereotypical Jewish studio head of the sort epitomized by Saxe in *What Price Hollywood?* (1932). The Hollywood milieu itself is drawn from the Coens' reading of Otto Friedrich's *City of Nets: A Portrait of Hollywood in the 1940s* along with well-known and off-repeated gossip about the studio moguls, their minions, and famous writers brought to Hollywood (60). (▶ Figure 6.22)

Assigned, as William Faulkner was, to write a generic wrestling picture for Wallace Beery but with "that Barton Fink feeling," Barton settles into the Earle Hotel, a locale with an increasingly surreal atmosphere, what with the strange desk clerk, Chet (Steve Buscemi), who slowly ascends from a trap door below his counter, the paper peeling off the walls of Barton's room due to the extreme heat, the mosquitos leaving bloody blemishes on his face, the noises of crying or lovemaking in the rooms next door that disturb his efforts to write (or that supply a reason for him not to do so), the elevators that burst into flames, and the picture on his wall of a "bathing beauty," which morphs into a real person on the beach whom Barton encounters in the film's final moments. (▶ Figure 6.23)

Then there is the man in the room next door. At the Earle, Barton befriends his neighbor, Charlie Meadows (John Goodman), an insurance salesman. (▶ Figure 6.24) Charlie is the "common man" who can tell Barton stories, as he repeatedly states, if Barton would ever listen, but the writer is too busy expounding upon his theory of a living art for the common man and "the life of the mind." As the film progresses, and Barton's wastebasket fills with crumpled sheets of typing paper, the line between reality and fantasy becomes progressively murky. Certainly by the time the hotel catches fire and Charlie walks through the flames, gunning down the two detectives who have come to apprehend him and screaming, "I'll show you the life of the mind," the film's verisimilitude, established in the opening scenes in New York City, has come undone. After his march down the long hallway, Charlie heads for Barton's room, where he bends the metal footboard of the bed to free Barton, who has been handcuffed there by the detectives, and enters his own room, while Barton leaves with the box that Charlie gives him, which may or may not contain a human head. Neither Charlie nor Barton pay attention to the flames surrounding him as he moves in and out of the burning corridor, so possibly the fire is symbolic and not literally happening, meant to signify that writing for Hollywood has been a descent into Hell for Barton Fink.

By this point in the film, too, we understand that Charlie is a serial killer, since the detectives tell Barton the salesman is "Madman Mundt," who has slain many people, including his doctor, the alcoholic writer W. P. Mayhew (John Mahoney), Mayhew's assistant and lover, Audrey Taylor (Judy Davis), and possibly even Barton's aunt and uncle back East; moreover the detectives suspect Barton may be Charlie's accomplice. The suspicion may not be out of line, at least thematically. R. Barton Palmer, in fact, proposes that "Charlie's frustration is the mirror reflux of Barton's. His is a voice from below stifled by institutional indifference rather than a voice from above [like Barton's,] that, confronting a semiotic tangle of 'readymades,' can find nothing to say about them" (Palmer 2004, 118). Yet while that is the case, it also begs the question of what is happening *narratively* since, given the postmodern texture of *Barton Fink*, reality and fantasy, like history and its representations, draw upon each other to cause a good deal of uncertainty.

For instance, is Charlie real and a vicious killer, or is he an externalization of Barton's unconscious, maybe even another personality acting out the writer's own violent impulses? Or if Charlie is not a multiple of Barton but a friend who helpfully disposes of Audrey's body, does that mean that Barton slaughtered her after they had sex? After all, Madman Mundt's m.o. is to blast his victims with a shotgun and cut off their heads; whereas Mayhew's corpse is headless—his missing head may be in the box Charlie gives to Barton—Audrey's is still attached when Barton wakes up. But why would Madman Mundt kill Mayhew? We can follow the accusation that he slayed his doctor since Charlie reports arguing with him over the bill. But Barton is the one furious at the writer's mistreatment of Audrey, especially once he learns that she has been ghostwriting his scripts and recent novels. Does Barton's fury extend to Mayhew for that same reason? Alternatively, are all the events in the Earle happening in Barton's mind? Indeed, are Charlie (who tries to teach Barton some wrestling moves), the serial killings, even the two detectives, all playing out in Barton's imagination as the material of the screenplay he finally turns in to Lipnick? The surreal style of *Barton Fink*, with its "irrational logic," as Joel Coen described it (Allen 2006, 49), makes all of these possibilities conceivable while contradicting them so that each one seems equally implausible.

Regardless of how one sorts out the real from the fantastic, *Barton Fink* approaches the protagonist's writer's block from two contrasting perspectives. To begin with, Barton's block arises from an internal cause, the constipated life of his mind. Barton seems inhibited by his condescending attitude toward the very class of people he wants to write about since all he can initially produce are clichés about fishmongers in the streets. As Charlie explains to Barton after shooting the two detectives, "I know what it feels like, when things get all balled up at the head office. It puts you through hell, Barton. So I help people out. I just wish someone would do as much for me." When Barton asks, "Why me?" Charlie shouts, "Because you *don't listen!*" Barton's unwillingness to hear the common man makes him unable to fill the blank page in his typewriter until, during Charlie's absence, he furiously writes, supposedly about the salesman, a fitting inspiration for the wrestler character to be played by Wallace Beery. Or, just as possibly, as the opening and closing lines of his script suggest, Barton recycles his stage play. Or perhaps he does both. In any event, at the USO club where he goes to celebrate his finished screenplay, Barton dances manically; when a sailor wants a chance to twirl with his anonymous female partner, Barton refuses, boasting of his superiority. "I'm a writer! I create!" He points to his head to show off his "uniform" and is promptly knocked down and bloodied. (▶ Figure 6.25)

On the other hand, the external "head office" in Hollywood is just as responsible for Barton's writer's block. (▶ Figure 6.26) After all, he is given an impossible task when assigned a wrestling picture for he knows nothing about film genres. Furthermore Lipnick repeatedly and furiously talks over Barton, professing his respect for writers but considering them a dime a dozen. "You think you're the only one who can give me that Barton Fink feeling," he shouts in their final meeting. "I got twenty writers under contract that I can ask for a Fink-type thing from.... You just don't get it, do you? You still think the whole world revolves around whatever rattles inside that little kike head of yours." Barton's screenplay does not please Lipnick because it is *too* serious. "I gotta tell ya, Fink, it won't wash," he bellows. Yet Lipnick is still planning to keep Barton under contract to Capitol, which will own everything he writes but never produce his scripts. "I want you in town, Fink," Lipnick yells, "and out of my sight!" Barton is, in a word, blacklisted. He will not own what he creates, and what he creates will never see the light of day but will be like those shelved scripts of the blacklisted writers after their banishment.

The invitation to connect the dots in this way, to supply a framework (but not a coherent narrative or allegorical explanation) taken from the mid-century Red Scare for this writer's *not* writing and then, when he does, for having his work suppressed, is there in Charlie's real name, Karl Mundt. According to Wikipedia, the historical Karl Mundt was a congressman from South Dakota and member of HUAC from 1943 to 1948 before moving on to the Senate, so Mundt was directly involved in the investigation of Communist "infiltration" of Hollywood. Furthermore, in 1948 he and Richard Nixon introduced a bill requiring Communists to register and forbidding them from holding public office, which ultimately became the McCarran Internal Security Act of 1950. The inspiration for Charlie's real name may be the joke behind his ruthlessly slaying detectives with Italian and German surnames and fascist inclinations. Thus Charlie's muttering "Heil Hitler" to Detective Deutsch, as he shoots him in the head, links the anger of the "common man"—of "the alienated, angry 'mass man' of a consumer-oriented capitalist society"—to the rise of European fascism (Adams 2015, 77–78), while also implying the connection of fascism to the origins of HUAC. Charlie's is the angry proletariat voice that the intellectual Barton hears but never listens to. As Joel Coen noted, "This is a movie about how much Barton does *not understand*" (qtd. in Allen 2006, 58, emphasis in original).

To be sure, only my admittedly sideways reading of *Barton Fink* discloses its relation to historical Hollywood of 1951 as well as 1941, and the film addresses the problematics of representation, creativity, and mass culture more directly, as critics like Palmer and Jeffrey Adams have well explained. By comparison, genuine Communist screenwriters inhabiting the early 1950s *do* populate and motivate the plotting of *Hail, Caesar!*

It is 1951, at least according to the copyright notice on the film-within-the-film starring Hobie Doyle, "The Stars Align." However, befitting how *Hail, Caesar!* plays with its historical (in)accuracies, according to a reference to the 1954 test of a thermonuclear device, which Cuddahy, the man from Lockheed, says the aviation company was part of, the film may be taking place in that year; or possibly, as his dialogue also implies, his reference mistakes the location of that later test for the first one, made in 1952; on the DVD, though, one of the film's stars, Channing Tatum, insists the year is 1951. In any event, the film's protagonist, Eddie Mannix (Josh Brolin), now heads Capitol Pictures in Hollywood. Eddie shares the name of the vice president, general manager, and notorious fixer at MGM, and he also reports by phone to Nick Schenck, who ran Loew's Inc. from New York City; however, this Eddie is nothing like his supposed real-life counterpart. Whereas Mannix was a brutal man who kept a mistress during his marriage to Toni Lanier—the characterization evident in *Hollywoodland* (2006), the backstudio about the mysterious circumstances surrounding the suicide of Toni's lover, George Reeves—the Coens depict Eddie as a respectable, soft-spoken, middle-class, Catholic, family man who has promised his wife not to smoke and whose confessions to his priest open and close the picture. Furthermore, whereas the Christian names of the real-life Mannix were "Joseph Edgar Allen John," Eddie's office door lists him as "Edward Mannix." In short, the Coens' Eddie Mannix is a kinder, gentler, and untrue version of the famous MGM fixer. And by 1951 (or 1954) Capitol Pictures has become much less Jewish too. (▶ Figure 6.27)

The other characters working at Capitol all have fictitious names but are more straightforward copies or composites of real people from Hollywood's Golden Age: swimming star DeeAnna Moran (Scarlett Johansson) recalls Esther Williams, with gossip about Loretta Young's adopting her own illegitimate child thrown in; musical star Burt Gurney (Channing Tatum), Gene Kelly, with a reminder of Kelly's leftish politics and long sojourn in Europe after making *Singin' in the Rain* to avoid HUAC; Latina bombshell Carlotta Valdez (Veronica Osorio), Carmen Miranda; the feuding twins Thora and Thessaly Thacker (Tilda Swinton), Louella Parsons and Hedda Hopper; singing cowboy Hobie Doyle (Alden Ehrenreich), Tim Holt and Roy Rogers; the fastidious gay director Laurence Laurentz (Ralph Fiennes), George Cukor and Vincente Minnelli; and the not-so-smart epic hero Baird Whitlock (George Clooney), Robert Taylor and Charlton Heston. As pastiche, *Hail, Caesar!* affectionately sends up these stars and their genres.

Eddie Mannix's door. (*Hail, Caesar!* ©2016 Universal)

DeeAnna's swimming number evokes Williams's water ballets in both *Bathing Beauty* (1944) and *Million Dollar Mermaid* (1952), for instance, just as Burt's number "No Dames!" makes explicit the queer subtext of Kelly's buddy musicals such as *Anchors Aweigh* (1944), and Baird's biblical epic echoes *Quo Vadis* (1951) and *Ben-Hur* (1959).

Another loose shaggy dog tale from the Coens, but without the surrealism of their earlier backstudio, *Hail, Caesar!* is held together by Eddie's character. He runs interference with the press and police for his errant stars, solving their offscreen troubles and squelching news about their peccadillos while viewing rushes, watching budgets, and meeting with Cuddahy, who, trying to hire Eddie to manage Lockheed, tells him the film business is "frivolous," whereas aviation is "the future." Eddie's main problem during the thirty-six hours covered by the film, though, is Baird's disappearance midway through a day of shooting another film-within-the-film, also called "Hail, Caesar!" A cell (or as they call themselves, "a study group") of Communist screenwriters has kidnapped the actor and now demands $100,000 in ransom. The note requesting the money also declares, "We are the future."

Baird is not made a prisoner with his eyes taped and his hands tied. Rather, over tea and sandwiches, the writers educate him in Marxist theory, led by a replica of the real-life Herbert Marcuse (John Bluthal), who has come down from Stanford to teach the writers how to move from "getting Communist content into motion pictures" to more "direct action" related to their own interests. "You see," the head Communist screenwriter (Max Baker) tells Baird, "if you understand economics you can actually write down what will happen in the future, with as much confidence as you write down the history of the past. Because it's science, it's not make-believe." Yet buried in the Communists' preaching to Baird is an undeniable truth about the infrastructure of Hollywood, one that has rankled screenwriters since the formation of their guild (and that is also reflected in Barton's servitude to Lipnick and Capitol Pictures). The head Communist explains to the star, "Just because the studio owns the means of production, why should it be able to take the money, our money, the value created by our labor, and dole out what it pleases?" After being told that they consider the ransom "payback," Baird asks if he can have a share, but he is told it would not be "ethical" for him to share in his own ransom. "What if I name names?" he asks. "If, uh, I just tell the truth?" He is silenced with the threat of their exposing how he got his first big role in "On Wings as Eagles," which gossip says was by sleeping with its director, Laurence Laurentz.

The writers' discourse makes them all seem rigidly ideological but also tendentious and pedantic, exactly as HUAC had painted the Communist writers in 1947. Indeed they confirm the Committee's suspicions that the radical left had snuck Communist content into Hollywood films, and they are all arrested after Hobie rescues Baird. Furthermore Baird's threat to "name names" or "just tell the truth" positions him in the room as a friendly witness, which the writers then counter with their reminder of the star's dubious sexual past, rumors of which Eddie has suppressed. The writers' plot to send the ransom money to Moscow comes to nothing, too, since Burt drops the satchel with the cash in the

Baird Whitlock (George Clooney) being tutored in Marxist theory. (*Hail, Caesar!* ©2016 Universal)

ocean when his dog, Engels, jumps into his arms as he boards the Soviet submarine that emerges from the deep not too far from Malibu beach. Burt, who does not seem like the sharpest knife in the drawer, is the most unlikely Red one can imagine; why he is leaving Hollywood—in the middle of shooting a picture and by submarine near the California coast, no less—is another preposterous event happening in the film. (▶ Figure 6.28)

With the reference to the screenwriters' status as writers for hire, which places copyright in the studio's hands, and Baird's threat of naming names, the kidnapping plot resonates not only with HUAC's return to Hollywood in 1951 and their attack on the Screen Writers Guild, which began in 1947, but with the Guild's history as well. The future of the Screen Writers Guild was not as clear at that historical moment since HUAC and the blacklist had left deep wounds within the organization's hierarchy and divided its membership. Nonetheless we know that the Writers Guild of America (formed when the Screen Writers Guild merged with several other guilds to represent TV scribes in 1954) would survive the demise of the studio system epitomized by Capitol Pictures and become a powerful union again. This may be how the writers' "science" understands "history," as conveyed by the writers' note declaring that *they* are the future. Conversely, in 1951 (or 1954) aviation may have seemed like the future, as Cuddahy tells Eddie, but hindsight should remind us that Lockheed was rocked by a series of bribery scandals that began in the 1950s, and the company needed a government bailout in 1971.

Neither aviation nor the radical politics of the Screen Writers Guild is the "future" from the perspective of the wacky historical past that *Hail, Caesar!* imagines. For ultimately, if still with tongue-in-cheek humor, Hollywood moviemaking triumphs over the Commies and jet propulsion. Back in Eddie's office, as Baird recapitulates in detail all that he has learned from the Communists about how "the studio makes pictures to serve the system," Eddie slaps him in the face when the star mentions the exploitation of labor that fills the pockets of "that fat cat, Nick Schenck." Eddie grabs Baird and slaps him a second time. "If I ever hear you bad-mouthing Nick Schenck again, it will be the last thing you say before I have you tossed in jail for colluding in your own abduction." Eddie slaps Baird once more and orders him to go finish "Hail, Caesar!" "You're gonna do it because you're an actor and that's what you do, just like the director does what he does, and the writer and the script girl and the guy who claps the slate. You're gonna do it because the picture has worth! And you have worth if you serve the picture, and you're never gonna forget that again....Go out there and be a star." Eddie's speech to Baird about gaining worth from a picture's worth appears to motivate the executive's decision to refuse Lockheed's job offer, even though its salary, stock options, shorter hours, and early retirement would surpass what he gets at Capitol.

Returning to his set, Baird portrays Autolochus staring at Christ on the cross, and his sincere acting causes crew members to watch attentively. This contrasts with the raucous and quite funny arguments between various religious leaders over Christ's divinity earlier in the film, when Eddie asks them to approve the epic's screenplay. "Why shouldn't God's anointed appear here among these strange people to shoulder their sins?" Autolochus asks his friend Graccus. "Why should He not take this form, the form of an ordinary man? A man bringing us not the old truths, but a new one....A truth beyond the truth that we can see. A truth beyond this world. A truth told not in words but in light. A truth that we could see if we had but...if we had but..." Baird tumbles on the final word, "faith." After the director yells "Cut," Baird says the word softly, then more loudly, slapping his head as noise from the crew clatters out of frame. (ⓔ Figure 6.29)

As they prepare for a retake, the film cuts to Eddie confessing again. His priest says Eddie is a good man and does not need to confess daily, but Eddie says he snuck two cigarettes, did not make it home for dinner, and struck a movie star in anger. After being absolved with five Hail Marys, Eddie asks the priest about the difference between an easy job like the one Lockheed has offered and a hard one like his position at Capitol. "Sometimes I don't know if I can keep doing it," he states, "but it seems right." The priest tells him, "God wants us to do what's right." (ⓔ Figure 6.30)

Eddie's scene in the confession box wittily connects him to "the ordinary man" of Autolochus's speech. For he is also "a man bringing us not the old truths, but a new one," namely, cinema: "A truth told not in words but in light." Indeed, in closing the film, the narrator (Michael Gambon) explains, "The stories begin. The stories end. So it has been. But the story of Eddie Mannix will never end. For his is a tale written in light everlasting." The camera shows a studio building; behind it, in the distance, is a water tower with the word "behold" painted on it. As a heavenly choir chants to the majestic orchestration of a score typical of biblical epics, the camera moves over roofs and then upward to take in big white billowing clouds in the bright blue sky, soaring upward still farther until the flash of a heavenly star burns bright and cuts to the end credits. Hail to this Hollywood Caesar! Have faith in the movies! (ⓔ Figure 6.31)

Truth to tell, unlike *The Way We Were, Guilty by Suspicion*, or *The Majestic, Hail, Caesar!* does not purport to recount the blacklist as a historical narrative of oppressed screenwriters. Rather, it uses the blacklist much as it uses genres like the biblical epic and the musical, as a way of situating itself in a historical period when the movie studios, as the film's cinematographer Roger Deakins puts it, "were like sausage factories, really. I mean they were just churning out movies like crazy." Deakins shot *Hail, Caesar!* on film, not digital, per the Coen brothers' insistence, but Deakins discovered "stock and lab problems" when using celluloid. "I don't want to do that again, frankly," he commented to *Variety*. "I don't think the infrastructure's there." After elaborating upon the challenges of shooting on film today, Deakins concluded the interview by stating, "As I say, just the technical problems with film, I'm sorry, it's over" (Tapley 2016).

The Coen brothers also appear to be sorry "it's over" insofar as *Hail, Caesar!* laces their pastiche of Old Hollywood genres and stars with a strong dose of nostalgia about the sausage factory that churned out one movie after another. The nostalgia here, though, is as much a backhanded avowal of the present conditions of filmmaking as it is an affectionate and witty remembrance of things past. In an era when the kind of middlebrow films made in the 1950s have, along with celluloid, pretty much been discarded except for a few A-list directors like the Coens, it *is* comforting to think in 2018 that "the story of Eddie Mannix will never end," isn't it?

1962: "This Industry Lives on Gossip and Scandal"

"This industry lives on gossip and scandal," Agatha Murphy (Shelley Winters), a fictionalized TV gossipmonger, declares to sexy blonde starlet Kelly Williams (Connie Stevens) in *The Sex Symbol* (1974), an ABC movie of the week adapted by former blacklisted writer Alvah Bessie from his 1966 novel, which in turn was inspired by the life of a well-known, deceased, very blonde film star in real-life Hollywood. For as Joyce Haber noted in her *Los Angeles Times* gossip column, "The film...shows Connie Stevens as the closest thing to the late Marilyn Monroe since Joe DiMaggio" (Haber 1974).

The Sex Symbol, which Douglas S. Cramer, then Haber's husband, produced for Columbia Pictures Television, was itself momentarily notorious for promoting gossip and scandal, as Haber reported in her daily column, not sparing readers any of the juicy details. In addition to exploiting and fictionalizing public knowledge about Monroe's career, failed marriages to a football (read "baseball") player and artist (read "playwright"), a longer theatrical version meant for Europe featured Stevens in full frontal nudity, while her character's sprawling suicide pose for American television pushed against broadcast standards by openly displaying the actress's nude body from the rear. A giant billboard on the Sunset Strip paraded that imagery too. Furthermore, for his screenplay Bessie invented a married lover of Kelly Williams, a senator with an Irish surname played by Don Murray (Monroe's costar in *Bus Stop* [1956], as it happened). Gossip in the press automatically assumed that the politician in the film was meant to be Robert Kennedy, not John, possibly because Norman Mailer's biography of Monroe, a patchwork of other accounts and his own speculation, had appeared just the year before. It was there that Mailer apparently fabricated his account of the star's affair with the younger Kennedy brother and theorized that the CIA and FBI murdered Monroe as a consequence, all in order to make the book more salable since he "needed money very badly" (Churchwell 2004, 290). Although those events have never been substantiated, both have subsequently become semicanonical in the Monroe biography.

Press accounts speculated that the sex scenes, or the female nudity at the end, or, most likely, the need to appease the Kennedy family was the unstated reason for ABC's abrupt postponement of the ninety-minute telefilm shortly before its initially scheduled broadcast of March 5, 1974. A reedited version of *The Sex Symbol* with much of the politician's backstory eliminated and Stevens's bare bottom covered up was finally broadcast later that same year.

A pretty routine backstudio, *The Sex Symbol* is still notable for registering the migration to American television of the female star narrative. Furthermore this TV movie inaugurated what has turned out to be an ongoing cycle of TV biopics about Monroe, "unquestionably Hollywood's most famous and most scrutinized casualty," whose "death put an end to what was left of the studio era in 1962" (Lewis 2017, 178, 180). Still characterized today by its blurring of facts and fictions, rumors and records, contradictions and controversies, Monroe's biography has risen to the level of cultural myth, to be sure, but the template of her life and death has also become central to how Hollywood perpetuates its mystique today by repeating an anachronistic image of female stardom, with the star's glamour and sexuality made inseparable from her abjection and pathology.

Not counting the numerous documentaries about her, a new Monroe biopic has appeared on broadcast or cable with clock-like regularity: Arthur Miller's autobiographical *After the Fall* on NBC in 1974, the same year that *The Sex Symbol* aired; *Marilyn: The Untold Story,* a three-hour adaptation of Mailer's highly speculative biography on *The ABC Sunday Night Movie* in 1980; still another ABC movie in 1991, this time dwelling on Monroe's supposed secret marriage to Robert Slatzer, called *Marilyn and Me*; an account of her rumored affair with Robert Kennedy on the USA network in 1993, *Marilyn & Bobby: Her Final Affair*; an HBO biopic in 1996, *Norma Jean & Marilyn*; a two night miniseries in 2001 on CBS based on Joyce Carol Oates's novelized account of the star's life, *Blonde*; and most recently, Lifetime's two-part *The Secret Life of Marilyn Monroe* in 2015. I also should mention that during its two-season run the NBC series *Smash* (2012–13) centered on the creation, casting, and production of a musicalized version of Monroe's life for the stage entitled "Bombshell."

Nor has the Monroe story been entirely neglected by theatrical backstudios. A few years before the star's death, the lead character of Paddy Chayefsky's *The Goddess* (1958) followed the known early family biography, the marriage to a sports figure, and the professional and public breakdowns already being reported about the star. A quickie exploitation film, *Goodbye, Norma Jean*, appeared in 1976, and the same writer-director returned to Monroe's death more than a dozen years later with *Goodnight, Sweet Marilyn* (1989). Monroe was the cultural icon behind the figure of "the Actress" in Nicholas Roeg's *Insignificance* (1985). An account of Monroe filming *The Prince and the Showgirl* (1957) with Laurence Olivier on location in England was the subject of the indie theatrical release *My Week with Marilyn* (2011).

It ought to go without saying that I am not bothering to list the scores of Monroe biographies in print.

Why all this fascination with Monroe? According to Sarah Churchwell's insightful analysis of what she calls "the many lives of Marilyn Monroe" as recounted by the numerous, often competing books about the deceased star (Churchwell does not pay much attention to the biopics), Monroe's star image is one of desirability and femininity but also one of controversy, pathology, fatality, and, most of all, uncertainty. "Uncertainty *is* the story of Marilyn's biographical life," Churchwell points out. "We don't know nearly as much about her as people may assume" (Churchwell 2004, 3). That "uncertainty," some of it apparently perpetuated by Monroe herself, invites the speculation and fabrication—the gossip and scandal alluded to by *The Sex Symbol*—motivating the many efforts to recount the life story and explain the person anew. As Churchwell goes on to demonstrate with her side-by-side readings of the major retellings of the star's life story, the familiar elements that pull together the Monroe biography as a coherent tale only pull the subject apart, which may be why the life story never appears whole and finished, why it promises "the truth" but ends up only "telling us what we already think we know" (5), and why Hollywood may feel that the audience's hunger for it is never sated, offering us one "untold story" and "secret life" after another.

As the many TV movies and miniseries base their claims of authenticity on one or more of the print biographies that Churchwell analyzes, they draw on a controversial documentary record, much of it complicated by the gossip and scandal that shape what I call, to reference the merging of fact and fiction, "the Monroe bio-persona." To be sure, one can readily tick off the familiar thematic elements, most of which are invariably present in nearly every biopic of the star: the family romance of the crazy mother and absent father; the Cinderella-like transformation of Norma Jeane (the preferred spelling from her birth certificate) into "Marilyn" and its negative image of the star's divided self; the marketing of female sexuality, the objectification of the female body, and Monroe's unashamed nudity; the suspicions about her promiscuity, abortions, and frigidity, which are juxtaposed with her innocence and naïveté, her "natural" attitudes toward sex, and her unsuccessful efforts to become a mother; the marriages and love affairs of an iconic sex symbol with equally iconic masculine types personifying patriarchy—sports hero, intellectual, politician; and finally, the unresolvable mystery of her death.

In one way or another, the biopics all share an underlying anxiety about female agency that motivates the constant retelling of Monroe's story—and our culture's obsession with it—and that still informs the complexity and currency of her bio-persona.

As Churchwell says about the numerous books, "The biographies respond on the whole by vitiating [Monroe's] power: she is trembling target of studio head wrath; passive beneficiary of the counsel offered by older, wiser, male heads; or a coy manipulator who exploits female sympathies" (Churchwell 2004, 215). Adding to this aspect of her bio-persona, the conspiracy theories arising from and around Monroe's death in 1962 seem to be practically *demanded* by her biography due to its uncertainty and "its sense of a secret, manipulative authority"—the studio, patriarchy, the Kennedys, possibly even Monroe herself— insofar as the theories posit "an author, someone... in charge, and in most of these stories it is not Monroe. Rather she is a character in her own life story, one being authored by other powerful people, who themselves are authored by the biographer" (318).

The Monroe biopics produced for TV and cable after *The Sex Symbol* make female stardom legible in ways consistent with the masculinist biases and institutional anxieties of Hollywood because the bio-persona also papers over Monroe's agency as a working actress. Rarely in the biopics is Monroe's inability to remember lines, her failure to show up, or her reliance on having her acting coach with her on set interpreted as her means of asserting herself, of doing a scene *her* way—although truth to tell, *Blonde* at least gestures toward this viewpoint by having Monroe ask several times to rewrite her own dialogue or claim to know her character better than the director does. As a template for representing female stardom in narrative terms, the Monroe bio-persona takes a female star, who has mastered her craft even while personifying glamour and sexuality, and fixes her permanently as the archetypal "sex symbol" for the ages, whose skill and intelligence are called into question and who is a victim of her own disturbed psyche and emotional instability, not patriarchal Hollywood and its sexist exploitation of women. Moreover, while the Monroe biopics equate their subject with her sexualized and eventually highly drugged body, most also follow fundamental conventions of the theatrical female star narratives from the studio era. To illustrate, I shall confine myself to the three most recent and complex of the TV biopics: *Norma Jean & Marilyn*, *Blonde*, and *The Secret Life of Marilyn Monroe*.

Monroe's early life and relatively brief career resonates with the different institutional anxieties operating upon the earlier theatrical cycles of fictional female star narratives discussed in chapters 3 and 4; while death gave her biography a determinate endpoint, it continues to give the story a false ending since it opens the life to seemingly endless speculations informed by gossip and scandal. Beginning with movie fandom as Norma Jeane's inspiration for alleviating through her hopes of stardom the abuse and sense of abandonment experienced during her youth and, once she becomes a star, then focusing on Marilyn Monroe's insecurities, addictions, and overdetermined relations with men, the biopics fuse the "star is born" and "star is worn" trajectories into a single storyline. "Norma Jeane" is like the ambitious, movie-struck heroine of the first cycle, whereas "Marilyn" resembles the excessive, tormented heroine of the second. Along with this star's considerable nostalgic value, then, for the biopics, "Norma Jeane" looks to the promise of Hollywood as an escape from an unhappy life and "Marilyn Monroe" ultimately confirms the institution's inability to live up to that promise.

Additionally, much like those backstudios that double their fictional stars with a secondary character who functions as a mirror, foil, or antithesis, the Monroe biopics emphasize the divided self resulting from the transformation of Norma Jeane Baker into Marilyn Monroe. *Norma Jean & Marilyn* exemplifies this split subjectivity by having two actresses in the leading role, with Ashley Judd playing a driven and manipulative Norma Jean and Mira Sorvino a version of Monroe based on her dumb blonde persona. "You're going to be famous even if it kills me," Norma Jean says to Monroe after the name change. Together the two figures do not make the star coherent and whole since even after stardom Norma Jean still "resides" in Marilyn as a scolding and divisive inner self. (▶ Figure 6.32)

Similarly, in *Blonde* characters refer to Monroe (Poppy Montgomery) as "Norma Jeane" in private while treating "Marilyn" as a construct or persona invented by the studio, her management, and Monroe herself. "Marilyn was mine, Marilyn was beautiful, and you had no right to spoil her," Monroe's agent, a surrogate for Johnny Hyde, exclaims after the nude calendar shots get discovered and publicized. "I swear, Whitey," the star later declares to her makeup artist, "I am a slave to Marilyn Monroe."

Conversely, in *The Secret Life of Marilyn Monroe* one actress (Kelli Garner) plays Monroe, who is pretty consistently called "Marilyn" after she changes her name, but this treatment emphasizes her relationship with her mother, Gladys (Susan Sarandon). Forgoing the usual longing for the absent, unknown father as the motive for why Monroe craves "being loved," *The Secret Life* pairs mother and daughter through their shared paranoid schizophrenia, so Gladys functions as Monroe's doppelganger in this account. "I don't want to become like my mother," Monroe screams, but she begins to hear voices almost as soon as she becomes noticed in pictures and ends up as distraught and confused as her mother. Late in this miniseries the daughter even has a fantasy of Gladys appearing in a platinum blond wig. If the Marilyns in other biopics don't want to be treated like a joke but become one to the men in Hollywood, this Marilyn does not want to be like her mother, a destiny she likewise cannot avoid. (▶ Figures 6.33–6.34)

Finally, the "uncertainty" that Churchwell claims is crucial to the Monroe biography allows for a high degree of fictionalization, so while the basic story remains the same in the biopics, details and even major events are fabricated, drawing on gossip and scandal for inspiration. For instance, who introduced Monroe to drugs? In *Norma Jean & Marilyn* she gets them from Ted Lewis. In *Blonde* a lover, Cass (Patrick Dempsey), introduces her to pills. In *The Secret Life of Marilyn Monroe*, Johnny Hyde (Tony Nardi) gives her drugs to calm her down on the set of *All about Eve* (1950).

Blonde may be the most obviously fictionalized. After all, drawing on its source in Oates's "novelization" of the biography, both parts of the miniseries begin with this disclaimer: "Although the following film depicts some actual persons and events, it is a work of fiction." In addition to moments of fantasy on Monroe's part and characters speaking directly to the camera, many major figures in her life either have made-up names, such as I. E. Shin (Wallace Shawn) for Johnny Hyde and Mr. R for Darryl F. Zanuck, or are referred to as a type, such as "the Baseball Player" (Titus Welliver) and "the Playwright"

(Griffin Dunne). A major story point here, moreover, which is absent in the other biopics, is Monroe's supposed sexual relation with "Cass" or Charles Chaplin Jr. and "Eddie G" or Edward G. Robinson Jr. (Jensen Ackles). Living with both men in a threesome arrangement, she gets pregnant by one of them but has an abortion when she realizes neither man will grow up and handle his drug addiction. (▶ Figure 6.35)

The other biopics similarly trade upon the uncertainty inherent in Monroe's bio-persona. In *Norma Jean & Marilyn* and *Blonde* her foster mother Grace (respectively, Beth Grant and Kirstie Alley as the surrogate version called "Elsie") sets up Monroe's first marriage to get the nubile sixteen-year-old out of the house and away from the lascivious interest of her husband; in *The Secret Life of Marilyn Monroe* Grace (Emily Watson) does so because she and her husband are moving away. In all instances, the reason for the marriage is the same, since otherwise the sixteen-year-old Norma Jeane would have to return to the orphanage.

But other expressions of the uncertainty at the heart of the Monroe bio-persona involve the indeterminate knowledge of her mental state throughout her life. *The Secret Life of Marilyn Monroe* recounts how her growing schizophrenia begins earlier than in the other biopics; Monroe already hears voices and cannot concentrate when preparing for her audition for *All about Eve*, so she starts taking the drugs from Hyde, as previously mentioned, to escape her voices. Whereas in *Blonde* the miscarriage of her baby with Arthur Miller occurs because she falls down the basement stairs when hallucinating that animals are there, in *Secret Life* the fetus starves, according to Miller's taunts, because of Monroe's addiction to drugs and liquor. As well as explicitly splitting Monroe into two distinctive figures, with Norma Jean "present" to her in so many scenes of Marilyn's life, whether at home or the studio, *Norma Jean & Marilyn* plays at times like a dreamy record of the tormented Monroe's fantasies. The film opens with a dream in which an adult Norma Jean is nude in church, and it goes on to feature many fantasized scenes, such as when Norma Jean and Marilyn team up to seduce and murder Monroe's biological father. As filmed, such fantasies first appear to be playing out as reality and only at their end is their imaginary basis revealed. This biopic, drawn from Ted Jordan's book about his purported relationship with Monroe, features his surrogate, Eddie Jordan (Josh Charles), who supplies a moral yardstick that at the same time distinguishes between masculine and feminine modes of achieving success in Hollywood. A lover whom Norma Jean deserts for his uncle, Ted Lewis, although the couple remain somewhat friendly and intimate afterward, Eddie wants to be a serious actor while, as Norma Jean avows, she will get in the movies "if I have to fuck Bela Lugosi to do it." Jordan does not appear in the other biopics.

For all their simultaneous inventions and adherence to the "record," the biopics do not focus on Monroe's professional success; instead, although they attribute different causes, they dwell upon her personal failures, her inability to be a fulfilled and normal woman, and these are failures for which *she* pretty much gets the blame—because as a child she was traumatized by her mother's absence and possibly molested or raped; because she shamelessly flaunted her body; because she was promiscuous and had abortions; because she was an alcoholic and drug addict; or because she was mentally disturbed, even clinically insane. In these biopics Monroe's excesses are rendered upon her famous, desirable, vulnerable, and very damaged body.

As for Monroe's film work, the biopics dramatize it by stressing her erotic value, which is manufactured by various men and shown to be hindered first by her insecurity as an ingénue, then by her ambition to become a serious actor, and finally by her excessive tardiness and inability to remember lines. "Don't make me a joke," Monroe pleads more than once to the men responsible for creating "Marilyn" in *Blonde*. And in the end of that miniseries, as she approaches the stage of Madison Square Garden to sing "Happy Birthday" to JFK, she mutters, "Here I am. The president's wound-up sex toy." But by the same token, all this Monroe does throughout *Blonde* is giggle girlishly or sob uncontrollably, so she *does* come off as something of a joke and a sex toy. In *Norma Jean & Marilyn* one persona is as hardnosed as a Joan Crawford character, while the other is all soft and fuzzy-minded. *The Secret Life* at times shows Monroe focused intently on her work—given her messy private life, her career is finally all she has, as she states—but she is doomed by her DNA, inheriting her mother's and grandmother's mental illnesses.

The Monroe biopics stand out from ones about celebrities in other professions, such as sports or politics, or ones about other female stars, such as Jayne Mansfield (broadcast in 1980), Rita Hayworth (1983), Elizabeth Taylor (1995), or Audrey Hepburn (2000), because their sheer number over the past several decades gives them a coherence of their own. Recycled in one TV biopic after another that claims to disclose new revelations and insights but mainly reiterates a lot of the same old ones, Monroe's life story has been kept current and seemingly authentic through the ongoing gossip about her sexual life and speculation about her death. Hence the paradoxical grounding of uncertainty as the hallmark of her bio-persona. Monroe died when only in her thirties, moreover, so her visual image remains the eternal epitome of the glamorous movie star and the Hollywood system that produced her. Imagery of her face and body appears in poster reproductions, on home video covers, in photographs and books, on coffee mugs, T-shirts, shower curtains, and other forms of memorabilia and merchandise, not to mention in auctions of her own clothing and possessions. The gossip about her affairs, abortions, and (possible or impossible) assassination reinforces her immortality because their truthfulness is always disputable and debatable, giving her life story its sense of ongoing currency.

Monroe's cultural significance as a mythic figure for historical backstudios has a lot to do with how the particularities of her star image, her life story, and the surrounding discourses have intersected and solidified over time. It is no accident that *Guilty by Suspicion* bends history a bit with its anachronistic inclusion of clips from *Gentlemen Prefer Blondes* since Monroe, more so than other stars from her era, is by now universal shorthand for movie culture of the 1950s. Yet as the protagonist in a narrative about female stardom in the heyday of Hollywood, Monroe also supplies an institutional perspective for shaping what had been the fictional star narrative template into a cautionary tale for today about an ambitious woman who tried to overstep her restricted position in the industry as a sex object. Monroe's stardom is at once timeless (through the omnipresence of her iconic imagery, which each biopic carefully reproduces, and the uncertainty of her inconclusive biography, especially regarding the cause of her death in 1962) and historical (through her indelible association with the studio system, the periodization of her career, and the definitive ending of her life in 1962). The value of the many Monroe biopics consequently has little to do with what they newly tell us about her life or career since they all recount the same familiar story; rather, the biopics use Monroe to keep the mystique of Hollywood in continuous play while locating the glamorous trapping of that mystique in the past as the summation of the industry's former excesses.

1962 Redux: "Got Gossip?"

A quarter-page advertisement from the *National Enquirer* in the October 28, 2008, issue of *Daily Variety Gotham* asked, "Got Gossip? We'll pay big $$ for your celebrity information." To be sure, "gossip" and the "accurate inside knowledge about top TV, movie and music stars" that the tabloid also wanted may seem antithetical, although gossip as a means of obtaining access to celebrity goings-on in Hollywood was and still is a very big business. As evident from the backstudios I have already examined in this chapter, gossip has repeatedly textured accounts of historical Hollywood.

Feud: Bette and Joan exemplifies how a historical backstudio seamlessly blends gossip and "accurate inside knowledge" into a documentary record. Shown on the FX cable network in the spring of 2017, this eight-episode miniseries focuses on the bitter rivalry between Bette Davis (Susan Sarandon) and Joan Crawford (Jessica Lange) during the making and promotion of *What Ever Happened to Baby Jane?* in 1962. *Feud* then follows the aftermath of their mutual antagonism with a faithful recreation of the 1963 Oscar ceremony, when non-nominee Crawford stole nominee Davis's thunder, and afterward it takes their animosity to its inevitable if volatile conclusion with the ultimately unsuccessful effort by *Baby Jane* director Robert Aldrich (Alfred Molina) to reteam the two feuding stars in *Hush...Hush, Sweet Charlotte* (1964). *Feud* concludes with the two stars at the end of their lives, each alone and clinging to the last vestiges of their careers, and embeds a fantasy on Crawford's part of their reconciliation.

Gossip about Davis's and Crawford's tit-for-tat and barely disguised antagonistic behavior before, during, and after the production has by now supplied an informing supplement to *What Ever Happened to Baby Jane?* Expectations of trouble on the set certainly provided the columnists with lines of print in the summer of 1962. As production began, even the staid *New York Times* published a feature article that described the harmonious working relations of the two stars while, given the appeal of watching "stars in temperamental collision," concluding that "those in Hollywood who revel in malice were optimistic" the anticipated explosion would eventually happen (Schumach 1962). Since the film's release, many viewers take great pleasure from watching how the stars' performances transparently reveal the dislike, anger, jealousy, and competitiveness that Davis and

Crawford *must* have felt toward each other. "They were like two Sherman tanks, openly despising each other," Aldrich subsequently recalled (qtd. in Considine 2017, 341). Several anecdotes about the production have been repeated so often that by now they are canonical: that during one violent scene Davis kicked Crawford so hard in the head that the latter required stiches, and that, to get back at her costar, in another scene, when Davis had to lift her off the bed and drag her out of the room, Crawford weighted herself down, severely hurting Davis's back; that during filming of the final scene on the beach Crawford kept retiring to her portable dressing room between takes, each time returning with ever larger falsies and more makeup tricks to hide her age and soften her physical appearance. (⊙ Figure 6.36)

Once *Baby Jane* was completed, the stars' feud intensified and went public, as Brooks Atkinson slyly predicted it might do in his review for the *Times* of their new autobiographies. Atkinson began his column by noting that if the two stars were to "come to blows" during their film's promotion, Davis would probably win hands down (Atkinson 1962). Yet he underestimated Crawford's passive-aggressive manner of beating back Davis's barbed wisecracks to the press. First, Crawford withdrew from the planned cross-country tour by both stars of theaters showing the film, so Davis went out solo. Second, in contrast to Davis and supporting player Victor Buono, Crawford was shut out of the Oscar competition, so (according to Davis) Crawford and Hedda Hopper played good and bad cop as they (supposedly) lobbied industry people to prevent Davis, considered the favorite in the Best Actress race, from winning. Third, Crawford arranged to accept the award for Geraldine Page or Anne Bancroft should either New York stage actress win, and when Bancroft won, Crawford acted as if she had been awarded the coveted statuette, even posing with it for photographs alongside the other winners, rubbing Davis's nose in her loss. (⊙ Figure 6.37) Reportedly, Crawford's behavior at the Oscars set Davis's ire in stone. In retaliation, Davis got Crawford uninvited from the group attending the Cannes festival, where *Baby Jane* had its European premiere. By the time of *Hush…Hush, Sweet Charlotte* Davis had arranged to have the upper hand, so Crawford's recourse was to feign illness at Cedars Sinai Hospital, hoping to shut down production, but her plan was thwarted once Davis's friend Olivia de Havilland took over Crawford's role.

Feud basically follows the through line of Shaun Considine's gossipy account of their long-standing rivalry in *Bette & Joan: The Divine Feud*, yet there are some key differences. Considine takes the feud back to the women's romantic rivalry over Franchot Tone, whom Crawford married, so *Baby Jane* is just one major episode in their long-standing hostility toward each other, while *Feud* adds Jack Warner's (Stanley Tucci) indirect manipulation of the two women. He instructs Aldrich to feed gossip to Hedda Hopper (Judy Davis) as a means of getting juicy publicity for *Baby Jane* prior to its release. Whereas most accounts of Davis or Crawford emphasize the star's intimidating iron will and ability in one way or another to endure, at times to thrive in, the patriarchal studio system, *Feud* asks us to view both women as passive victims of Hollywood.

With this backstory, the writers of *Feud* ambiguously crisscross the lines separating truth and speculation. According to *Feud*, Warner had more direct input as a producer of the film than he may have really had since *What Ever Happened to Baby Jane?* was produced and financed by the Seven Arts company (which five years later would merge with Warners by buying Jack Warner's controlling interest) in conjunction with the Associates and Aldrich Company, and filmed at and around the Producer's Studio on Melrose, not at the Warners lot in Burbank. But *Feud* uses Warner to personify the studio boss who controls all aspects of the production, including the purse strings, and who has a fractious relationship with both women from when they were under contract to his studio and defied his authority.

In the first several episodes, during the production of *Baby Jane* Warner repeatedly emasculates Aldrich, forcing him to keep his stars at war with each other by exploiting their insecurities. While relations between the stars were initially cordial, creator Ryan Murphy told the *Hollywood Reporter* after the second episode, things became rockier when Crawford realized that Davis had the showier role and was making the most of it. "So that's when it turned and when the calm began to turn sour. And based on research that's because Jack Warner knew that two women pitted against each other would probably sell more tickets. So a lot of that was created by the system, by the columnists. What they did still happens today with women." But when asked if he had found "any actual evidence" about Warner and Aldrich's collusion to leak gossip to Hopper, as dramatized in the second episode, Murphy replied, "Actual documented research? It's not like the Zapruder film, you can't go back and look at a document, but based on our research that's what we thought and intimated" (Dowling 2017a).

Then in episode 6 Aldrich finally tells off Warner, informing the studio head that Twentieth Century-Fox has made a better offer for *Hush...Hush, Sweet Charlotte*. Showrunner Tim Minear's carefully worded explanation to the *Reporter* about the historical basis of the men's dialogue in this scene likewise oscillates between revealing and recanting its fictiveness. What is at issue here is why Warner Bros. did not also release the follow-up, as the company had distributed *Baby Jane*. "There's pretty much not anything in the show that could not have happened the way we presented it," Minear states. "A lot of it is taken from actual quotes, documentaries, eyewitnesses. We re-created this world and the story very faithfully." However, there was no actual record of Warner's and Aldrich's negotiations, Minear adds, "so a lot of that is imagined but it ends up being a faithful story of [why] this picture didn't go to Warner, it went to 20th. It's my version of that." In more practical terms, too, "it felt like a plausible way to end the story between Bob and Jack...and still have Stanley Tucci in the episode" (Dowling 2017b).

Imagining or intimating—or, more accurately, inventing—"a faithful story" of the institutional forces determining the women's feud underscores Murphy's publicized goal of making a "feminist" statement about the industry's sexist and ageist mistreatment of women, as true of 2017 as it was back in 1962. "Men age, they get character. Women age, they get lost," a masseuse tells Crawford in the first episode. One cannot underestimate the ageism openly at work when it came to maturing female actors like Davis and Crawford, so from start to finish *Feud* dwells upon the sadness and fear at the heart of their choices at this later stage of their careers, including their animosity and mistrust of each other. Yet a weakness of *Feud*'s portrayal of the women is that it hammers this message repeatedly and reductively.

But I also do not mean to take Murphy or Minear to task for drawing on gossipy speculation in their research or for imagining conversations and dialogue that could conceivably have taken place or just as conceivably may not have happened as they depict it. Inventing events, dialogue, and composite characters is what biopics like *Feud* do routinely. Still, it is worth noting that, after the series concluded and right before her 101st birthday, Olivia de Havilland sued the producers for including her (as played by Catherine Zeta-Jones) and "putting false words" into her mouth to create "the impression that she was a hypocrite who sold gossip to promote herself" (Cullins 2017). In reply, Fox 21 Television Studios, the producing entity, declared that the series was "meticulously researched," that the Davis-Crawford feud was "well-documented," and that "the law on this is very clear.... Docudramas, such as this one, are original narrative works, based on real, verifiable facts and events" (Littleton 2017).

True or false, what intrigues me most about *Feud* is that, for all the publicized claims by Murphy and Minear of documenting the eight episodes with their careful research and attention to accuracy, their treatment of the Davis-Crawford feud implicitly relies as much upon *What Ever Happened to Baby Jane?* as their template for characterizing these two famous historical personalities. Like two mirrors facing each other, the fictional *Baby Jane* reflects the feuding duo as a supplementary text for understanding the characters of sisters Jane (Davis) and Blanche (Crawford), while *Feud* itself reflects its characterizations of the two real-life stars through those two fictional characters. The final episode of *Feud* even borrows its title from what Jane says following her sister's big reveal that she herself was to blame for the car accident that crippled her: "You mean all this time we could have been friends?"

At every opportunity, Murphy repeatedly mentioned in interviews his lengthy conversation with Davis toward the end of her life as one of his firsthand sources for the scripts, yet while *Feud* essentially takes her side by showing Crawford as the crazy has-been and Davis as the saner survivor, it gives Jessica Lange, apparently Murphy's TV muse, more scenes and the showier part. Lange's Crawford personifies the movie star known primarily for her beauty, which increasingly fails to cover over completely the personal history of abuse, promiscuity, alcoholism, anxieties about her talent, and desperation to remain beautiful and appealing as younger stars like Marilyn Monroe take her place.

One can also see this subtext in the characterization of shut-in Blanche Hudson, surrounded by photographs of her halcyon days as a Hollywood star, as she watches the revival of her old films on afternoon television—which Crawford similarly does in the final episode of *Feud*. And like Blanche, who has fed her sister's guilt for some twenty-five years to create the monstrous Baby Jane, this version of Crawford antagonizes Davis into behaving abusively toward her. Much as Blanche secretly plots to put her sister in a home and sell their house, in the second and third episodes Crawford covertly allows Hopper to print blind items about the production in her column, thereby rupturing the tentative alliance that, according to *Feud*, the two stars had formed as production began—a rupture that Davis interprets as a declaration of war. Crawford's passive-aggressive behavior toward her costar then culminates in the events leading up to and occurring at the Oscars in the fifth episode.

Like Blanche, too, who is cloistered in her bedroom due to her paralysis, which enables Jane to get under her skin, *Feud*'s Crawford repeatedly drops her persona and lets her insecurities flood out, often but not exclusively with her maid, Mamacita (Jackie Hoffman). In no small way, this picture of Crawford seeks to revise the posthumous impression created by daughter Christina Crawford's notorious tell-all, *Mommie Dearest*, published in 1978, and the subsequent 1981 screen adaptation with Faye Dunaway, which has since been a camp cult film. *Feud* plays up the pathos of Crawford's functional alcoholism but forgoes the usual impression of the star, crystallized by Dunaway, as a hard, tough-minded, and controlling woman. Lange's Crawford wears her desperation and narcissism on her sleeve; while she swears a lot and throws things, her voice keeps betraying a softness and vulnerability more in keeping with Blanche's deliberately modulated dialogue with the housekeeper, Elvira (Maddie Norman), or Jane, upon whom she is dependent, than with Crawford's own deeper and carefully deliberated speech, with its underlying toughness. (⊙ Figure 6.38)

Feud polarizes Crawford and Davis much as *Baby Jane* opposes the Hudson sisters in the film's two prologues, which first shows Baby Jane as the famous child star in vaudeville as her bitter sister is sidelined and ignored, and then depicts Blanche as the big Hollywood star while a jealous Jane boozes, sleeps around, and acts in pictures so bad that they rarely make it to U.S. theaters. At first glance *Feud*'s Davis is not at all like Baby Jane, to be sure. For if once upon a time Crawford was the most beautiful woman in Hollywood, as we hear many times in *Feud*, then Davis was the greatest screen actress of her generation, an epithet repeated just as often. But not satisfied with being the talented one, Sarandon's Davis is extremely insecure about her beauty. She worries that, as far as the industry is concerned, she has become her Baby Jane character, the ghoulish figure with the white face mask. (⊙ Figure 6.39) In the seventh episode, she confesses to Aldrich about her "first screen test with Jack Warner": "I stuck around and I hid behind a door because I wanted to hear his reaction." Uninterested in her acting talent or her "brave attack on the scene," the crass mogul said Davis had "zero sex appeal." "Guess who he said he wished I looked like?" she asks Aldrich, who at this moment is undressing her. "Joan Crawford."

For all of Davis's accolades and stature as a serious actress, *Feud*'s version of a sexualized but unattractive Davis evokes Jane's jealousy of her sister's movie stardom, which is contrasted with her own short time in the spotlight as a child star. "I am a character actress," Davis repeatedly if defensively states, although Crawford finally admonishes her outside her hotel room during the location shoot of *Hush...Hush, Sweet Charlotte*: "The answer to feeling unattractive isn't to make yourself even uglier." As they begin production of *Sweet Charlotte*, *Feud*'s Davis does get "uglier" due to her treatment of Crawford.

Just as Jane keeps Blanche in solitude, confined to her second-floor bedroom, Davis isolates Crawford from the rest of the cast, with whom Davis parties in her hotel room in the evening; conspires with Aldrich in front of Crawford on the set; cuts Crawford's speeches from the shooting script; and belittles Crawford's performance in front of everybody. And while Davis's responsibility for the slights Crawford experiences on location in Louisiana is uncertain—no one meets Crawford at the airport, her room is not ready when she arrives at the hotel, and she awakens from a nap in her trailer to find that everyone else has left the location and she has to have her maid call a city taxi—Crawford suspects her costar's hand in these affronts.

Most of what I have been describing in *Feud* probably did happen, and the historical traces of gossip about the stars' feud, some of it fomented and fanned by Davis herself in interviews years afterward, helped the writers fill out the details. Likewise, *What Ever Happened to Baby Jane?* has shaped memories of Davis and Crawford, influencing how later generations of viewers have come to understand these two women psychologically through the characters they played and the gossip about their film's production, which has since become legend. "Gossip," Jennifer Frost writes in her book about Hedda Hopper, "is 'private talk'—true or false talk about private life—voiced, often illegitimately, in the public realm" (Frost 2011, 3). As gossip spreads through private networks of conversation, including the seeming "personal" space of celebrity gossip columns by journalists like Hopper, what is gossiped about gets layered with embellishments in each retelling. The effectivity, more than the veracity, of gossip is at issue when it comes to the record of the film industry's past, as the backstudios discussed in this chapter illustrate.

With fictional histories like *Hollywood Story, Guilty by Suspicion*, and *Hail, Caesar!* the incorporation of gossip as the source of inspiration for fictional characters and situations gives to the screenplay's inventiveness a sense of simulated truthfulness, of a shadowy referential ground in real Hollywood history. With backstudios like *Feud* and the Monroe biopics drawing on real people, gossip becomes even more inseparable, even indistinguishable from the historical record. But as important, the traces of gossip in the record encourage viewer investment in the ongoing Hollywood project. For in contrast with the uninitiated viewer, those knowledgeable in the gossip achieve a privileged point of entry into the historical Hollywood being depicted. Whether explicitly incorporated (as in *Feud*) or more genially alluded to (as in *Hail, Caesar!*), historical backstudios draw on well-known and much-repeated gossip to invite a knowing viewer to share in, and hence assent to, the filmmakers' perspective on the past.

Regardless of the period they take for their setting, most historical backstudios aim to sustain the continuity of the present in the past and vice versa, and this purpose has taken on even more importance, even urgency, for Hollywood in our era of conglomerate ownership of the studios, transnational productions, global address of the product, and new media portals for distribution. Returning to the studio era, historical backstudios reiterate for audiences an identification of filmmaking with Hollywood in its dream factory setting, despite the fact that "Hollywood" itself no longer has a fixed material referent either in Los Angeles or the movie industry.

7

Virtual Hollywood

The Congress (2013), an indie backstudio that is half live action and half animation, pushes further the premise of *S1m0ne* (2002). Whereas the latter imagines the possibility of a computer-generated movie star, *The Congress* posits a film industry that scans stars for future use as virtual creations, their three-dimensional likenesses digitized for and commodified by Miramount, a fictional composite of an indie company (Miramax) and a major (Paramount). The protagonist of *The Congress* is Robin Wright, played by the real-life Robin Wright. If scanned, she would become the intellectual property of Miramount, which would own her public identity for twenty years. Although Robin insists that scanned performers lose the "gift of choice," her agent, Al (Harvey Keitel), reminds her that she has always been "a puppet" of the system, told what to do by "all of them, the producers, the directors." "This is your gate to freedom," Al informs her. Reluctantly, Robin accepts Miramount's offer and is scanned. "Robin Wright" ceases to be a flesh-and-blood actress and becomes the studio's "character" in a series of sci-fi action flicks.

Twenty years later Miramount invites an older and now anonymous Robin Wright to the restricted Animation Zone, where an inhaled drug turns her into a cartoon figure. Here, in this colorful and surreal setting, Miramount wants to extend Robin's contract while adding a new clause since "movies are old news." The Miramount-Nagaski labs have created a means of selling Robin's "character" as a pure "substance" that consumers can eat or drink, enabling them to imagine "Robin Wright" as they wish and the company to receive royalties from their fantasies about the character. But a rebellious uprising occurs against the monolithic corporation, during which the animated Robin suffers from "extreme hallucination contamination," is frozen for another twenty years to await discovery of a cure, and eventually awakens. After sprouting wings and unsuccessfully searching for her son, Aaron, she decides to leave this world where inhaling a drug gives one freedom to live in (or to imagine one lives in) whatever animated form one wishes.

Robin looks for her son on "the other side," where, not unlike in *The Matrix* (1999), "truth" resides. A dissolve reveals the "truth" behind the animated world, namely, that on this "other side" the wildly colorful animated figures are in truth crowds of drably dressed, mute, emotionless people. (▶ Figures 7.1–7.2) Robin learns that Aaron, fearing she would not be returning, has himself entered the animated world, so she goes back there. In an animated montage recapping Aaron's birth and life from *his* viewpoint, Robin imagines herself in his body, yet she also sees Aaron as an independent figure working on a flying machine. Robin calls his name and the screen freezes on a close-up of his face.

The Congress is an absorbing yet often obscure backstudio that comments on, among other themes, the commodification of stars as branded intellectual properties, the drug-like escapism of twenty-first-century mass entertainments, and the impenetrable heft of the corporations producing them. Robin's career as a film star has been characterized by her many "lousy choices"—"all those irrational, abrupt walkouts" usually determined by her concern for Aaron's welfare since he is slowly losing his hearing and vision from Usher's syndrome—yet to her they are evidence of her "gift of choice." Miramount, by contrast, functions as a state apparatus that is both ideological and repressive. Throughout the animated section we see recurring imagery that associates Miramount-Nagasaki with Nazi storm troopers, German blimps, firing squads, and the Nuremburg Rally.

Yet like *S1m0ne*, *The Congress* is also that rare backstudio that addresses the state of motion pictures in our era of digital creation and manipulation. It juxtaposes real-life Hollywood and a virtual reality rendered in a surreal mixture of old-time cartoon styles from the 1930s and 1940s and imagery inspired by Keith Haring's prints and drawings. Bodies in the Animation Zone are vividly colored and fluid; some resemble famous movie stars like Monroe, Sinatra, and Eastwood; some look like mythological, religious, and historical icons; some are half-human creatures or shape-shifters; and a few draw upon the actors supplying their voices.

Additionally, in its premise of stars being scanned in the live-action section, *The Congress* imagines a virtual Hollywood, the product of computer-generated simulation. The fellow who samples Robin is a former cinematographer, signifying that the digitized virtual image has replaced the analogical photographic one. The scene of her being sampled alludes to how CGI creates the illusionism of contemporary films, as when actors perform in front of a green screen for elaborate special effects or are scanned for motion-capture technology. (▶ Figure 7.3) In the Animated Zone, Dylan Truliner (voiced by Jon Hamm) reveals that he had a prior life on "the other side" as head of the Robin Wright Department for Miramount. Having fallen in love with his digital creation then, and despite her insistence on not being her digitized character, Dylan does not distinguish between the real and the virtual Robin Wright, just as he sees no difference between his computer creation and the animated woman he meets in the Zone. He rescues Robin during the uprising, waits twenty years for her to become unfrozen, and they become lovers before she crosses back to "the other side." To Dylan the virtual *is* the real. (▶ Figure 7.5)

As well as encouraging us to think about the disaggregation of the digitized cinematic image from a referential ground on "the other side" of the screen, *The Congress* asks us to reconsider our identification with escapist cinema and to ask how Hollywood functions as an ideological apparatus in soliciting our culture's strong investment in such films. Other backstudios raise these issues by representing virtual Hollywood, but they do so in more "analog" terms. This final chapter looks at two such expressions of simulated moviemaking in films from the past several decades that anticipate themes of *The Congress*: "immersive Hollywood," when fictional characters interact with real-life actors, crossing the boundary separating the reel from the real as epitomized by the screen; and "appropriated Hollywood," when an apparatus of the state—the police, the FBI, the CIA, the White House—fabricates a film production as its cover story for a sting operation that draws out the equivalence of Hollywood's practices and those of the national security state.

Immersive Hollywood

In its mixture of live action and animation, *The Congress* calls to mind an earlier backstudio, *Who Framed Roger Rabbit* (1988), in which humans dynamically cohabit with cartoon figures in 1947 Hollywood. The Animated Zone in *The Congress* is utopian because of newer and more effective drugs. Aaron's doctor tells Robin before she returns there, "Nothing has changed; once they masked the truth, now they reinvent; the drugs have just gotten better. Over here one waits for death; over there, one hallucinates and dreams." By contrast, although Judge Doom (Christopher Lloyd), the villain in *Roger Rabbit*, turns out to be an evil Toon masquerading as a human, he appears to be the sole exception. The cartoon world here is a utopian alternative to the more conflicted and anguished human world, which in its plot and human protagonist, the disgruntled and hard-drinking private eye Eddie Valiant (Bob Hoskins), is rendered as film noir, a genre now identified with Hollywood output from the late 1940s.

Toons in *Who Framed Roger Rabbit* are childlike if also transgressive and perverse in their elastic bodies and anarchical impact. They exist to make audiences laugh or feel joy and wonder—that is, to experience the very pleasures of watching a movie as celebrated by the end of *Sullivan's Travels* (1941). Eddie Valiant, on the other hand, is drowning in alcohol after his brother's death (a Toon dropped a piano on Teddy; the killer turns out to have been Doom). But as he gets more involved in solving Marvin Acme's murder and proving the innocence of Roger Rabbit (voiced by Charles Fleischer), Eddie's body becomes increasingly Toonlike. In fact, there are a few moments in Toontown when a "hand-drawn double" of Bob Hoskins replaces him in "a shot that would have been too dangerous for a real actor" (Wolf 2003, 49), as when Eddie collapses flat like a pancake in the elevator operated by Droopy. (▶ Figure 7.5) Along with his knowledge of Toon behavior and Toon props, Eddie's quickness and athleticism, not to mention his body's seeming pliability, enable him to defeat the judge in their final showdown at the Acme warehouse. Afterward Eddie shows what he has learned about the ameliorating value of Toons. Roger gives him a smooch in the kisser, and a hush goes over the crowd of animated characters as they watch for his response. Unlike his early scenes with the manic rabbit, when the sourpuss detective was unfriendly and unsympathetic, Eddie returns the kiss with just as much comic gusto.

Toons, however, are still second-class citizens in Hollywood, and Toontown, while a riot of color and song just on the "other side" of Maroon Studios and Acme's warehouse, is their ghetto, evoking the situation of African Americans in the 1940s. The Ink and Paint Club features a Toon review starring Donald and Daffy, Hollywood's most famous Ducks, as well as Toon doormen and servers such as Betty Boop. Like Harlem's Cotton Club, the club is "strictly humans only," as R. K. Maroon informs Eddie when the detective balks at going there to get proof of Jessica Rabbit's (voiced by Kathleen Turner) infidelity in order to resolve Roger's anxiety about his marriage, which is causing the rabbit's missteps on set in the film's opening sequence.

The narrative stake of *Who Framed Roger Rabbit* is the future of the Toons and Toontown and, by implication, of the innocent pleasures of moviegoing and moviemaking. It does not seem mere coincidence that the film takes place in the year the war boom ended, the countdown of the studio system's demise was about to begin, and HUAC came to town—although in 1947 the seriousness of these events was not yet apparent. Instead *Who Framed Roger Rabbit* spins its conspiracy story out of the LA myth that the automobile industries, led by General Motors, colluded to end the use of electric streetcars and trolleys in favor of a network of freeways, privileging the motor car and buses running on diesel (Adler 1991; Bianco 1998). As sole owner of Cloverleaf Industries, Judge Doom buys the Red Car company to dismantle its inexpensive public transportation system; he likewise murders the owners of Maroon Studios and Toontown to gain possession of and then demolish the buildings there. Doom knows about the City Council's plans for a new freeway that will go right through those two properties, echoing the destruction in the neighborhood necessitated by the construction of the Hollywood Freeway, and he envisions the businesses the new freeway will generate as cars get on and off, day and night: "a string of gas stations, inexpensive motels, restaurants that serve rapidly prepared food, tire salons, automobile dealerships, and wonderful, wonderful billboards reaching as far as the eye can see! My God, it'll be beautiful!" His description evokes the ugly shopping strips on new highways that emerged in cities and suburbs across the United States after 1947.

As well as representing the capitalism driving postwar expansion beyond the urban centers downtown, where studios controlled most first-run exhibition, Doom, much like Miramount's fascist regime in *The Congress*, is a dictator ruling over the Toons. Acting as their judge, jury, and executioner when it comes to sentencing them to the dreaded "Dip," the chemical mixture that can erase them, Doom is the reason Roger tells Eddie, "There's no justice for Toons anymore." Doom intends to wipe out Toontown altogether with Dip—hence the filmmakers at first thought of calling the mixture "the Final Solution" (Rosenbaum 1988, 33). Eddie not only causes Doom's demise and exonerates Roger, but, when he realizes how, with invisible ink, Acme has concealed his will, which leaves Toontown to its inhabitants, Eddie also saves the Toons and their community for future generations.

The film's groundbreaking immersion of animation in live-action scenes enables Toons and humans to inhabit the same time and space, believably interacting with each other, as when Eddie walks by the cast of *Fantasia* (1940) on the Maroon studio lot; Betty Boop shuts his open mouth after Jessica Rabbit appears on stage in the Ink and Paint Club; Roger handcuffs himself to Eddie, who hides the rabbit in soapy water as Doom's weasels come looking for him; Eddie and Roger elude the weasels, driving off in Benny the Cab; and Eddie pursues Jessica into Toontown after Maroon is shot. (▶ Figure 7.6) Moreover *Who Framed Roger Rabbit* imagines signature cartoon figures like the two Ducks or Bugs Bunny and Mickey Mouse "rubb[ing] shoulders for the first time," thereby "crossing studio boundaries and fusing disparate styles and sensibilities" (Rosenbaum 1988, 34) as a means of equating the Toons and Toonland with Hollywood at large.

A sense of nostalgia for the Golden Age of animation is obvious in the many cameos of famous cartoon characters from multiple studios, some of whom have dialogue or appear in a short sequence and some of whom make a fleeting appearance in the background. Nostalgia is also an inescapable if unintentional effect of the film's technological breakthroughs in merging animation and live action so convincingly. As Mark J. P. Wolf observes, "Although *Who Framed Roger Rabbit* represented the cutting edge of compositing technology and a dazzling display of the optical printer's creative power, ironically it appeared at a turning point in compositing history when compositing began the transition from the optical printer to the digital technology of the computer. Thus, the film now stands as a monument to a dying technology, the pinnacle of its achievement" (Wolf 1995, 45). In its optical engineering of a convincing virtual Hollywood where Toons and humans interact, the innovations of *Who Framed Roger Rabbit* were already becoming a sign of Hollywood's past, just as they were being lauded and awarded with Oscars.

A less technologically complex but more provocative immersion of Hollywood in the real world of its audience occurs in *The Purple Rose of Cairo* (1985), which takes place in New Jersey during the Depression. Cecilia (Mia Farrow), an abused wife and inept waitress, finds solace for her unhappy life by going to the neighborhood movie theater. One day Tom Baxter (Jeff Daniels), a supporting character in the film-within-the-film also called "The Purple Rose of Cairo," suddenly leaves the screen, wanting to meet Cecilia because he has become intrigued by her gaze and the fact that she has seen the film five times already. Tom's abrupt departure causes consternation on- and offscreen. "You're on the wrong side of the screen!" one of the film's players shouts at him; soon the ensemble argue over whose story is most central, and they start to talk back to the remaining audience members. In the meantime, theatergoers complain that the actors, who cannot move the story forward without Tom, "sit around and talk. There's no action." One dissatisfied spectator moans, "I want what happened in the movie last week to happen this week. Otherwise, what's life all about anyway?" In Hollywood the producer Raoul Hirsch and his lackeys are upset about the legal implications for them of a fictional character in one of their films walking offscreen and interacting with real people; losing control over this character, they are afraid he may rob or rape someone and worry that more Tom Baxters will start leaping off the screen in other cities.

Tom Baxter (Jeff Daniels) leaps off the screen to meet Cecilia (Mia Farrow). (*The Purple Rose of Cairo* ©1985 Orion)

Cecilia readily succumbs to Tom's charm and gallantry, but also becomes "confused," as she tells his portrayer, Gil Shepherd (also Jeff Daniels). "I'm married. I just met a wonderful man. He's fictional, but you can't have everything." (▶ Figure 7.7) Tom's fictiveness, however, defines what makes him both attractive and shallow, since he can only know, feel, and say what has been written into his character. His sense of wonder at the world beyond the screen, along with his innocence of the human emotions, weaknesses, suffering, and brutality that characterize the real world, illuminates the appealing unreality of much Hollywood product during the Depression. For instance, he thrives on what Cecilia recognizes is "movie talk." Faced with his lack of a job, he states, "Well then, we'll live on love." Likewise Tom may know how to give a "perfect" kiss to Cecilia, but he becomes puzzled when there is no fade-out afterward. He not only discovers that cars don't start without an owner's key but that the wad of prop money in his pocket has no value offscreen. Cecilia takes him into a church to explain the concept of God, but Tom can understand the concept of a divinity only in terms of the two screenwriters who created him. When her husband, Monk (Danny Aiello), and Tom get into a fight inside the church, the latter is seriously beaten yet shows no signs of his injuries afterward.

In the meantime, Gil Shepherd travels to New Jersey because Tom's liberation from the screen threatens his career. Since it appears the actor has lost control of his character, causing a scandal his agent compares to Fatty Arbuckle's, no one will now risk making a picture with Gil. Right before he meets Cecilia by accident, when she at first mistakes him for Tom, we overhear Gil's gruff, insistent, and worried responses on a long-distance phone call to Hollywood. After meeting Cecilia, however, he quickly picks up on her infatuation with his character as well as her naïveté. As she compliments Gil's acting and comments on his "magical glow" onscreen, he gets all "gosh," "golly," and "gee" in his responses, in effect performing Tom Baxter for her. (▶ Figure 7.8) In the music store, after telling her that movie professionals know how to fake-kiss, he kisses her and mutters with a giggle, "Oh, my goodness," asking her to feel his beating heart. Gil eventually clinches the deal by telling her, "Look, I love you. I know that only happens in the movies, but I do," and he asks her to come with him to Hollywood. But after winning Cecilia away from his fictional alter ego, who returns to the screen in disappointment, Gil departs for the coast without her. "He couldn't wait to get outta here," the theater manager tells Cecilia when, leaving her husband and their marriage, she goes to the movie house to meet Gil. "He said this was a close call for his career," the manager continues. Gil Shepherd, it turns out, is a very good actor indeed.

Cecilia's figure mediates these reel and real Hollywood lovers. As she says, "Last week I was unloved. Now two people love me, and it's the same two people." Tom keeps telling her she is unhappily married, offering to carry her away where they can live on love, so he functions as her fantasy projection of a romantic male, a stark contrast with her brutish, selfish, and unemployed husband, Monk. Since he lacks real money, Tom takes her into the fictional world of his movie, where they go out nightclubbing in a montage modeled on countless such scenes in 1930s films; the montage closes with a rear shot of the couple in a taxi, her head resting on his shoulder. (▶ Figures 7.9–7.10) "My whole life I've wondered what it would be like to be this side of the screen," Cecilia remarks as their evening together winds down. Despite how Tom personifies Hollywood product as an unrealistic alternative to her unsatisfying marriage and unhappy life, the movie hero articulates for Cecilia what she has feared acknowledging to herself—which is also to say that Tom projects *her* fantasy of escaping from Monk. Not simply a critique of Hollywood, then, the imaginative situation at the heart of *Purple Rose of Cairo* indicates a significance for movies that lies beneath the surface of their passive, escapist appeal.

When Tom and Gil demand that Cecilia choose between them, the character states, "I'm honest, dependable, courageous, romantic, and a great kisser," whereas the actor forgoes such a checklist and simply says, "I'm real." His reality inevitably trumps Tom's virtual existence. As Cecilia tells Tom, "In your world things have a way of always working out right. See, I'm a real person. No matter how tempted I am, I have to choose the real world." As part of that real world, though, Gil is as dishonest and exploitative of Cecilia's good nature as is her husband. After Gil's desertion, with nowhere else to go and postponing the inevitable return to Monk, Cecilia enters the movie theater. Overwhelmed and paralyzed by the shock of Gil's betrayal, she finds a seat; as she watches Fred and Ginger dance, Cecilia's expressionless face gradually forms a radiant smile, and she becomes sutured to the screen. (▶ Figure 7.11)

The Purple Rose of Cairo juxtaposes the insularity of Depression-era movies, which follow an unrealistic logic all their own, and the external conditions of the real world in the 1930s, which in its harshness and scarcities is diametrically opposed to the screen's gloss and glamour, but this difference exceeds a simple illusion/reality polarity. That Tom and Gil are, as Cecilia says "the same two people" suggests they are two sides of the same coin: the (escapist) representation and its (corporate) manufacturer. As a Hollywood fabrication, Tom's behavior and understanding of the world may be limited by how he was written. Yet his innocence enchants not only Cecilia but also the hookers he meets, since he is unlike any other man they have encountered: his gentlemanly demeanor critiques real men's brutish behavior toward women. On the other hand, as a Hollywood professional looking out for his career, Gil is a smooth operator; he adeptly manages Cecilia once he realizes what qualities in his "Purple Rose" character, which he played "with a kind of poetic idealistic quality" and "with a cheerful bravado," appeal to her. His "real" figure is more resonant of Hollywood's manipulation of an audience than the "reel" character of Tom, a Hollywood creation. Yet despite Cecilia's desolation at the end, followed by her total absorption as a viewer, she was the one who compelled Tom to leave the screen, inciting him to break free of Gil's—and Hollywood's—control, and she is the one who sends him back there because she knows she must choose "the real world." Hollywood may churn out films that bear scant resemblance to the real world inhabited by audiences, offering them escapist fantasies, but it cannot determine how those consumers ultimately make sense of what they watch by connecting those fantasies to their everyday lives.

Last Action Hero (1993) tries for a similar understanding of moviegoing but with less subtle humor and more self-contradictory results. Nick (Robert Prosky), an old-fashioned projectionist, gives young Danny Madigan (Austin O'Brien) a magic ticket that the older man had received from Houdini as a child but had been afraid to use. "It's a passport to another world," Nick states, adding that the famed magician told him, "This ticket has a mind of its own. It does what it wants to do." The ticket transports Danny from the dilapidated Times Square movie house where Nick works into the sunny LA world of the action flick "Jack Slater IV." Only in the last forty minutes or so does the fictional movie hero (Arnold Schwarzenegger), a lone-wolf cop who typically goes rogue to defeat criminals, enter the youngster's real world: a dark, gloomy, impersonal, and dangerous New York City.

The opening of *Last Action Hero* sets up the dualism of benign Hollywood product and the sinister "real world" of the child moviegoer. We first watch a scene from an earlier entry, "Jack Slater III," in which Jack single-handedly bucks authority to rescue a group of children, including his own son, held hostage by the Ripper (Tom Noonan) on a high-rise rooftop. As Jack dispatches the slasher, the movie goes out of focus because Nick has fallen asleep in the projection booth. The auditorium is practically empty; aside from Danny, there are a handful of homeless people scattered about the huge hall. Outside the theater, a sign announces that a new Loews multiplex will soon be occupying the site. The next morning, Danny sidles in late to class, where a lesson on *Hamlet* has begun. As Laurence Olivier's version is being screened by the teacher (played with a wink and a nod by Olivier's widow, Joan Plowright), Nick settles into a daydream in which Jack Slater becomes Hamlet in a mock trailer: "Something is rotten in the state of Denmark, and Hamlet is taking out the trash." Picking up the Oedipal theme of *Hamlet* at the point when "Jack Slater III" went out of focus, we later learn that the Ripper dragged Jack's son off the roof with him. The fictional world justifies Jack's finding a surrogate son in Danny, just as the child finds a surrogate father in the movie hero.

Once Danny enters "Jack Slater IV" with the magic ticket during a special midnight preview that Nick runs just for him in the old movie palace, *Last Action Hero* tropes Hollywood as the land of eternal sunshine, blue skies, and beautiful people. Everyone has a 555 phone number. Jack cannot use vulgar language because he exists in a PG-13 film. The police station where he works looks more like a Vegas casino or lavish ultramodern hotel lobby. "I was just in a real police station, and this one's way nicer," Danny remarks. (▶ Figures 7.12–7.13) Here he encounters stars like Sharon Stone, who passes by in her costume from *Basic Instinct* (1992), and animated characters like Whiskers, with whom Jack and his captain, Lieutenant Dekker (Frank McRae), interact without losing a beat. A desk sergeant calls out assignments, incongruously pairing cops like the blond Krause with an orthodox rabbi. Much violence occurs throughout this long section of the film, during which Danny unsuccessfully tries to convince Jack that they are in a movie—people are shot, punched, thrown against or through walls, cars explode—but there are few fatalities and little bloodshed, just physical damage to buildings and motor vehicles.

Whereas the movie world of "Jack Slater IV" occurs mostly in bright sunlight, the action in New York City happens mostly at night, emphasizing the city's anonymity. Here Danny has no friends, he cuts school, his widowed mom can barely keep track of him due to her work hours, and he slips out late at night to watch movies at the old movie palace on 42nd Street. As Danny is about to sneak out against his mother's orders for a special midnight preview of "Jack Slater IV," a burglar breaks into their apartment and handcuffs the child to the toilet, which is why he has been to a real police station prior to entering the movie world.

The film's main villain, Benedict (Charles Dance), also uses the magic ticket, having taken it from Danny. To escape from Jack, who inevitably defeats him in reel life, Benedict enters the real world. Here he discovers that people steal and prostitute themselves; that no sirens sound when he shoots someone in cold blood; that no one pays attention to gun fire or his screaming that he has just killed someone; and that, as he later boasts to Jack in their final showdown, "in this world, the bad guys can win." Moreover Benedict realizes that if he uses the magic ticket to bring the Ripper into the real world to kill Arnold Schwarzenegger at the premiere of "Jack Slater IV," the fictional character will disappear from the movie world and he and his accomplice can return there, unstoppable. (▶ Figure 7.14)

After Danny and Jack follow Benedict into the real world, the youngster has to keep explaining to the detective that, as Benedict has discovered, "things work differently here." Jack hurts his hand when he breaks a car window; cars don't explode when he shoots them; a cab driver goes through the windshield after a crash with Jack's car and the hood is covered in blood; and Jack gets shot with real bullets. Additionally Danny's mother makes Jack "a wuss" in her son's eyes by introducing the detective to Mozart and giving him the opportunity to talk sincerely with a woman for the first time. But in placing Jack in this real world, *Last Action Hero* simply confirms the generic formula of numerous buddy cop films. When Dekker, suspicious of Danny's intimate knowledge of the Jack Slater movie series, makes him Jack's partner so that they can keep an eye on him, Danny tells Jack, "I'll teach you to be vulnerable. You'll teach me to be brave." Unsurprisingly, this conventional wisdom proves true.

Comparing *Last Action Hero* with *Purple Rose of Cairo*, Christopher Ames notes, "Both movies present tempered cautionary tales in which excessive investment in filmgoing is depicted as harmful, while movies are still celebrated for the imaginative alternative they offer to the struggles of everyday life" (Ames 1997, 112). However, unlike *Purple Rose* (or *Who Framed Roger Rabbit*, for that matter*)*, *Last Action Hero* uncertainly goes back and forth between smugly satirizing and uncritically valorizing its own outlandishness. It uses the trope of immersion to riff self-reflexively on both its leading man's stardom and its own genre, indicating the waning currency of each in the early 1990s, but the film never complicates or criticizes Danny's extraordinary faith in his hero. At the premiere of "Jack Slater IV," the real Schwarzenegger boasts to the press of its lower body count (48 dead in contrast with the 119 killed in the previous installment) and assures fans that this new film pays more attention to character and plot development. When the actor meets Jack there, the former compliments the latter for being the best celebrity look-alike the studio has yet gotten, though the character proclaims, "I don't really like you. You've brought me nothing but pain." (▶ Figure 7.15) Further advancing the way *Last Action Hero* turns on itself, Jack gets to redo the conclusion of "Jack Slater III" in the finale. After the Ripper throws Danny off the roof, and as the boy hangs perilously from a gargoyle, Jack kills the slasher, as he does in the movies, yet this time the detective saves his "son" with a gesture echoing the end of Hitchcock's *North by Northwest* (1959). Together Jack and Danny go on to defeat Benedict, but not before Benedict shoots Jack. With Jack bleeding profusely from the wound, Danny has to return his surrogate father to the movie world, where the fatal chest injury will prove to be only a flesh wound.

In its final moments, *Last Action Hero* wants to have it both ways. Jack tells Danny to remain in the real world because he has a real life, yet since Danny insists, "You're real to me," the detective swears in turn that his surrogate son's faith in him will continue to give him a reality in "reel" life. Thus, while in the real world Jack gets depressed when he discovers that he is a made-up character and that the tragic loss of his son was a writer's invention—the reason he blames Schwarzenegger for his pain—once back onscreen in the reel world, the movie hero shows what he has learned from his experience of the real New York. With his wound completely healed, Jack exclaims to the blubbering, hyperventilating Dekker, "You know why you're shouting? Because it's in the script. You're the comic relief. Yes, and you know what else? I'm the hero, so shut up!" He winks in direct address to Danny, shown in reverse shot on the other side of the screen, and continues, revealing his new vulnerability: "You see, Hollywood is writing our lives, and you know something? I don't want to shoot people anymore and blow up buildings." As Jack's voice fades out in the distance, Danny returns the magic ticket stub to Nick, but his friend, about to be dispossessed of his job by the wrecking ball, tells the child that the ticket is his now and that the magic that brought the movies to life was his as well.

These three "immersive" backstudios are less critical than *The Congress* about the fantasy worlds that Hollywood constructs for its audiences; while acknowledging the ideologies operating through such fantasies, in varying degrees they each celebrate the value of films and filmgoing. Each stages the exuberant vitality of movies through imaginary characters—Roger Rabbit, Tom Baxter, Jack Slater—who not only come to life but are larger than life offscreen, interacting with real characters in ways that break the screen's customary fourth wall. While *Who Framed Roger Rabbit* does not imagine an obsessive spectator like Cecilia or Danny, it too collapses the difference between real people and reel characters: Roger is as "real" as Eddie, just as that human character is as "reel" as the animated rabbit. And while Hollywood product may be depicted as superficial and escapist, in each case, as the "reel" makes direct contact with the "real," their interaction offers at least temporary compensation for the hand that reality has dealt the protagonists. Eddie moves past grieving his brother's murder; Cecilia comes to terms, for better or worse, with her unhappy marriage; Danny finds a father figure who teaches him how to be brave, a skill necessary for survival in the real world of New York. As a trade-off for its unabashed interpellation of them in a fantasy world, Hollywood is therefore shown giving these characters an imaginative site for learning a valuable lesson about their real worlds. Eddie rediscovers the joyfulness of Toons and learns to laugh again; Cecilia (at least momentarily) confronts the difference between reality and the fantasies spun each week by the movies; and Danny is made to see that his imagination is what brings the movies to life. What these characters learn, though, does not diminish how each backstudio restricts its understanding of the movies to escapist fare nor how, produced during a period—the blockbuster era—when such films dominated the box office year after year, each depicts Hollywood as a fantasy machine.

Appropriated Hollywood

Four backstudios from the past several decades that imagine a virtual Hollywood through some form of analogic simulation—*F/X* (1986), *F/X 2* (1991), *The Last Shot* (2004), and *Argo* (2012)—depict the appropriation of the industry's filmmaking practices by a state agency, drawing parallels between the process of making a movie and corrupt or covert governmental activities.

As indicated by their titles, *F/X* and its sequel concern themselves with Hollywood's special effects. As a peeved actress says at the start of *F/X*, "Nobody cares about making movies about people anymore. All they care about is special effects." She correctly describes the attention paid to special effects by these two backstudios. Each begins with a scene that could be really happening but turns out to be a film shoot relying on simulated violence. *F/X* starts with a man in a raincoat and fedora entering a crowded restaurant where he begins shooting wildly; screaming patrons jump for cover and hide beneath tables; blood spurts from corpses; the venue's multiple lobster tanks explode, with crusta-ceans, water, and shattered glass flying everywhere. The shooter moves in on a young woman seated with a man at a rear table; apparently she is his unfaithful mistress or spouse; the shooter blows her away—after which we learn this entire scene has been a film shoot with special effects planned out and executed by Rollie Tyler (Bryan Brown). (▶ Figures 7.19–7.21)

F/X 2, by comparison, opens with a street scene that promises a different genre. A woman crashes her car and, when stopped by a drunken homeless man who tries to wash her windshield, reveals herself to be an ugly, angry, cross-dressing cyborg; it throws the homeless man into the glass front of a liquor store as police arrive; they shoot off the cyborg's arm, leg, and part of its face, but it unleashes a missile at the cop car—at which point the special effects fail since the car explodes after the director yells "Cut." Rollie is not the FX artist on this sci-fi flick but a bystander, watching the shoot occur on a "real" New York City street with young Chris, his girlfriend Kim's (Rachel Ticotin) son. Having left film work, Rollie now makes expensive toys that draw on his expertise in special effects. (▶ Figures 7.19–7.21)

Both backstudios have men from law enforcement—Martin Lipton (Cliff De Young) and Colonel Mason (Mason Adams) in the first film, Ray Silek (Philip Bosco) and Mike Brandon (Tom Mason), Kim's ex and Chris's father, in the second—entangle Rollie in a convoluted scheme that relies on his great proficiency as an effects artist. In *F/X*, Mason and Lipton of the Justice Department hire Rollie to stage a convincing hit in a restaurant on a mobster, Nicholas DeFranco (Jerry Orbach), who is willing to testify if he can be kept alive. The plan is to fake his death and hide him until trial. In *F/X 2*, Silek of the NYPD solicits Rollie's help to catch a sex predator by transforming Mike into a double of the real woman who will initially be used as bait. In both *F/X* and *F/X 2* the staged scene engineered with finesse by Rollie echoes the film shoot at the beginning, just as in both it quickly goes awry. It looks like Rollie has killed DeFranco for real, although the gangster has been secreted away by Lipton and Mason so they can share in the $15 million that DeFranco stole from the mob and deposited in a Swiss bank. Rollie himself is considered a loose end needing to be eliminated, but he escapes when Lipton tries to kill him, so Mason brings in a professional to finish the job. Similarly, an assassin shoots Mike during his drag undercover act because he has gotten too close to uncovering Silek's criminal activity in arranging to sell to the mob rare gold medallions stolen from the Vatican. The assassin escapes as Silek kills the suspected predator, making it look like his team ar-rived too late to save Mike from his knife. Since Rollie stumbled upon the assassin as he left and has an incriminating video of Silek covering up the assassination by making it look like Mike died from knife wounds, our hero once again turns out to be a loose end needing elimination.

The two films take as their starting point the appropriation of Hollywood's know-how by a corrupt legal agency of the state—the Justice Department, the NYPD—for its own purposes, after which Rollie uses his expertise to defeat them. As Rollie foils Lipton's and Mason's efforts to subdue him in *F/X*, he reminds them why he was hired—"For my particular genius"—which he successfully deploys to outwit their brute force tactics. Both films betray some of the secrets used by real FX artists in creating effects not with computers but with plastics, makeup, explosives, electronics, screens, stuntmen, rigged automobiles, and so forth. In *F/X*, for example, we watch the steps by which Rollie manufactures for DeFranco a face mask with lines of fake blood that will spill when triggered by a remote-control transmitter as the shooter in the restaurant fires a gun with blank cartridges. Later on, in order to steal his van from the impound lot and elude the numerous cop cars in pursuit, Rollie calls out to his assistant the names of films they have made together ("Hellraisers," "Skidball Express," etc.), his way of telling her what effect to use as they make their getaway. In *F/X 2*, Rollie demonstrates to Mike step by step how he will trick the predator by transforming the detective into a woman. Afterward, when the assassin locks Rollie, Kim, and Chris in a supermarket, Rollie becomes a bricoleur as he fashions numerous ordinary household items into special effects that distract their pursuer as they run through the store in search of an exit. Both films conclude with the bad cops and their gangland conspirators in a remote mansion, where Rollie, secretly arriving there with his big bag of tricks, rolls out elaborate effects to distract and eliminate the various gunmen one by one.

In this pair of backstudios Hollywood magic jumps off the screen and into the streets, where FX illusions have real effects on people and property. Yet significantly neither plot concludes with a public vindication of Rollie's innocence, and his violent behavior in retaliating against his antagonists is no different from theirs. As well as killing several people in each film, he sends the main villain to certain death in the climax. Rollie superglues a gun to Mason's hands and pushes the man out of the mansion to face a waiting crowd of police, who shoot him despite his pleas. Silek takes off in a helicopter

Rollie (Bryan Brown) making a plaster cast of DeFranco (Jerry Orbach) as part of a scheme to use movie special effects to fake the mobster's death. (*FX* ©1986 Orion)

that turns out to be piloted by a remote-controlled cyborg clown, which Rollie directs to jump into the water below, leaving a terrified Silek by himself, certain to crash since he does not know how to operate the controls.

Likewise, with the aid of the filmmakers' genuine special effects, both backstudios stage brutal and overlong fights between Rollie and the man hired to kill him. In both films, the killer seems vanquished midway through but comes back to life a minute or two later to continue fighting. In the first *F/X* the professional, a black ops sharpshooter, kills Rollie's girlfriend (Diane Venora), and, after a vicious battle that tears up her apartment, Rollie finally slays him. In the second *F/X* the assassin escapes after fighting with Rollie in a scene that ratchets up the destruction, this time of his workshop, but catches up with him in the supermarket later on. In both films, too, Rollie forces information out of his enemy by torturing him. In *F/X* Rollie locks Lipton in the trunk of his car and, in a deserted junk yard, repeatedly rams the back of the auto into pillars and other cars to get information about Mason's whereabouts. In *F/X 2* Rollie captures the assassin in the supermarket and covers the man's face with meat-packing plastic, forcing him to divulge information about Silek under the threat of suffocation. In both instances, we have to infer that Rollie leaves his enemy for dead afterward since each man then disappears from the film.

For all his quick thinking in deploying special effects, which self-reflexively mirrors the filmmaking process, Rollie is like a Stallone or Bronson character in action films of the 1980s. Deceived by the law, with someone close to him dead and his own life endangered, he functions as a vigilante, getting some assistance from a detective who "pisses people off," Leo McCarthy (Brian Dennehy). Leo's investigation in *F/X* parallels Rollie's efforts to get at the truth, save his own skin, bypass ineffective and headline-seeking colleagues, and bring down DeFranco, whom he is convinced is still alive. Since the two men have shared DeFranco's loot at the end of *F/X*, in the sequel Rollie turns to Leo for help in figuring out why Silek had Mike murdered. At the end of this second installment, Rollie substitutes phony medallions for the real ones, but it turns out the mob was buying them to return them to the church, so in a coda we see Rollie and Leo placing the heavy gold pieces in a Vatican collection basket. However, they apparently keep for themselves the small fortune that the mob paid to Silek for the medallions. Rollie, in short, demonstrates the clever use of Hollywood's special effects in the real world, but, appealing to the hip cynicism of their era, in both films his expertise helps him get away with murder and a lot of money.

The Last Shot and *Argo*, in comparison, recount true stories in which the FBI and CIA, respectively, each used a fake movie production as the cover for a sting operation. Of the two, *The Last Shot* is the more self-reflexively fictionalized. Its opening pivots between real and reel perspectives. A title announces, "December 1985. New York City. Based on a true story." On a rainy night a man waiting in a car gets out of the vehicle, approaches two men departing a limo, and shoots them dead. We will shortly learn that, as in real life, this was Paul Castellano and his bodyguard, an assassination ordered by John Gotti. The camera moves in on the headlight of Castellano's car, and the image dissolves to a brightly lit theater marquee, which begins the film's titles, as credits appear on different signs of moviegoing: Matthew Broderick's name is on a ticket stub, Alex Baldwin's on a Coke Classic can, Toni Collette's on a theater seat, Tony Shaloub's on a hot dog. Other names show up on debris littered on the floor, such as those of featured actors on a used mustard packet, the costume designer's on a box of spilled candy, the editor's and cinematographer's on a newspaper page, the producer's on a bucket of popcorn. The bucket spills and rolls toward the light with the name of the writer and director, Jeff Nathanson. A shot of the auditorium follows; the audience watches an advertisement for the theater's refreshment stand as the camera moves behind the screen, returning us to the "real" world, this time Houston, Texas.

There gangsters are torturing an FBI agent, Joe Devine (Alec Baldwin), warning him they will cut off his finger in three minutes during the opening credits of the feature attraction if he does not tell them where the money is. Two gangsters debate whether the proper term is "opening credits" or "opening titles." *The Last Shot* then moves from the backstage of the movie house to a van outside, where Joe's team is recording what is happening. They argue over whether to step in before Joe loses his finger or to wait until the amputation gives them ample evidence for an arrest, since that may be the reason Joe has not yet given his safe word to be rescued. The next scene, though, establishes this backstudio's wackier tone: Joe, his severed finger sewn back on, returns home to discover that his beloved dog, Sasha, lonely and despondent, committed suicide by throwing herself in the Jacuzzi.

Transferred to Providence by his brother Jack (Ray Liotta), head of the FBI, Joe convinces his superiors there to let him set up a fake movie production in order to get Gotti's second cousin, Tommy Sanz (Tony Shalhoub), on a racketeering charge for taking a bribe to bypass union regulations for the shoot. Going to Hollywood to learn how to act like a producer, Joe encounters sad sack Steven Schatz (Matthew Broderick), who has a script called "Arizona" about a woman dying of cancer in the desert, which the agent purchases to give his scheme credibility. With Steven hired to direct as well, Joe's next task is to convince him to make "Arizona" in Providence because, he explains, "the dentists" financing the project have made a deal with the Rhode Island Film Commission. Joe reassures Steven; he has been to both states, "and you'd be amazed at the similarities." Soon Joe not only gets evidence of Tommy's racketeering, but he persuades "the dentists" to continue with the sting, nicknamed "Dramex," arguing that he can use Sanz to get Gotti and even nail the entire mob family in the tiny state. Furthermore, as the production gives every appearance of really happening, Emily French (Toni Collette), a former Oscar nominee fresh out of rehab, travels to Providence to beg for the leading role of Charlotte, which Steven had promised to his psycho girlfriend (Calista Flockheart). Real-life actors Pat Morita and Russell Means also join the cast.

It turns out, though, that Jack has used his brother's sting operation as a decoy to nab Gotti in New York. With the mob leader in custody, the FBI head arrives in Providence to shut down Dramex. "What about the movie?" Joe asks his brother, who replies, "We're the FBI. We don't make movies." However, Joe has become hooked by moviemaking and knocks his brother unconscious so that production may begin. Steven starts to film the last shot in the picture, a dying Charlotte in front of a huge painted backdrop of the Arizona desert, but FBI helicopters stop the filming. (▶ Figure 7.22) In a coda occurring some time later, we learn that Emily French has had a triumph directing "Leaving Arizona," "a movie about making another movie that was a sting operation." As for Joe, no longer with the agency, he arrives with a peace offering at Grauman's Chinese, where Steven has returned to his job as a manager; before departing the FBI, Joe stole from the evidence locker the bit of "Arizona" that Steven shot before the helicopters brought filming to a halt. Joe apologizes and starts to explain his real identity, but Steven stops him, saying he has seen Emily's movie: "And by the way, I thought Tom Berenger captured you beautifully." The two men watch the "Arizona" footage twice in the empty theater. Afterward Joe intrigues Steven with his sketch of a screenplay he has himself started to write. *The Last Shot* closes with the expectation that the two will collaborate on it.

The Last Shot takes potshots at the insincerity and pretentiousness of industry types, most notably through the brash, vulgar, bullying character of Fanny Nash (Joan Cusak), a producer who instructs Joe's team on how to act convincingly as Hollywood players. "If you wanna carry yourself like you're in the movie business," she states, "you need to act like the big dog, Clifford, and remember that everyone in the entire world is desperate to play with your big red balls." Joe's field experience as an FBI agent translates into his easily becoming a manipulative, dishonest, ballsy Hollywood producer, while acting like such a producer for Dramex appears to up his game as an agent. As Joe takes Steven around Providence to scout locations that "resemble" Arizona, the film gets many laughs from the sheer absurdity of their shooting in the Northeast a film whose storyline depends on Southwestern locations. (▶ Figures 7.23–7.24)

Steven, meanwhile, is satirized as the archetypal Hollywood outsider, a milquetoast desperate to crash the movies as a filmmaker but lacking the imagination and assertiveness to do so. The closest he has so far gotten to Hollywood is his job at the Chinese theater. He lives next door to a kennel that caters to the stars in the hopes of making a connection there, and his wannabe actress girlfriend plays piano at Nordstrom's, which is not just any store but "where every casting agent shops." When Jack prevents her from strangling a barking dog at the kennel, someone asks, "Are you some kind of good Samaritan?" "No," he replies, "I'm a Hollywood producer." His answer causes Steven's eyes to light up. With Dramex Joe enables Steven to fulfill his dream of making it in Hollywood—and the agent and his associates get swept up in his dream as well.

"I'm not really making a movie, sir," Joe tells one of his bosses. "I'm producing one." His hair-splitting here defines "producing" as the act of going through the motions, of faking it. An added irony, though, is that unbeknownst to Joe (at least to start with, since his team is recording everything), "Arizona" is itself a fake script. Steven claims Charlotte's story is true, but he and his cowriter, his estranged brother, Marshal, never had a sister named Charlotte who died in Arizona for they have made up every detail in their script. "You can't fool Hollywood. They can smell a fake a mile away," Marshal warns. But apparently the FBI can be fooled. Joe and his associates become their own patsies as they get seduced by the same heady appeal of Hollywood that captivates Steven. Although he has enough evidence to nail Tommy, Joe agrees to have the mobster sign on as an executive producer of "Arizona," thereby holding off on arresting him so that production can continue, and the mobster too falls for the mystique of Hollywood. After "Arizona," Joe wants to go from state to state producing more films to catch additional racketeers. His team wants to get in on the act as well. The agent filming auditions from behind a one-way mirror wants to run the camera when production starts, momentarily forgetting that "Arizona" will not be a real movie. Most outrageously, "the dentists" themselves are swept up by the movie business. Joe's bosses in Providence give him detailed notes after reading the script, sign him to a three-picture deal, and argue with him over who will get merchandising rights. (▶ Clip 19)

Drawing humor from the equivalence of an FBI sting operation and Hollywood hustling, *The Last Shot* reverses what happens in the two *FX* films, where Rollie uses Hollywood's special effects to defeat corrupt lawmen. Although Marshal insists that you can't fool Hollywood with a fake script, in *The Last Shot* Hollywood itself is all fakery. Furthermore, since an agent covertly films everything happening in Providence, including the auditions, production meetings, and Steven's tense encounter with his brother, the FBI *does* make movies, Jack Devine's denial notwithstanding. In *Argo*, on the other hand, the movie business provides a cover story for engineering the escape from Iran of six Americans who had successfully fled from the U.S. embassy in Tehran when students overran it and took everyone else hostage in November 1979. As Tony Mendez (Ben Afleck), a specialist in CIA exfiltration operations, says, "We think everyone knows Hollywood people. And everyone knows they'd shoot in Stalingrad with Pol Pot directing if it would sell tickets." Although his ruse of having the six Americans pose as a group of Canadian filmmakers scouting locations in Iran exploits the global fame and reach of the movie business, *Argo* shows that Hollywood is still a very American enterprise.

Argo was controversial for emphasizing the United States' seeming total control of the escape plan, downplaying Canada's role and fictionalizing the rescue to make it more thrilling. "In 1980, 'the houseguests' cover story had in fact never really been tested and in some ways proved irrelevant to their escape. Emigration officials barely looked at the Americans and their documentation as they passed smoothly through the airports" (Shaw and Jenkins 2017, 109). Much of *Argo*, however, recounts Tony Mendez's efforts to convince the State Department to approve his plan, his roundabout entry into Iran via Turkey, his persuading the six people to trust him, his dangerous excursion with them into the Grand Bazaar to meet a representative of the Ministry of Culture, his defiance of the State Department's last-minute abortion of the operation followed by a reversal, his taking his six charges to the airport, their passage through a tense sequence of checkpoints, and finally the Revolutionary Guards chasing the Swissair plane as it taxis down the runway. But approaching *Argo* as a backstudio picture and not a political thriller enables me to call attention to what it registers about the currency of Hollywood in 1980 and for 2013.

As with Joe's sting in *The Last Shot*, before traveling to Asia Tony needs to confer with real Hollywood people, find a script, and establish the credibility of his fake movie. He meets with (real-life) special effects artist John Chambers (John Goodman), who has worked with Tony and the CIA before. When Tony tells Chambers that he needs him "to help me make a fake movie," the latter responds, "You've come to the right place," for, like Rollie in *F/X*, Chambers is a master of analog special effects, winning an honorary Oscar for the prosthetic makeup that convincingly transformed actors into simians in *Planet of the Apes* (1968). It appears there isn't much difference between faking an ape's appearance and faking an entire movie since the film business is nothing but appearances, which is what Tony is relying upon to fool the Iranian revolutionaries. After Chambers hears the plan, he comments, "So you want to come to Hollywood, act like a big shot…without doing anything?" He smiles and adds, "You'll fit right in."

Chambers next sets Tony up with Lester Siegel (Alan Arkin), a longtime producer with credits to his name who will produce the fake movie for free and can be trusted with classified information. Unlike Chambers, the fictional Siegel is a composite of real-life Hollywood figures; to borrow phrasing from *The Last Shot*, this character has mastered the art of acting like the big red dog, as evident when he successfully negotiates for the script of a science-fiction picture entitled "Argo." Chambers and Siegel partner on the fake movie to establish its validity. They get an office in the Producers' Building at the Burbank Studios, business cards, and a poster. But Tony insists that is not enough to fool the Iranian guards at the airport; they have to do something big, "and it has to have something that says it is authentic." "If you want to sell a lie," Chambers begins to tell Tony, using Rock Hudson's straight reputation as his example, but Siegel interrupts, finishing the thought: "you get the press to do it for you." They set up a press event at the Beverly Hilton with actors in costume doing a table read of the script. (▶ Figure 7.25) Their goal is achieved when, much like what happens with the fake movie in *The Last Shot*, coverage in a Hollywood trade confirms the authenticity of "Argo," with a two-column article focusing on Chambers and Siegel as its producers and noting the start of production in the spring. The story appears opposite a full-page advertisement for the fake film.

Argo views Hollywood through a dual lens. On one hand, the movie business is all outward show with no substance. What is authentic is the appearance of authenticity, the cliché about Hollywood that Tony's plot relies on, that Chambers's sarcasm confirms, and that the table read of "Argo" stages. On the other hand, what also stands out about Hollywood in *Argo* is that the two characters associated with it, Chambers and Siegel, seem past their prime in the business, and so for the most part do the minor figures they interact with. The film is set in 1980, when the industry was itself in a state of transition. One of the first establishing shots of the movie capital is the dilapidated Hollywood sign visibly and sadly needing repair. Another shot of a familiar water tower shows that the Warners lot has (temporarily, as it would turn out) been renamed Burbank Studios. Chambers and Siegel, moreover, seem most to enjoy kibitzing about the old days. The movie business in *Argo* has a nostalgic layer beneath its fakery, which

A story and advertising in *Daily Variety* give credibility to the fake movie "Argo." (*Argo* ©2012 Warner Bros.)

substantiates the appearance of authenticity that is Hollywood. If the suggestions of nostalgia for old-time Hollywood at a point of its diminishment in 1980 don't revive the movies' mystique, at least they invite one to remember when the mystique had more substance. (▶ Figures 7.26–7.27)

Personifying both views of Hollywood, Lester Siegel is the most memorable character in *Argo* because he is larger than life in comparison with the somber Tony and the numerous people working for the CIA and the Department of State. Siegel is brusque, loud, crotchety, vulgar, wisecracking, funny, and old. When Chambers brings Tony to meet him, Siegel is on his way to receive a lifetime achievement award, although he bellows, "I'd rather stay home and count the wrinkles on my dog's balls." At the press event a reporter keeps asking what the title signifies, since it sounds like a shortened version of "Argonaut"; after saying it is just a space ship, an exasperated Siegel shouts, "Argo fuck yourself," which becomes his slogan for their project. Siegel's ego is on the line despite the unreality of this project, since he declares, "If I'm doing a fake movie, it's gonna be a fake hit." Representing an older Hollywood, Siegel gets the best lines, which may be why his portrayer, Arkin, was singled out by the Academy with the only acting nomination for *Argo*.

The one time we see actual filmmaking occur is the night the State Department cancels the operation only to reverse itself after Tony disobeys and takes his group to the airport anyway. Siegel and Chambers decide to go for drinks rather than shut down the office and clear out, as per their new instructions from the CIA. On their way back, as Siegel reminisces with Chambers, finishing a conversation about something that would "go all the way throughout the thirties," they have to wait for an outdoor fight scene on the studio lot to finish shooting. Another take is required, but an impatient Siegel tells the assistant who has stopped them, "Sorry, pal, we're gonna be in the movie. Call my agent." The editing intercuts this scene with those of the CIA strong-arming State into reversing its cancelation of the operation and trying to reach Chambers again, Tony and the six Americans going through the three stages of immigration clearance at the airport, and a Revolutionary Guard making the phone call. The delay at the studio and Siegel's ultimate refusal to continue waiting fortuitously allow Chambers to take the call from Iran, authenticating Tony's cover story, thereby enabling him and the six Americans to board their flight. The grouchy, sarcastic old men of Hollywood, in short, save the day. (▶ Figure 7.28)

Like Jack Devine's comment in *The Last Shot* that the FBI does not make movies, before giving the official go-ahead, the CIA director asks Tony, "You're telling me there is a movie company in Hollywood right now that is funded by the CIA?" Both *Argo* and *The Last Shot* feature characters in authority positions who disclaim the parallels with Hollywood that each backstudio nonetheless advances. With the success of the "Argo" operation, Tony receives the Intelligence Star but cannot keep it since the award is classified. "So they're going to give me an award and then take it back?" he asks his boss, Jack O'Donnell (Bryan Cranston). "If we wanted applause," Jack replies, "we would have joined the circus." "I thought we did," Tony responds. Their exchange harks back to comments made when Tony first pitched his idea of the fake movie to State. One staff member warned, "Flamboyant cover identities should be avoided, as it increases operational visibility," and another added, "You wanna blend in with the population, you don't look like a rodeo clown." On one hand, *Argo* recognizes that the CIA relies upon its invisibility; flamboyance and rodeo clowns are not its trademark by any means. Public credit for the daring exfil operation thus goes to Canada and, we are told in an end title card, the agency's role in the daring escape was not known until President Clinton declassified the mission in 1997. On the other hand, Tony and Jack's exchange suggests that the circus—and the flamboyance, costumes, clowns, and spectacle of a circus call to mind the table read of "Argo" for the press—works well as a fitting metaphor for what they do. (▶ Figure 7.29)

Though one is a thriller and the other a comedy, *Argo* and *The Last Shot* draw parallels between the smoke and mirrors of Hollywood and the CIA and FBI. Concealing their real missions, in both films the two agencies put on a show that rivals Hollywood's, yet the film industry is also being co-opted by the state to serve its purposes. To be sure, the industry has long had content censored by numerous watchdog agencies, such as its own Production Code Administration, the Legion of Decency, and, during World War II, the Office of War Information. The CIA and the Pentagon have routinely scrutinized scripts too, and their vetting practices continues (Jenkins 2012; Alford and Secker 2017). In both backstudios, with Hollywood subordinated to the state's covert purposes, the hierarchy registers onscreen a subtle new sense of the Americanness of filmmaking in our century: not, as usually understood, Hollywood's role in manufacturing cultural myths that create a unified American identity through mass entertainment, but Hollywood's subordination to the political interests and machinations of the U.S. government. *Wag the Dog* (1997) raises this issue more boldly with a prescient satire conflating Hollywood and politics that still has pertinence for today.

"It's Like the Oscars"

Wag the Dog begins with the current president facing a sex scandal because a Firefly girl has accused him of molesting her in a private room adjacent to the Oval Office. With his probable reelection happening in just under two weeks but now hanging in the balance, he summons spin doctor Conrad "Connie" Brean (Robert De Niro) to distract attention from the disastrous accusation. Connie's motto is "Change the story, change the lede." His tactic, made up on the fly, is to have the administration float and then deny rumors about an imaginary B-3 bomber, and then to declare war on Albania, chosen because few Americans know or care about that country. When the president's adviser Winifred Ames (Anne Heche), contends, "We can't afford a war," Connie explains, "We're not gonna have a war. We're gonna have the appearance of a war." The people will find out, she insists, so he asks, "Who's gonna tell 'em?" This premise immediately casts suspicion on real-life presidential military actions that can distract the public from scandals closer to home.

Connie and Winifred travel to Hollywood to commission the big-time producer Stanley Motss (Dustin Hoffman) to produce their fake war. "I'm in show business, why come to me?" he inquires, rising from his tanning bed and sipping a veggie shake. Connie mentions several slogans, such as "Remember the Maine," "Tippecanoe and Tyler Too," and "54, 40, or Fight," and explains that people recall those mottos, but not the wars they refer to, because "war is show business." As additional proof, he cites iconic imagery of previous wars, such as the marines hoisting the flag on Iwo Jima, the V for Victory poster from World War II, and the young naked girl covered in napalm from the Vietnam War. He then raises the possibility that the signature image of the Gulf War, "smart bomb falling down a chimney," may have been forged in a Virginia studio. "Is that true?" Stanley asks. "How the fuck do we know?" Connie replies, making his point about the indeterminacy of media representations. When Stanley realizes that he is being asked to produce a war, Connie corrects him: "It's not a war, it's a pageant. We need a theme, a song, some visuals. It's a pageant. It's like the Oscars. That's why we came to you." (▶ Figure 7.30) (▶ Clip 20)

The Congress disaggregates both the scanned movie star and inhabitants of the Animated Zone from their referential connections to the real world on "the other side," but they still retain an iconic relation to what they represent. *Wag the Dog*, on the other hand, completely divorces the manufactured image, which still looks like "reality," from a source in real life. The film bases its satire by exaggerating the equivalence of Hollywood razzle dazzle and the government's manipulation of the media in an era when imagery of news events can be digitally manufactured much like in the movies, as happens when Stanley produces a video of a young Albanian woman running from terrorists. With the actress filmed against a blue screen, a team of effects people place a village behind her, adding a burning bridge and a stream, the sound of screaming and sirens, and a kitten instead of the bag of chips she held while being filmed. Furthermore, this scene confirms that the president, who overrides Stanley's choice and makes the final decision about the kitten's color, knows full well what Connie is doing. Several hours later the footage airs on the evening news. When the CIA, who knows there is no war, sends an agent (William H. Macy) to interview Connie and Winifred as possible threats to national security, Connie declares, "Of course there's a war. I'm watching it on television." (▶ Figures 7.31–7.36)

The plotting of *Wag the Dog* then complicates Connie's scheme due to unexpected shifts in the fake war narrative. After leaving Connie and Winifred, the CIA makes a deal with the president's election opponent and declares the war has ended. To keep the fake war going, Stanley creates a hero, "Old Shoe," who was left behind enemy lines. (▶ Figure 7.37) William Schumann (Woody Harrelson), the real soldier cast in that role, turns out to be a criminally insane prisoner who had raped a nun, among other unnamed offenses; after he is handed over to Winifred in chains, the plane returning them crashes in a storm; all survive, but the crash delays Old Shoe's publicized arrival. (▶ Figure 7.38) Finding refuge on a farm, Connie, Winifred, and Stanley momentarily lose sight of Schumann, who attempts to molest a young woman and is shot by the farmer, her father. Stanley then plans a big military funeral for the "hero."

Each time the fake war narrative takes what seems a disastrous turn, in short, Stanley comes up with a creative solution; as this happens his excitement grows, in contrast to Winifred's despair and Connie's stoicism. Stanley exclaims time and again, "This is nothing" because "This is producing!" Producing is problem-solving, he explains; it is thinking ahead. The lesson, he says as the war narrative winds down, is "Never give up. The show must go on." With the president's poll numbers soaring by the end of the film, Stanley watches on TV Old Shoe's military funeral, which effectively ends the pageant, and declares to Connie, "That is a complete fucking fraud and it looks a hundred percent real. That's the best work I've ever done in my life because it's so honest." According to Andrew Doyle, "The closer that the fantasy war looks like reality, the more enamoured Motss is of it....Motss has become part of reality, in contrast to his work as a master of unreality" (Doyle 2009, 119). But for Stanley Motss, a creature of Hollywood, the appearance of reality on screen, be it in a movie theater or on television or a computer monitor, has always been reality to him. The reverse of Doyle's formulation therefore seems just as credible: the more

Connie Brean (Robert De Niro) and Stanley Motss (Dustin Hoffman) toast to the success of their "pageant." (*Wag the Dog* ©1997 New Line)

Stanley's fake war looks like a Hollywood movie, the more enamored he is of it. That is why he believes that "a complete fucking fraud" can nonetheless be "so honest."

To his mind, what Stanley creates with the fake war is another motion picture. When the CIA announces the war is over, he declares, "The war isn't over until I say it's over. This is *my* picture, it's not the CIA's picture." He not only conflates his production of a fake war with the production of a movie—"They can't shut down my picture," he insists, his anger rising—but he also equates politics with moviemaking. "This is politics at its finest," he boasts to Winifred's staff, even though the politics he has in mind comprise his production of the fake war, its aftermath, and the speech he writes for the president about Old Shoe's captivity, all based on the timeworn Hollywood principles of classic narrative structure and ballyhoo. Hence Stanley's great disappointment when it first appears that his fake war narrative will have only a first act with the fighting in Albania, and his subsequent excitement when he gets to complete a three-act structure with Old Shoe's being left behind and rescue as act 2 and then his death and funeral as act 3. His knowing how structure works to engage spectators is also the basis of his warning Winifred that she is making a mistake in bringing Schumann back from captivity too early. "Sweetheart," he says, "Schumann is the shark, okay? Schumann is Jaws, you know? You have to tease them. You gotta tease them. You don't put Jaws in the first reel of the movie. It's the contract, sweetheart. The contract of the election, whether they know it or not, is 'Vote for me Tuesday, Wednesday I'll produce Schumann.' See, that's what they're paying their seven bucks for."

Stanley's wanting credit for producing the fake war, however, threatens to make visible the government's secret manipulation of the electorate's patriotism. He tells Connie about producing, "You do your job right, nobody should notice. But when you fuck up, everything gets full of shit." By the same token, what is a producer without public recognition of his work? Stanley Motss has produced the Oscars—why Connie sought him out in the first place—but he has never won one for producing. "You know you're a writer, that's your script. You're a director. But if you're the producer," he complains, "what'd you do? See, nobody knows what you do. The producer, I mean, all he's got is the credit." The contradiction Stanley inhabits as a Hollywood producer in *Wag the Dog* is his knowing that good producing is invisible work while, at the same time, his needing the work credited to make it noticeable *as* work. After all, credit is Hollywood's currency.

Despite the obvious bond that has developed between the two men, because Stanley finally declares he is going to get his credit, Connie reluctantly authorizes his assassination. (▶ Figures 7.39–7.40) Although Stanley has repeatedly stated that he wants the credit, Connie has previously shut him down with a dire warning, a reminder of their agreement of secrecy, and a promise of an ambassadorship. However, after the funeral procession for Old Shoe, TV pundits discount the causal effect of the Albanian war on the president's great popularity, attributing his 89 percent approval rate to the spin given to the events and the fear driving the public, which is assuaged by the banal commercials that ask, "Why switch horses in midstream?" The host agrees, concluding, "The president is a product." Stanley, whose fake war has effectively banished the Firefly girl's accusation from the news and assured the president's reelection, becomes enraged at these remarks. For one thing, as a Hollywood professional he has been criticizing the amateurish quality of those campaign ads since meeting Connie and Winifred. For another, he hears the two young pundits taking credit for the president's surge in popularity through their interpretation of it. But if anyone should get credit it should be him, Stanley Motss. "I did it—pure Hollywood!" he shouts.

But also pure Beltway. When the two men first met at Stanley's mansion, Connie raised questions about the factual basis of the Gulf War, suggesting that what was shown to the American public was possibly manufactured for TV. "One video of one bomb, Mr. Motss, the American people bought that war," Connie stated. He further raised suspicions about memories of previous wars due to their reduction to slogans and iconic images. Connie's skepticism here voices a deep mistrust of historical memory, which *Wag the Dog* implies is in no small way Hollywood's fault for inspiring Washington. Losing its stable ground in facts and records, historical memory has instead become partial, distorted, ephemeral, subjective, and possibly, probably fictional. Connie's comments, moreover, suggest that historical memory is inherently political because what is remembered may not have happened in reality but still serves a political end. One of the slogans he mentions, "Tippecanoe and Tyler Too," was not a war catchphrase but a motto referring to the Whig candidates William Henry Harrison and John Tyler in the election of 1840. While perhaps simply an error on the screenwriters' part, this slogan's inclusion alongside the others symptomatically indicates how war and elections have always been linked in American politics, just as it is symptomatic of how historical memory loses adherence to historical facts over time.

Given that suspicion, *Wag the Dog* fittingly ends on an ironic note with an apparent real invasion of Albania. A news anchor announces, "This just in. A group calling itself 'Albania Unite' has claimed responsibility for the bombing moments ago of the village of Klos, Albania. The president was unavailable for comment, but General William Scott of the Joint Chiefs of Staff says he has no doubt we'll be sending planes and troops back in to finish the job." The irony here is doubly layered. It first arises from fake and real events colliding. The fake war eventually causes genuine fighting on the ground, but it is still not clear why "Albania Unite" bombed Klos, why the United States needs to return "to finish the job," what that job is exactly, and if Scott "has no doubt" of future military action only because the fake war had appeared to land U.S. troops there in the first place. The premise of *Wag the Dog* then compounds this irony: could the bombing and "Albania Unite" be part of a setup by Connie Brean to continue distracting the press and the public from the Firefly girl's accusation—or, more ominously, by the CIA or Pentagon or White House to justify a military presence in Albania to further U.S. global politics?

There is an additional extrafilmic coda of sorts to *Wag the Dog*. Shortly after the film's release genuine political events intruded upon its outrageous premise, circumstantially indicating how life imitates art. *Wag the Dog* opened for Christmas in 1997, and the Monica Lewinsky scandal broke the following month. Although during filming no one involved in the making of *Wag the Dog* had any reason to know of President Clinton's relation with the intern, the photograph in the film of the president and the Firefly girl was taken from "the same angle (over the president's right shoulder looking down at the girl) as the most famous piece of video of Clinton and Lewinsky." Likewise, "in the video, as in the picture, both the girl and Lewinsky are wearing a black beret." The political context drove up grosses, turning *Wag the Dog* into "a cultural icon" (Stempel 2005, 63). Additionally, later that year Clinton, acting on what turned out to be dubious information about its affiliation with al Qaeda, ordered the bombing of the Al-Shifa pharmaceutical factory in Sudan to retaliate against bombings of American embassies in Kenya and Tanzania. Republicans in Congress and pundits chided him for "wagging the dog" since he was about to testify under oath before Kenneth Starr, which eventually resulted in Clinton's impeachment by the House for perjury and obstruction of justice.

A few years later the influence of *Wag the Dog* was felt again when doubt about the veracity of the Pentagon's official version of Jessica Lynch's rescue from Iraq paralleled Connie Brean's suspicion about the authenticity of Gulf War imagery. As a writer in *The Guardian* put it, "Her rescue will go down as one of the most stunning pieces of news management yet conceived. It provides a remarkable insight into the real influence of Hollywood producers on the Pentagon's media managers, and has produced a template from which America hopes to present its future wars" (Kampfner 2003). Did the Pentagon specifically learn from *Wag the Dog* about the value of staged military events? In *Argo* and *The Last Shot* the state agencies exploit Hollywood, using it for their own purposes while fooling the film industry at large into authenticating their fake movie. With Stanley Motts's manufacturing of a fake war, which conflates what Hollywood and the government each do in engaging the public through manipulated representations, *Wag the Dog* speculates about the extent of Hollywood's active complicity in the government's manufacturing of propaganda.

The currency of *Wag the Dog* continues. Renewed interest in the film occurred in 2017 from the rampant circulation of fake news throughout social media, as well as the mistrust of the media's veracity, disregard for historical facts, and the biased spinning of disputable "truths" by politicians going up the food chain to the White House. Pundits now wonder if every action, not to say tweet, coming from Pennsylvania Avenue means to serve as a distraction from what is happening in Washington. It therefore came as no surprise when the *Hollywood Reporter* interviewed *Wag the Dog* director Barry Levinson about the parallels between his twenty-year-old film and the present moment. "*Wag* was in the area of satirical absurdism," the director concluded, "and now we are living in absurdism" (Shanley 2017a). Two weeks after that interview, HBO announced its development of a series based on *Wag the Dog*. Working with Levinson, who would executive produce the series and direct the pilot, the cable channel stated that its adaptation would be "an ode to the classic film but moving the weapons of mass destruction beyond politics and into business, entertainment and yes, nonprofits. In the 21st century with the tools of social media at their hands, nothing is off limits to a small group of operators when it comes to manufacturing reality. Fake news is so yesterday" (Shanley 2017b).

As I write this, there is no certainty that a series will result, but what interests me about HBO's initial description is its effacement of the state's political "manufacturing [of] reality," and possibly Hollywood's as well. After all, the satire in *Wag the Dog* begins with political spin doctor Connie Brean going to Hollywood precisely because the film industry has the necessary skills that the government lacks in 1997, namely, Stanley Motss's expertise in producing a pageant, honed by his blockbuster movies as well as the Oscars ceremony. Stanley knows how to balance narrative and spectacle in engaging representations of a virtual reality, the cinema. Hence the ease of his calling the fake war his motion picture. Yet with the mention of "a small group of operators" and the series' movement "beyond politics" and "into business, entertainment and yes, nonprofits," it seems as if HBO intends to privatize the dog-wagging. In softening the political satire and its cautionary warning about the state's manipulation of reality through its weapons of mass misdirection (as opposed to the weapons of mass destruction referenced in error by the press release), HBO appears to be locating its planned adaptation of *Wag the Dog* in an apolitical arena. Knowing series television, I suspect that the "small group of operators" will be neither agents working for the state in any capacity nor Hollywood producers like Stanley, but independent spin doctors, freelance entrepreneurs whose talents and technological know-how will be for hire.

We all know that motion pictures have never not been political, of course. Whether with respect to their form or their content, they always come shaped by an ideological viewpoint, not only of their makers but of the institution from which they originate, as *The Congress* overtly dramatizes through the corporate power of Miramount-Nagasaki and as the other films discussed in this chapter have in their own way implied, whether by immersing characters in a movie world or by appropriating Hollywood's special talents to fight corruption or to serve political objectives. Furthermore, in every sort of backstudio, from the genre's beginnings to the present day, Hollywood never eludes its reputation as a fabulous dream factory, as the films discussed in this chapter also illustrate. Both factors account for the enduring appeal, but also insularity and dangers, of the Hollywood mystique.

Conclusion

The backstudio picture is a long-lived genre. Its value, I have argued, arises from its function in defining what Hollywood signifies as a place, an industry, and a fantasy. For some filmmakers, a backstudio story has no doubt offered them a venue for settling scores or exploring cinematic creativity. But I have for the most part discounted the personal intentions of individuals throughout this book and instead have focused on the backstudio picture as a product turned out with great regularity from the silent era to the present day. The genre's importance exceeds the commercial success or failure of individual backstudios at the box office, moreover, since it has been a cumulative phenomenon, the effect of numerous backstudios coming out in a single year time and time again. Viewed as a robust genre, the backstudio picture has worked to keep visible the centrality of Hollywood to American filmmaking.

The backstudio picture has historically solicited viewers to the movies by inciting and then playing on their fascination with Hollywood as a site of glamour, modernity, consuming, and leisure. In doing so, it brands the making of American motion pictures with the Hollywood mystique. What the backstudio genre recounts about Hollywood onscreen, I suspect, it has also helped the industry to achieve, for better and worse: ambitious young people irresistibly drawn to Los Angeles in search of work, from the movie-struck girls of the 1920s and 1930s, who saw Hollywood as an escape from the confinement of their home life, to the movie-struck fan boys and girls of the twenty-first century heading west after college with their eye on a career in films. As shown onscreen, Hollywood signifies an exciting professional life that offers class mobility for the lucky few with the right amount of talent, nerve, and luck.

Onscreen, while leisure may be romanticized for its Bohemianism, domesticity in Hollywood is aligned with bourgeois tastes in consumption and bourgeois morality in (mis) behavior. For this reason the backstudio picture refracts historical changes in class-bound tastes and morality as well. The screen image of Hollywood in backstudios superficially conforms to coverage by the popular press, whether as featured in the fan magazines and Sunday supplements of yesterday or the tabloid news shows and websites of today. But the many different stories about success and failure in filmmaking—star narratives about young women making it and older women pushed to the wayside, historical accounts of the industry's development tinged with nostalgia, satires about frustrated filmmakers—expand the image of Hollywood beyond the pages of *Photoplay* or episodes of *Entertainment Tonight*.

Hollywood as an industry is further defined onscreen by its inclusion of a lucky few and exclusion of the unfortunate, those unable to make it there in the first place or those whom the institution has chewed up and spit out. The backstudio picture imagines Hollywood as a utopian space where work in the dream factory overcomes alienated labor or a dystopian one when that work is interfered with or prevented. Backstudios also imagine Hollywood as a privileged space where stars and filmmakers inhabit a state of mind peculiar to the film colony. To see backstudios depicting Hollywood as a state of mind—a mode of thinking, feeling, desiring, believing, and valuing—is to see how its mystique works as an ideology that incorporates filmgoers and filmmakers alike in the institution's worldview.

But equally important is how the backstudio genre has chronicled the film industry's history. Its cyclical renewals over the past hundred years register, sometimes directly and sometimes indirectly, economic transformations of the industry, changes that the genre treats with equal degrees of transparency and disavowal. Both responses help to normalize depictions of the major shifts in the industry's political economy, as evident in the nostalgic historical backstudios that dominated the 1970s and 1980s, when the infrastructure and ownership of American filmmaking was being dramatically altered after the studio era. Given the initial dominance of female star narratives, which then greatly diminished in numbers as the genre became fixated on male filmmakers and male audiences in the 1970s, the backstudio picture's own history chronicles the unequal status of gender in the industry's ongoing sexual politics. Along with its gendering of Hollywood and alignment of the leisure and domestic lives of stars and filmmakers along class lines, the backstudio picture further documents how Hollywood has constructed its own whiteness, which is as unacknowledged as such onscreen as it is made explicit by its near exclusive presence. As the backstudio picture holds a mirror up to the industry, the genre routinely sees the whiteness of the institution reflected back, another instance in which the insider view holds as a principle of exclusion for Hollywood.

Although it now includes all the multimedia entertainment industries—television and cable, Internet streaming, recordings, even gaming, as well as theatrical motion pictures—the backstudio genre continues to identify Hollywood with the production of motion pictures. The backstudios released now every year defensively testify to the importance of movies while indicating their uncertain standing in the hierarchy of entertainment product being manufactured by multimedia Hollywood. This is why the historical backstudio, looking back to periods when motion pictures dominated the entertainment scene, still has such great purchase. At the same time, a historical vantage point has given filmmakers more license to expose sexual vices of the present, albeit indirectly, by dwelling on their prevalence in the past. While backstudios seldom openly address the sexism and harassment that have always characterized the industry and continue to do so in this century, the newer versions focused on real women from Hollywood's past, such as the Monroe biopics and *Feud*, are more revelatory of the abusive behavior of Zanuck, Warner, and other old movie moguls.

But the backstudio picture always projects an imaginary Hollywood, which does not necessarily diminish the significance of its representations of the film industry on-screen. For instance, as a Hollywood fixer Eddie Mannix in *Hail, Caesar!* has obvious parallels with Connie Brean in *Wag the Dog*. The comparability of the two fixers under-scores the more disturbing implications of what it means to identify "Hollywood, USA" with the nation not only as a unified society and culture but as a political institution, an undercurrent that most backstudios have sought to repress. The two figures suggest the comparability of Hollywood and Washington in using the media to cover up bad sexual and political behavior, spinning news to shine more favorably upon the institution that each personifies, as when the real-life Mannix covered up the rape of Patricia Douglas in 1937 at a party for MGM's salesmen, destroying her credibility when she filed charges and then burying her as far as the industry was concerned.

It does not necessarily follow, however, as writer Pamela Hutchinson maintains in *The Guardian* when she mentions Mannix and Douglas, that *Hail, Caesar!* "substantially sanitised his work, covering up this and many more studio scandals" (Hutchinson 2017). To be fair, Hutchinson was writing in 2017 about the industry's long history of sexual mis-conduct by its moguls in the wake of the numerous allegations about Harvey Weinstein, but in doing so she dismissed (and miscategorized) *Hail, Caesar!* as "a lighthearted mu-sical comedy about Mannix." However, with the deliberate renaming of Mannix from "Joseph Edgar Allen John" to "Edward," the Coens' film epitomizes a backstudio picture's *imaginary* relation to the world it represents. The inspiration in a real historical figure for Charlie Mundt's name in their *Barton Fink* has a similar resonance even as it alludes, albeit incongruously since the film is set a decade earlier, to the conditions of the black-list. There is always that slippage from fact to fiction, however minor, even when details claim a fidelity to truthfulness, so the referents of images, characters, and stories are inev-itably and always imaginary. That, the backstudio picture has shown again and again, is the basis of Hollywood's aura and the self-reflexive ground of its mystique.

Works Consulted

Adams, Jeffrey. 2015. *The Cinema of the Coen Brothers: Hard-boiled Entertainments*. London: Wallflower Press.

Adler, Sy. 1991. "The Transformation of the Pacific Electric Railway: Bradford Snell, *Roger Rabbit*, and the Politics of Transportation in Los Angeles." *Urban Affairs Quarterly* 27, no. 1: 51–86.

Alford, Matthew, and Tom Secker. 2017. *National Security Cinema: The Shocking New Evidence of Government Control in Hollywood*. N.p.: Drum Roll Books, Kindle e-book.

Allen, Robert C., and Douglas Gomery. 1985. *Film History: Theory and Practice*. New York: McGraw-Hill.

Allen, William Rodney. 2006. *The Coen Brothers Interviews*. Jackson: University Press of Mississippi.

Alderton, Walter Gregg. 1933. *Official Souvenir Book: Hollywood at A Century of Progress International Exhibition*. N.p.: George W. Weatherby.

Altman, Rick. 1999. *Film/Genre*. London: BFI.

Ames, Christopher, 1997. *Movies about the Movies: Hollywood Reflected*. Lexington: University Press of Kentucky.

Ames, Christopher. 2008. "The Hollywood Novel at the End of the Twentieth Century." *Literature/Film Quarterly* 36, no. 3: 164–70.

Ames, Christopher. 2013. "Jazz Heaven: Woody Allen and the Hollywood Ending." In *A Companion to Woody Allen*, ed. Peter J. Bailey and Sam B. Burgis. Malden, MA: Wiley Blackwell.

Anderson, Patrick Donald. 1976. "In Its Own Image: The Cinematic Vision of Hollywood." PhD dissertation, University of Michigan.

Anderson, Patrick Donald. 1978. *In Its Own Image: The Cinematic Vision of Hollywood*. New York: Arno Press.

Anselmo-Sequeira, Diana. 2015. "Screen-Struck: The Invention of the Movie Girl Fan." *Cinema Journal* 55 (Fall): 1–28.

Atkinson, Brooks. 1962. "Critic at Large: Autobiographies of Bette Davis and Joan Crawford Evoke Some Observations." *New York Times*, September 18.

Banks, Miranda J. 2015. *The Writers: A History of American Screenwriters and Their Guild*. New Brunswick, NJ: Rutgers University Press.

Barbas, Samantha. 2001. *Movie Crazy: Fans, Stars, and the Cult of Celebrity*. New York: Palgrave.

Bart, Peter. 2009. "Tweet Titan Sweetens Brand." *Daily Variety Gotham*, October 12.

Basinger, Janine. 1995. *A Woman's View: How Hollywood Spoke to Women, 1930–1969*. Hanover, NH: Wesleyan University Press.

Behlmer, Rudy, ed. 1973. *Memo from: David O. Selznick*. New York: Avon Books.

Behlmer, Rudy, and Tony Thomas. 1975. *Hollywood's Hollywood: The Movies about the Movies.* Secaucus, NJ: Citadel Press.

Bianco, Martha J. 1998. "Kennedy, *60 Minutes*, and *Roger Rabbit*: Understanding Conspiracy-Theory Explanations of the Decline of Urban Mass Transit." *Center for Urban Studies Publication and Reports,* Paper 17, July 2017. http://pdxscholar.library.pdx.edu/cus_pubs/17.

Bingham, Dennis. 1994. *Acting Male: Masculinities in the Films of James Stewart, Jack Nicholson, and Clint Eastwood.* New Brunswick, NJ: Rutgers University Press.

Boozer, Jack. 2013. "Novelist-Screenwriter versus Auteur Desire: *The Player*," *Journal of Film and Video* 65, nos. 1–2: 75–86.

Braudy, Leo. 2011. *The Hollywood Sign: Fantasy and Reality of an American Icon.* New Haven, CT: Yale University Press.

Brody, Richard. 2017. "What 'Feud' Misses about Bette Davis, Joan Crawford, and the Art of Movies." *New Yorker*, March 23. http://www.newyorker.com/culture/richard-brody/what-feud-misses-about-bette-davis-joan-crawford-and-the-art-of-movies.

Broe, Dennis. 2009. *Film Noir, American Workers, and Postwar Hollywood.* Gainesville: University Press of Florida.

Caldwell, John Thornton. 2008. *Production Culture: Industrial Reflexivity and Critical Practice in Film and Television.* Durham, NC: Duke University Press.

Carman, Emily. 2016. *Independent Stardom: Freelance Women in the Hollywood Studio System.* Austin: University of Texas Press.

Charles, Jeffrey, and Jill Watts. 2000. "(Un)Real Estate: Marketing Hollywood in the 1910s and 1920." In *Hollywood Goes Shopping*, ed. David Desser and Garth Jowett. Minneapolis: University of Minnesota Press.

Christensen, Jerome. 2012. *America's Corporate Art: The Studio Authorship of Hollywood Motion Pictures.* Stanford, CA: Stanford University Press.

Churchwell, Sarah. 2004. *The Many Lives of Marilyn Monroe.* London: Picador.

Cohan, Steven. 2005. *Incongruous Entertainment: Camp, Cultural Value, and the MGM Musical.* Durham, NC: Duke University Press.

Cohan, Steven. 2010. "Star Spangled Shows: History and Utopia in the Wartime Canteen Musical." In *The Sound of Musicals*, ed. Steven Cohan. London: British Film Institute.

Cohan, Steven. 2012. "Teaching Film Genre(s)." In *Teaching Film*, ed. Lucy Fischer and Patrice Petro. New York: Modern Language Association.

Cohen, David S. 2012. "Digital Allows Creative Use of Frame Rates." *Daily Variety*, June 7.

Cohen, David S. 2016. "Bias below the Line." *Variety*, August 9.

Considine, Shaun. 2017. *Bette and Joan: The Divine Feud.* N.p.: Graymalkin Media. Originally published, New York: E. P. Dutton, 1989.

Cullins, Ashley. 2017. "Olivia de Havilland Sues FX over 'Feud' Portrayal." *Hollywood Reporter*, June 30. http://www.hollywoodreporter.com/thr-esq/olivia-de-havilland-sues-fx-feud-portrayal-1018306.

Dargis, Manohla. 2011. "Hollywood's Own Hollywood Endings." *New York Times*, December 4.

Davis, John. 1977. "Inside Hollywood." In *Movies about Movies / Chicago '77*, ed. Sharon Kern. Chicago: Film Center, School of the Art Institute of Chicago.

Desjardins, Mary R. 2015. *Recycled Stars: Female Film Stardom in the Age of Television and Video.* Durham, NC: Duke University Press.

D'haeyere, Hilde. 2014. "Slapstick on Slapstick: Mack Sennett's Metamovies Revisit the Keystone Film Company." *Film History* 26, no. 2: 82–111.

Dowling, Amber. 2017a. "'Feud': Ryan Murphy on Aging in Hollywood, Sexuality and the Sadness of 'Lost Potential.'" *Hollywood Reporter*, March 12. http://www.hollywoodreporter.com/live-feed/feud-ryan-murphy-aging-hollywood-sexuality-sadness-lost-potential-985267.

Dowling, Amber. 2017b. "'Feud' Boss on Staying True to the 'Baby Jane' Sequel and Joan's Descent." *Hollywood Reporter*, April 9. http://www.hollywoodreporter.com/live-feed/feud-boss-baby-jane-sequel-joans-descent-991820.

Doyle, Andrew. 2009. "Competing Realities in *Wag the Dog*." *Screen Education*, no. 56: 115–21.

Feuer, Jane. 1993. *The Hollywood Musical*. 2nd edition. Bloomington: Indiana University Press.

Fischer, Lucy. 2013. *Body Double: The Author Incarnate in the Cinema*. New Brunswick, NJ: Rutgers University Press.

Fischer, Lucy. 2016. "Screen Test: Celebrity, the Starlet, and the Movie World in Silent American Cinema." *Feminist Media Histories* 2, no. 4: 15–63.

Fox, Charles Donald. 1925. *Mirrors of Hollywood*. New York: Charles Renard.

Fox, Terry Curtis. 1985. "The Hollywood Novel." *Film Comment* 21, no. 2: 7–13.

F.R. 1921. "Pictures and the Girl Question." *Camera! The Digest of the Motion Picture Industry* 4, no. 1: 3.

Frost, Jennifer. 2011. *Hedda Hopper's Hollywood: Celebrity Gossip and American Conservatism*. New York: New York University Press.

Gilbert, Andrew. 2012. "The Death of Film and the Hollywood Response." *Senses of Cinema*, April 18. http://sensesofcinema.com/2012/feature-articles/the-death-of-film-and-the-hollywood-response/.

Gomery, Douglas. 2005. *The Coming of Sound*. New York: Routledge.

Grainge, Paul. 2008. *Brand Hollywood: $elling Entertainment in a Global Media Age*. London: Routledge.

Haber, Joyce. 1974. "Sex Symbol Due in Nation's Homes." *Los Angeles Times*, July 25.

Hall, Jeanne. 2001. "The Benefits of Hindsight: Re-visions of HUAC and the Film and Television Industries in *The Front* and *Guilty by Suspicion*." *Film Quarterly* 54, no. 2: 15–26.

Hall, Jeanne Lynn. 2006. "Opposites Attract: Politics and Romance in *The Way We Were* and *Speechless*." *Quarterly Review of Film and Video* 23, no. 2: 155–69.

Hallett, Hilary A. 2013. *Go West, Young Women! The Rise of Early Hollywood*. Berkeley: University of California Press.

Harold, Christine. 2007. *Our Space: Resisting the Corporate Control of Culture*. Minneapolis: University of Minnesota Press.

Harvey, Stephen. 1989. *Directed by Vincente Minnelli*. New York: Harper.

Haskell, Molly. 1974. *From Reverence to Rape: The Treatment of Women in the Movies*. Baltimore: Penguin.

Haver, Ronald. 1980. *David O. Selznick's Hollywood*. New York: Knopf.

Horne, Gerald. 2001. *Class Struggle in Hollywood, 1930–1950: Moguls, Mobsters, Stars, Reds, and Trade Unionists*. Austin: University of Texas Press.

Hoxter, Julian. 2014. "The New Hollywood, 1980–1999." In *Screenwriting*, ed. Andrew Horton and Jilian Hoxter. New Brunswick, NJ: Rutgers University Press.

Hozic, Aida. 2001. *Hollyworld: Space, Power, and Fantasy in the American Economy*. Ithaca, NY: Cornell University Press.

Hutchinson, Pamela. 2017. "Moguls and Starlets: 100 Years of Hollywood's Corrosive, Systemic Sexism." *The Guardian*, October 20.

Jenkins, Tricia. 2012. *The CIA in Hollywood: How the Agency Shapes Film and Television*. Austin: University of Texas Press.

Jurca, Catherine. 2012. *Hollywood 1938: Motion Pictures' Greatest Year*. Berkeley: University of California Press.

Kampfner, John. 2003. "The Truth about Jessica." *The Guardian*, May 15. https://www.theguardian.com/world/2003/may/15/iraq.usa2.

Kaufman, J. B. 1990. "'Fascinating Youth': The Story of the Paramount Pictures School." *Film History* 4, no. 2: 131–51.

Kenaga, Heidi. 2011. "Promoting *Hollywood Extra Girl* (1935)." *Screen* 52 (Spring): 82–88.

Kern, Sharon, ed. 1977. *Movies about Movies / Chicago '77*. Chicago: Film Center, School of the Art Institute of Chicago.

Kernan, Lisa. 2004. *Coming Attractions: Reading American Movie Trailers*. Austin: University of Texas Press.

Klein, Amanda Ann. 2011. *American Film Cycles: Reframing Genres, Screening Social Problems, and Defining Subcultures*. Austin: University of Texas Press.

Klein, Naomi. 2000. *No Logo*. New York: Picador.

Larson, Allen. 2007. "1937: Movies and New Constructions of the American Star." In *American Cinema of the 1930s: Themes and Variations*, ed. Ina Rae Hark. New Brunswick, NJ: Rutgers University Press.

Lev, Peter. 2013. *Twentieth Century-Fox: The Zanuck-Skouras Years, 1935–1965*. Austin: University of Texas Press.

Lewis, Jon. 2016. Introduction to *Producing*, ed. Jon Lewis. New Brunswick, NJ: Rutgers University Press.

Lewis, Jon. 2017. *Hard-Boiled Hollywood: Crime and Punishment in Postwar Los Angeles*. Oakland: University of California Press.

Littleton, Cynthia. 2017. "Fox Vows to 'Vigorously Defend' Olivia de Havilland 'Feud' Lawsuit." *Variety*, July 26. http://variety.com/2017/tv/news/fox-feud-olivia-de-havilland-lawsuit-1202507022.

Mainar, Luis Miguel García. 2002. "Genre, Auteur and Identity in Contemporary Hollywood Cinema: Clint Eastwood's *White Hunter, Black Heart*." *Miscelánea: A Journal of English and American Studies* 26: 21–37.

Maltby, Richard. 2003. *Hollywood Cinema*. 2nd edition. Oxford: Blackwell.

Mann, William J. 2014. *Tinseltown: Murder, Morphine, and Madness at the Dawn of Hollywood*. New York: Harper, Kindle edition.

Mast, Gerald. 1987. *Can't Help Singin': The American Musical Onstage and Screen*. Woodstock, NY: Overlook.

Melton, Mary. 1998. "There's Something about 'Sammy'; Hollywood May Finally Be Ready for 'What Makes Sammy Run?'" *Los Angeles Times*, September 6.

Meyers, Richard. 1978. *Movies on Movies: How Hollywood Sees Itself*. New York: Drake.

Moran, Kathleen, and Michael Rogin. 2000. "'What's the Matter with Capra?': *Sullivan's Travels* and the Popular Front." *Representations* 71 (Summer): 106–34.

Nadel, Alan. 2017. *Demographic Angst: Cultural Narratives and American Films of the 1950s*. New Brunswick, NJ: Rutgers University Press.

Naremore, James. 1993. *The Films of Vincente Minnelli*. New York: Cambridge University Press.

Navasky, Victor. 1991. "Has 'Guilty by Suspicion' Missed the Point?" *New York Times*, March 31.

Neale, Steve. 1999. *Genre and Hollywood*. London: Routledge.

Nugent, Frank S. 1937. "Another Dance of the Seven Veils: The Screen Reveals Its Mysteries to the Public, Yet Manages to Hide behind the Cloak of Illusion." *New York Times*, October 10.

Ortner, Sherry B. 2009. "Studying Sideways: Ethnographic Access in Hollywood." In *Production Studies: Cultural Studies of Media Industries*, ed. Vicki Mayer, Miranda J. Banks, and John Thornton Caldwell. New York: Routledge.

Palmer, R. Barton. 2004. *Joel and Ethan Coen*. Urbana: University of Illinois Press.

Parrish, James Robert, and Michael R. Pitts, with Gregory W. Mank. 1978. *Hollywood on Hollywood*. Metuchen, NJ: Scarecrow Press.

Paul, Andrew. 2013. "Making the Blacklist White: The Hollywood Red Scare in Popular Memory." *Journal of Popular Film and Television* 41: 209–18.

Rosenbaum, Jonathan. 1988. "Reviews: *Who Framed Roger Rabbit?*" *Film Quarterly* 42 (Fall): 33–37.

Schatz, Thomas. 1988. *The Genius of the System: Hollywood Filmmaking in the Studio Era*. New York: Pantheon.

Scheuer, Philip K. 1954. "Star Judy Garland Is 'Born' Again in Film's New Version." *Los Angeles Times*, August 29.

Schulberg, Budd. 1990. *What Makes Sammy Run?* New York: Vintage Books.

Schumach, Murray. 1962. "Hollywood T.N.T.; Potential Explosion Seen in Pairing of Bette Davis and Joan Crawford." *New York Times*, July 29.

Shanley, Patrick. 2017a. "'Wag the Dog' Director Barry Levinson Sees Those Trump-Era Comparisons." *Hollywood Reporter*, April 12. http://www.hollywoodreporter.com/news/wag-dog-director-barry-levinson-sees-trump-era-comparisons-q-a-993067.

Shanley, Patrick. 2017b. "'Wag the Dog' TV Series in the Works at HBO (Exclusive)." *Hollywood Reporter*, April 27. http://www.hollywoodreporter.com/live-feed/wag-dog-tv-series-works-at-hbo-998140.

Shaw, Tony, and Tricia Jenkins. 2017. "From Zero to Hero: The CIA and Hollywood Today." *Cinema Journal* 56 (Winter): 91–113.

Shiel, Mark. 2012. *Hollywood Cinema and the Real Los Angeles*. London: Reaktion Books.

Siegal, Mark. 1985. "Ozymandias Melancholia: The Nature of Parody in Woody Allen's *Stardust Memories*." *Literature/Film Quarterly* 13, no. 2: 77–84.

Sklar, Robert. 2012. "Hollywood about Hollywood: Genre as Historiography." In *Hollywood and the American Historical Film*, ed. J. E. Smyth. New York: Palgrave Macmillan.

Slide, Anthony. 1995. *The Hollywood Novel: A Critical Guide to Over 1200 Works with Film-Related Themes or Characters, 1912 through 1994*. Jefferson, NC: McFarland.

Smith, Paul. 1993. *Clint Eastwood: A Cultural Production*. Minneapolis: University of Minnesota Press.

Smyth, J. E. 2006. *Reconstructing American Historical Cinema: From* Cimarron *to* Citizen Kane. Lexington: University Press of Kentucky.

Spiro, Elaine. 1998. "Hollywood Strike—October 1945." *Film History* 1: 415–18.

Springer, John Parris. 1995. *Hollywood Fictions: The Dream Factory in American Popular Literature*. Norman: University of Oklahoma Press.

Stahl, Matt, 2009. "Privilege and Distinction in Production Worlds: Copyright, Collective Bargaining, and Working Conditions in Media Making." In *Production Studies: Cultural Studies of Media Industries*, ed. Vicki Mayer, Miranda J. Banks, and John Thornton Caldwell. New York: Routledge.

Stamp, Shelley. 2000. *Movie-Struck Girls*: *Women and Motion Picture Culture after the Nickelodeon*. Princeton, NJ: Princeton University Press.

A Star Is Born press book. 1937. Distributed by United Artists for Selznick-International. Author's collection.

Stempel, Tom. 2005. "The Collaborative Dog: *Wag the Dog* (1997)." *Film & History* 35: 60–64.

Studlar, Gaylyn. 2015. *Precocious Charms: Stars Performing Girlhood in Classical Hollywood Cinema*. Berkeley: University of California Press.

Sullivan, John L. 2009. "Leo C. Rosten's Hollywood: Power, Status, and the Primacy of Economic and Social Networks in Cultural Production." In *Production Studies: Cultural Studies of Media Industries*, ed. Vicki Mayer, Miranda J. Banks, and John Thornton Caldwell. New York: Routledge.

Tapley, Kristopher. 2016. "Roger Deakins on 'Hail, Caesar!,' Old Hollywood and Going Back to Celluloid." *Variety*, January 25. http://variety.com/2016/artisans/in-contention/hail-caesar-roger-deakins-celluloid-1201687528.

Taylor, Aaron. 2007. "Twilight of the Idols: Performance, Melodramatic Villainy, and *Sunset Boulevard*." *Journal of Film and Video* 59 (Summer): 13–31.

Tieber, Claus. 2010. "The Way He Wrote: Dalton Trumbo and Sixteen Unused Pages for *The Way We Were*." *Film International* 8, no. 4: 51–64.

Trope, Alison. 2011. *Stardust Monuments: The Saving and Selling of Hollywood*. Hanover, NH: Dartmouth College Press.

Weiler, A. H. 1959. "By Way of Report: Schulbergs' 'Sammy' to 'Run'—Other Items." *New York Times*, January 18.

Wiggins, Benjamin. 2012. "'You Talkin' Revolution, Sweetback': On *Sweet Sweetback's Baadasssss Song* and Revolutionary Filmmaking." *Black Camera* 4, no. 1: 28–52.

Wilder, Billy. 1999. *Sunset Boulevard*. Facsimile edition of the screenplay by Charles Brackett, Billy Wilder, and D. M. Marshman Jr. Berkeley: University of California Press.

Wolf, Mark J. P. 1995. "In the Frame of *Roger Rabbit*: Visual Compositing in Film." *Velvet Light Trap*, no. 36 (Fall): 45–59.

Wolf, Mark J. P. 2003. "The Technological Construction of Performance." *Convergence* 9, no. 4: 48–58.

Filmography

A Girl's Folly (1917); Maurice Tourneur; Paragon Films
The Extra Girl (1923); F. Richard Jones; Mack Sennett
Souls for Sale (1923); Rupert Hughes; Goldwyn
Merton of the Movies (1924); James Cruze; Paramount
Ella Cinders (1926); Alfred E. Green; First National
The Last Command (1928); Josef von Sternberg; Paramount
Show People (1928); King Vidor; MGM
The Studio Murder Mystery (1929); Frank Tuttle; Paramount
Free and Easy (1930); Edward Sedgwick; MGM
Showgirl in Hollywood (1930); Mervyn LeRoy; First National
The Lost Squadron (1932); George Archainbaud; RKO
Movie Crazy (1932); Clyde Bruckman; Paramount
Once in a Lifetime (1932); Russell Mack; Universal
Make Me a Star (1932); William Beaudine; Paramount
What Price Hollywood? (1932); George Cukor; RKO
Bombshell (1933); Victor Fleming; MGM
Going Hollywood (1933); Raoul Walsh; MGM
Lady Killer (1933); Roy Del Ruth; Warner Bros.
Let's Fall in Love (1933); David Burton; Columbia
Lucky Devils (1933); Ralph Ince; RKO
Sitting Pretty (1933); Harry Joe Brown; Paramount
365 Nights in Hollywood (1934); George Marshall; Fox
Hollywood Party (1934); Alan Dwan; MGM
In Person (1935); William A. Seiter; RKO
Music Is Magic (1935); George Marshall; Twentieth Century-Fox
Hollywood Boulevard (1936); Robert Florey; Paramount
The Preview Murder Mystery (1936); Robert Florey; Paramount
It Happened in Hollywood (1937); Harry Lachman; Columbia
Pick a Star (1937); Edward Sedgwick; MGM
Stand-In (1937); Tay Garnett; United Artists
A Star Is Born (1937); William A. Wellman; United Artists
Boy Meets Girl (1938); Lloyd Bacon; Warner Bros.

Crashing Hollywood (1938); Lew Landers; RKO
The Goldwyn Follies (1938); George Marshall; United Artists
Hollywood Hotel (1938); Busby Berkeley; Warner Bros.
Hollywood Cavalcade (1939); Irving Cummings; Twentieth Century-Fox
Honolulu (1939); Edward Buzzell; MGM
Star Dust (1940); Walter Lang; Twentieth Century-Fox
Never Give a Sucker an Even Break (1941); Edward Cline; Universal
Sullivan's Travels (1941); Preston Sturges; Paramount
Holiday Inn (1942); Mark Sandrich; Paramount
Best Foot Forward (1943); Edward Buzzell; MGM
Crazy House (1943); Edward F. Cline; Universal
Star Spangled Rhythm (1943); George Marshall; Paramount
Thank Your Lucky Stars (1943); David Butler; Warner Bros.
The Youngest Profession (1943); Edward Buzzell; MGM
Hollywood Canteen (1944); Delmer Daves; Warner Bros.
Anchors Aweigh (1945); George Sidney; MGM
The Jolson Story (1946); Alfred E. Green; Columbia
Without Reservations (1946); Mervyn LeRoy; RKO
Merton of the Movies (1947); Robert Alton; MGM
The Perils of Pauline (1947); George Marshall; Paramount
Miracle of the Bells (1948); Irving Pichel; RKO
On an Island with You (1948); Richard Thorpe; MGM
Dancing in the Dark (1949); Irving Reis; Twentieth Century-Fox
It's a Great Feeling (1949); David Butler; Warner Bros.
Jolson Sings Again (1949); Henry Levin; Columbia
Slightly French (1949); Douglas Sirk; Columbia
You're My Everything (1949); Walter Lang; Twentieth Century-Fox
In a Lonely Place (1950); Nicholas Ray; Columbia
Sunset Boulevard (1950); Billy Wilder; Paramount
Hollywood Story (1951); William Castle; Universal International
Starlift (1951); Roy Del Ruth; Warner Bros.
The Bad and the Beautiful (1952); Vincente Minnelli; MGM
Dreamboat (1952); Claude Binyon; Twentieth Century-Fox
Singin' in the Rain (1952); Gene Kelly and Stanley Donen; MGM
The Star (1952); Stuart Heisler; Twentieth Century-Fox
The Barefoot Contessa (1954); Joseph L. Mankiewicz; United Artists
A Star Is Born (1954); George Cukor; Warner Bros.
Susan Slept Here (1954); Frank Tashlin; RKO
The Big Knife (1955); Robert Aldrich; United Artists
Love Me or Leave Me (1955); Charles Vidor; MGM
Hollywood or Bust (1956); Frank Tashlin; Paramount
The Buster Keaton Story (1957); Sidney Sheldon; Paramount
Jeanne Eagles (1957); George Sidney; Columbia
The Fuzzy Pink Nightgown (1957); Norman Taurog; United Artists
Man of a Thousand Faces (1957); Joseph Pevney; Universal-International
Will Success Spoil Rock Hunter? (1957); Frank Tashlin; Twentieth Century-Fox
The Female Animal (1958); Harry Keller; Universal-International
The Goddess (1958); John Cromwell; Columbia
Too Much Too Soon (1958); Art Napoleon; Warner Bros.
Beloved Infidel (1959); Henry King; Twentieth Century-Fox
The Errand Boy (1961); Jerry Lewis; Paramount
The George Raft Story (1961); Joseph M. Newman; Allied Artists

Sweet Bird of Youth (1962); Richard Brooks; MGM

Two Weeks in Another Town (1962); Vincente Minnelli; MGM

What Ever Happened to Baby Jane? (1962); Robert Aldrich; Warner Bros.

The Carpetbaggers (1964); Edward Dmytryk; Paramount

Paris When It Sizzles (1964); Richard Quine; Paramount

Harlow (1965); Alex Segal; Magna

Harlow (1965); Gordon Douglas; Paramount

Inside Daisy Clover (1965); Robert Mulligan; Warner Bros.

The Oscar (1966); Russell Rouse; Embassy

Valley of the Dolls (1967); Mark Robson; Twentieth Century-Fox

Fade-in aka *Iron Cowboy* (1968); Jud Taylor; Paramount

The Legend of Lylah Clare (1968); Robert Aldrich; MGM

The Comic (1969); Carl Reiner; Columbia

Alex in Wonderland (1970); Paul Mazursky; MGM

Myra Breckinridge (1970); Michael Sarne; Twentieth Century-Fox

What's the Matter with Helen? (1971); Curtis Harrington; United Artists

The Last of Sheila (1973); Herbert Ross; Warner Bros.

*The Long Goodbye (*1973); Robert Altman; United Artists

The Way We Were (1973); Sydney Pollack; Columbia

The Phantom of Hollywood (1974); Gene Leavitt; CBS

The Sex Symbol (1974); David Lowell Rich; ABC

The Day of the Locust (1975); John Schlesinger; Paramount

Gable and Lombard (1976); Sidney J. Fury; Universal

Goodbye, Norma Jean (1976); Larry Buchanan; Cinema Shares

Hearts of the West (1975); Howard Zieff; MGM–United Artists

Play It Again, Sam (1975); Herbert Ross; Paramount

The Wild Party (1975); James Ivory; American International

The Last Tycoon (1976); Elia Kazan; Paramount

Nickelodeon (1976); Peter Bogdanovich; Columbia

Silent Movie (1976); Mel Brooks; Twentieth Century-Fox

W. C. Fields and Me (1976); Arthur Hiller; Universal

Won Ton Ton, the Dog Who Saved Hollywood (1976); Michael Winner; Paramount

Valentino (1977); Ken Russell; United Artists

The World's Greatest Lover (1977); Gene Wilder; Twentieth Century-Fox

Fedora (1978); Billy Wilder; United Artists

Hooper (1978); Hal Needham; Warner Bros.

Stardust Memories (1980); Woody Allen; United Artists

The Stunt Man (1980); Richard Rush; Twentieth Century-Fox

Mommie Dearest (1981); Frank Perry; Paramount

S.O.B. (1981); Blake Edwards; Paramount

Under the Rainbow (1981); Steve Rash; Orion

Best Friends (1982); Norman Jewison; Warner Bros.

Frances (1982); Graeme Clifford; Universal

Star 80 (1983); Bob Fosse; Warner Bros.

Malice in Wonderland (1985); Gus Trikonis; CBS

*The Purple Rose of Cairo (*1985); Woody Allen; Orion

FX (1986); Robert Mandel; Orion

Sweet Liberty (1986); Alan Alda; Universal

Hollywood Shuffle (1987); Robert Townsend; Samuel Goldwyn

Sunset (1988); Blake Edwards; Tri-Star

Who Framed Roger Rabbit (1988); Robert Zemeckis; Buena Vista

The Big Picture (1989); Christopher Guest; Columbia

Postcards from the Edge (1990); Mike Nichols; Columbia
White Hunter, Black Heart (1990); Clint Eastwood; Warner Bros.
Barton Fink (1991); Joel Coen; Twentieth Century-Fox
FX 2 (1991); Richard Franklin; Orion
Guilty by Suspicion (1991); Irwin Winkler; Warner Bros.
The Hard Way (1991); John Badham; Universal
Mistress (1992); Barry Primas; Rainbow
The Player (1992); Robert Altman; Fine Line
The Last Action Hero (1993); John McTiernan; Columbia
Get Shorty (1995); Barry Sonnenfeld; MGM/UA
Living in Oblivion (1995); Tom DiCillo; Sony Pictures Classics
Norma Jean & Marilyn (1996); Tim Fywell; HBO
L.A. Confidential (1997); Curtis Hanson; Warner Bros.
Wag the Dog (1997); Barry Levinson; New Line
Burn Hollywood Burn (1998); Alan Smithee; Buena Vista
Gods and Monsters (1998); Bill Condon; Lionsgate
Twilight (1998); Robert Benton; Paramount
Bowfinger (1999); Frank Oz; Universal
Introducing Dorothy Dandridge (1999); Martha Coolidge; HBO
The Muse (1999); Albert Brooks; USA Films
Notting Hill (1999); Roger Michell; Universal
RKO 281 (1999); Benjamin Ross; HBO
State and Main (2000); David Mamet; Fine Line
The Last Producer aka *The Final Hit* (2000); Burt Reynolds; USA Network
America's Sweethearts (2001); Joe Roth; Columbia
Blonde (2001); Joyce Chopra; CBS
Life with Judy Garland: Me and My Shadows (2001; Robert Allan Ackerman; ABC
The Majestic (2001); Frank Darabont; Warner Bros.
Mulholland Drive (2001); David Lynch; Universal.
These Old Broads (2001); Matthew Diamond; ABC
Adaptation (2002); Spike Jonze; Columbia
The Cat's Meow (2002); Peter Bogdanovich; Lionsgate
Hollywood Ending (2002); Woody Allen; DreamWorks
S1m0ne (2002); Andrew Niccol; New Line
Looney Tunes: Back in Action (2003); Joe Dante; Warner Bros.
The Aviator (2004); Martin Scorsese; Miramax
Baadasssss! (2004); Mario Van Peebles; Sony Pictures Classics
The Last Shot (2004); Jeff Nathanson; Buena Vista
Straight Jacket (2004); Richard Day; Regent
The Dying Gaul (2005); Craig Lucas; Strand
For Your Consideration (2006); Christopher Guest; Warner Independent
Hollywoodland (2006); Allen Coulter; Focus
Tropic Thunder (2008); Ben Stiller; DreamWorks and Paramount
What Just Happened? (2009); Barry Levinson; Magnolia
The Artist (2011); Michael Hazanavicius; Weinstein Company
Hugo (2011); Martin Scorsese; Paramount
My Week with Marilyn (2011); Simon Curtis; Weinstein Company
Argo (2012); Ben Affleck; Warner Bros.
The Girl (2012); Julian Jarrold; HBO
Hitchcock (2012); Sacha Gervasi; Fox Searchlight
The Congress (2013); Ari Folman; Drafthouse
Birdman or (the Unexpected Virtue of Ignorance) (2014); Alejandro G. Iñárritu; Fox Searchlight

The Last of Robin Hood (2014); Richard Glatzer and Wash Westmoreland; Goldwyn

Top Five (2014); Chris Rock; Paramount

Entourage (2015); Doug Ellin; Warner Bros.

The Secret Life of Marilyn Monroe (2015); Laurie Collyer; Lifetime

Trumbo (2015); Jay Roach; Bleecker Street Media

Café Society (2016); Woody Allen; Lionsgate

Hail, Caesar! (2016); Ethan and Joel Coen; Universal

La La Land (2016); Damien Chazelle; Lionsgate

Rules Don't Apply (2016); Warren Beatty; Twentieth Century Fox

Feud: Bette and Joan (2017) Gwyneth Horder-Payton, Helen Hunt, Liza Johnson, Ryan Murphy, and Tim Minear; FX

Index